MODERN BUSINESS CORRESPONDENCE

Kutipan Pasal 44:
Sanksi Pelanggaran Undang-undang Hak Cipta 1987

1. Barangsiapa dengan sengaja dan tanpa hak mengumumkan atau memperbanyak suatu ciptaan atau memberi izin untuk itu, dipidana dengan pidana penjara paling lama 7 (tujuh) tahun dan/atau denda paling banyak Rp 100.000.000,— (seratus juta rupiah).

2. Barangsiapa dengan sengaja menyiarkan, memamerkan, mengedarkan, atau menjual kepada umum suatu ciptaan atau barang hasil pelanggaran Hak Cipta sebagaimana dimaksud dalam ayat (1), dipidana dengan pidana penjara paling lama 5 (lima) tahun dan/atau denda paling banyak Rp 50.000.000,— (lima puluh juta rupiah).

Modern Business Correspondence

*A comprehensive guide to business writing
and related office services*

L. GARTSIDE

MBE, BCom, FSCT

FOURTH EDITION

Pitman   Binarupa Aksara

First published in Great Britain in 1963
by Pitman Publishing Limited
A Longman Group Company

© Pitman Publishing Limited 1986

First published in Indonesia in 1989
by Binarupa Aksara

This edition of *L. Gartside* : **Modern Business Correspondence,
Fourth Edition** is published by arrangement with
Pitman Publishing, London

Printed and bound in Indonesia by
Binarupa Aksara

Binarupa Aksara, P.O.Box 69, Grogol, Jakarta Barat, Indonesia

Preface to the Fourth Edition

Continuous advances in communications technology have greatly extended the choice of media for transmitting information and ideas. The text of this fourth edition has been fully updated to take account of the new technology and its effects on office processing practices.

Oral communication has the advantage of immediate feedback, but communication in writing, though slower, has the advantage of precision and certainty and is necessary where records are required for future reference; it also provides valuable legal evidence in the event of disputes. If only for these reasons the business letter continues to play an essential part in the business communications system.

The book is arranged in two parts. Part I deals with the principles of good business writing. It takes account of the grammatical disciplines that make for correct writing, but is much less concerned with these things than with the choice of words and forms of expression as means of appropriate and effective writing. The emphasis throughout is on the kind of letters that not only achieve the response sought, but which in the process also help to foster a spirit of friendliness in those with whom we seek to do business.

Part II deals with the practice of letter writing and other forms of communication in business. It includes example letters and reports, and deals with such correspondence-related activities as data processing, reproduction work, mailing, telecommunications and with filing and retrieval systems. There is also a chapter written specially for the typist. Appendix C comprises a 50-page Glossary of Business Terms which may be expected to have something rather more than a passing interest.

Besides providing a text for readers who are interested in good standards of business writing, the book has an important secondary role as a reference source. Subject matter throughout is arranged under clearly displayed headings and subheadings. This makes for quick and easy reference when used with the detailed index provided.

It is hoped that the changes made in this new edition will increase the usefulness of the book as a guide and source of reference to what is generally accepted as sound practice in modern business writing.

1985   LG

Acknowledgments

My thanks are due to the examining bodies whose names appear below for permission to include questions from past examination papers in the exercises.

The varied nature of the matters dealt with has entailed references to many sources, including books, journals, government departments and business concerns, and to all of these I gladly acknowledge my indebtedness for the ideas and information they have provided.

I am grateful to HM Stationery Office for permission to use in the text the extracts from *Plain Words* by Sir Ernest Gowers (pp. 86 and 180–1), to Methuen and Co. Ltd. for the extract from *In Search of England* by H. V. Morton (p. 121), and to the Royal Bank of Canada for the paragraphs on *Creative Writing* from *Monthly Letter* (p. 325). The extract from the *ABC Code Book* (pp. 307–8) is reproduced by courtesy of ABC Telegraphic Codes and Pitman Ltd.

I am grateful also to British Telecom and to several manufacturers of office equipment for supplying material for the illustrations bearing their names, to Miss Josephine Shaw, Director of Teaching Aids Ltd., to my publishers for valuable help and guidance, and finally to my late wife for help in reading the proofs of earlier editions.

EXAMINATION QUESTIONS

AEB	Associated Examining Board
ICSA	Institute of Chartered Secretaries and Administrators
LCCI	London Chamber of Commerce and Industry
NCTEC	Northern Counties Technical Examinations Council
NWRAC	North West Region Advisory Council
RSA	Royal Society of Arts
UEI	Union of Educational Institutions
ULCI	Union of Lancashire and Cheshire Institutes

Contents

PART I:
THE ENGLISH BACKGROUND

CONTENTS

List of Illustrations

PART I

THE ENGLISH BACKGROUND

CHAPTER ONE

Communication in Business

> If a wise man were granted a life of abundance of everything material, so that he had leisure to contemplate everything worth knowing, still if he could not communicate with another human being he would abandon life.
>
> Cicero

THE MEANING OF COMMUNICATION

Communication comes from the Latin *communico* (to share) and is the act of sharing or imparting a share of anything. In its vital sense it means a sharing of ideas and feelings in a mood of mutual understanding. It is a two-way process in which a speaker must have a listener and a writer a reader with whom to share the experience. This understanding is achieved only if the parties "speak the same language"—only, that is, if the words communicated mean the same thing to both. If a customer asks the shopkeeper for a metre of cloth or a kilo of sugar, it doesn't matter very much how long a metre is or how heavy a kilo. What does matter is that *metre* or *kilo* mean the same thing to both. This identity of meaning is at the heart of all effective communication; it is the key to the proper use of all language in business and society.

THE ROLE OF LANGUAGE

Language has been described as "the vehicle of thought". It is indeed almost the sole means we employ for communicating thought and feeling. There are others of course. It is possible to

1

communicate pleasure by a smile, approval by a nod, direction by a sketch and pain by a groan, and the deaf have evolved a complete sign-language of their own. Even so, in its spoken and written forms, language remains by far the commonest and most important means of communication. For business purposes of every kind and at every level of performance, whether routine or administrative, efficiency is liable to turn, from time to time, on communication in speech or writing. In some of the professions, as in religion, law and politics, language is the very essence of their activity. Nor have advances in mechanization lessened the importance of speech and writing. The telephone may have lessened our dependence on writing, but it has increased our dependence on speech, while the typewriter and the teleprinter have provided but another means of writing. We cannot do without language as a means of communication. Indeed, the need for higher standards of clear, precise and purposeful expression grows constantly with the increasing size and complexity of business.

THE COMMUNICATION PROCESS

The growth of large-scale undertakings has extended the lines of management and supervision and created special problems of communication within the undertaking. As businesses have grown in size these problems have become increasingly difficult. The economic and political influences of trade unions at both national and local level have given rise to demands from employees for information about all sorts of matters affecting their work and terms and conditions of employment, and it is no longer sound policy for employers not to give it. There is now a widespread feeling among employees that they have a moral right to be kept informed of events and policies bearing upon what they regard as their legitimate interests as partners in the production process.

The last half century has seen great changes in the character of the management–worker relationship. One of the most important aims of this altered relationship is to create mutual understanding and co-operation. This inevitably focuses attention on the means of communication, and in industry today all the traditional media of mass communication are used wherever possible by management to convey information. The result has been a great multiplication of house magazines, employee handbooks, news sheets, notice boards, films and propaganda campaigns, and meetings addressed by executives. These are the techniques of down-the-line communication most commonly found in industry today. They are valuable means of circulating information among employees, but by themselves they are not enough to achieve the degree of understanding and co-operation they are designed to promote. In the field of industrial relations effective communication is a two-way process that not only circulates information among employees, but also gives them opportunities to make their views and feelings known to management, by the flow of information up the line, or through the interchange of views in schemes of joint consultation.

THE ESSENCE OF COMMUNICATION

The *Oxford English Dictionary* (*OED*) defines communication as the action of conveying or exchanging information and ideas. But communication is effective only if it reflects in the mind of the receiver a true image of the thoughts conveyed by the sender. A person writing a letter must therefore be at pains to express himself clearly and make his reader's task as easy as possible. He must use words his reader will be sure to understand without waste of time and effort. If a writer fails to make his meaning clear he is liable to be misunderstood, and this is something no businessman can afford. To write clearly he must think clearly and have a clear awareness of the purpose of his letter and of what he wants it to achieve. Is it to seek information, to give information, to place an order, to promote a sale, or to establish good will? Only when he is clear about what he wants his letter to do can he begin to think clearly about what to say. Clear thinking and clear writing go hand in hand. He must choose words that say exactly what he wants them to say and use them in sentences framed to leave no room for misunderstanding. For example, he must not say: *Your account must be sent to me for payment not later than 12th October* when what he means is: *Your account must be sent to me not later than 12th October*—possibly for payment at some later date. Nor must he say: *Let me know the number of children attending the classes before the end of this month,* when he means: *Let me know before the end of this month the number of children attending the classes.* He must not say: *I am writing to advise you* when he means *inform you,* or *feel* that an offer is unreasonable when he means he only *thinks* it is. Nor must he confuse a *proposal* (an offer) with a *proposition* (something suggested for discussion), *continuous* (without a break) with *continual* (recurring frequently), or *capacity* (power to receive or retain) with *ability* (power to do). Even when the words he uses are exactly the right ones there is no certainty that his correspondent will read exactly the same meaning into them. Much will depend upon his correspondent's level of understanding, but at least the writer will have discharged his primary duty of trying to make his meaning clear.

THE ELEMENTS OF GOOD COMMUNICATION

Study your correspondent

Communication is effective only if the message received is understood in the sense intended by the writer. This is true equally of relationships within an organization and of relationships between the organization and the outside world. If your message takes the form of a business letter it will be a good letter only if it promotes the response you hoped for or expected. One of the advantages of communication by speech lies in the subtle colouring that can be given to words by tone of voice, stress, gestures and facial expression. As a writer you cannot draw upon these ancillary sources of spoken communication. To convey your feelings as a writer you have to rely solely on the words you choose and the way in which you use them.

To get from your reader the response you seek you must take into account his personality and level of understanding. If you don't already know him, try to imagine what he is like, using as clues the letter he has written, or the way he spoke on the phone. Put yourself in his place. By imagining yourself to be the reader rather than the writer try to sense the feelings your letter is likely to arouse and the reaction it is likely to set up. Only then can you choose the best way of saying what you have to say. This ability to "stand in the reader's shoes" is one of the hall-marks of all successful letter writing.

Failure to look at things from the reader's angle is one reason why letters so often fail to do their job. Try therefore to approach your letter-writing from his standpoint. Write to him at what you feel to be the level of his vocabulary. Avoid using words he may not understand. If for example you are writing to a foreigner keep your language simple enough for him to grasp its meaning at first reading; but if he is a specialist you can safely use the specialized terminology of his particular field of work. Think clearly what you want your letter to achieve and, especially if it is a lengthy letter, first jot down the main points of what you want to say. Then arrange them in what you feel to be the most suitable order.

Choose your language with care

The words used

A written word is not merely a symbol displayed on a piece of paper; it is a valuable tool of communication. It is important that the same word holds precisely the same meaning for your reader as it does for you. This is the very essence of effective communication. There can be no true "meeting of minds" between two people who understand the same word in different ways.

Words such as *book, house* and *flower* are names of things that are readily identifiable because they possess attributes or characteristic qualities of their own. They are *concrete words* denoting something tangible. They present no communication problem since they carry the same meaning for everyone. But this is not so with words like *truth, freedom, democracy* and *gratitude*. Unlike concrete words they denote qualities or conditions we can think about but cannot see or touch. They are *abstract words* denoting something intangible. Such words often mean somewhat different things to different people. Because of this they need to be used with special care. Concrete words and abstract words are both needed in communication, but one of the commonest faults in present-day writing is excessive use of the abstract. This is bad because abstract words, besides being vague, often lead to roundabout statements. For example:

The *preparation* of new salary scales is in hand.

(Say instead: New salary scales are being prepared.)

Due to the unusual *nature* of the request.

(Say instead: Because the request is unusual.)

Avoid abstract nouns whenever possible and, using the concrete as in the above examples, reconstruct your sentences as may be necessary.

Repetition in the same sentence of an important word that has different areas of meaning is also bad and must be avoided. You must not say:

How do you *account* for the fact that the *account* is wrong?

(Instead of *account for*, say *explain*)

We shall take a *firm line* with the *firm's* agent.

(Instead of *firm line*, say *strong line*)

But in the effort to avoid repetition you must not make the opposite mistake of confusing your reader by using different words to express the same meaning. Don't say in the same letter that goods have been *sent, forwarded* and *despatched,* and if you begin your letter by referring to a *firm,* don't convert it into a *concern,* or a *business,* or an *organization* as you go along. If you do, you will leave your reader wondering whether you intend something different.

Tone and style

The tone of a letter must suit both your correspondent and the subject-matter, being firm, persuasive, conciliatory or friendly, and so on, according to the impression you want to convey. Many people who are warm and friendly by nature become persons of another sort as soon as they sit down to write or dictate a business letter. They seem to think that business letters call for a special kind of impersonal and starchy language. They forget that a letter is a sort of "conversation by post" and resort to impersonal constructions that produce the cold and aloof tone evident in the following extract:

> Your letter has been received and your complaint is being investigated. When all the facts are known a further letter will be sent to you.

Personal constructions with the emphasis on the personal *you, we* or *I* produce the warmer and friendlier tone more suited to letter-writing. Instead of the above it is much better to write:

> I have received your letter and am investigating your complaint. When all the facts are known I will write to you again.

One of the most important things we all look for as customers is a spirit of friendliness in those with whom we seek to do business. The whole secret of good business letter-writing is to write in an easy natural way—like one friendly human being talking to another. Make your letters sound as much as possible like good conversation. You wouldn't say on the phone: *It is regretted that the goods cannot be sent today.* You would say: *I am sorry we cannot send the goods today,* so why not say it in a letter?

To write in the style of good conversation does not mean that you must always "write as you would speak". There are many expressions in everyday conversational use that are not acceptable in good business letters. You must not say, for example, *The deal isn't on* (say, *is not acceptable*); *I'm not with you* (say, *I don't understand you*); *It is up to you* (say, *your responsibility*); *They pulled a fast one on me* (say, *deceived me*). And don't describe a firm with financial problems as being *on the rocks*. What writing in the style of good conversation does mean is that you must express yourself naturally and say quite simply in plain language just what you mean. The great merit in all business writing is to be clear—to write in terms that give the reader no excuse for misunderstanding. He may not agree with what you say, but at least you do your duty if you make it clear what you are saying.

Business letter-writing calls for a plain style—a style that is simple, clear and easily understood. Your aim is after all to express your thoughts and not to impress your reader with the range of your vocabulary. Therefore keep your language simple.

Instead of	Say
accomplish	do
communication	letter, order
come to a decision	decide
express a preference for	prefer
in the near future	soon
at this point in time	now, at present

THE IMPORTANCE OF VOCABULARY

If we fail to convey our thoughts clearly we lay ourselves open to misunderstanding. We must say exactly what we mean in terms that leave no doubt as to our intentions, and for this we must have an adequate vocabulary.

The power to use words effectively is a precious possession and, in business, a most desirable accomplishment. But for business purposes it is the quality rather than the range of vocabulary that matters. Ability to use a limited number of words with exactness is more important than to have a vague familiarity with a larger number. Merely to be able to identify a word in its context is not enough; before it can be properly used its exact meaning must be known. We all know the difference between an *imitation* and a *forgery*, between a *lie* and a *misstatement* and between an *infant* and a *child*, but are we sure about the differences between the following?

alternately (first one, then the other)	and	alternatively (offering a choice)
appropriate (suitable)	and	relevant (applicable)
bankrupt (destitute)	and	insolvent (unable to pay)
comprise (to include)	and	compose (to form)
disinterested (impartial)	and	uninterested (not interested)
infer (to draw a conclusion)	and	imply (to express in an indirect way)

There are many such words with almost but not quite the same meaning. Each has its own special meaning—a meaning that distinguishes it from all other words similar to it. Reflect for a moment on the different shades of meaning expressed by the synonyms (i.e. words with similar meanings) of a simple word like *said* in the following sentence:

He said (stated, asserted, suggested, claimed, maintained, declared) that the firm was in difficulties.

In loose conversation we may use such alternatives without much harm, but they signify important differences. *Say* means to express in words; *state*, to express in a formal manner; *assert*, to express strongly; *suggest*, to present an idea; *claim*, to express as being true; *maintain*, to uphold; *declare*, to make known. Such differences may appear trifling, but if we wish to think clearly and express ourselves clearly (and which of us does not?) we must respect them. *Large, huge, vast* and *great* all have their own shades of meaning, which reference to any good dictionary will quickly reveal.

Reading and the patient use of the dictionary are the best means we have of improving our knowledge and use of words. Chapter Six explains how this can be done. It is an excellent, and indeed an essential, practice to make a list of unfamiliar words as you come across them, learn their meanings and use them in speech and writing when the opportunity occurs. Only by actual use will new and unfamiliar words become part of your vocabulary.

EXERCISES

1. Write the following words and phrases in a column and at the side of each write a single word that has the same meaning. The part-words in brackets may help you.

dispute (con . . . . . rsy)	letters sent and received
indispensable (ne . . . . . ry)	(corr . . . . ce)
foretell (pr . . . . t)	altered appearance (dis . . . . e)
of lower rank (sub . . . . . . te)	onlooker (sp . . . . . . r)
have faith (be . . . . e)	drive out (ex . . l)
cannot be blotted out	
(ind . . . ble)	(*RSA*)

2. Form abstract nouns from the following words (e.g. from *tame* we form *tameness*): sure, move, genuine, keen, critic, infringe, aristocrat, neighbour, vulgar, condemn.   (*RSA*)

3. Rewrite or type the following sentences, substituting a single word for those in italics:

(a) A general meeting of shareholders is held *once a year*.

(b) He left the employment of his former company *of his own free will*.

(c) The meeting arranged for next Tuesday has been *put off to a later date*.

(d) At the end of the financial year we shall have to arrange for an *official examination of the accounts*.

(e) What was the amount of the *money paid as an instalment to confirm the contract*?

(f) The office manager was a *man who looks on the best side of things*.

(g) He spoke for half an hour *without preparation*.

(h) He was not noted for arriving at the office *at the appointed time*.

(i) The chief clerk was asked to arrange for a *list or schedule of items* to be prepared.

(j) If the firm is to make a profit next year it will be necessary to *cut down expenses*.

4. Replace each of the following expressions by a single word:

(a) gift under a will;
(b) yearly grant;
(c) unable to pay one's debts;
(d) spoken without preparation;
(e) paid appointment involving no work or duties;
(f) could not be recalled under any circumstances;
(g) numerical facts systematically collected;
(h) one entrusted with the carrying out of the terms of a will.

(RSA)

5. Explain *briefly* the difference in meaning between the words in each of the following pairs:

lay, lie	define, refine
practice, practise	uniform, dress
principal, principle	a right, a duty
insistent, consistent	independent, interdependent
profession, work	out-dated, out-moded

(RSA)

CHAPTER TWO

The Grammatical Background

Let schoolmasters puzzle their brain,
    With grammar and nonsense and learning,
Good liquor, I stoutly maintain,
    Gives genius a better discerning.
                Goldsmith: *She Stoops to Conquer*

GRAMMATICAL DISCIPLINE

Grammar is the name given to the system of rules underlying the use of language. It is concerned with *accidence* (changes in the form of single words) and *syntax* (the arrangement of words to form sense groups). To use a word in its wrong form, or to link words in a way contrary to accepted practice, is to be guilty of bad grammar.

There are certain rules that govern all good writing. These rules must be followed if we would write correctly, but we must not allow ourselves to become slaves to the finer points of grammar at the expense of that naturalness and warmth of tone which is the essence of all good writing. Grammar must be our servant and not our master. Even so, it is important to remember that the letters we write in business are expected to be in good English and that good English will generally be the kind of English that conforms to the accepted rules of grammar. These rules are, after all, the result of long experience and are based on common sense. They are a summary of what experienced writers have found to be the best safeguard against vague and ambiguous expression, and we cannot ignore them. Except therefore where usage clearly sanctions departures from the rules, the disciplines of grammar must be accepted and the rules must be observed. But let it be said at once that ability to write good English does not depend upon an intimate knowledge of grammar. Nevertheless, no-one can write correctly without understanding at least the basic principles of sentence construction and their practical application.

A person may claim that he knows nothing about grammar and yet be able to write perfectly good English. What he really means is that he is ignorant of the technical terms used in discussing language structure, and that he writes and speaks without being aware of the rules he is unconsciously following. Through speech and reading he has acquired the forms of correct expression, whose use has become second nature to him. True, a knowledge of grammar should lead to greater accuracy in expression, but a little common-sense is often all that is needed to rid us of many of the mistakes we sometimes make, as the following examples show:

Sentence (The correct expressions are placed in brackets)	Fault
(a) *Replying* to your enquiry, *the goods* were sent by post. (Say: *Replying to your enquiry, we* sent the goods by post.)	*Replying* is wrongly attached to *the goods.* It is the writer and not the goods who is replying.
(b) *As a regular customer* (say: *As you are a regular customer*) *we* will allow you a special discount.	The opening phrase is wrongly attached to the pronoun *we.* It is not the person writing who is the regular customer.
(c) I did not see the sign, travelling in the dark. (Say: *Travelling in the dark, I did not see the sign.*)	Departure from the natural order of expression.
(d) I laid (say: *lay*) my head on the pillow and slept soundly.	Confusion between the verbs *lay* and *lie.*
(e) *The reason why* a current account does not earn interest *is* because the money is repayable on demand. (Omit words in italics.)	The opening phrase means *because* and is tautological (i.e. unnecessarily repetitive).
(f) Quite a lot (say: *many,* or *a large number*) of us were surprised at the result.	*Quite* is an adverb, but is wrongly used as an adjective.
(g) He took a note from his wallet and put it on the table. (If the note, say: *From his wallet he took a note and ...*)	Sentence ambiguous. Is it the note or the wallet that is put on the table?

THE PARTS OF SPEECH

The words used in a sentence perform different functions. Some words give names to things; others describe things; still others tell what happens to them. There are in all eight of these functions and corresponding to them we have what are called the eight parts of speech, known by their technical names as nouns, pronouns, adjectives, verbs, adverbs, prepositions, conjunctions and interjections.

The rest of this chapter is devoted to a short account of each of these parts of speech. You will find the account sufficient to enable you to understand the work of sentence building dealt with in the next chapter.

The noun
A noun is the name we give to anything or anyone we want to say something about, e.g. *typewriter* (an object), *honesty* (a quality), *Southend* (a place), *Mary* (a person). There are different kinds of nouns, but it will be sufficient to note only three of them:

(a) *Common nouns.* These are names common to *any number of things of the same kind*, e.g. *girl, town, month.*

(b) *Proper nouns.* These are names for *particular things* that are distinct from every other, such as names of persons, places and any other objects that possess particular individual qualities, e.g. *Emily, Winchester, November.* Proper nouns always take an initial capital letter.

(c) *Collective nouns.* These are names given to *groups of similar things*, the group being regarded as one whole, e.g. *herd, flock, firm, council, audience, congregation, parliament.*

The pronoun
The pronoun is a word used *pro*, that is *for* or *instead of*, a noun (e.g. *I, me, mine, he, him, his, she, her, hers, it, its,* (not *it's*)) or several nouns (e.g. *we, us, ours, they, them, theirs*).

Mr Watson told his secretary to take the letter to the manager.
          HE   HER   IT   HIM

The value of the pronoun is that it avoids needless repetition and makes sentences easier to understand.

I saw the typist and asked the typist if the typist would type a letter.
                    HER   SHE

Like nouns, pronouns are of different kinds, but here again we are concerned with only three of them.

(a) *Personal pronouns* are those which represent persons or things. They are *I, you, he, she, it, we, they, me, him, her, us, them.*

I tell *you* I saw *him* do *it. We* left *them* with *her.*

(b) *Relative pronouns* are those which *relate* to some noun (or another pronoun) previously mentioned, called the *antecedent* because it *goes before.* They are *that, which* and *who* (with the forms *whose* and *whom*) and *what.*

The storekeeper, *who* was a careful man, always checked the invoices *that* came in.

In this sentence the respective antecedents of *who* and *that* are *storekeeper* and *invoices.*

The relative pronouns may also join sentences together and thus serve as conjunctions:

This is the typewriter *that* I bought. (i.e. This is the typewriter. I bought it.)
John Groves is a customer *whose* account is still unpaid. (i.e. John Groves is a customer. His account is still unpaid.)

(c) *Possessive pronouns* are those which denote possession. They are *mine, ours, yours, hers, its,* (not *it's*) *theirs.*

CAUTION: Take care not to confuse the relative pronoun *whose* with *who's* (meaning *who is*), or the possessive pronoun *its* with *it's* (meaning *it is*).

EXERCISES

1. Pick out the relative pronouns in the following sentences and name the antecedent of each.

(a) An account that is not regularly made up, presented, and settled is termed a current account.
(b) The receipt that you sent me was for an amount exceeding £2, but it need not now be stamped.
(c) The girl who answered the phone is my secretary.
(d) He is a man whom I have often wished to meet.
(e) The clerk whose car was stolen this morning works in the accounts department.
(f) The pen that you found in the corridor is mine.
(g) The book which I recommended is worth reading.
(h) The agent whom we appointed last year has now terminated his agreement.

(i) The results of the examination for which we sat during the summer are not yet published.

(j) The terms of the settlement that were arranged through your Mr Parker provided for a quarterly account.

2. Copy the following letters, making them read sensibly and smoothly by replacing nouns in parentheses by appropriate pronouns:

(a) Dear Mr Williams

> (Mr Parker and I) have received your letter of 5th July and will call on you next Monday. (Mr Parker and I) shall then be prepared to discuss the claim of the manufacturers against (Mr Parker and me) and make (the manufacturers) an offer of compensation.
>
> Mr Parker and I very much regret that (the manufacturers) should have had any cause for complaint concerning the consignment referred to by (Mr Williams). There have been no complaints about the earlier (consignments) and it is most unfortunate that there should now be dissatisfaction with the present (consignment).
>
> Yours faithfully
> F. Johnson

(b) Dear Mr Bowden,

> (Mr Parsons and I) were glad to receive an enquiry from (Mr Bowden) concerning Du Pont & Co. (Mr Parsons and I) have known this firm for many years, (Du Pont & Co.) are in fact very old customers of (Mr Parsons and me), and you may rely upon (Du Pont & Co.) as being a very respectable firm. (Du Pont & Co.) pay their accounts well within the time (Mr Parsons and I) allow for payment of (the accounts), and (Mr Parsons and I) do not hesitate to allow (Du Pont & Co.) credit to an amount considerably beyond the sum mentioned by (J. Bowden).
>
> Yours faithfully
> R. Spencer

The adjective

An adjective is a word that describes a noun or pronoun and so adds to its meaning. Each time we add an adjective to a noun we reduce the number of things to which the noun can refer:

(a) a pen
(b) a *fountain* pen
(c) a *black fountain* pen
(d) *my black fountain* pen

Sometimes the adjective expresses an attribute or quality

directly and stands with, or before, its noun; sometimes it follows and is used with a verb to form the predicate of the sentence, i.e. that part of a sentence which makes a statement about the subject:

(a) the *red* pencil (an attributive adjective)
(b) the pencil is *red* (a predicative adjective)

When two or more words are combined to denote a single quality, they are joined by a hyphen and form a *compound adjective*:

a *well-known* author; an *up-to-date* office

EXERCISES

1. Supply adjectives corresponding to the following nouns:

access	economy	presumption
account	error	pretence
advantage	example	probation
benefit	felicity	problem
column	habit	regret
commerce	island	remedy
comparison	labour	reputation
conscience	opportunity	secretary
contribution	discipline	spectacle
crisis	practice	terminus

2. Copy the following sentences, inserting any necessary hyphens (*Caution*: not all sentences require them):

(a) Arrange for the timber to be cut into one metre lengths.
(b) Even the most prejudiced anti trade unionist cannot object.
(c) I wish to make a long distance call.
(d) A first class ticket to Manchester will cost £14.50.
(e) As a player he is first class.
(f) A well written article on the subject appeared in *The Times* last week.
(g) The suggested advertisement will occupy a full page.
(h) A full page advertisement will cost £800.
(i) Various government financed projects have been suggested.
(j) Additional staff have been appointed, both full time and part time.

The verb

A verb is a word that makes a statement about something:

A postman *delivers* letters.

It may also give a command, or ask a question:

Write to Mr Smith after lunch. (A command)
Have you *paid* the bill? (A question)

When, as in the last example, the verb consists of more than one word, one of them (e.g. *paid*) will be the principal verb; the other word or words (e.g. *have*) are called *auxiliary* verbs because they "help" the principal verb to do its work.

Agreement with subject

A sentence is a group of words that express a complete thought and make complete sense. All sentences, whether long or short, consist of two parts—the *naming* part, or subject, and the *doing* part, or predicate. The predicate must include a verb since without a verb it is not possible to frame a sentence or express a thought. The verb used must always be in agreement with the subject as to both *number* (i.e. singular or plural) and *person* (i.e. the person or thing speaking, spoken to or spoken about, known respectively as first, second and third person).

Agreement is obtained by changing the form of the verb:

> I *hope* (first person singular).
> You *hope* (second person singular).
> He *hopes* (third person singular).
> We ⎫
> You ⎬ *hope* (plural, all three persons).
> They ⎭
> A telephone *is* necessary (third person singular).
> Telephones *are* necessary (third person plural).

Finite and non-finite verbs

Because the verb forms *hope* and *hopes* in the above examples are restricted to particular subjects they are said to be *finite*, i.e. limited to particular subjects. *Hopes*, for example, can apply only to third person singulars (e.g. *he, she, it* or their noun equivalents—*the man, the woman, the dog*). It cannot be used with first and second person subjects or with plural subjects (e.g. *I, you, we* or *they*, or their equivalents).

Non-finite verbs are those which, by themselves, cannot say anything about a subject. They take the following three forms:

(a) *to hope*, known as the infinitive,
(b) *hoping*, known as the present participle (which always ends in *-ing*),
(c) *hoped*, known as the past participle (which usually ends in either *-ed* or *-n*, as in *broken*).

These non-finite forms of the verb may be converted into finite verb forms by using them in association with auxiliary verbs:

I *shall* (to) hope (omitting the preposition in brackets).
I *was* hoping.
I *had* hoped.
We *have* broken.

Active and passive verbs

Verbs may also be classified as *active* or *passive*. Active verbs are these whose subject *does something* to something or someone else.

Our carrier *delivered* the goods yesterday.

Passive verbs are those whose subject is said to *suffer something* from something or someone else.

The goods *were delivered* by our carrier yesterday.

Verbs used passively tend to make a statement more impersonal. They are sometimes used in this way to convey unpopular news which the person communicating does not wish to be personally associated with.

Your claim for compensation *cannot be allowed*. (Passive)
rather than
We *cannot allow* your claim for compensation. (Active)

The adverb

We saw earlier that adjectives are used to describe nouns and pronouns. To modify any other part of speech we use *adverbs*:

Some people find it *very* hard to spell *correctly* (*very* modifies the adverb *hard*, and *correctly* modifies the verb *spell*).

He is an *unusually* keen man of business (*unusually* modifies the adjective *keen*).

She types *remarkably* well (*well* is itself an adverb and is in turn itself modified by the adverb *remarkable*).

The catalogue is *immediately* behind you (*immediately* modifies the preposition *behind*).

We offer this discount *only* because you are a good customer (*only* modifies the conjunction *because*).

To avoid ambiguity adverbs should be placed as near as possible to the words they modify:

Mr Watson *only* borrowed £5 (i.e. he did not seek the money as a gift).

Mr Watson borrowed *only* £5 (i.e. he borrowed £5 and no more).

Only Mr Watson borrowed £5 (i.e. he and no-one else).

Special care is needed with the adverb *only*. Its correct grammatical position is next to, preferably before, the word it qualifies, as in the above examples. But if there is no ambiguity, *only* may be allowed to take what is felt to be its natural, rather than its grammatical, place in the sentence. We can say, for instance:

She *only* sang one song.

which sounds more natural than the strictly correct

She sang *only* one song.

CAUTION: The adverb *all right* must always be written as two words, and never as *alright*.

EXERCISES

1. Construct sentences using each of the following commercial terms as (i) a noun, (ii) a verb:

(a) combine, transfer, report, credit, guarantee.
(b) order, return, market, supply, stamp.
(c) refund, commission, sample, tender, export.
(d) stock, invoice, estimate, advance, account.
(e) contract, discount, indent, mortgage, share.

2. Take the verb corresponding to each of the following commercial terms and use it to construct a sentence:

buyer	compensation	consumption	contribution
co-operation	correspondence	depreciation	economy
invoice	negotiability	production	protection
quotation	registration	remuneration	speculation
subsidy	typewriter	valuation	warranty

3. Copy the following sentences, selecting from the alternatives given in brackets the correct form of the finite verb:

(a) The entire system of road and rail communications (appear, appears) to be closely co-ordinated.

(b) It is one of the finest tributes that (has, have) been paid to any man.

(c) *Tales from Shakespeare* (was, were) written by Charles and Mary Lamb.

(d) We have received two reports from our surveyor neither of which (seem, seems) encouraging.

(e) Everyone, as all are aware, (know, knows) the answer.

(f) A large crowd of men, women and children (is, are) gathered in the square.

(g) The chairman, with the directors, (deny, denies) the reports circulated.

(h) Your car, and mine too, (need, needs) overhauling.

(i) Economics (is, are) nowadays included as a subject in most professional examinations.

(j) A large number of applications (has, have) been received.

4. Answer both *(a)* and *(b)*:

(a) The past participle of the verb "give" is "given". (Past participles can be used after "I have", e.g. I have *given*.)

Write down the past participles of the following verbs: drive; buy; seek; rage; sweep; spring; come; lie; cut; do.

(b) The past tense of the verb "give" is "gave".

Write down the past tense of the following verbs: beat; fall; go; know; kick; see; spring; lie; write; raise.

(RSA)

The preposition

A preposition (*pre-position* means a position in front of) always precedes a noun (or its equivalent) and shows the relation in which one thing stands to another:

The book is *on* the table (*under* the table; *behind* the table).

On, *under* and *behind* are all prepositions associating *book* with *table*.

Certain words are always followed by their own special prepositions. The use of these special prepositions is a matter of what is called *idiom*, i.e. what is customary, and no definite rules can be given. Apart from custom, there often seems to be no particular reason for using one preposition rather than some other, yet the use of the correct preposition is one of the principal tests of ability to speak and write good English.

The following is a list of the more common prepositional phrases:

absolve *from* (blame)
accede *to* (a request)
accompanied *by* (not *with*, e.g., a friend)
acquiesce *in* (a suggestion)
acquit *of* (a charge)
adapt *to* (a thing)
adapt *for* (a purpose)

adapt *from* (something previously done)
adequate *to* (or *for*)
agree *to* (a proposal)
agree *with* (a person)
agree *upon* (a plan)
analogous *to* (a thing)
angry *at* (a thing)

angry *with* (a person)
anxious *for* (someone's recovery)
anxious *about* (an event)
approve *of* (a thing)
averse *from* (or *to*)
centre *in* (or *on*, never *round*, e.g. the mind)
compare *to* (when comparing one thing to another)
compare *with* (when comparing resemblances and differences between two things)
compatible *with* (a condition)
compensate *for* (a loss)
comply *with* (a request)
concerned *at* (some occurrence)
concerned *for* (someone's welfare)
concur *in* (not *with*, e.g. a suggestion)
confer *on* (a subject)
confer *with* (a person)
confide *in* (i.e. place confidence in)
confide *to* (i.e. to entrust to)
conform *to* (a pattern)
connive *at* (an act)
conscious *of* (a circumstance)
consequent *upon* (an event)
consist *of* (i.e. composed of)
consist *in* (defines the subject referred to)
contemporary *with* (a person or thing)
conversant *with* (a thing)
correspond *to* (a thing)
correspond *with* (a person)
defer *to* (an opinion)
differ *from* (a person in some quality)
differ *with* (a person in opinion)

different *from* (no longer *to*)
divide *between* (two)
divide *among* (more than two)
encroach *on*(or *upon*)
enter *upon* (a duty)
enter *into* (an agreement)
impatient *with* (a person)
impatient *at* (an event or circumstance)
impatient *of* (criticism)
interfere *in* (a matter)
interfere *with* (a person)
invest *in* (an enterprise)
invest *with* (authority)
jump *at* (a bargain)
jump *to* (a conclusion)
oblivious *of* (not *to*, e.g. his surroundings)
opposite *to* (a thing)
part *from* (a friend)
part *with* (money)
personal *to* (an individual)
preference *for* (a thing)
presume *on* (a kindness)
prevail *upon* (not *on*, e.g. a person)
profit *by*.(experience)
profuse *in* (apologies)
reconcile *with* (a friend)
reconcile *to* (a condition)
replace *by* (not *with*, e.g. something else)
similar *to* (a thing)
substitute *for* (not *by* , e.g. something else)
suitable *for*
synonymous *with* (a thing)
tendency *to* (an action)
tendency *towards* (a state)
typical *of* (a person or thing)

There is a half-hearted rule that the preposition, being a link word, should not come at the end of a sentence. For formal written work this may be good advice, but strict observance of the rule frequently produces a forced artificiality that it is better to avoid.

What are you doing that FOR? has a smoother flow and a more natural ring than FOR *what are you doing that*? and *It is something I will not put up* WITH is certainly better than *It is something up* WITH *which I will not put.*

EXERCISES

1. Supply the correct prepositions to fill the gaps in the following sentences:

A

(a) John deferred ___ Mr Harvey's greater experience and did not press his preference ___ a bolder policy.

(b) Yours is a very different story ___ the one I heard yesterday.

(c) The employer was averse ___ giving details concerning the profits of the firm.

(d) Genius consists ___ an infinite capacity for taking pains.

(e) We may correspond ___ them on the subject, but politely point out that their accusations do not correspond ___ the facts.

(f) I agree ___ you ___ the proposals for an extension to the premises.

(g) My friend was impatient ___ me, and also ___ the suggestion I made.

(h) This sketch has been adapted ___ the play by us, and is quite suitable ___ children.

(i) The whole question centres ___ the results of the examination.

(j) He is likely to be acquitted ___ stealing.

B

(a) I will confide the powers ___ you.

(b) I will make an early opportunity to confer ___ the family ___ the matter raised.

(c) It is typical ___ him that he should wish to be reconciled ___ his friend.

(d) I hope to prevail ___ her not to replace the model ___ a more recent one.

(e) Every typist should be conversant ___ the basic rules of grammar.

(f) The smaller amount was divided ___ the two sisters, and the larger ___ the four brothers.

(g) Engrossed in her novel she was oblivious ___ the storm outside.

(h) I take the precisely opposite view ___ the one you yourself hold.

(i) The children entered ___ the task of memorizing the poem.

(j) It would be unwise to interfere ___ the couple ___ the plans they are making for their holiday.

2. We *accuse* a person *of* some wrongful act. What prepositions are used after the following:

adequate; amenable; acquiesce; associate; confide; compatible; conduce; derive; desist; contrary. (RSA)

The conjunction

A conjunction is a word used to join together either (a) other words or (b) sentences. The two conjunctions most commonly used are *and* and *but*:

Clear speech *and* legible handwriting are the good manners of language (joins words).

I will call, *but* I cannot stay long (joins sentences).

The conjunction must not be used to connect ideas that are not related. We cannot for example say:

The directors will interview the applicants *and* there will be a full moon tonight.

since there is no connection between the two ideas expressed.

Other conjunctions in common use include *as, when, since, if, or, otherwise, because,* and the phrases *as well as, as soon as*:

I must go soon, *otherwise* I shall be late.

Let me know *as soon as* you are ready to go.

The following conjunctions are always used in pairs; each must always be accompanied by its own partner:

> both ... and
> either ... or
> neither ... nor
> not only ... but also
> not merely ... but even
> if ... then
> rather ... than
> whether ... or

She is *not only* a good typist *but also* a competent shorthand-writer.
I would *rather* travel by train today *than* by plane tomorrow.
I am undecided *whether* to go tomorrow *or* wait until next week.

Conjunctions used in pairs in this way are known as *correlative* conjunctions, because each is related to the other.

EXERCISES

1. Use each of the following conjunctions in a sentence of your own construction:

although	that
because	then
both ... and	therefore
neither ... nor	unless
otherwise	yet

2. The following paragraphs consist of short sentences. Improve them by combining some of the sentences in order to produce a more fluent style. (Avoid the too frequent use of *and* and *then*.)

(*a*) We received your letter of 15th January. Your order has not been overlooked. The goods are now being packed. They should reach you by the beginning of next week. We are sorry about the delay. We have had a great deal of sickness among the staff.

(*b*) I regret to inform you that a fire broke out last night. It occurred in the storage shed. The damage is estimated at £3,000. The stock consists mainly of textile materials. Fortunately, the books were not destroyed. The value of the damaged stock can therefore be ascertained without difficulty. Please arrange for your representative to call. I should like him to do so at once if possible. Let me have your instructions regarding salvage.

(*c*) I regret that you have ignored my previous applications for a settlement of your account. It was rendered on 1st June last. It was for the sum of £37.50. Your cheque must reach me before the morning of 30th November. Unless it does so I shall take immediate steps to enforce payment.

(*d*) I am pleased to inform you that I have taken Mr S. Wright into partnership with me. The reason is the large increase in the business. Mr Wright was my senior traveller. He has represented the firm for the past twenty years. He is thoroughly conversant with the details of the business. The name of the firm will remain unchanged.

(*e*) I am pleased to support the application of Miss J. Rowse for a post with you. She was employed by me for fifteen years. She was my secretary. I found her to be most trustworthy. She was steady and reliable. She was also a first-class shorthand writer and typist. Her only reason for leaving me was that I accepted a post in Scotland. She did not see her way to leave London. All her interests and connections were there. I can thoroughly recommend her.

The interjection
An interjection is a word used either to call attention (e.g. Hi! Hello!) or to express some feeling or emotion (e.g. Oh! Good! Really! Splendid!). Interjections are sometimes *interjected* or *thrown into* a sentence, but form no part of its grammatical structure:

Heavens! It's four o'clock already.

The interjection takes a capital letter and is always followed by an exclamation mark, as in the above examples.

For a more detailed account of the parts of speech the reader is referred to the author's *English for Business Studies.** The two most important are the noun (or pronoun) and the verb; both are in fact indispensable, for without either of them intelligible communication between persons is impossible. The other parts of speech serve the purpose of extending the use of the noun or the verb to convey different shades of meaning.

* Macdonald & Evans (3rd edn.), 1983.

CHAPTER THREE

Sentence Building

By being so long in the lowest form [at Harrow] I gained an immense advantage over the cleverer boys ... I got into my bones the essential structure of the ordinary British sentence—which is an honourable thing.

Winston S. Churchill: *My Early Life*

THE KINDS OF SENTENCE

A sentence is a combination of words expressing a complete thought and making complete sense. It may be any one of four kinds:

(a) It may make a statement: Transport brings us food from all over the world.

(b) It may ask a question: How much will it cost to send the goods by air?

(c) It may issue a command: Let me have your decision by the weekend.

(d) It may take the form of an exclamation: What a pity delivery was held up!

The exclamation sentence is not normally used in business correspondence, but it is just as well to be familiar with its construction.

Whatever its form, and however long or short, the sentence always consists of two parts—the *naming* part or subject, and the *doing* part or predicate. As in example *(c)* above the subject may be omitted as being understood.

Subject	Predicate
(a) Transport	brings us food from all over the world.
(b) It	will cost how much to send the goods by air?
(c) (You)	let me have your decision by the weekend.
(d) (It	is) what a pity delivery was held up!

24

PHRASES AND CLAUSES

The phrase

From the above examples it is clear that a sentence must not only have both a subject and a predicate but also make complete sense. A phrase has neither of these qualities. It is a group of words with no finite verb and therefore cannot by itself make sense. Consider the following sentences:

   (a) *My bank account* is overdrawn.
   (b) The car *in the garage* is mine.
   (c) You will find the papers *on my desk*.

In each of these sentences the words in italics form a phrase. In sentence (a) the phrase forms the subject of the sentence and is therefore equivalent to a noun. (It is a *noun phrase*.) In sentence (b) the phrase identifies the car and is therefore equivalent to an adjective. (It is an *adjectival phrase*.) In sentence (c) the phrase explains *where* and is therefore equivalent to an adverb. (It is an *adverbial phrase* modifying the verb *find*.)

The clause

When two or more sentences are combined to form a longer sentence, they cease to be called sentences and, in relation to the longer sentence of which they become part, are known as *clauses*, each with its own subject and predicate. Take the following three sentences:

He had a fortnight's holiday.
He went to Spain.
He did not enjoy himself.

Using conjunctions, these sentences may be combined to form one, thus:

He had a fortnight's holiday and (he) went to Spain,
       Clause 1   Clause 2
      but (he) did not enjoy himself.
             Clause 3

Clauses, like phrases, may serve as nouns, adjectives and adverbs:

WE REGRET *we cannot deliver the goods immediately*.
(The words in italics form a *noun clause* serving as the object of *regret*.)
THE GOODS *you delivered yesterday* ARE NOT SATISFACTORY.
(In this example, an *adjectival clause* explaining which goods.)
WE WILL DESPATCH YOUR ORDER *as soon as we can*.

(In this example, an *adverbial clause* explaining time of despatch.)

In each of these sentences the clause in capitals makes the main statement and is known as the *main clause*; the clause in italics adds to the meaning of the main clause and is known as a *dependent* (or *subordinate*) *clause*.

EXERCISES

1. Place in three groups the adverbs, adverbial phrases and adverbial clauses printed in italics in the following sentences:

(a) I will meet you at *two o'clock tomorrow afternoon.*
(b) *As soon as the new session begins* we shall join typewriting classes.
(c) The tribunal dealt with the case *fairly.*
(d) You will find the papers *in the right-hand tray on my desk.*
(e) *Now and then* I am required to help in the wages office.
(f) We shall attend to your order *as soon as supplies are received from the manufacturers.*
(g) *The urgent letters having been dealt with,* we were able to relax.
(h) She writes shorthand *nearly as fast as I do.*
(i) *When* will you be taking up your new post?
(j) The consignment was delayed *because of the dock strike.*

2. Write out the main clauses in the following passages:

(a)   *Letter of Introduction*
I have much pleasure in introducing Mr James Hawkins, who has been a member of the clerical staff of this firm for the past five years. Owing to his wife's illness it is necessary for him to remove to the south coast, where he hopes to obtain work as a book-keeper.

If you have a vacancy in your accounts department I should like you to consider Mr Hawkins. He has had good accounting experience with us and we have always found him to be very conscientious and trustworthy.

(b)   *Letter of Recommendation*
In reply to your enquiry of 3rd April, I am glad to be able to report favourably on Messrs Du Pont & Co. They are a small but highly respectable firm and very old customers of ours, and have been established for nearly thirty years.

They do not as a rule qualify for cash discounts, but on the other hand they pay their accounts promptly. We ourselves have no hesitation in giving them credit to an amount considerably beyond the sum you mention.

(c)   *Circular Letter*
We regret to inform your that our premises at 17 Broad Street were partly destroyed by fire earlier this week. Fortunately, we have been

able to obtain temporary factory accommodation at 25–27 Morley Road and hope by the end of this week to be able to fulfil the orders we now have on hand, including your own.

Although the damage to our premises is serious, production will not be unduly hampered, and we look forward to a continuance of your own custom, which we have always valued.

3. Construct sentences to include each of the following clauses *(i)* as an adjectival clause, *(ii)* as an adverbial clause, *(iii)* as a noun clause:

    (a) when the work is completed
    (b) where the secretary lives
    (c) when I receive your cheque
    (d) where the meeting is to be held

STRUCTURE OF THE SENTENCE

The structure of a sentence may be:

    (a) simple
    (b) compound
    (c) complex
    (d) compound-complex

The simple sentence
This is the sentence in its simplest form. It contains only one finite verb and can therefore make one, and only one, complete statement:

The creation of good will *is* an important function of the business letter.

A sentence may have several subjects, but so long as it makes only one statement about them it is still a simple sentence:

Clarity, simplicity, sincerity and courtesy *have* a place in all good business letters.

And just as a verb may have more than one subject, so it may have more than one object; in the following sentence *provides* has three:

The Post Office *provides* postal services, banking services, and remittance facilities.

Notwithstanding the three objects, this is still a simple sentence since it contains only one finite verb.

The compound sentence

A sentence is said to be *compound* when it consists of two or more coordinate main clauses (that is independent clauses of equal grammatical status) and no dependent clauses:

I applied for the post but (I) was not successful.

     Main clause   Main clause

Neither of these two clauses depends in any way on the other; each makes a statement that stands by itself, and to form the sentence they are linked by a conjunction.

The complex sentence

A sentence is said to be *complex* when it contains one main clause and one or more dependent clauses:

The traveller who called yesterday promised he would call again.

| (Subject of main clause) | (Dependent adjec- tival clause qualifying *traveller*) | (Predi- cate of main clause) | (Dependent noun clause, the object of *promised*) |

The compound-complex sentence

A sentence is said to be *compound-complex* when it contains two or more main clauses (i.e. compound) and one or more dependent clauses (i.e. complex):

If you hope to succeed you must work hard and pass your examination

   Dependent clause   Main clause   Main clause
                                                   (*you must* understood)

EXERCISES

1. Say whether each of the following sentences is simple, compound or complex:

(a) The ship, carrying a load of timber from the Baltic, put into Kiel for repairs.

(b) The ship, which was carrying a load of timber, put into Kiel.

(c) The ship was carrying a load of timber and put into Kiel for repairs.

(d) There have been disturbances in Algeria, which may have the effect of bringing about an improvement in prices.

(e) The disturbances in Algeria may have the effect of raising prices.

(f) There have been disturbances in Algeria and a rise in prices is likely to be the result.

(g) The paper we have been using is unsatisfactory inasmuch as it will not keep its colour on the walls.

(h) Because of its tendency to fade the paper we have been using is unsatisfactory.

(i) The paper does not keep its colour on the walls and is therefore unsatisfactory.

(j) The paper, being liable to discoloration, is unsatisfactory.

2. Turn each of the following sentences into a compound or complex sentence, stating whether your sentence is compound or complex:

(a) Having dealt with the firm for so many years I have no hesitation in recommending them.

(b) I had the pleasure of meeting your director yesterday for the first time.

(c) The premises in Victoria Park are for sale.

(d) The ship sailed from the Port of London at dawn.

(e) We are enclosing samples showing the various colours we stock.

(f) Prices, including delivery to your works, can be arranged.

(g) Acting on the instructions of the chairman, the secretary signed the contract.

(h) To help you to decide we are sending you samples by separate post.

(i) Having heard of your recent removal into the district we are sending you a copy of our catalogue.

(j) We thank you for your letter enclosing a copy of your latest price-list.

3. Analyse the following complex sentence into its constituent clauses, writing each one out in full. State what kind of clause each is, and show its connection with the rest of the sentence.

Here is the sentence:

When I asked the boys if they would be responsible for any damage that might occur while they were using the premises, they said they hadn't thought about that. (RSA)

THE FORM OF THE SENTENCE

Writing would soon become monotonous if sentences were always built to the same pattern. Variety is just as necessary in letter-writing as it is to an attractive garden. Some of the ways in which we can vary the construction of sentences to make our letters more interesting and attractive will now be considered.

The form of a sentence may be loose or periodic and this is determined by its principal statement.

The loose sentence
The distinguishing characteristic of the *loose* sentence is that it makes the principal statement at the beginning. It consists in fact

of a grammatically complete statement followed by one or more explanatory or qualifying phrases or clauses. It continues to run on after grammatical completeness has been reached and when it may be thought that the sentence has come to an end:

We are not surprised to learn that the cheque has been dishonoured,/as there have been rumours that the financial position of the drawers is unsatisfactory / on account of their inability to raise capital / necessary to finance their new extensions.

The main idea in this sentence is contained in the first clause. The sentence is grammatically complete at the word *dishonoured* and could have finished there. It could also have finished at either of the other two divisions indicated.

The periodic sentence

The distinguishing characteristic of the *periodic* sentence is that it reserves the principal statement for the end. It is not grammatically complete until the end of the sentence is reached, and in consequence the mind of the reader is kept in suspense until the sentence is finished:

As there have been rumours that the financial position of the drawers is unsatisfactory on account of their inability to raise capital necessary to finance their new extensions, *we are not surprised to learn that the cheque has been dishonoured.*

Loose and periodic sentences compared

Loose	Periodic
I had an interview as soon as I arrived.	As soon as I arrived, *I had an interview.*
The price of tea rose owing to rumours of a bad crop.	Owing to rumours of a bad crop, *the price of tea rose.*
Please let me know immediately should you be unable to deliver the goods.	Should you be unable to deliver the goods, *please let me know immediately.*

The periodic style is more dignified and forceful than the loose style. It tends to induce brevity and precision and above all to maintain the unity of the sentence. It leaves one with a sense of completeness. On the other hand it demands greater concentration, and if the sentence is long the thread of the various subordinate statements made may have been lost by the time the main statement at the end of the sentence is reached.

The loose sentence has the advantage of being easy, flowing and natural, and is thus admirably suited to a plain straightforward style of narrative. It is more in keeping with the style of the spoken language and calls for less effort on the part of the reader. It is therefore particularly suitable for business letter-writing. Its danger is that it may degenerate into slipshod construction and become involved and obscure.

Whether the loose or the periodic style is preferable depends upon the context in which it is used. Each form of sentence has its own special advantages and drawbacks, and neither can be regarded as superior to the other. The practice of the best writers is to use both forms, though for letter-writing it is better that the loose form should tend to predominate.

EXERCISES

1. Recast the following loose sentences in periodic form:

(a) He gave me an order the first time I called, and with little or no trouble on my part.

(b) Cost of production is a vital factor for the manufacturer, in fact just as vital a factor as the selling price.

(c) The chairman's report provided almost unlimited opportunities for questions and criticism, and this was not surprising in view of the difficult time through which the company had just passed.

(d) We should be very glad to go into this matter in greater detail on receiving further particulars from you, including the submission of drawings and estimates.

(e) At today's sale the price of tea made a sudden jump owing to rumours that a severe drought had adversely affected the crop.

2. Recast the following periodic sentences in loose form:

(a) As soon as I arrived, and almost before I had sat down, the office manager began asking me about my previous job.

(b) In spite of all the indications to the contrary present trends in market prices are likely to be reversed.

(c) Although the conduct of the accountant in the matter of the loans was open to criticism, no one doubted his honesty.

(d) Although, looking back, it seems only like yesterday, it is now five years since we placed our first order with you.

(e) Before the railway authorities will accept any parcels for dispatch they require a consignment note to be signed.

THE LENGTH OF THE SENTENCE

The length of a sentence is a matter of no less importance than its form, but there is no hard-and-fast rule as to what the length should be.

The short sentence has the merit of simplicity; it is easy to understand and is more suitable for business letters than the long sentence, which calls for skill and practice as well as ability to think ahead clearly. A business enterprise deals with hard facts, and these are more easily grasped if presented in short sentences written to the point. Only rarely should it be necessary to write sentences of more than about twenty words. Moreover, the longer the sentence the more are grammatical errors likely to creep in. For example:

> The report on the finances of the firms referred to in your letters of 5th and 13th March *suggest* the need for a cautious credit policy.

Here, the verb *suggest* has been made to agree with the plural nouns preceding it instead of with the subject, *The report*, to which the verb properly belongs.

If you have not yet had much experience in writing, you are advised to keep your sentences short until you have gained enough command of language to lengthen them without getting lost in a tangle of grammatical precepts and confused thinking. Note, however, that a succession of short sentences tends to produce a disagreeable jerky effect:

> We have sent you a consignment of cotton by SS *Arabia*. We enclose the bill of lading and bill of exchange. The latter requires acceptance. It should be returned immediately.

Monotony of this kind is avoided by using sentences of varying length. A judicious mixture of long and short is called for so that the drowsy monotony of long sentences is broken by the occasional use of a short sharp sentence that revives drooping attention. For example:

> We regret to have to complain that you have not yet delivered the goods ordered a month ago (*medium*). They are now urgently wanted (*short*). The customer for whom we ordered them threatens to cancel his order unless he receives the goods by the end of this month at the latest (*long*). Please therefore do all you can to deliver them at once (*short*).

Broadly speaking, a preponderance of long sentences sets a dignified and lofty style, and a preponderance of short sentences a style that is light and conversational. The short sentence is there-fore more suitable for letter-writing though, to avoid monotony, there must be a discreet blending of the short with the long.

EXERCISES

1. Combine each of the following groups of short sentences into not more than two sentences each, making only minor changes:

(a) The train ran through the station. It was a fast train. It did not stop. There were crowds of passengers. The passengers were waiting on the platform. Most of the passengers were in a great hurry.

(b) The old man settled in his chair. It was his favourite armchair. He was tired. He had done a hard day's work. He had reached home. His wife was busy. She was preparing his tea. (RSA)

2. Rewrite each of the following groups of sentences as one long sentence. Do not use *and, but, so* or *then.* No information must be omitted, but the order of the sentences may be changed:

(a) The garden was beautiful. It contained flowers of many different colours. I was very impressed by it.

(b) The letter was long. It was very badly written. I did not read it.

(c) The man worked hard. He deserved to succeed. He never gave up trying. He had failed many times. (RSA)

3. Show your skill at sentence structure by combining the following sentences in the most interesting and suitable ways:

The word "electric" comes from the Greek word "elektron". This word means "amber". Amber is the name given to a fossil. This fossil is made of resin. This substance must be briskly rubbed. Then it attracts other substances. These must be small and light. William Gilbert first studied frictional electricity. He lived at Colchester. This is a town in England. He has been called "the father of electricity". He wrote a book. It was published in the year 1600. It concerned the magnet, magnetic bodies and our earth as a magnet. All over Europe, men became interested in electricity. Sometimes progress was made. Chance played a certain part. There is an example. Two Germans tried to electrify water. They took a hand machine. This machine could produce electricity. They suspended an iron chain from it. The other end of the chain was dipped into water. This was in a jar. The result was interesting. It was the starting point. From this point were developed condensers. These condensers play a part today. They are important. They are used in wireless apparatus and in telephones.

(RSA)

CHARACTERISTICS OF THE GOOD SENTENCE

Unity

Sentences must be built to a regular plan, with each part grammatically related to some other part. But this grammatical unity is not by itself enough. In addition, there must be unity of thought, that is to say a sentence must contain one, and no more than one, main idea, with each of the several parts closely related to the main thought the sentence is intended to convey. It would be logical to write:

> We sent you a cheque for £25 yesterday and hope you received it safely.

because the second statement is related to the first. But we cannot write:

> We sent you a cheque for £25, and we begin our summer sale next week.

since the sentence contains two main ideas—the cheque and the sale—that are in no way related. The sale has nothing whatever to do with the cheque. Each of these two main ideas should appear in a sentence of its own.

The following is a less obvious example of false unity:

> The Bank of England, which employs a staff of about 5,000, acts as financial adviser to the British Government.

The separate facts stated here are inappropriately linked, since there is no logical connection between the number of staff employed and the Bank's advisory function. The two ideas should therefore be expressed in separate sentences:

> The Bank of England employs a staff of about 5,000. It acts as financial adviser to the British Government.

Coherence

Coherence here means that the component parts of a sentence must be arranged in good logical order. Incoherence may result either from lack of balance or from failure to observe the rule of proximity (*see* below).

Balance

The balanced sentence is a stylistic device by which those parts of a sentence similar *in thought* are made similar *in form*.

> Reading maketh a *full man*; conference a *ready man*; writing an *exact man*.   (Bacon)

Every lesson is a *lesson in English*, and every teacher is a *teacher of English*.

A well-balanced sentence has an attraction of its own: it makes for simplicity and sounds well. It is useful in making comparisons and contrasts, but it must not be taken to excess because it tends to become monotonous with overuse. It must therefore be used with moderation.

Proximity

It is a rule of correct writing that qualifying words and phrases must be placed as close as possible to others to which they belong in the sentence, otherwise the sentence may convey a meaning not intended. This is known as the *Rule of Proximity*.

Please let me know the number of clerks on duty *by the end of the month*.

Does the writer mean that he wants the information by the end of the month? If he does, then the phrase in italics should be placed immediately after the verb *know*, to which it belongs.

Lack of proximity may also produce ambiguity:

He took a note from his wallet, and with an angry gesture *threw it on the counter*.

Threw what: the note or the wallet? If as seems probable it was the note, then the sentence should be rearranged so that *threw it on the counter* follows *note*, thus:

From his wallet he took a note and, with an angry gesture, threw it on the counter.

The need for special care in placing the adverb *only* has already been referred to in Chapter Two.

Emphasis

The normal order of words in a sentence is

subject + predicate + object

with qualifying words and phrases placed as near as possible to the words to which they belong. Variation of normal word order is an effective way not only of avoiding the monotony born of sameness, but also of securing emphasis since words placed abnormally attract attention, especially when placed at the beginning or the end of a sentence.

Normal order	Emphatic order
The amount owing on your account is £25.	On your account the amount owing is £25. (Emphasizes *your* account)
I met your representative yesterday	Yesterday, I met your representative. (Emphasizes the day)

Emphasis is also achieved by using *It is, It was* to introduce statements.

Normal	Emphatic
We note with surprise the content of your letter.	*It is with surprise* that we note the content of your letter.
Unfortunately the goods did not arrive in time.	*It is unfortunate* that the goods did not arrive in time.

Variety of expression

To avoid monotony in writing is not difficult since most ideas can be expressed in a number of different ways:

We will certainly pay you promptly if we can.
Certainly, we shall pay you promptly if possible.
If we are able to pay you promptly, we shall certainly do so.
If it is at all possible, we shall certainly pay you promptly.
Unless prevented from doing so, we shall certainly pay you promptly.

EXERCISES

1. Point out the ambiguity or absurdity in each of the following sentences and, by changing the order of the words or phrases and making any other necessary changes, rewrite or type the sentences to give the meaning probably intended:

(a) Every now and again the trader goes for a talk with his manager to find out how he stands.

(b) The accounts should be passed to me for payment not later than 30th September.

(c) The manager told his clerk he was a careless man, and could not keep his accounts properly.

(d) Bills are requested to be paid in advance.

(e) I shall return the copy of the book which you sent me for inspection during the course of next week.

(f) I should be glad if you would let me know the number of children attending the classes before the end of the month.

(g) We learnt that the parcel reached you with much satisfaction.

(h) The speakers for next week will be found pinned on the notice board.

(i) The daughter of a retired Indian civil servant, educated in England, seeks employment as a secretary.

(j) He gave an account of his travels soon after his return to one of the leading newspapers.

2. Recast the following sentences so as to improve them in any way you think necessary:

(a) Goods that are easily broken are not advised to be sent by rail.

(b) Goods taken by road is a much better form of transport than goods taken by rail.

(c) Until we receive confirmation of this information I do not think it should be made public.

(d) The enclosed sample of cloth is the nearest we can supply to the colour required, from stock, which we trust will meet with your approval.

(e) Without transport motor cars would not have been able to be produced in the first place.

(f) The importance of transport in connection with commerce is so great it could not function properly without it.

(g) The bank provides a safe place to deposit money instead of keeping it in the house.

(h) Without transport goods, if they were perishable, would be no use at all.

(i) A current account does not usually earn interest, the reason being because it is not kept by the bank for a long period.

(j) A department store often has a restaurant which is very convenient and also very reasonable prices.

3. Explain two ways in which each of the following sentences can be interpreted. Rewrite each sentence so that it has only one possible meaning:

(a) The manager was as anxious to please his customers as his staff.

(b) The appeal for the founding of a scholarship fund by the staff representative is worthy of consideration.

4. Express each of the following statements in as many different ways as you can:

(a) If it is at all possible we shall deliver the goods tomorrow.

(b) We cannot despatch the goods as promised because of the railway strike.

(c) We hope you will send us a trial order so that you can test our claims against the facts.

(d) By imparting information to customers, the catalogue performs much the same function as the salesman.

(e) Because of their warmth continental quilts are rapidly becoming very popular.

CHAPTER FOUR

The Paragraph

A tale should be judicious, clear, succinct:
The language plain, and incidents well link'd.
William Cowper: *Conversation*

FUNCTION

A paragraph may consist of a single sentence, as it often does at the conclusion of a letter:

We hope the goods will reach you in good time and that we may have the pleasure of further orders from you.

But what is generally understood by paragraphing is the arrangement of sentences into groups to make the reader's task easier. Besides, a page of typed or printed matter arranged in paragraph form looks much less forbidding than if presented in a solid block.

The sentences grouped to form a paragraph must be closely related to one another in thought and deal with the same subject-matter—the same topic or theme, or at least a different aspect of the topic. Each paragraph should deal with only one idea, and every sentence in the paragraph should have a distinct bearing upon the sentences that precede and follow it. As soon as the idea dealt with is exhausted another paragraph should be begun.

The function of the paragraph is best understood if we think of a chain as consisting of a number of separate links. Each link is a complete unit in itself, but it serves also to connect the links immediately before and immediately after it. In the same way each paragraph is a unit since it deals with only one topic; at the same time it serves to carry the reader forward to the next stage in the development of the writer's theme.

ESSENTIAL QUALITIES

The essential qualities of a good paragraph, like those of a good sentence, are unity and coherence.

Unity

Unity means that the paragraph deals with only one main point or topic, and that nothing is introduced unless it has a bearing on that topic. This concentration of the paragraph upon a single topic makes the reader's task easier. It helps him to follow the writer's train of thought one step at a time and thus makes for clarity and assists comprehension. For each new topic there should be a new paragraph. Consider the following letter:

27 May 19..

Mr N A Ford
25 Clive Avenue
Sheldon
Devon TQ14 0HA

Dear Sir

We are pleased to offer you an appointment as our representative in South-West England on a commission basis of five per cent. Hotel, travelling, and miscellaneous expenses will be paid in addition.

It is not our policy to dispute every unusual item of expenditure and, as long as results justify them, expenses incurred will be refunded immediately

The special features of your territory make it necessary for us to leave a great deal to your discretion in such matters as discounts and terms of credit to be allowed. Provided therefore that the arrangements you make are in keeping with our interests, we propose to give you a free hand.

You will of course realize that we are placing a good deal of confidence in you, and we trust that the amount of business you are able to find for us will justify our estimate of your ability.

Yours faithfully

T F Johnson

This letter deals with four separate ideas:

    (a) the appointment and its terms:
    (b) the firm's policy concerning expenses;
    (c) the agent's freedom of action; and finally,
    (d) an expression of hope.

This letter is therefore set out in four paragraphs each dealing with its own separate idea.

Coherence

It is not by itself enough that the sentences forming a paragraph should relate to the same point. They must be placed in logical order so that one sentence leads naturally to the next, the next taking up the point where the preceding one left it. In other words, each sentence is a unit complete in itself and must be so linked with other sentences that the writer's thoughts move smoothly and naturally from one statement to the next.

The following paragraph fails to develop its point naturally and so lacks coherence:

> *(a)* Punctuation in business is usually left to the typist. *(b)* Not infrequently a sentence will be dictated that depends for its meaning upon the punctuation marks used. *(c)* Such sentences may not be good sentences, *(d)* but it is the typist's duty to see that the punctuation used conveys the meaning intended. *(e)* The typist is taught punctuation as part of her professional training.

Following the natural sequence the paragraph would be improved if recast in the order *(e)*, *(a)*, *(b)*, *(c)*, *(d)*, as follows:

> Punctuation is taught to the typist as part of her professional training, and in business is usually left to her. Not infrequently a sentence will be dictated that depends for its meaning upon the punctuation marks used. Such sentences may not be good sentences, but it is the typist's duty to see that the punctuation used conveys the meaning intended.

THE TOPIC SENTENCE

As we have seen, a well-constructed paragraph will deal with only one point or topic. This will usually be announced in one of the sentences, the remaining sentences serving merely to extend or elaborate the point made in the *topic sentence*, as it is called.

Because of its importance it is usual to place the topic sentence at the beginning of the paragraph. This has the advantage of telling the reader what the paragraph is about and so helps him to follow the writer's train of thought without trouble.

Consider the following letter (topic sentences in italics):

Dear Mr Loeber

We contemplate publishing a new edition of our 800-page, blue-bound, English and Shorthand Dictionary. Our first problem is to find someone able and willing to prepare a list of new words that have come into general use since the Dictionary was last edited, and to delete those that have fallen into disuse to such an extent that their inclusion in a dictionary of this kind could not reasonably be expected.

The purpose of this letter is to invite you to undertake the required revision for us at a fee to be agreed upon. Until a start has been made on the work it is impossible to estimate the length of time it is likely to take, and consequently I am unable to suggest a fee. It occurs to me, however, that the most satisfactory arrangement would be to base payment upon an agreed rate of so much a day, and to leave it to you to decide what constitutes a day's work.

The dictionary position in this country, though better now than formerly, is not entirely satisfactory. In recent years, many new words have found their way into the accepted vocabulary but, as yet, not into many dictionaries. Even the Oxford Dictionary with its half-million references can never be up to date. Some of the smaller single-volume dictionaries, however, have recently been revised and of these the most useful appears to me to be Chamber's Twentieth Century Dictionary.

I hope you will be able to accept my invitation. May I suggest that you join me at lunch one day next week when, after a discussion of some of the problems involved in the revision, you could perhaps give me your decision.

I look forward to hearing from you.

Yours sincerely

In this letter each paragraph deals with only one topic. As each new topic is introduced a new paragraph is begun, the writer's thoughts moving naturally from one point to the next—from publication in the first paragraph, to invitation in the second, to the dictionary position in the third, and on to the final appeal. Each paragraph is introduced by a sentence that refers so suitably to the subject-matter that the reader is left in no doubt as to what the paragraph is about.

A paragraph in which the topic sentence appears at the beginning is said to be *loose*; one in which the topic sentence appears at the end is said to be *periodic*. (Compare loose and periodic sentences, explained in Chapter Three.) It is much less usual for the topic sentence to appear at the end, but when it does the paragraph will begin by clearing up some preliminary matter. The aim may be to marshal facts leading to a conclusion or an effective climax. For example (topic sentence in italics):

Dear Sirs

We understand that you have been established in South America for many years, and that you have built up a wide connection with buyers there. We also understand that you specialize in marketing electrical appliances and machinery. Having recently extended our factory in Birmingham we are now anxious to widen the market for our increased output. *We are therefore writing to invite you to accept appointment as our sole agents for South America on terms to be arranged, and hope you will accept.*

Yours faithfully

LENGTH OF THE PARAGRAPH

There is no hard-and-fast rule about the length of the paragraph but be careful to use paragraphs of varying length. This helps to give your letters an interesting and attractive appearance that otherwise would give way to uniformity and dullness if paragrpahs of equal length were used. Length will vary with the circumstances and be determined by the unity of the thought to be expressed. The modern trend favours the fairly short paragraph, which has the merit of presenting ideas clearly and is easy to follow. Long paragraphs, like long sentences, tend to become involved and are less readily understood than short ones. It is therefore better to avoid paragraphs of more than about half a dozen lines of typing; depending on circumstances some paragraphs may consist of only two or three lines. One of the advantages of using short sentences is that they divide more easily into paragraphs of suitable length than long ones.

The fairly short paragraph is well suited to the style of the business letter. Quite apart from helping the reader to grasp the writer's points more quickly, it helps to give the letter an attractive appearance. A solid unbroken text has an uninteresting look. It makes for slow and hard reading and may well irritate the reader. To divide the same text into paragraphs gives it a touch of lightness and stimulates interest. On the other hand, too many very short paragraphs must be avoided because of the disjointed effect they tend to produce. Far from helping the reader, a long series of very short paragraphs may prove to be a hindrance. The paragraph is essentially a unit of thought; length is controlled by the idea to be expressed. But if treatment of a single idea requires a sequence that means an unreasonably long paragraph, then the paragraph may be split. On the other hand, paragraphs that do not form units of thought must not be combined to form a paragraph, even though this may result in what may seem to be unduly short paragraphs.

DISPLAY

If it is to serve its purpose of helping the reader the paragraph must be displayed so as to "catch the eye". With sentences this is done by leaving a space (two or three strokes of the space bar in typewriting) after the full stop. In paragraphing it is done by beginning the first sentence on a new line and by displaying the paragraph in a variety of ways. Four different display devices are used.

The indented paragraph

The first word of the paragraph is set back from the left-hand margin—in typewriting, five spaces for pica type and six for élite type, though more extensive indentations are sometimes preferred:

```
Dear Sir

        I enclose the catalogue of typewriters for which you ask in your
letter of 5th February.  It includes particulars of portables by a number
of makers.  We think the Olivetti "Studio 44" is a machine that would suit
your purpose very well.

        This machine weighs 4 kg and is heavier than most portables, but even
so it is conveniently portable when carried in its case.  A type-face
suitable for cutting stencils could be supplied.

        We have one of these machines in stock and, if it is convenient for
you to call, we shall be pleased to let you try it.

                        Yours faithfully
```

This style served as the traditional form of display for the business letter, but has now largely been replaced by the blocked form.

The blocked paragraph

In this type of display each line of the paragraph, including the first line, begins at the same vertical point in the paper. It is the type of display used for inset paragraphs, as in the example below, and for quotations that appear within the body of the text, and in recent years has come to be adopted also for business letters on the ground that the absence of indentations reduces typing time. Those who dislike this style claim that it is side-heavy and unbalanced and that the absence of indentations occasions a loss of clarity. For example:

Dear Sir

We are pleased to confirm the agreement reached during our discussions last month and look forward to a happy and successful working relationship with you. Before drawing up the formal contract for signature we should like to confirm the main points upon which we reached agreement, namely:

(1) That you act as our sole agents for a period of three years, commencing on 18th September next.

(2) That we pay you a commission of ten per cent on your sales of our products.

(3) That you undertake not to sell the competing products of other manufacturers, either on your account or on that of other suppliers.

(4) That you render monthly statements of sales and accept drafts we draw on you for the net amount due.

(5) That you maintain a full range of our products in your showrooms.

Upon receiving your letter confirming these points we will arrange for the contract to be drawn up and sent to you for signing.

Yours faithfully

The hanging paragraph

This type of paragraph is used only as a special device. Its effect is to throw the first few words into prominence. The first word of the paragraph begins at the left-hand margin, the remaining lines being indented—usually two to five spaces in typewriting. It is thus a reversal of the device used for the indented paragraph:

When you write a letter you are trying to convey a meaning from your
mind to the mind of your reader.

The mechanics of letter-writing may be important, but it is the message
that matters. We certainly need punctuation, clear expression and
grammatical construction as servants, but our purpose in using them
is to write so that we shall be understood in the spirit in which
we write.

Headed paragraphs

If a letter is lengthy, containing a number of paragraphs each dealing with a separate point, it may be convenient either to

number the paragraphs or to give them headings, or even both.
This makes subsequent reference easier, and is an advantage
where subsequent correspondence is likely to deal with the
various points separately. The following is an example:

```
Dear Sir

I thank you for your order for the installation of a gas-fired boiler to
replace the existing solid fuel boiler in your home, and have pleasure
in confirming the following details:

    (1)  Boiler.  Removal of existing solid fuel boiler and flue pipe
         and replacement by one Excelda, automatic gas-fired boiler,
         rated at 15.2 kw, and complete with gas governor, flame-
         failure safety device and boiler water thermostat.

    (2)  Clock control.  Installation of a Timex 103 clock control to
         give automatic operation of the central heating system at
         predetermined times.

    (3)  Flue.  Lining with suitable material of existing brick flue
         stack, and fitting of a GC.2 terminal.

    (4)  Electrical work.  Provision of all materials to enable
         electrical wiring and other necessary connections to be made.

    (5)  Exclusions.  Our quotation does not include the painting of
         any pipe-work, making good of decorations, replacing carpets
         or linoleum, or lifting any special types of floor, e.g.
         tongue and groove, parquet, or rubber tiled.

    (6)  Price and terms.  For the installation as described, supplied
         and fitted....£950. including Value Added Tax.

Yours faithfully
```

   If numbers are used for the paragraphs they may or may not
be placed within brackets. An unbracketed number is followed
by a full stop, but numbers within brackets are sufficiently distinctive to make the use of full stops unnecessary.
   Paragraph headings may be typed in either upper-case or
lower-case characters, followed by a full stop or colon, or even by
a dash. If lower-case characters are used they should be under-
lined to make clear the distinction between heading and text.

Subsidiary paragraphs

For inset or subsidiary paragraphs any one of the first three forms of paragraph display may be used. To emphasize the distinction it is, however, advisable to adopt different forms of display for main and subsidiary paragraphs, the blocked form of subsidiary paragraph being the one most commonly used with indented main paragraphs.

EXERCISES

1. Rewrite the following passage in one paragraph made up of not more than *four* longer sentences. Minor changes may be made, provided the general meaning of the passage is not affected:

He picked his way across the floor by the light of the torch. The floor was strewn with sleeping bodies. He had remembered to bring his torch. The child lay there asleep. He lifted up the child. He took no notice of the other sleepers. He hurried down the stairs. He reached the street. The carriage was waiting. He carried the child to the carriage. The street was quiet and empty. A few cats could be heard quarrelling at the street corner.   (*RSA*)

2. As secretary of a commercial college draft a circular letter containing five short paragraphs dealing in turn with:

   (*a*) advantages of a full-time secretarial and commercial training;
   (*b*) outline of courses provided;
   (*c*) qualifications for admission;
   (*d*) enrolment arrangements and fees;
   (*e*) examinations prepared for.

3. Type, or write, five short paragraphs on the career you would like to follow, dealing in turn with each of the following topics:

   (*a*) the kind of career;
   (*b*) reasons for choosing it;
   (*c*) the qualifications needed;
   (*d*) how you propose to prepare yourself;
   (*e*) the prospects it holds out.

4. Type, or write, a short paragraph on each of the topics included under the headings given below:

A. *Commerce*	B. *Cheques*
Meaning of commerce	What a cheque is
Branches of commerce	Comparison with other forms of money
Benefits from commerce	Reasons for popularity

C. *Money*	D. *Retail trading*
Meaning of money	Meaning of "retail" trade
Types of money	Types of retail organization
Services performed by money	Self-service selling

E. *Banking*	F. *Insurance*
Importance of modern banking	Spreading risks
Kinds of banks	Forms of insurance
Services rendered by banks	The insurance contract

G. *Transport*

Importance
Various types
Transport in the future

5. Read carefully through the following letters and decide the points at which new paragrpahs should begin. Then type, or rewrite, them, using blocked paragraphs:

A

Application for a Post

Dear Sir

I am writing to apply for the post of private secretary advertised in today's *Daily Telegraph*. I am twenty-four years of age, received my general education at the Walthamstow County High School, and my secretarial training at the Bloomsbury Secretarial College. My secretarial training included shorthand, typwriting, English, office practice, accounts, and general principles of English law, and in the examinations held at the end of the course I was awarded the college secretarial diploma, with speeds of 120 and 50 words a minute in shorthand and typewriting respectively. Upon completion of my training I obtained a post as shorthand-typist with Messrs Baxter, Lloyd & Smithson, Solicitors, 125–129 High Road, Woodford, and for the past three years have been private secretary to Mr Baxter, the senior partner. He seems to have been well satisfied with my work and would I feel sure, give me a good recommendation. I enclose copies of two testimonials—one from my former Headmistress, and one from the Principal of my secretarial college, and hope that my qualifications and experience will commend themselves to you. I should be pleased to attend for an interview at your convenience, when I could give you further details concerning myself.

Yours respectfully

B

A Testimonial

Dear Sir

In reply to your enquiry of 21st September, I have much pleasure in supporting the application of Miss R. Golding for the post of private secretary to your director. She joined my staff five years ago, and for the past three years has been my personal secretary. I have been greatly impressed by her conscientious attitude to her work, by her patience, her tact, and unfailing good humour. Her shorthand is very good, and her standards in typewriting I have not seen equalled for a long time. She holds the Teacher's Certificates of the Royal Society of Arts in both these subjects. Miss Golding is a very competent person in all she undertakes, and is thoroughly reliable in every way. Although I should be very sorry to lose her services I can recommend her to you with every confidence for the post she now seeks with you.

Yours faithfully

C
A Letter of Complaint

Dear Sirs

We are sorry to inform you that, on opening up the ten cases of glass delivered here yesterday by Messrs Brash & Jones, we found about 10 per cent of the glass to have been broken, nearly half shows bubbles, and most is badly scratched. I should be glad if you would arrange for your London agents to inspect the consignment and report to you upon it, because I am afraid we shall have to claim on you for a 30 per cent reduction in the amount of your invoice—the balance representing our estimate of the value of the glass as it stands. As we are under contract to deliver assorted sizes of this kind of glass immediately and are awaiting your decision before cutting up, I should be glad if you would kindly give your immediate attention to the matter, and let me know when your representative may be expected to call.

Yours faithfully

6. Show your skill in sentence structure by combining the following sentences into a well-arranged paragraph:

Water for irrigation comes from rivers or wells. The level is usually below that of the surrounding land. A barrage is constructed. Sometimes it is called a weir. It stretches across the bed of the river. The level of water is thereby raised. It flows along canals. The intakes to these lie above the level of the weir. There may be surplus flood water. This can pass over the crest of the structure. It may go through sluices. Some rivers derive their water from melting snow. These rivers are seasonal. Much of their water is wasted. It rushes down in torrents. To conserve this water a dam may be built. It will be suitably located. The floods come. Immense quantities of water are impounded behind the dam. This will be released later. The release will be gradual. It will supplement the shrunken natural flow.

(RSA)

CHAPTER FIVE

Common Errors in Business writing

Error is a hardy plant; it flourisheth in every soil.
Martin F. Tupper: *Proverbial Philosophy*

The preceding chapters provide only a very short summary of the main rules of good English writing, but you will find they give you all the information you need to enable you to understand many of the mistakes that commonly creep into business letters and to avoid them in your own writing. Some mistakes occur so often that they deserve special attention.

ERRORS WITH PRONOUNS

The main fault in the use of pronouns lies in confusing the subject forms (*I, he, she, we, they, who*) with their corresponding object forms (*me, him, her, us, them, whom*).

Following the verb "to be"
The different parts of this verb (*am, is, are, was, were*) are always followed by the subject form of the pronoun:

It was *she* (not *her*) who received the message.
We are *they* (not *them*) who signed the cheque.

Although it is grammatically wrong to say *It is me*, the expression has established itself as acceptable idiomatic English and may now be defended on the ground of widespread usage.

Following "than" and "as"
The subject form of the pronoun is also used after *than* and *as* in comparisons:

I am not as good a typist as *she* (not *her*).
Our competitors have been more successful than *we* (not *us*).

49

Any grammatical difficulty disappears if we write the sentences out in full and say, *as she is, than we have been.*

"Who" and "whom" distinguished

Whether to use the subject form *who* or the object form *whom* depends upon whether the pronoun is the subject or the object of its clause:

> This is our new chief clerk, *who* (not *whom*) has just been appointed (i.e. *he* has just been appointed).

but:

> This is our new chief clerk, *whom* (not *who*) we have just appointed (i.e. we have just appointed *him*).

"Which"

When used as a relative pronoun, i.e. When it refers to some previous noun or pronoun, *which* must have an antecedent (*see* Chapter Two). To use it without antecedent is quite wrong. We cannot, for example, say:

> He completed his report in good time, *which* pleased the directors.

The pronoun *which* in this sentence is without antecedent; it refers neither to *report* nor to *he* (the only preceding noun and pronoun), but to the fact of *completion*. The sentence should therefore be reconstructed in one of the following ways:

> His completion of the report in good time pleased the directors.
>
> OR
>
> By completing his report in good time he pleased the directors.
>
> OR
>
> The directors were pleased by his early completion of the report.

The wrong use of *which* can often be avoided by substituting the pronoun *this* or *these*. The example sentence above could then be re-written correctly as:

> He completed his report in good time, *and this* pleased the directors.

One more example:

> The fire spread rapidly, *which* caused considerable damage.

Which in this sentence does not refer to *fire*, but to the *rapid spread of the fire* and *which* is once more without antecedent. To put this right we must say:

> The fire spread rapidly, *and this* caused considerable damage.

or better still:

The rapid spread of the fire caused considerable damage.

Which is sometimes used quite unnecessarily. For example:

The report on the examination will be issued as soon as it has been approved by the examining board, *which will be* at the beginning of next month.

The sentence is improved by leaving out the phrase in italics and so getting rid of the relative altogether.

"One"

The indefinite pronoun *one* must not be mixed in a sentence with one or other of the personal pronouns. If we begin with *one* we must continue with *one* and not slip into *he* or some other pronoun. The use of pronouns within a sentence must be consistent:

One can often see another's faults, but rarely *one's* (not *his*) own.
One must work hard if *one wishes* (not *they wish*) to succeed.

"Its" and "it's" distinguished

These two forms are commonly confused. *Its* without an apostrophe is a possessive pronoun; with the apostrophe it is an abbreviation meaning *it is* or *it has*.

It's (It is) the best machine of *its* kind.
It's (It has) proved *its* worth and served *its* purpose.

EXERCISE

A few only of the following sentences are correct. Identify them, and then copy the remaining sentences, making such corrections as may be necessary.

A

(a) He is the person whom we thought was to blame.
(b) One must safeguard his own interests.
(c) I decline to do business with dealers who I know are dishonest.
(d) They blame me for the mistake, which is most unjust.
(e) Someone, we don't know whom, addressed the parcel wrongly.
(f) I can type faster than she.
(g) Who do you think called yesterday?
(h) His car broke down, which caused him to be late.
(i) If I were him I should be disappointed.
(j) The trader had little or no capital, which I suspected.

B

(a) He examined Mr Brown's letter, who expressed himself in strong terms.

(b) One must be tactful as well as capable if they wish to succeed.

(c) I hope I can do the job as well as he.

(d) I am certain it was not him who phoned.

(e) He is hard-working and in consequence has been more successful than me.

(f) I suggest you and me try to settle this matter amicably.

(g) The girl whom you met just now is my secretary.

(h) She is not nearly as good a typist as me.

(i) Mr X is retiring, which will be a big blow to his firm.

(j) This is an excellent site, and which we should like to acquire.

ERRORS WITH ADJECTIVES

When making comparisons

In words such as *quick, quicker, quickest;* and *good, better, best,* we have three degrees of comparison, known respectively as *positive, comparitive* and *superlative.*

We use the comparitive when comparing two things and the superlative when comparing three or more:

> The *quicker* (or the *better*) of the two.
> The *quickest* (or the *best*) of the three.

A very common mistake is to use the superlative when the comparative would be correct.

"Either" and "any"

Either is used to refer to any one of two; *any,* to refer to any one of three or more:

> *Either* (not *any*) of these two patterns will do.
> You will find *any* (not *either*) of these three methods satisfactory.

"This", "that", "these", "those"

This and *that* (singular) with *these* and *those* (plural) must agree with their nouns in number:

> We have had *this sort* (or *these sorts*) of excuse before (not *these sort*).
> They prefer *that type* (or *those types*) of desk (not *those type*).

Misuse of "same"

Same is an adjective (e.g. the same desk, the same person) and must never be used as a pronoun as in the sentence:

We thank you for *same*.

Say, *We thank you for the book, the letter,* or whatever has been received.

The "two first" and "two last"
There cannot be more than one first or one last of anything. Say, *the first two, the last three,* etc.

EXERCISE

Some of the following sentences are correct; others are not. Identify the correct sentences, and then copy the remaining ones, making such corrections as may be necessary:

(a) Of the two proposals we think the first is the most attractive.

(b) I have chosen the willow pattern and wish you to deliver same next week.

(c) Of the three clerks, Thompson is by far the more reliable.

(d) I dislike those sorts of complaints more than I can say.

(e) The oldest of the two partners is the one with the grey beard.

(f) I sent him half-a-dozen samples, but he was unable to choose from either.

(g) I regret that the three last pages are missing.

(h) Having received your cheque this morning, we are writing to thank you for same.

(i) These kind of ribbons are more expensive, but they last longer.

(j) Which is the best to do—to buy now or to wait a while?

ERRORS WITH VERBS

Verbs with double subjects
When two singular nouns joined by *and* refer to the same thing, or are closely related in meaning, they take a verb in the singular:

New plant and machinery *was* (not *were*) installed (meaning *new equipment* was installed).

But when two nouns are joined by any word or words other than *and* the verb agrees in number with the first:

Bank rate, together with other interest rates, *moves* (not *move*) in response to government policy.

but

Rates of interest, including bank rate, *reflect* (not *reflects*) the demand for money.

With "each", "everyone", "either", "neither"
These and other pronouns that refer to each individual in a group take a verb in the singular:

> Each of the rooms *has* (not *have*) a telephone.
> Everyone *knows* (not *know*) the manager.
> Neither of the offers *is* (not *are*) good enough.

With collective nouns
Collective nouns (i.e. nouns denoting a group of similar things) take verbs in the singular when we are thinking of the group as a whole, and verbs in the plural when we are thinking of the individuals forming the group:

> The firm *has* just celebrated its centenary (i.e. the business).
> The firm *were* unanimous in accepting the offer (i.e. the partners).

But there is no hard-and-fast rule about the foregoing. The important thing is not the choice of verb, but the consistent use of the singular or plural throughout the same piece of writing.

With relative pronouns
The verb used with a relative pronoun must always agree in number with the antecedent to which the pronoun refers:

> It is one of the machines that *were* delivered last week (not *was*, because *that* refers to *machines*).
> He is one of the few who *are* always on time (not *is*, since *who* refers to *few*).

Error of attraction
When a noun in the plural depends upon a singular noun that precedes it, the true subject is the singular noun and the verb must agree with it:

> A *block* of flats *is* (not *are*) being built.
> A *choice* of tools *was* (not *were*) available.

On the same principle, when a noun in the singular depends upon a plural noun that precedes it, the verb is in the plural:

> *The first results* of the experiment *were* (not *was*) disappointing.

Wrong tense sequence
The main uses of *shall* and *will* are as auxiliary verbs to express future time:

> I *shall phone* him at once.
> You *will enjoy* the concert.
> They *will consider* the proposal.

When these uses are reversed, *shall* and *will* no longer express the future, but have a special significance denoting such feelings as willingness, compulsion or determination:

I *will phone* him at once (expresses willingness or intention).
You *shall return* all you borrowed (expresses compulsion).
They *shall have* their reward (makes a promise).

When a sentence contains an *If* clause the sequences *shall/will, should/would* and similar sequences must be observed. In other words, the verbs in the separate clauses must be in the same mood or manner. Thus:

I *shall* be glad if you *will* (or *can, may*).
I *should* be glad if you *would* (or *could, might*).

Shall, will, can and *may* are all in the indicative mood; the corresponding verbs *should, would, could* and *might* are in the subjunctive mood. In conditional sentences of the kind illustrated the two moods must not be mixed.

The mood of a verb shows the mood or manner in which the action of the verbs is performed. The *indicative mood* makes statements or asks questions; the *subjunctive mood* expresses doubt, or indeed anything but a fact.

Abbreviated forms

In informal circumstances such as everyday speech, *I will* and *I shall* may be shortened to *I'll*, and similarly with *you'll, he'll she'll, it'll, we'll* and *they'll*. These and similar shortened forms of expression (e.g. *aren't, won't* and *didn't*) form no part of good business writing and should not be used in business letters.

"Lay" and "lie"

Lay (with the past *laid*) and *lie* (with the past *lay*) are two quite different verbs. Confusion can be avoided if it is remembered that *lay* always requires an object (expressed or understood), whereas *lie* does not:

He *lays bricks* for a living. ⎫
She *laid the telegram* on the desk. ⎭ (With object)
She *lies* down after dinner. ⎫
She *lay* down because she was tired. ⎭ (Without object)

"Loan" and "lend"

Loan is a noun and should not be used as a verb (though it is so used in the United States):

I will *lend* (not *loan*) you the money you need.

The split infinitive

It is a generally accepted rule that the infinitive form of a verb
(e.g. *to consider, to phone, to understand*) should not be split by the
intrusion of any word between *to* and the rest of the verb. It is
quite natural to say *to consider carefully, to phone at once,* and *to
understand clearly,* and so these forms are to be preferred to *to
carefully consider, to at once phone,* and *to clearly understand.* But the
principle of non-splitting must not be pushed too far. *The members are said to favour strongly a strike* is an awkward construction
and it is better to split the infinitive and say *to strongly favour.*

EXERCISE

A few only of the following sentences are correct. Identify them, and
then copy the remaining sentences, making such corrections as may be
necessary:

A

(a) Each of the parts have been made separately.
(b) If neither of them are to be trusted there is little point in referring to them.
(c) He lay in bed until ten o'clock yesterday morning.
(d) Every member of the club have their own views on the matter.
(e) Neither Mr Brown nor Mr White were at the meeting.
(f) He is one of the keenest buyers that has ever been here.
(g) A new set of records have been prepared.
(h) He is one of those who is never happy unless he is in the limelight.
(i) His bread and butter are at stake should he lose his job.
(j) Tact and discretion is an essential part of a secretary's make-up.

B

(a) He laid there for an hour, as if in a dream.
(b) A suite of furnished rooms were available, but at a prohibitive
rent.
(c) The committee adds these comments to their report.
(d) He enquired whether either of the applicants were suitable.
(e) I am not one of those who never makes a mistake.
(f) Gloucester has one of the finest cathedrals that is to be found in
Britain.
(g) The number of employees have increased by more than half.
(h) The United Nations charter is one of the most important documents that has ever been prepared.
(i) The great variety of styles we are able to offer to customers ensure
our ability to please.
(j) All being well we will be able to complete the work by Saturday.

ERRORS WITH ADVERBS

"Less" and "Fewer"

Less refers to quantity and *fewer* to number. It is a very common fault to use *less* where *fewer* would be correct:

Fewer (not *less*) than a dozen members came to the meeting.

"Scarcely" and "hardly"

These two adverbs should be followed by *when* and not, as so often happens, by *than*:

Scarcely had I arrived *when* (not *than*) the phone rang. We had *hardly* been gone five minutes *when* (not *than*) fire broke out.

"Quite"

Quite means completely, entirely, perfectly. It is an adverb and should come immediately before the word it modifies:

The work to be done was *quite easy*.
It's *quite warm* today.

The practice of using *quite* as an adjective to qualify nouns is one to be avoided:

We had *quite a surprise* when the results were announced. (Say instead: *We were very surprised*).
Quite a number of us disagreed with the changes made. (Say instead: *A large number*, or *many*.)

However, the informal use of *quite* in *quite a lot, quite a few, quite a surprise* and similar expressions is now sanctioned by usage.

EXERCISE

Recast the following sentences to include any necessary corrections:

A

(a) One member of staff only arrived late this morning.
(b) We received less than half a dozen letters by this morning's post.
(c) It will be quite a problem to get the work finished in time.
(d) Scarcely had I replaced the receiver than the phone rang again.
(e) We only deliver in your district on Tuesdays.
(f) In winter we find ourselves with less than ten hours of full daylight.
(g) Quite a lot of responsibility falls on the deputy.
(h) He had hardly begun dictating than he was called away.
(i) The newly appointed assistant is quite a good typist.
(j) There were less of us at the meeting than usual.

B

(a) Mathematical tables can only be learned by rote memorization.

(b) There is quite a lot of truth in what you say.

(c) Hardly had I arrived than I was invited to play.

(d) The school only taught commercial subjects at the elementary level.

(e) The present economic position calls for more rather than for less restrictions.

(f) That is quite a different story.

(g) I had scarcely reached home than it began to rain.

(h) The value of the experiment can only be measured by results.

(i) Although we work less hours and less hard than formerly, we enjoy a higher living standard.

(j) His late arrival created quite a problem.

ERRORS WITH PREPOSITIONS

"Between" and "among"

Between refers to two; *among* refers to three or more:

> Profits are shared equally *between* the two partners.
> The cheque was found *among* the papers in the tray.

"Due to" and "owing to"

Due to means *caused by* and, with the one exception stated below, is always associated with a noun.

Owing to means *because of* and is always associated with a verb:

> His late *arrival* was *due* to lack of transport.
> He *arrived* late *owing* to lack of transport.

NOTE: The parts of the verb "to be" always take *due to*:

> The rise in price *is* probably *due to* rising costs.

"Except", "without" and "like"

All these words are prepositions and must not be used to join sentences as if they were conjunctions:

> We cannot quote *unless* (not *except* or *without*) you provide a sample.
> The machine was expensive, *as* (not *like*) we expected.

EXERCISE

Recast the following sentences to include any necessary corrections:

(a) We are able to reduce prices due to a lowering of costs.

(b) Prepare a credit note, just like the one you did yesterday.

(c) We cannot increase wages except we increase output.

(d) Due to a blackout the works were plunged into darkness.

(e) He was energetic and capable, just like his father was.

(f) The delay in replying is owing to the secretary's illness.

(g) X, Y and Z shared the profits equally between them.

(h) This youth does not work like his brother did.

(i) Without his parent signs it the agreement is of no legal value.

(j) The makers informed us they could not deliver tomorrow like they had hoped.

ERRORS WITH CONJUNCTIONS

Mention has already been made that certain conjunctions (called *correlatives*) are always used in pairs (see p. 22). Not only must each conjunction in the pair always be accompanied by its own partner, but each must also be followed by *the same part of speech*.

We cannot for example say:

He *not only built* houses, *but also flats*.

because the first correlative is followed by a verb (*built*) and the second by a noun (*flats*).

We must therefore alter the position of *not only* and say:

He built *not only houses, but also flats*.

Both correlatives are then followed by a noun. Nor can we say:

He *neither cares* what games he plays *nor which* subjects he studies.

because the first correlative is followed by a verb (*cares*) and the second by an adjective (*which*). We must say instead:

He cares *neither what* games he plays *nor which* subjects he studies.

Both correlatives are then followed by adjectives (*what* and *which*).

EXERCISE

Recast the following sentences to include any necessary corrections:

(a) The book you are seeking is neither in the desk nor the book-case.

(b) The secretary may either be in his office or in the warehouse.

(c) His success is neither due to hard work nor to unusual abilities.

(d) A study of trends both within the national economy and the undertaking itself has become necessary.

(e) You can either pay me now, or later.

(f) The proposed changes not only apply to shorthand but to type-writing also.

(g) He is neither inclined to listen to advice nor to act for himself.

(h) The two schools differ considerably both in outlook and achievement.

(i) The agent's principal must either be named or clearly identified in some other way.

(j) The organization is not only concerned with attaining its objectives in the present, but in the future.

ERRORS WITH PARTICIPLES

A participle may be either past or present (*see* p. 16). It is a common fault to start a sentence with a participle and to fail to provide it with its noun (or pronoun), thus leaving it unrelated or, as we sometimes say, *loose* or *unattached*:

> While *studying* the report, the telephone rang.
> While *engaged* with the chairman, the sun came out.

Both these sentences are faulty. The participles *studying* and *engaged* clearly relate to some person, but as this person is not mentioned, the participles wrongly associate themselves with *the telephone* and *the sun*— the subjects of the main clauses that end the sentences. The sentences should be rewritten as follows:

> While *I was* (*he was*, etc.) studying the report, the telephone rang.
> While *I was* (*he was*, etc.) engaged with the chairman, the sun came out.

The same kind of fault is frequently found in business letters in both the opening and the closing phrases.

Opening phrases
Failure to provide such opening phrases as *Referring to your letter*, *Replying to your enquiry* with their appropriate nouns or pronouns is a common fault:

> Referring to your enquiry, *you* will be glad to know ...
> Replying to your letter of yesterday, *the goods* were despatched ...

In these examples *Referring* is wrongly associated with *you*, and *Replying* with *the goods*. They must be rewritten as follows:

> *Referring* to your enquiry, *we* wish to inform you that ...
> *Replying* to your letter of yesterday, *I* am writing to inform you that ...

The participles *Referring* and *Replying* are then correctly associated with their respective subjects, *we* and *I*.

Closing phrases

Another fault of the same kind is to bring a letter to a close by phrases beginning with *Hoping, Trusting, Thanking, Regretting* and other participles. Unless these phrases are supported by such expressions as *I am, We are, I (We) remain*, the participle is left unattached. This type of closure is now old-fashioned and is best avoided.

Participial closure	Say instead
Thanking you for your help,	I thank you (or *am grateful*)
I am	for your help.
Yours sincerely	Yours sincerely
Hoping to hear from you soon	We hope to hear (or *look forward*
We remain	*to hearing*) from you soon.
Yours faithfully	Yours faithfully

EXERCISES

1. Recast the following sentences to include any necessary corrections:

(a) Referring to the account you sent us last week, you have omitted to allow the usual trade discount.

(b) Having established a good business connection, an effort is now being made to extend operations.

(c) Thanking you for your interest in the matter, Yours truly

(d) Hoping to hear from you very soon, Believe me, Yours faithfully

(e) Having been advised of the ship's arrival, a busy time may now be expected.

(f) Having labelled the parcels, they were taken to post.

(g) Being an old friend of mine, I did my best to help him.

(h) After enjoying the dance, all thoughts turned to supper.

(i) Being Saturday, the trains were packed.

(j) Arriving late, our attendance at the meeting wasn't recorded.

2. Rewrite the following sentences correctly:

(a) The financial results were as good and even better than ever.

(b) You would be wise to carefully reconsider your proposal.

(c) Every man, woman and child have a right to be considered.

(d) We have a wider selection than any firm in the town.

(e) His way of doing things is very different to his manager's.

(f) Who are you typing that letter for?

(g) We found it necessary not only to provide him with clothes but also with money.

(*h*) Being the only product of its kind on the market, we are naturally optimistic concerning sales.

(*i*) Walking home last night a car nearly knocked me down.

3. Rewrite the following correctly, and give reasons for your corrections:

(*a*) Due to your not writing last month, everybody in the bank thought you were seriously ill.

(*b*) In every branch, customers exist at whom we all sneer yet secretly admire.

(*c*) Referring to your letter of the 13th instant, details of the proposed mortgage were despatched to you last month.

4. Correct the following sentences and give reasons for any alterations you may make:

(*a*) Having only received your order today, it is impossible to despatch the new machine before next week.

(*b*) To effectively dispose of this problem, the result of the shareholders' meetings should have given more authority to him and I.

(*c*) The reason why the new sales programme failed was because it had not been planned as it should have been.

5. The following letters contain a number of grammatical errors. Recast the letters, making whatever corrections you consider to be necessary:

A. *Application for a Post*

Dear Sir

Having seen your advertisement in the "Daily Telegraph", my qualifications and experience may interest you.

I am 25 years of age, have had eight years' office experience and am quite an experienced shorthand-typist. The promise of better prospects, together with easier travelling, are my main reasons for wishing to change my present job. I have recently applied for two other posts nearer my home, but neither were to my liking.

My present employer is one of those men who is always willing to help those who work for him to improve themselves. I am therefore sure that he will be willing to give me a reference should you approach him for one. He and myself have now worked together for the past five years, which has been very enjoyable. Everyone, however, should broaden their experience, and that is another reason for my present application.

Should you wish to interview me I could call to see you on either of the three first days of next week.

Yours respectfully

B. *Letter reporting Damage*

Dear Sirs

Referring to your advice note of the 18th July, the lantern slides arrived yesterday in a badly damaged condition; quite a number were broken. We do not know who to blame for the damage, but we shall make a full investigation, which should enable us to place the responsibility. Each of the carriers concerned are aware that they will be liable for any damage due to their negligence. The two first to handle the package have already informed us that they have had no less than three other complaints of a similar nature during the past month, but that in each case the goods complained about were alright when they passed them on.

We not only feel concerned about the amount of damage that has occurred, but also about the number of occasions on which we have had similar cause to complain.

Hoping however that we will soon have information that will enable us to lodge a claim in the right quarter.

Yours faithfully

C. *Letter of Complaint*

Dear Sirs

Replying to your letter of 20th January, our customers now inform us that the shirting supplied last November was too light in shade, which is unfortunate, since they are customers who we do considerable business with. They also report finding quite a deterioration in the quality of some of the rolls, owing, they suggest, to breaks in the thread during spinning.

This complaint, together with others we have recently received from several other customers, are a matter of serious concern to us, and we will be grateful for your assurance that you will take all possible steps only to supply shirting of first-class quality against future orders. We look forward to you doing everything you can to ensure this.

Hoping there will be no further difficulties of this kind.

Yours faithfully

CHAPTER SIX

Effective Business Writing

> Vigorous writing is concise. A sentence should contain no unnecessary words, a paragraph no unnecessary sentences, for the same reason that a drawing should have no unnecessary lines and a machine no unnecessary parts.
>
> Wm. Strunk Jr.: *The Elements of Style*

THINK CLEARLY

Words are the symbols we use to express our ideas. They are the tools of effective communication. Their importance lies in the power they have, when suitably chosen and arranged, to convey our thoughts to other people in language that is unmistakably clear and readily understood. To write effectively you must choose the right words and use them to express yourself simply, concisely and directly, avoiding the temptation to show off by using the long and unfamiliar words and roundabout phrases that some writers continue to prefer.

In your choice of words be guided by the three essential qualities of accuracy, clarity and simplicity. First be clear about what you want to say. You cannot express clearly an idea you have not yet fully and clearly formed. Clear thinking and clear writing go together. Once you know what you want to say the words with which to say it will come all the more readily. Perhaps Lewis Caroll had this in mind when he parodied the well-known proverb and cautioned us to "take care of the sense and the sounds will take care of themselves". The more clearly you think, the more clearly you will write and the more clearly will your reader understand. You cannot expect him to grasp the meaning of what you say if you are not yourself clear about what you are trying to say. Once you are clear about the idea you want to pass on and the impression you want to create in your reader's mind, say simply what has to be said in words appropriate to the understanding level of your reader, choosing your words wisely and imaginatively. They will then convey not only the sense of your message but also the spirit of it as well.

PREFER THE SIMPLE WORD

One of the main faults in present-day business writing is the tendency to prefer what is complicated and roundabout to what is simple and direct:

Instead of	*Say*
We shall be in a position to effect delivery.	We can (*or* shall be able to) deliver.
If you come to a decision regarding the installation of the machine.	If you decide to install the machine.
We express the hope that you will deal with the matter expeditiously.	We hope you will deal with the matter promptly.

Preference for the roundabout phrase is linked with a preference for the long word rather than the short. But if it serves equally well the short word is better. It is simpler, it is clearer and more in keeping with good English writing style. Your choice of words cannot be dictated by hard-and-fast rules, but it is well to have some rules. The rule to prefer the short and familiar to the long and unfamiliar is a sound rule for general occasions, but it is a rule to be followed with discretion. If the choice lies between two words that serve your meaning equally well, one short and familiar and the other long and unusual, choose the short. But a longer and more unusual word should not be rejected merely on that account if it more aptly expresses what you want to say. It is the unnecessary use of long and unfamiliar words that you must guard against. Make it a rule therefore never to use a longer word if there is a shorter word that serves equally well. Instead of *acquainting* your customer with the details, *tell* him about them; don't *solicit* his custom, *invite* it; and instead of *despatching* the goods, *send* them to him.

The shorter words in the following list express the meanings of their longer often overworked equivalents and are generally to be preferred, though there may be times when to use the longer words provides a welcome change.

Instead of	*Say*	*Instead of*	*Say*
acquire	gain, get	desire	wish
approximately	about	diminish	reduce
ascertain	find out	donate	give
assist	help	endeavour	try
commence	begin (which is less formal)	experience	feel
		forward	send
communicate	write	implement	carry out
description	kind, sort	inform	tell

Instead of	Say	Instead of	Say
initiate	begin, start	render	give
locality	place	request	ask
majority	most	requirements	needs
materialize	occur, take place	sufficient	enough
peruse	read	terminate	end
practically	nearly, almost	transmit	send
prevent	stop	utilize	use
purchase	buy	visualize	imagine
remunerate	reward, pay		

Nor should you use *feel* as if it were the same thing as *think*; *feeling* is the result of intuition, and business decisions, which should result from reasoning, should not be expressed as if they were the results of intuition.

By writing simply and avoiding what is elaborate and complex you not only convey your meaning more clearly, but also create a feeling of sincerity and integrity. For who can be suspicious of a person who writes and speaks plainly?

EXERCISES

1. Study the following synonyms, and frame sentences to illustrate the different shades of meaning in each set:

    (a) abbreviate, abridge   *(f)* find, discover
    (b) centre, middle   *(g)* fault, mistake
    (c) association, society   *(h)* advise, inform
    (d) balance, surplus   *(i)* receive, acquire
    (e) produce, product   *(j)* renew, repair

2. Improve the following sentences by using simpler words and phrases for those in italics:

(a) We *discovered* the lorry *in close proximity* to our premises.

(b) The accident is likely to *impair his capacity* for work.

(c) The changes made will appeal to *the great majority* of our customers.

(d) Clerical employment does not *involve the necessity of obtaining* a medical certificate.

(e) *The position with reference to the shortage of labour* is now very serious.

(f) We shall be glad to *render you any assistance in our power*.

(g) When asked if she had typed the report she *answered in the affirmative*.

(h) Because of the recent floods delivery of the goods by rail is not a *practical proposition*.

(i) We regret the enclosure was *inadvertently omitted*.

(j) The damage caused by the fire was *of a very far-reaching character*.

3. Express the following sentences in simpler form without changing the meaning:

(a) We despatched the goods to you yesterday per passenger train.

(b) If you will advise us of your requirements we will do our utmost to assist you.

(c) When we received your communication we experienced a sense of deep disappointment.

(d) We anticipate being able to place an order with you for approximately 500 tables.

(e) We venture to express the hope that you will deal with the matter as expeditiously as possible.

(f) The difficulties we had expected to encounter in acquiring the site did not materialize.

(g) The enclosed brochure contains full details of the operations we have in mind, and we trust you will peruse it at your convenience.

(h) We wish to terminate the service agreement to which you make reference in your letter.

(i) There is insufficient work to enable us to utilize the services of a third shorthand-typist.

(j) The order for shirts, which you despatched to us last Friday, has been transmitted to our factory for attention.

AVOID SUPERFLUOUS WORDS

To use more words than are needed to do the job generates woolly expressions most of which are mere padding. Unnecessary words waste time, add nothing to meaning and contribute nothing to the reader's perception of what is written. On the contrary, by making complex what should be simple they cloud meaning and add to the reader's task.

Adjectives and adverbs

Use adjectives only when they contribute to the meaning of what is said. A thing that is *right* is no more correct when it is claimed to be *definitely right*; nor is *delay* more prolonged merely because it is *undue*.

Take care, too, to use adjectives and adverbs with their proper meanings. Do not use *incidentally* to introduce a piece of essential information, nor talk of a *fantastic salary* or a *fabulous holiday*. Fantastic means *fanciful* or *unreal*, and *fabulous* pertains to *fable* or what is *not true*.

Adjectives

Adjectives that denote *kind* are more likely to be correctly used than adjectives that denote *degree*. You can write correctly about a *social problem, good-humoured opposition, unexpected danger* or a *train disaster*, but need to take care with adjectives in phrases such as a *real problem, considerable opposition, substantial danger* and *major disaster*. They are not necessarily wrong, but they are often used when it would be better to leave them out.

Choose those words that say what you mean. When a person says he *loves* kippers, *loves* tennis and *loves* Julie he is using the same word to express quite different feelings, a word that means only one thing—affection. But one can hardly have an affection for kippers, or even for tennis. The meaning may be clear enough to those who are accustomed to such loose expressions, but loose and vague expressions are out of place in a business letter, where what is meant must be said. If we *like* kippers, or *enjoy* tennis we must say so, and reserve our affection for those we really love.

Adverbs

What applies to adjectives applies equally to adverbs—you must use them sparingly and with care. By all means say "It is *exactly* four o'clock", "I am *completely* puzzled", "I will see you *presently*", "It is *rather* cold", where the adverbs mean something, but keep a watchful eye on the use of such adverbs as *considerably, definitely, unduly, relatively, comparatively, somewhat* and *rather* in expressions such as *considerably overdue, definitely harmful, unduly prolonged, relatively few, comparatively soon, somewhat rare, rather think*, where they contribute little or nothing to the sense. Beware, too, of such overworked adverbs as *absolutely, actually* and *perfectly*.

Vague words, especially adverbs, are always useless; they mean nothing of value. They form a kind of barricade behind which the timid take shelter from the risks to which clear statement and precise promises would expose them. The following example is typical:

> We *hope* (whatever that means) to send a *substantial percentage (whatever that may be) of the goods ordered at an early date* (whenever that is).

Such a statement tells the customer nothing helpful. If only the writer had put *relatively* before *substantial*, and *comparatively* before *early*, his security would have been complete.

Use *relatively* and *comparatively* only when you compare one thing with another. Instead of saying *relatively* or *comparatively few, relatively* or *comparatively small*, state how many or what size. Thus, it is quite correct to say:

In the accident yesterday fifty people w.   .
seriously.

where the number injured seriously is co.   with
ber injured. But you must not say:

In the accident yesterday *relatively few* people w

since no comparison is made.

Prepositional phrases

Another common failing in business letter-writ   is to use
phrases where a single word would do. Phrases ending with
prepositions are often no more than cumbersome substitutes for
single words that do the work simpler and better:

Instead of	*Say*
approve of	approve
by means of	by, through, with
consequent upon	after
for the purpose of	
in connection with	
in respect of	for
on behalf of	
having regard to	concerning
in spite of	although
in the case of	by, for
in the course of	during
in the event of	if
prior to	before
shall take steps to	shall
in order to	
so as to	
with a view to	to
with the object of	
in relation to	
on the question of	
on the subject of	about, concerning
with reference to	
with regard to	

Before using a phrase ending with a preposition make sure that
you cannot replace it by a single word meaning the same thing.
The following are examples of the unnecessary use of such
phrases, the word that should be used being shown in brackets:

[...]e increased prices *in order to* (TO) reduce our losses.
[...]e equipment is needed *in connection with* (FOR) the new office block.
I have received your letter *on the subject of* (CONCERNING) the new machinery.
We are *in a position* (ABLE) to supply the goods immediately.
Please insert particulars *in respect of* (FOR) last week.
I am writing *on behalf of* (FOR) Mr Watson.
With regard to the question of (CONCERNING) insurance, we are informed that premium rates have been raised.

and finally:

During his speech he talked *about* security.

is certainly simpler and much better than:

In the course of his speech he talked *on the question of* security.

Introductory phrases

Nowhere does padding show itself more plainly than in the *that* phrases still frequently used to introduce new paragraphs:

It should be noted that	It may be stated that
It is expected that	I am to add that
It is appreciated that	I am further to state that
It is true that	I may mention that

This form of padding is easily recognized and is not difficult to resist. You should avoid all such phrases.

Just as recognizable and as easily avoided are such obvious padders as *for your information, in this connection, in the circumstances, as a matter of course, as a matter of fact, in view of the fact, the fact of the matter.*

Instead of	Say
We thank you for your enquiry and *for your information* enclose a copy of our catalogue.	Omit *for your information*.
We misunderstood your terms of payment and *in the circumstances* should be grateful if you would allow us to defer payment.	Omit *in the circumstances*.
In view of the fact that payment is already two months overdue, we shall *as a matter of course* have to disallow our usual discount.	Since payment is already two months overdue I regret we cannot allow you our usual discount.
Urgent delivery is required and *in this connection* we suggest you send the parcel by express delivery service.	As urgent delivery is required we suggest ...

Padding often takes much more subtle forms than those illustrated, but perhaps enough has been said to warn you not to use unnecessary words. You can do much to improve your writing by being self-critical. Ask yourself these questions:

    (a) Is this word or this phrase necessary?
    (b) Does it improve the meaning of what I want to say?
    (c) Does it contribute to the reader's understanding?
    (d) Is it likely to get from him the response I seek?

EXERCISES

1. Examine critically the use of the words and phrases in italics in the following sentences, and recast the sentences in good English:

    (a) We have in stock a *considerable quantity* of folding tables, which we can offer you *at a reasonable price*.

    (b) *It is expected that* work on the new site will be completed *at a comparatively early date*.

    (c) The *true facts* are as given you in my letter last week.

    (d) The contractors have been informed *of the likelihood of substantial delay* in the delivery of the steel girders.

    (e) The gradual rise in prices *represents a real threat* to the standard of living.

    (f) We *are necessarily anxious* to do everything we can to help.

    (g) We *rather hope* you will not allow the lower prices offered by our competitors to *unduly influence* your policy.

    (h) Since the workmen arrived *there has been relatively little opportunity* to deal with correspondence.

    (i) We *are somewhat at a loss to* understand why we have received no orders from you during the past six months.

    (j) There is likely to be *an appreciable rise in price* within the next year or so.

2. Avoiding the words and phrases in italics, rewrite the following sentences in good English:

    (a) *In spite of* its importance the meeting was attended by *relatively* few shareholders.

    (b) You were *definitely* right in thinking that *consequent upon* the visit conditions would improve.

    (c) *In the event of* continued inflation the authorities face a very *real* problem.

    (d) *Having regard to* the strike, delivery is likely to be delayed, but not *unduly*.

    (e) *In the course of* his address the chairman, *on behalf of* the board, expressed appreciation of the work of the staff.

    (f) *With the object of* restoring good business relations the suppliers have approved *of* a special discount *in the case of* textiles.

(g) I must mention that having regard to the size of your order we are unable to supply all the goods from stock.

(h) I am to point out that in the course of our phone conversation it was agreed that *in the event of* a strike we could not be responsible for any delay in delivery.

(i) I am bound to say that our policies are drafted *with the object of* giving maximum cover to policy holders.

(j) In the event of payment not being received by the end of this month we shall take steps *with a view to* recovering the amount due.

AVOID ABSTRACT NOUNS

The need for care in using abstract words was referred to in Chapter One. In *The Complete Plain Words** Sir Ernest Gowers condemns the use of the abstract as "the greatest vice of present-day writing". It causes to be said in roundabout and complicated ways what might otherwise be simple and straightforward. The message of a letter must be clear. It is much less likely to be so if it is hedged about by superfluous words. To say *Last winter there was a shortage of coal* is a perfectly plain statement that is readily understood, so why cloud its meaning in the language of a Government White Paper, which referred to the shortage as *a tight situation in the supply of coal*? We cannot do without abstract words, but more often than not what needs to be said can be said more plainly and clearly by using concrete words. Concrete words are more specific; they name their objects clearly, simplify the use of language, and since they have the same meaning for both writer and reader present no communication problem. Wherever possible, therefore, avoid the abstract word and use the concrete, reconstructing your sentences as may be necessary.

Rules have been made for the *avoidance* and *settlement* of disputes.

(Say: Rules have been made for avoiding and settling disputes.)

Achievement of the results looked for will not be possible without the co-operation of the staff.

(Say: The expected results will not be achieved without the co-operation of the staff.)

Your *entitlement* to pension will be dependent upon length of service.

---

* HMSO (2nd edn.), 1973.

(Say: Whether or not you are entitled to pension will depend upon length of service.)

The italicized words in these sentences are all abstractions and lead to unsatisfactory ways of saying something that is said more simply and effectively if the sentences are recast as shown.

Large numbers of words ending in *-tion* and *-sion* are abstract; you should give them careful thought before accepting them. *Position* and *situation* are among the common snares:

The *position* in regard to the supply of coal may become serious.
(Say: There may be a serious coal shortage.)

The *situation* with reference to the supply of skilled engineers is not likely to improve.

(Say: The shortage of skilled engineers is likely to continue.)

Conditions in reference to employment are more favourable than for many years past.

(Say: Employment prospects are better than for many years past.)

Application of the new salary scales has caused disappointment.

(Say: The new salary scales have caused disappointment.)

I will arrange for the *preparation* of the programme at once.

(Say: I will arrange to prepare the programme at once.)

EXERCISE

Rearrange the following sentences in plain, straightforward English, without using the abstract nouns and the phrases in italics.

A

(a) There is early *expectancy* of a vacancy on the technical staff of the power station.

(b) Most of our customers *express a preference for* the modern style of TV cabinet.

(c) *The use of* road maps is a *necessity* for the modern motorist.

(d) There will have to be a careful *perusal* of the estimates before *a decision on the matter can be arrived at.*

(e) It will be for members of the technical staff to decide on the *suitability or otherwise* of the new machine.

(f) We *express regret* that we cannot accept *responsibility* for the mistake *that has occurred* in the delivery of the goods.

(g) We *have pleasure in announcing* that on 31st July we shall be taking over the business of Blake and Nunn, estate agents.

(h) The *appointment* of a new office manager will be made by the Board at their meeting next Thursday.

(i) *In all probability* we shall need a *considerable quantity of* new typewriters after the end of this year.

(j) We are glad *to have your assurance* that the work on the new plant will be completed by the end of August.

B

(a) We hope to *give consideration to* your request *in the very near future*.

(b) *The possession of* many books by no means implies that the owner is a person of *education*.

(c) *The prevention of* evil is better than its cure.

(d) In the rush of modern life *relaxation* is regarded as essential for both factory and office workers.

(e) The *authorization* of the expenditure is a matter for the Finance Committee.

(f) *Owing to the expiration* of our lease we have moved to new premises at the above address.

(g) *There is little variation in* the quality of the various samples which you enclosed with your letter.

(h) We are glad *to have your assurance* that work on the site will begin next week.

(i) *The inspection of* the damaged boiler will be carried out by our chief technical adviser.

(j) *I have no hesitation in saying* that Miss Clarke has proved to be a most loyal and competent assistant in every way.

AVOID EXAGGERATION

Be discreet in your choice of words and avoid any that exaggerate. Hyperbole, as gross exaggeration is called, is a figure of speech that may be all very well in popular language when it is recognized as such, but there is no place for it in the business letter. In conversation we often exaggerate to produce a striking effect and attract attention. To offer a *thousand apologies*, to make a *terrific effort*, to *kill oneself with laughing* are expressions that may be harmless enough in speech, but they are of the kind that seldom appear in the written vocabulary, and certainly have no place in the business letter. In business letters attention must be attracted by original ideas and the clarity with which they are expressed, and not by using strong and often ill-fitting words.

Exaggeration tends to weaken rather than strengthen the effect of a statement intended to be taken seriously since it calls in question the writer's general regard for sincerity and accurate statement. Avoid especially such expressions as *stupendous, tremendous, immeasurable* and *gigantic* when you mean no more than *big, large* or *considerable,* or *unbearable* and *intolerable* when you merely mean *annoying:*

The storm caused *immeasurable* (say *heavy* or *considerable*) damage to the factory.
The shortage of skilled labour is creating a *tremendous* (say *serious* or *grave*)problem.

Avoid also the popular though improper use of such qualifying words as *awfully, dreadfully, terribly* and *jolly* for *very* in connections like *awfully busy, dreadfully sorry, terribly inconvenient* and *jolly good effort;* and don't write *scores of times* for *several times, exhaustive enquiries* for *careful enquiries, disastrous results* for *serious results,* or express *astonishment* when you are merely *surprised.* Strong words lose their power when used unnecessarily. Besides, if you refer to a lost cricket match as a *disaster,* or to a sleepless night as *terrible,* what have you left that is vivid enough to describe a plane crash, an earthquake or an atom bomb?

EXERCISE

Improve the following sentences by using more reasonable expressions for the exaggerations printed in italics:

(a) Considering the bad state of trade our turnover last year was *truly magnificent.*
(b) If I've told him once about coming late I've told him *hundreds of times.*
(c) Wait for me downstairs; I'll be with you in *half a second.*
(d) Meetings can waste such a lot of time and I *simply hate them.*
(e) The applause following his speech *literally brought the house down.*
(f) It is *ages* since we last heard from you.
(g) It's *absolute heaven* to work in our new office block.
(h) A good secretary is *worth her weight in gold.*
(i) He is a director of six companies and has *tons of money.*
(j) "One picture is worth *ten thousand words.*" (Chinese proverb.)

AVOID FOREIGN PHRASES

The English language is usually rich and vivid enough to say all that needs to be said. When there are English expressions that serve just as well, foreign expressions, especially Latin tags, are out of place in the business letter. *Au fait* (well acquainted), *inter alia* (among other things), *per annum* (yearly), *pro rata* (in proportion), *pro tem* (for the time being), *status quo* (the present position) and *vice versa* (conversely) are all phrases that can be replaced equally well by the English equivalents shown in brackets, greatly to the benefit of the reader, who may be less familiar with foreign phrases than you are. These phrases have no special merit to commend them. They say nothing that cannot be said more simply and clearly in the plain English for which they stand. True, a few foreign phrases, such as *per cent* (in every hundred), *bona fide* (in good faith), *en route* (on the way) and *ex officio* (by virtue of office), have established themselves in the technical vocabulary of business, probably because of the economy with which they express the ideas they stand for. It would therefore be against reason to deny them a place in the business letter when it is appropriate to use them.

To use foreign phrases is not a sign of superior education; they have become much too hackneyed and commonplace for that, and in the interests of that simplicity which is one of the marks of the good business letter they should never be used merely for the sake of effect.

AVOID TAUTOLOGY

Tautology means repetition, especially the use of words that add nothing to the sense. It takes a number of forms, but for our purpose may be taken to embrace all forms of needless repetition and redundant writing. In the phrases *joint* partnership, *entire* monopoly, *voluntary* offer, *surrounding* circumstances, return *back*, the words in italics are redundant and should be omitted. *Partnership* means a joint venture, *monopoly* means sole control, an *offer* is an unsolicited proposal, *circumstances* means the surrounding situation, and *return* means send back.

Avoid, too, associating such adverbs as *quite, very* and *most* with adjectives like *unique, perfect, ideal* and *excellent,* which in themselves express the highest degree possible. You cannot, for example, logically refer to something as being *quite unique, very perfect, most ideal* or *most excellent.* Nor must you use such expressions as *often in the habit, give mutual help to each other,* and *the reason is because,* in which *often, mutual* and *because* are all redundant. Some other examples of redundancy are given below, the superfluous words being enclosed within brackets:

He declined (*to accept*) our offer.	*Decline* means not to accept.
The goods must be restored (*again*) to their rightful owner.	*Again* suggests that the goods have been restored more than once.
He received the news with equanimity (*of mind*).	*Equanimity* is evenness of mind.
He deserves (*condign*) punishment.	*Condign* means well deserved.
There was universal recognition (*by all*).	*Universal* means by everyone.
He travelled with three (*fellow*) companions.	A *fellow* means a companion.
The (*true*) facts are not known.	A *fact* is necessarily true.
I am a (*new*) beginner.	A *beginner* is necessarily new.
In (*close*) proximity	*Proximity* means nearness.
(*A high degree of*) perfection.	*Perfection* is the highest form attainable.
To co-ordinate (*together*).	*Co-ordinate* means to bring together.

EXERCISES

1. The following sentences all contain unnecessary words. Rearrange each sentence, improving it by using fewer and simpler words, but without changing the sense:

A

(a) He was completely inaudible, and no one could hear him.

(b) We were sitting alone, all by ourselves, when he arrived.

(c) We enjoyed our holiday this year equally as well as last year's.

(d) It is very doubtful as to whether he will gain the promotion he is expecting.

(e) Applicants for employment in our factory abound in great numbers.

(f) There is no question whatever but that the mistake was his own.

(g) Our traveller will call on you if and when you ask him to do so.

(h) When the new clerks arrive each will be told what his respective duties are.

(i) A quite unique feature of the firm's new lorries is their low petrol consumption.

(j) We have received your letter and the same shall have our urgent and immediate attention.

B

(a) She has resigned from her post as invoice clerk.

(b) One way out of the difficulty still remains open.

(c) In the event of your wishing me to do so, I will call on you next week.

(d) I have been unable to reply before owing to the fact that I have only just returned from abroad.

(e) The two assistants were mutually antagonistic to each other.

(f) His appointment dates as and from March 1st.

(g) The two vehicles collided with each other at considerable speed.

(h) The true facts of the situation are not yet in our possession.

(i) As a shorthand-writer she has attained a high standard of perfection.

(j) I asked him to call and see me, but he declined to accept my invitation.

2. Improve the following sentences by omitting superfluous words, indicating in each case the reason for your omission:

(a) His future prospects were not very promising.

(b) As chairman of three different companies he possessed very unique experience.

(c) The surrounding circumstances do not justify an advance of more than £2,000.

(d) The company has a complete monopoly of the market.

(e) We were warmly welcomed as soon as we entered into the room.

(f) Descending down the staircase she slipped and hurt herself.

(g) The repairs you asked us to carry out are now quite completed.

(h) The production of cassette tapes has now reached a high degree of perfection.

(i) We enclose herewith a copy of the report.

(j) We managed to trace the original source of the quotation.

YOUR DICTIONARY

New words

Regular use of the dictionary will help you to extend your knowledge of words and your ability to use them correctly. Make it a rule never to pass a new word without looking it up and making a note of it. Avoid the temptation, always present, to guess the meaning of a word from its context, otherwise you run the risk of using it wrongly not only in conversation but also, and what is worse still, in your correspondence. Having noted its meaning use it both in conversation and in writing when it is appropriate. Only by doing so will new words become an effective part of your vocabulary.

Any worthwhile dictionary will indicate how words should be pronounced. Correspondence is not of course concerned with pronunciation, but many business contacts are of the personal kind or by telephone, and if you are to create a good impression with educated business acquaintances correct speaking is essential.

Words pronounced alike

One class of words that is a source of frequent trouble consists of those with similar pronunciations but different spellings and different meanings. *Complement* (a supplement) and *compliment* (an expression of praise); *draft* (a rough copy) and *draught* (a current of air); *licence* (a noun) and *license* (a verb) are among many words of this class. The following are others frequently used in correspondence:

air	heir	its	it's
ascent	assent	meter	metre
born	borne	naught	nought
boy	buoy	passed	past
broach	brooch	peace	piece
canvas	canvass	plain	plane
cession	session	practice	practise
check	cheque	principal	principle
complacent	complaisant	rain	reign, rein
council	counsel	rapt	wrapped
cubicle	cubical	sew	sow
currant	current	shear	sheer
die	dye	son	sun
faint	feint	stationary	stationery
flair	flare	their	there
forbear	forebear	to	too, two
hoard	horde	who's	whose

These and similar words are particularly troublesome in dictation. When typing from dictated material you must first think of the word in its context before you can choose the right spelling.

Words spelt alike

Sometimes the transfer of stress from one syllable to another alters the meaning of a word as well as its grammatical function. Thus, *ab'stract*, with the stress on the first syllable, is a noun and means *a summary*, while *abstract'*, with the stress on the second syllable, is a verb and means *to take away*. Many other words behave in this way. You will find further examples in the following Exercise 3 on p. 81.

Words bearing resemblance

Then there are those words that bear some resemblance and which in consequence are often confused. They include such words as *accept* (to receive, or agree) and *except* (to exclude); *affect* (to produce an effect) and *effect* (to bring about, to accomplish);

precede (to come or go before) and *proceed* (to continue). Words of this class are considerable and call for special care:

advice (a noun)	advise (a verb)
amend (to correct)	emend (to delete)
artist (a painter, etc.)	artiste (an entertainer)
biannual (twice yearly)	biennial (two-yearly)
confidant (a close friend)	confident (assured)
definite (exact)	definitive (final)
distinct (separate)	distinctive (characteristic)
elicit (to draw out)	illicit (unlawful)
enquiry (a question)	inquiry (an investigation)
ensure (to make certain)	insure (to guarantee)
farther (more distant)	further (in addition)
lightening (making lighter)	lightning (an electrical discharge)
prescribe (to recommend)	proscribe (to outlaw)
stimulant (a drug)	stimulus (an incentive)

Words with several meanings

And finally, the passage of time has not only given birth to new words but also provided new meanings to old ones, and so the same word has progressed through a number of changes and come to mean a number of different things. These words have what we call different *areas of meaning*. Reference to a dictionary tells us, for example, that the word *bar* may mean a number of quite different things, including:

> a pole; an obstruction; a strip of metal below the clasp of a medal; a bank of sand at the mouth of a river; the place in Court where prisoners stand; the profession of a barrister; a room in a tavern where liquor is served; and in music, a vertical line on the stave.

Most words have more than one meaning and a great number, such as *bar*, have many. This may appear confusing, but in practice the context in which a word stands provides the clue to the meaning intended, and this with a little common sense can usually be found from the dictionary without much trouble. If we say *No drinks are served in this bar after 22.00 hours*, there is no doubt as to the meaning intended.

EXERCISES

1. The following paragraph has been abstracted from a dictionary. Explain it fully.

WHILE, whīl, *n.* A space of time.—conj. During the time that.—v.t. pret. & pp. *whiled,* whīld; ppr. *whiling,* whīling. To cause to pass pleasantly; usually with *away.* (*RSA*)

2. (*a*) The following paragraph has been copied from a dictionary. Explain in detail what it means.

TILL, til, *n.* A drawer for money in a shop—*prep.* To the time of—*v.t.* To cultivate.

(*b*) Explain *briefly* and *clearly* the difference between a dictionary and an encyclopaedia. (*RSA*)

3. In each of the following words the stressed syllable is marked by an immediately following dash. Use each word in a sentence to show the different meanings of the words forming each pair:

| (*a*) | appro'priate | com'bine | con'duct | con'flict | con'tract |
| | appropriate' | combine' | conduct' | conflict' | contract' |

| (*b*) | del'egate | discrim'inate | elab'orate | ex'port | min'ute |
| | delegate' | discriminate' | elaborate' | export' | minute' |

| (*c*) | pres'ent | prod'uce | sub'ject | subord'inate | trans'port |
| | present' | produce' | subject' | subordinate' | transport' |

4. Replace each of the following phrases by a single word. (The first and last letters and the number of letters in the word required are given in brackets.)

(*a*) A document issued by a company charging its assets with the repayment of a loan. (d . . . . e)

(*b*) A prepared set of written questions for the purpose of compiling or comparing information. (q . . . . e)

(*c*) A detailed list or schedule of goods, furniture, etc. (i . . . . y)

(*d*) The official numbering of a country's population. (c . . . . s)

(*e*) The needless use of words that merely repeat something already said. (t . . . . y)

(*f*) Not bearing upon or related to the matter in hand. (i . . . . t)

(*g*) A formal written order for the supply of goods or materials. (r . . . . n)

(*h*) Not biased in favour of either side in a contest or argument. (i . . . . . . l)

(*i*) The fall in value of a thing due to wear and tear. (d . . . . n)

(*j*) A person to whom money is paid. (p . . . e)

5. Select five of the following phrases and show that you understand their meaning:

appropriate remedy	cursory examination
circumstantial evidence	equitable arrangement
collective responsibility	fallacious reasoning

6. By using them in sentences distinguish between the meaning of the following pairs of words:

> alternate   bankrupt   deprecate   moral   presumptive
> alternative insolvent   depreciate   morale   presumptuous

7. Explain the meaning of the following expressions:

> an emotive situation   remedial treatment
> a capitation grant   a laissez-faire policy
>   to beg the question

ENCROACHING WORDS

Your ability to choose and use the right words depends upon the range of your vocabulary, and this will be adequate only if you take opportunities to talk with educated people, to read criticlly, and to use and study your dictionary.

Some words tend to encroach on others that are better. The use of such encroaching words is something you must try to avoid. In the list that follows are a number of these words, and of others that are frequently misused:

Do not confuse this	*with this*
achieve (to attain by effort)	get, reach (to obtain, possibly without effort)
acquaint (to make aware)	inform (to tell)
address (formal, and may be written)	speech (less formal, and presumed to be spoken)
advise (to offer counsel)	inform (to tell)
aggravate (to make worse)	annoy (to irritate)
allude (to refer to something indirectly)	mention (to call attention to)
alternately (first one, then the other)	alternatively (offering a choice)
amateur (not professional, but may be highly skilled)	novice (a beginner)
answer (relates to questions)	reply (relates to arguments and statements)
anticipate (to act in advance, to forestall)	expect (to wait, to look for)
appreciate (to set value on anything)	realize (to understand clearly)
appropriate (fitting, suitable)	relevant (applicable)
audience (hearers)	spectators (onlookers)
capacity (power to receive or retain)	ability (power to do)
comprise (to contain, include)	compose (to put together)

Do not confuse this	*with this*
conference (a meeting, esp, large)	talk (conversation)
confirm (to verify, make sure)	corroborate (to make double sure)
continuous (without a break)	continual (recurring frequently)
credible (believable)	creditable (praiseworthy)
defective (lacking in quality)	deficient (lacking in quantity)
dependant (a person)	dependent (an adjective)
discreet (prudent)	discrete (separate, distinct)
disinterested (unbiased, impartial)	uninterested (not interested)
distinguish (to recognize a difference)	discriminate (to make fine distinctions)
effective (producing a result)	effectual (answering its purpose)
e.g. (for example)	i.e. (that is)
equable (devoid of extremes)	equitable (just and fair)
exceptional (unusual)	exceptionable (objectionable)
expect (to wait, look for)	believe (to accept as true)
evidence (proof)	testimony (a sworn statement)
ingenious (clever)	ingenuous (free from deception)
kind (sort)	description (as described)
feasible (practicable, capable of performance)	probable (likely)
feel (to perceive by intuition)	think (to be of opinion)
find (to come across)	discover (to uncover, detect)
imply (to mean indirectly)	infer (to deduce)
individual (has a disparaging flavour)	person (a human being)
integrate (to combine the parts of, to form a whole)	co-ordinate (to range together)
judicial (legal)	judicious (prudent)
likely to (probably)	liable to (suggests something detrimental)
loan (something lent)	lend (the act of lending)
meantime (noun)	meanwhile (adverb: say *meanwhile*, but *in the meantime*)
mutual (reciprocal)	common (applying to many)
neglect (a careless omission)	negligence (habitual neglect)
negligent (careless)	negligible (of little importance)
nice (exact)	attractive (inviting, charming)
official (properly authorized)	officious (meddling)
party (a legal term)	person (a general term)
practical (useful in practice)	practicable (feasible)
practically (opposite to theoretically)	almost (nearly)
pretence (make-believe)	pretension (advancement of a claim)
proposal (an offer)	proposition (something proposed for discussion)
quantity (how much)	number (how many)

Do not confuse this	*with this*
remember (to recall without conscious effort)	recollect (to recall with conscious effort)
requirements (wants)	requisites (essentials)
site (a specific spot)	situation (general surroundings)
state (to present formally)	say (to speak)
transpire (to become known, come to light)	occur (to come to pass).

The following examples illustrate the right and wrong use of some of these words frequently used in business correspondence.

Wrong	*Right*
Advise, inform	
We will *advise* you as soon as the goods are ready (say *inform*).	We *advise* you not to accept the price offered (i.e. give you counsel).
Allude, mention	
The matter *alluded* to in your letter will be considered at our next meeting (say *mentioned*).	He was *alluding* to one of us (i.e. hinting at someone not actually mentioned)
Anticipate, expect	
We do not *anticipate* any difficulty in meeting your request (say *expect*).	We *anticipated* your request for quick delivery and sent the goods this morning (i.e. acted in advance).
Appreciate, realize	
You will no doubt *appreciate* that we cannot allow a discount (say *realize, understand*).	Your help is very much *appreciated* (i.e. valued).
Appropriate, relevant	
We shall study the part played by the *appropriate* financial institutions in providing the capital needed (say *relevant*).	The speech made by the chairman was not *appropriate* for the occasion (i.e. not suitable).
Capacity, ability	
He has an unusual *capacity* for organizing (say *ability*).	His *capacity* for foreign languages is quite remarkable (i.e. his power to acquire).
Compensate, remunerate	
We shall *compensate* you for the work done (say *remunerate*).	We shall *compensate* you for any loss sustained (i.e. make good any loss).

Wrong	*Right*

Comprise, compose

The five members who *comprise* the committee all hope to be present (say *compose*, or better still, *form*).

The committee *comprises* five elected representatives (i.e. includes).

Depreciate, deteriorate

Perishable goods *depreciate* quickly unless carefully stored (say *deteriorate*).

The pound *depreciated* under pressure on the foreign exchanges (i.e. fell in value).

Disinterested, uninterested

As I have attended all meetings you can hardly accuse me of being *disinterested* (say *uninterested*).

We suggest the matter be referred to someone who is *disinterested* (i.e. not biased).

Expect, believe

We *expect* you were quite right to decline the offer (say *believe*).

We *expect* to hear from you soon. (i.e. like to hear from you).

Feel, think

I cannot help *feeling* that the terms are unreasonabe (say *thinking*).

Despite the absence of evidence I *feel* he has acted wisely (i.e. feel instinctively).

Individual, person

He is a most reliable *individual* (say *person*).

A distinction must be drawn between the *individual* and the group (i.e. the single person).

Integrate, co-ordinate

The formation of a pool will *integrate* the work of the typists (say *co-ordinate*).

The advertising department will now be *integrated* with the sales department under the sales manager (i.e. will form one with the sales department).

Likely, liable

We are *likely* to fail in our attempts to increase profits (say *liable*).

It is *likely* that she will take offence if you criticize her (i.e. probable).

Loan, lend

We are willing to *loan* you £200 for a month (say *lend*).

The Council will grant a *loan* of £200 (i.e. a sum of money).

Wrong	*Right*
Meantime, meanwhile	
I shall be away until Friday; *meantime*, perhaps you will complete this report (say *meanwhile*, or *in the meantime*).	The manager will return next Monday; *meanwhile* (or *in the meantime*). Mr X will act as his deputy.
Mutual, common	
We refer you to our *mutual* friends, Messrs X & Co. (say to *X & Co., who are well known to both of us*).	We are glad to think that our *mutually* good relations will not be impaired by the difficulties that have arisn (i.e. our relations with each other).
Practical, practicable	
To complete the work by the time stated is not *practical* (say *practicable*).	What is *practicable* is not always *practical* (i.e. what is possible is not always profitable).
Transpire, occur	
The accident *transpired* as he left the meeting (say *occurred*).	It has *transpired* that the directors could not agree (i.e. become known).

To provide a fitting close to this chapter it is apt to quote from the advice given by Sir Ernest Gowers in his book* that everyone concerned with business letter-writing would do well to read:

"What we are concerned with is not a conquest for a literary style as an end in itself, but to study how best to convey our meaning without ambiguity and without giving unnecessary trouble to our readers."

He then proceeds to give rules for writing:

"Use no more words than are necessary to express your meaning, for if you use more you are likely to obscure it and to tire your reader. In particular do not use superflous adjectives and adverbs and do not use roundabout phrases where single words would serve."

"Use familiar words rather than the far-fetched, if they express your meaning equally well; for the familiar are more likely to be readily understood."

"Use words with a precise meaning rather than those that are vague for they will obviously serve better to make your meaning clear; and in particular prefer concrete words to abstract, for they are more likely to have a precise meaning."

* *op. cit.*, p. 72.

EXERCISES

1. Complete the following sentences by selecting from the words in brackets the one that expresses the appropriate meaning:

(a) After a long and arduous climb they (*reached, achieved, got to*) the summit.

(b) On (*achieving, reaching*) retirement age all employees qualify for pension.

(c) I will (*acquaint, inform*) him (*with, of*) the facts.

(d) I am writing to (*acquaint, inform*) you that our traveller will be in your district next week.

(e) The appointment of a new secretary will not (*affect, effect*) my plans for visiting the Continent.

(f) I hope the appointment of a new secretary will (*affect, effect*) an improvement in the administration.

(g) Threats only serve to (*aggravate, annoy*) those to whom they are made.

(h) The medicine supplied only served to (*aggravate, annoy*) his condition.

(i) The journey to the United States can be made by air or (*alternately, alternatively*) by sea.

(j) They spent the evening at home and (*alternately, alternatively*) listened to music and watched television.

2. Contrast the meanings of the words included in each of the following pairs by using each word in a sentence. (*Refer to your dictionary as may be necessary.*).

(a) address, speech
(b) amateur, novice
(c) answer, reply
(d) neglect, negligence
(e) quantity, number
(f) requirements, requisites
(g) site, situation
(h) accept, except
(i) confirm, corroborate
(j) exceptional, exceptionable.

3. Referring to your dictionary as may be necessary, give in your own words a short definition of each of the following commercial terms:

(a) agent, amalgamation, annuity, auctioneer, barter;
(b) budget, broker, cartel, company, consignment;
(c) contract, credit, currency, debenture, demurrage;
(d) depreciation, endowment, factor, guarantee, indemnity;
(e) insolvency, invoice, lien, monopoly, notary;
(f) option, overdraft, partnership, rebate, requisition;
(g) revenue, subsidy, tariff, trustee, wharfinger.

4. Find single words for the following definitions. The initial letters of the words required are given.

(a) an exact copy of a document made by photographic means (p...);
(b) able to use either hand with equal skill (a...);

(c) a typed version of shorthand or sound-recorded notes (t...);
(d) bond on which the interest is a prior charge on assets (d...);
(e) a possible future event in business (c...);
(f) total money income (r...);
(g) business obligations (l...);
(h) use of money to buy shares, property, bonds, etc. (i...);
(i) tireless; incapable of feeling weariness (i...);
(j) sudden, unexpected increase in a company's cash resources (w...).
                                                                (*RSA*)

5. *(a)* Each of the following words may be stressed in two ways. In each case a change of stress from the first syllable to the second brings an alteration of meaning. Write *ten* sentences, *two* for each word to show the various meanings:

> col'lect and collect'   com'pound and compound'
> con'cert and concert'   com'press and compress'
> in'valid and inval'id

(b) Write the negative form of the following words (e.g. like—dislike):

prove, regular, noble, merit, arrange, legal, similar, trust, wind, capable.   (*RSA*)

6. Substitute one word for those printed in italic type in each of the following sentences. The first and last letters of the words are given in brackets at the end of the sentences. Do not write out the sentences:

(a) He was very disappointed that the stamp was only a *clever immitation of the genuine stamp*. (c.........t)
(b) After a very successful season the tennis player decided to become a *player who earned money through playing the game*. (p..........l)
(c) The son regarded his father as a *man to whom he could turn for advice*. (c........r)
(d) The writer's outlook was *free from any national prejudice*. (c..........n)
(e) He was praised for his *ability to look always on the bright side of things*. (o......m)
(f) Jim should *come before* his younger brother in the procession. (p.....e)
(g) No one *derived any advantage* from this. (b.......d)
(h) The prisoner's evidence was *such that it could not be understood*. (i..............e)
(i) The statesman passionately believed in *government by the people* (d.......y)
(j) He was very interested in *the study of prehistoric remains*. (a.........y)

7. Words printed in italics in the following letter are used in the wrong sense. Recast the letter substituting the correct words probably intended.

Dear Sir

We have received an *anomalous* letter from a customer who has a grievance that, I assure you, is quite *imaginative*. The *inflammable* tone of the letter suggests that the writer is very angry. His complaint refers to an *incidence* that occurred during the period when work in our factory was *temporally* suspended owing to an *unofficious* strike. The letter is written in French and I am enclosing a *literary* translation of it.

It is not our *practise* to treat *anomalous* letters seriously, but in this *instant* we feel the nature of the complaint to be such that an *inquisition* should be made into the alleged circumstances. We should therefore be glad if you would *precede* to make *judicial* enquiries to find out who the writer is. We *fervidly* hope your *inquisition* will enable him to be identified, because we are most anxious to preserve *harmonical* relations with our customers, and to do business with them on terms that are both fair and *equable*.

Yours faithfully

CHAPTER SEVEN

Style in Business Writing

Style is the dress of thoughts; and a well-dressed thought, like a well-dressed man, appears to great advantage.

Lord Chesterfield: *Letters*

WHAT IS STYLE?

The words used in a business letter and the way in which they are arranged express the writer's personality and give the letter what is called its style. Style in writing as in other walks of life is a quality peculiar to the individual, for no two people write alike. It is determined by background, training and experience and the way a person thinks. Being so much a personal matter it cannot be copied, nor are there any set rules for acquiring it. Just as there is style in literary writing so there is style in business letter-writing, and in any summary of its desirable elements sincerity, simplicity and clarity certainly have a place. To these must be added an adequate vocabulary, for without a competent knowledge of words and a sufficient mastery over their use it is not possible to weave the elements of style into the fabric of a good letter.

There is no special kind of writing to which the business letter should conform, but only the kind of writing that observes the rules of good writing, and is free of the jargon and cliché-ridden phrases of an earlier age. Style itself does not depend on rules; it springs from a deeper source—the writer's personality and the sincerity with which he writes.

SINCERITY

Whether a person is writing a piece of literary composition or a mere business letter, he needs to write with sincerity. The business letter may seem to be a drab and commonplace piece of writing offering little scope for originality; even so, it must have originality of the sort that expresses the thoughts of its writer in his own words in his own way. This is the essence of genuine style. It consists in saying naturally what one feels in language that is simple and concise, and fittingly related to the reader's needs and level of comprehension. If all business letters were modelled to a set style they would make wearisome reading.

SIMPLICITY

Don't be ashamed of simplicity; it goes with naturalness of tone and freshness of viewpoint to make readable writing. If it is appropriate the short word is preferable to the long; it draws less attention to itself as a word and enables the reader to concentrate attention on the idea denoted by it. But this does not mean that you must never use long words. One good reason for the short word is that it has a greater impact than the longer word:

> drunk is more emphatic than *intoxicated*
> dead is more emphatic than *deceased*
> rude is more emphatic than *discourteous*
> sad is more emphatic than *sorrowful*

But there are times when the short word is not strong enough to convey the writer's feeling; the longer word is then more appropriate:

> *violent* is stronger than rough
> *enormous* is stronger than big
> *powerful* is stronger than strong
> *exhausted* is stronger than tired

Nor does the use of simple language mean that short simple sentences are always best. Your reader will not enjoy a style of writing that always leaps and never flows. What is called for is a prudent blending of both the long and the short so that the monotony of a series of long sentences is broken by the occasional use of a short sharp sentence that "keeps the reader awake".

It is in the choice of the most appropriate word and the judicious mixture of short and longer sentences that vocabulary is an important element in style. High-sounding words and phrases are to writing what ostentation is to dress—merely a means of drawing attention and showing off. They reveal the writer for what he is—superficial, conceited and certainly lacking in good taste. To *express a preference for*, to *give consideration* to, or *arrive at a decision* when all that is meant is *prefer, consider,* or to *decide* is to elaborate needlessly what ought to be simple. The following are further examples:

Instead of	Say
in the normal course	normally, usually
we are of the opinion that	we think
in view of the fact that	since, because
at all times	always
in the near future	soon
at the present time	now
grant approval	approve
make a revision	revise
we are aware of the fact	we know
in spite of the fact that	although
it affords me great pleasure to inform you	I am glad to tell you

Business letter-writing calls for a plain style—a style that is simple, clear and easily understood, one that makes use for the most part of short and familiar words. Such is the style of much of our greatest literature.

CLARITY

When we write letters dealing with such concrete things as orders, shipments and payments the dominant need is for exactness expressed in terms that are absolutely clear. We owe it to our readers to write clearly and to make their task of comprehension as easy as possible at first reading. We fail in this if we abandon simplicity. First be clear about what you want to say and then say it simply and straightforwardly. Clear writing and clear thinking go hand in hand, and a person who thinks straight will usually be able to write straight, building words into sentences that express his thoughts exactly and clearly. Clarity is achieved through natural forms of expression, the use of familiar words, and straightforward sentences grouped in paragraphs each with one central idea. The tone of the letter should be conversational and the language used as natural as everyday speech, but without its colloquialisms and slang expressions. Write as plainly as you would speak, but remember that we do not always speak as clearly as we might.

Clarity is also promoted by what is termed parallel structure, i.e. the placing of related ideas of equal importance in parallel positions in the sentence, as in the following examples:

The booklet contains *instructions for adjusting* the machine and *suggestions for operating* it.

Transport charges vary with *weight of package* and *distance of transmission*.

They decline not only *to pay the account* but also *to return the goods*.

Besides making for clarity, parallel structure carries ideas forward in a way that sounds well.

Make sure to write sentences capable of only one interpretation. It is surprisingly easy to write sentences that appear to their writers to have only one meaning, but in which their correspondents see a quite different meaning. For example:

The manager gave his secretary a cheque, and her husband a watch.

Does this mean:

(a) The manager gave his secretary a cheque, and her husband presented her with a watch?

OR

(b) The manager gave a cheque to his secretary and a watch to her husband?

It is a golden rule of writing that those parts of a sentence which are closely connected in thought should be placed in the sentence as near to one another as possible, so that their mutual relationship is clear. Failure to observe this rule is a frequent cause of ambiguity. In the sentence:

I can recommend him for the post he applies for with complete confidence.

are we to understand that he applies for the post with complete confidence, or that he is recommended with complete confidence? If the latter, then the phrase *with complete confidence* should be placed immediately after *recommend him*.

And again:

No child shall be employed on any weekday when the school is not open for a longer period than four hours.

Does this mean that no child must be employed when the school is not open for more than four hours, or that no child must be employed for more than four hours when the school is not open? The latter is presumably intended and the phrase *for a longer period than four hours* should be placed immediately after *employed*.

When you write or dictate a letter it is an excellent idea to jot down the points you wish to make and to place them in order; in other words, to "write to a plan". About this more will be said in Chapter Twelve. Planning helps to produce the orderly kind of letter that creates a good impression because its message is clear. If your correspondent has to read your letter a second time before he can understand it, the chances are that it is not a good letter.

COHERENCE

Coherence is an essential part of clarity. What was said in Chapter Four about coherence in paragraph structure applies to coherence in letter structure. Logical arrangement, the topic sentence and the use of connective terms all have a part in coherence.

Logical arrangement

For its full effect we saw that the paragraph depends upon the orderly arrangement of its component sentences in a logical sequence. And so with the business letter, whose overall effectiveness depends upon the orderly arrangement of its component paragraphs. Each paragraph must flow smoothly into the next to form a series that represents a coherent whole in which the mutual relationships of the paragraphs are manifest.

The topic sentence

The business letter on pp. 40–1 illustrates the part played by the topic sentence as a factor in coherence. Placed at the beginning the topic sentence serves to link its paragraph with the one before it and to prepare the reader for what is to follow. It promotes the smooth flow of ideas as one topic blends naturally with the next, giving coherence to the communication as a whole. It has been said that the reader can get the gist of a well-written letter by reading the topic sentences, and while this may be an exaggeration it is certainly true that skilful use of the topic sentence assists comprehension in a very real way.

Use of connective terms

Coherence is also achieved by using conjunctions, adverbs and phrases as connectives. There is a feeling among some that sentences and paragraphs should not begin with conjunctions, but this view is not supported by the practice of good writers. After all, if what is written is to form a connected whole, there must be some means of carrying on the thought from one sentence or paragraph to another, and what could be more appropriate than to make use of such connectives, or transitional words, as *but, for, although, because, therefore, consequently, however, otherwise, nevertheless,* besides many others, or even transitional phrases such as *in addition, for example, on the other hand, on the contrary, on the whole,* etc.? Even complete sentences may be used as connectives, of which an example will be found in the second of the following two letters.

The first of these letters is composed of short, poorly-connected paragraphs, which fail to flow smoothly for want of suitable connectives.

Dear Sir

We are sorry to learn from your letter of 12th October that you have had complaints from customers about our vases. Your letter has caused us a great deal of concern. We are glad you have brought the matter to our notice so promptly.

These vases are made from pure Chinese porcelain. They are renowned for their exquisite design and fine craftsmanship. There is a very promising market for them. It is unfortunate that the consignment supplied to your last order should have included a number of defective items.

We suggest that you return all items still unsold from this particular consignment. We will then replace them free of charge.

We deeply regret the inconvenience you have been caused. Please accept our apologies.

Yours faithfully

Now compare the above with the following reparagraphed letter.

Dear Sir

We are sorry to learn from your letter of 12th October that you have had complaints from customers about our vases. We are very concerned, *but nevertheless* glad that you have brought the matter to our notice so promptly.

As you know, these vases are made from pure Chinese porcelain *and* are renowned for their exquisite design and fine craftsmanship. It is *therefore* unfortunate that the consignment supplied to your last order should have included a number of defective items.

We feel sure you will wish to continue to stock these vases as there is a very promising market for them, *and in the circumstances* suggest that you return for replacement free of charge all items still unsold from this particular consignment.

Meanwhile, we deeply regret the inconvenience you have been caused *and* ask you to accept our apologies.

Yours faithfully

The connective or transitional expressions in this second letter are printed in italics. They take the writer's thoughts forward smoothly and naturally and make for comfortable reading.

COURTESY

Not only must your letter style be sincere, simple and clear; it must also be courteous and sympathetic. In the rush of modern business this is sometimes forgotten. There are some who seem to regard bluntness as a token of strength, when it is in fact a sign of bad breeding. Courtesy makes friends, and friends in business are no less necessary than in the wider life. If, then, you receive a rude and sharp letter resist the temptation to retaliate; reply with understanding and courtesy to criticisms, however unjust or stupid they may be. You belittle your dignity if you allow your correspondent to set the pattern for your reply. With a little care and considerateness you can convey criticism, disapproval and even rebuke without giving offence or creating hard feelings. "A soft answer turneth away wrath", and the considerateness of your reply may put your correspondent in a more reasonable and even in a favourable frame of mind; if you don't make a friend you will at least avoid making an enemy.

EXERCISES

1. The following is a reply to a letter from a customer regretting his inability to settle his account, the reason given being the small demand for goods recommended as a good selling line by the supplier's traveller. Reconstruct it so as to improve its tone as you think necessary:

Dear Sir

We beg to acknowledge receipt of yours of yesterday's date, in which you intimate that you are unable to make a settlement just now, but hope to remit part of it in a week or two. This is not satisfactory. Far from the goods being slow-selling, we have had from dealers in your town no less than fourteen repeat orders, some of them for large amounts. We cannot but think that had you actively pushed the sale of our goods you would long ago have exhausted your stock. Anyhow, it is hardly fair that you should expect us to suffer from your own failure; and, though we have no desire unduly to press you for payment, we must ask you to remit us the whole amount due, on or before the 16th of next month.

Yours faithfully

2. The following is a rude and angry letter sent to a firm of heating engineers who failed to complete a central-heating installation by the promised date. Replace the letter by one more suitable and more courteous, stressing the inconvenience to which you are being put and pressing for early completion of the work:

Dear Sir

I have received your letter explaining why you did not complete the installation of the central heating by the date promised. I am afraid I am not at all satisfied with the reasons you give for the delay; they sound very much like excuses and are not in the least convincing.

I now wonder whether, when you promised to complete the work by 9th May, you really felt you could do so. Your later promise to recommence work on the installation you have also failed to keep, nor have I received the courtesy of an explanation why. It is evident that the promises you make are not to be relied upon.

My only concern now is to get the installation finished and in working order as soon as possible, and I now hope you will do something about it. I propose to give you another ten days in which to complete the work, and if by that time you haven't done so I shall take it out of your hands and arrange for it to be completed by another contractor.

Yours faithfully

3. Read the following letter:

15 Carlton Road
SHEFFIELD
S10 2UA
12 October 19..

The Secretary
Jones & Whiteside Ltd.
Paragon Printing Works
MANCHESTER M1 6EB

Dear Sir

English for the Office

In the account I received from you on 8th October I found included a charge of £42.90 for corrections and alterations to the proofs for this title.

I feel there must be some mistake since most of the corrections were due to printers' errors. Other corrections and alterations were relatively few.

I shall be glad if you will send me a detailed explanation of the charge.

Yours faithfully
H. Mayall

As Secretary to Jones and Whiteside reply to Mr Mayall and explain that the charge is correct and does not include printers' errors and corrections. Nor does it include corrections and alterations within the limit of 10 per cent of the cost of typesetting provided for in the agreement made last January. Mention that the corrections and alterations were greatly in excess of the 10 per cent limit and enclose a detailed statement.

4. Read the following letter:

5 Crescent Road
CHINGFORD
E4 6AT
12 May 19..

Messrs King & Chadwick
Solicitors
25 Bryanston Street
LONDON W1A 2AZ

Dear Sirs

Mr James Ashton, my next-door neighbour, has expressed his intention on a number of occasions to use his portion of the adjoining land to build four cottages for his farm workers, and last week informed me that he had already made plans with a local builder for the work to be started.

I have always understood that neither his portion of the land nor my own could be used for building purposes, and I strongly oppose the arrangements he has made.

Would you please advise me what steps I should take in the matter.

Yours faithfully
W. Dawson

As a partner in the firm of King & Chadwick write to Mr Dawson and say that Mr Ashton cannot build on the land. The land was sold as one lot by Lady Campbell about twenty-five years ago and the title deeds state clearly that it is not to be used for building of any kind. Her son and heir is abroad and may be difficult to trace. Even so, it is doubtful whether he could alter the present arrangement if he wished. As matters stand it is most unlikely that the local authority will allow the proposed building to take place. Advise Mr Dawson to register his objection with them.

5. Write a letter to a tourist agency, whose newspaper advertisements you have seen, asking for their advice and assistance in arranging a holiday abroad for yourself and a friend. Give all necessary particulars.
(*UEI*)

6. Write a letter to the owner of some field or park, asking for permission to use it for a fête, garden party, or sports, the proceeds of which are for local charity. Give precise particulars and undertake to make good any damage. (*RSA*)

7. You have recently bought a new typewriter, but it is not giving you satisfaction.

(*a*) Write a letter to the makers, giving reasons for your dissatisfaction, and asking them to send a representative to call on you.
(*b*) Prepare the reply of the maker to the foregoing letter, expressing his confidence in the machine, and stating that he is arranging for a representative to call to examine the machine and advise you about its use and care.

CLICHÉS

Cliché is a French word used in English to denote a phrase that has become stereotyped and threadbare through excessive use. A cliché is another of the faults in style that must be avoided in business correspondence; it indicates poverty of language and an unwillingness to think for oneself. Letters packed with clichés can never be fresh and original, since by its very nature a cliché is something that is second-hand.

A cliché that is unacceptable as standard English becomes slang; if it is frequently used as part of the vocabulary of a particular branch of writing, business correspondence for example, then it becomes what is known as jargon.

The following are some of the commoner clichés many of which find their way into business letters:

as a matter of fact	bound to admit
as a rule	by and large
at all events	by the way
axe to grind	conspicuous by its absence
be that as it may	cut out the dead wood
bear in mind	explore every avenue
better half	face facts

fact of the matter
for the time being
for your information
goes against the grain
if the worst comes to the worst
in any shape or form
in point of fact
in the first place
in the meantime
in the near future
in view of the fact
in well-informed circles
inclined to think
it goes without saying
last but not least
leave no stone unturned
let us face it

look on the bright side
make the most of the opportunity
mince matters
need hardly say
needless to say
no room for complacency
on the contrary
over and above
plus the fact
psychological moment
rising generation
second to none
shrewd suspicion
take the rough with the smooth
the man in the street
to all intents and purposes
unparalleled success

What is a cliché is a matter of opinion. If the phrase is used because it is the fittest way of expressing what one wants to say there can be no objection to it; otherwise it should be avoided. If at any time you find yourself about to slip into a familar phrase think twice before using it, and then use it only if it is the best way of saying what you have to say.

SLANG

The *Shorter Oxford Dictionary* defines slang as "language of a highly colloquial type, considered as below the level of standard educated speech". *Slanguage* is a term recently coined to describe the use of slang in speech and writing. Words and phrases that are unacceptable as standard English are often used in familiar and informal speech, and in moderation and in their proper place there is no harm in so using them. But they are certainly out of place in business letters and in serious writing. In conversation you can say *on the dot* for *precisely*, *OK* for *all right*. *Do the needful* for *Do what is necessary*, *Get a move on* for *Hurry up*, and *It is up to you* for *It is for you to decide*. These and similar expressions are entirely the language of informal conversation, to which their use must be confined. On no account must you give them a place in the business letter.

The dictionary contains hundreds of words noted as slang. Most of us can recognize them at once and would not hesitate to condemn them out of hand as offending good taste. We should no more think of using *bilge, cushy, hooey* and *posh* in our letters than we should *quids* for *pounds*, *grand* for *a thousand pounds*, or *blower* for *telephone*. We don't tell our correspondent he has *had it, put his foot in it*, or *fallen for it*. We say he has *been unfortunate, made a mistake*, or *been deceived*.

At all costs, then, avoid using slang in the business letter.

JARGON

True jargon consists of the technical terms and specialized terminology of some profession, trade or occupation. But jargon in the popular sense has come to mean long-winded and involved expressions used for their own sake. It is a term now applied to a style of writing that is pompous, obscure and verbose, full of clichés and hackneyed expressions that add little or nothing to the meaning of what is written, and which are sometimes hard to understand.

Jargon in this sense was the characteristic feature of the business letter of half a century ago, with its stereotyped, roundabout and meaningless terminology—a legacy from the correspondence of our Victorian ancestors, who wallowed in such monstrosities as *beg to advise, your esteemed enquiry, your valued favour, your good self, your earliest convenience, meets with your approval, we beg to say, Awaiting the favour of your esteemed commands, Thanking you in anticipation,* and *Assuring you of our best attention at all times.*

In more recent times we have come to recognize how absurb and futile is this style of writing. But although standards of business and official letter-writing have much improved, expressions we should do better without still linger in the vocabulary of some of our correspondence. Perhaps in time the growing awareness of what is good style in letter-writing will enable us to write *We have received* rather than *We are in receipt of* without feeling that our behaviour is unusual.

EXERCISES

1. In the following sentences substitute fresher expressions for those printed in italics:

(a) We hope the new design will appeal to *the man in the street*.

(b) *It stands to reason* that when prices rise the value of money falls.

(c) You may not agree with his views, but *when all is said and done* he is the expert.

(d) At the meeting last night the Member for Oxbridge was *conspicuous by his absence*.

(e) The speech he made after dinner was *too funny for words*.

(f) *It goes without saying* that a good name is better than riches.

(g) The suggestion to build another garage is *without rhyme or reason*.

(h) *As a matter of fact* I shall be in Manchester on business next week.

(i) *Believe it or not* his salary is now over £15,000 a year.

(j) Her shorthand wasn't *up to scratch* and as a result she *missed the bus*.

2. Distinguish between a cliché, slang, and jargon, and give two examples of each.

3. Copy the following letter, and underline the phrases that consist of clichés and jargon:

Dear Sir

Needless to say we are pleased to receive your esteemed favour of 5th August enclosing illustrated catalogue, which arrived at the psychological moment. There is no doubt whatsoever that good orders could be obtained for many of the items in your catalogue, but on the whole we feel you are severely handicapping both yourselves and us by requiring cash settlement. As a matter of fact nearly all business in this area is done on a credit basis, the period of credit varying from as little as one month to as much as three months and more often than not to six months. It goes without saying that custom will be discouraged unless credit can be given.

We further respectfully suggest that the prices you quote are for the most part too high, and by and large you will find it difficult to compete with other manufacturers unless you reduce them.

We trust you will give favourable consideration to our suggestions with respect to both credit and price.

Assuring you of our best attention at all times.

We are
Yours faithfully

4. Express in good English the letter given in Exercise 3.

5. Translate each of the following slangy sentences into good conversational English.

(a) Do dry up.   (f) It's a beastly bore.
(b) I'm broke to the wide.   (g) I'm fed to the back teeth.
(c) Do you get me?   (h) It's a regular wash-out.
(d) What's the damage?   (i) He went off the deep end.
(e) He's got the wind up.   (j) He's got a screw loose.

(RSA)

COMMERCIALESE

Like most other activities, business has acquired its own technical terms, and these you must use whenever necessary, because they replace what you would otherwise have to say in many words. Most of these terms are now represented by recognized abbreviations such as *COD* (cash on delivery), *E and OE* (errors and omissions excepted), *fob* (free on board), *cif* (cost, insurance and freight). Others such as *carriage forward, paid on account* or *in full settlement,* and *drawn payable to order* are universally accepted and well understood within the business community. Apart from these and similar specialized terms the common usage of English provides all that is necessary for business correspondence; ordinary language is good enough. Secretaries deal with ordinary people and there is no advantage in avoiding the ordinary friendly words of common speech.

The old-style business letter was shrouded in a jargon that came to be termed *commercialese,* or *commercial English.* Even in the modern business letter some of the influence of the old style remains to keep writers in a strait-jacket of remote and meaningless expressions, hampering their efforts to write the kind of letters they wish to write. The following are among the expressions still sometimes used by writers who seek to make their letters sound more official than they would if written in plain English:

Instead of	Say
Openings:	
Adverting to your favour	Referring to your letter
Re your letter	*or*
Replying to your letter	Thank you for your letter
The writer wishes to acknowledge	I (We) acknowledge, *or* Thank out for your letter
We are in receipt of	
We beg to acknowledge receipt of	We have received
We have to acknowledge	
We beg to inform you	We are writing to inform you
We respectfully inform you	
We beg to thank you	We thank you
Your esteemed favour to hand	
Your letter to hand	We have received your letter
Yours to hand	

Endings:

The favour of your early reply will oblige	I shall be glad to hear from you soon
Assuring you of our best attention at all times	
Thanking you in anticipation	
We beg to remain	
We remain	*Omit all these.*
Awaiting the favour of your early reply	
Trusting our action meets with your approval	

Miscellaneous:

as per	according to, as stated in
at your earliest convenience	as soon as possible
enclosed please find	I (We) enclose (are enclosing)
of even date	of today
only too pleased to	very glad to
per	by
please be good enough to advise us	please tell us, inform us
prior to	before
same	your letter, the goods, etc.
take an early opportunity	as soon as possible
under consideration	being dealt with
idem., inst., prox., ult.	name the month
your communication	your letter, phone message, etc.
your good self	you
your favour	your letter, order
under separate cover	separately; *or better still*, by registered post, etc.

Hereto, herewith, thereto, therein, thereof, therewith are also expressions to be discouraged. They introduce into letters a legal flavour that is best avoided. A slight rewording of the sentence is usually all that is necessary to avoid them:

Instead of	*Say*
in the First Schedule *hereto*	in the First Schedule
we enclose *herewith*	we enclose
the information contained *therein*	the information it contains
any information relative *thereto*	any information relating to it

Avoid also such unnecessary phrases as *It should be noted that, It will be appreciated that, I am to point out that.* Such expressions are mere padding. They contribute nothing to the meaning of what is said, in no way help the reader and are a blemish on style. Omit them; go straight to the point and say simply and directly what has to be said:

Instead of	*Say*
It will be appreciated that owing to fluctuations in price, it is impossible for us to give you a quotation.	Owing to frequent price changes we cannot give you a quotation.
It should be noted that all prices include delivery.	
I am to point out that the prices quoted are subject to a trade discount of 25 per cent.	*Omit the words in italics.*

The use of stereotyped and hackneyed phrases makes it difficult for letters to be, as they should be, friendly, sincere, and natural. Could what you have said in a letter be said to someone on the telephone and still sound natural? If so, it is a good letter. *We are sorry to tell you* sounds more natural than *We regret to inform you; We are sending separately* is better than *We are sending under separate cover,* and *as soon as possible* is certainly preferable to *at your earliest convenience.*

A good business letter will be written to the point and will use no more words than are necessary to convey a clear message. But this does not mean that it need be discourteous. It is no discourtesy to say *Will you please send* instead of *We should esteem it a favour if you would kindly send,* or to say *as soon as possible* instead of *at the earliest possible moment.*

The following letter is a typical piece of commercialese:

We beg to acknowledge receipt of your favour of the 26th inst. with regard to the estimate and plans required for the erection of a bungalow on the vacant site in close proximity to the Argosy Theatre, and shall have pleasure in arranging for our architect to call on you with a view to a discussion of the matter on Friday next, the 3rd prox., at three o'clock, which we trust will meet your convenience. In the meantime, we enclose herewith plans of a type of bungalow we can recommend, and beg to remain.

Yours truly

The writer of such a letter would no doubt claim that there was no time in business to adopt the style of good literature; but it is because so many of our letters fail to include the qualities of good literature that they not only fall short of being good

English but also lack the essential qualities of a good business letter, by failing to be clear and to the point.

The foregoing letter is set out below with a corrected version in the right-hand column:

Instead of	*Say*
We beg to acknowledge receipt of your favour	We have received your letter
of the 26th inst.	of 26th February
with regard to the estimate and plans required	requesting an estimate and plans
for the erection of a bungalow	for erecting a bungalow
on the vacant site in close proximity to the Argosy Theatre	on the vacant site near the Argosy Theatre
and shall have pleasure in arranging	We will arrange
for our architect to call on you	for our architect to call
with a view to a discussion of the matter	to discuss the matter
on Friday next, the 3rd prox., at three o'clock	next Friday, 3rd March, at three o'clock
which we trust will meet your convenience	if convenient to you
In the meantime	Meanwhile
we enclose herewith	we enclose
plans of a type of bungalow we can recommend	plans for a bungalow we recommend
and beg to remain	(*omit this*)

Now read through the two versions and see which is the better. The second says all that is said in the first, and in fewer words—57 instead of 94. It has the further merit of being clearer. Although much shorter, it contains no suggestion of discourtesy.

To summarize the suggestions given in this and the preceding chapter—cultivate a good vocabulary; express yourself concisely and to the point; prefer the short word to the long, and the concrete word to the abstract; use adjectives sparingly, reserving them for occasions when precision is called for; and finally, avoid commercialese. Short, simple statements, well arranged, are what your correspondent will best understand.

EXERCISES

1. Rearrange the following letters replacing the words in italics by expressions in straightforward English:

A

Dear Sir

We beg to refer to our communication of 12th October, and shall be glad to learn whether you have yet *arrived at any decision regarding the installation* of the Chain Drives for which we *had the pleasure of quoting*.

We have *executed a number of contracts for the installation* of these transmissions in several factories in the Midlands, and *have pleasure in stating* that in all cases they have proved satisfactory.

We should be very glad to give you fuller information *regarding* these Chain Drives on *receipt of* further details of your *requirements*.

Trusting that we shall hear further from you, and that you will *favour us with your valued order*.

We are

Yours faithfully

B

Dear Sir

Your esteemed enquiry of 29th ult. is duly to hand. We now beg to quote you for the supply of 20 tonnes of Zinc Ashes, as requested.

We shall be in a position to effect delivery at your works by 29th July for the inclusive price of £50 *per* tonne. This is a very *advantageous* price for the quality of ashes you need, and one we are not likely to be able to repeat.

If you decide to favour us with your valued order, we shall do our utmost to *execute it to your entire satisfaction*, and shall look forward to further dealings with you.

The favour of your early reply will oblige.

Yours faithfully

2. Reconstruct the following letters in good English, correcting any faults in style:

A

Dear Sirs

We have to acknowledge receipt of your letter of the 1st inst. and thank you for the kind offer contained therein, which we are very glad to accept with full appreciation of your kind consideration in this matter.

We remain

Yours faithfully

B

Dear Sir

As you will see from a perusal of the circular enclosed herewith, I have been taken into partnership by Mr A. Waugh, and shall consequently have to deny myself the privilege of a regular call upon you. I feel confident, however, that you will accord to my successor, Mr Thomas Holding—whom I hope to have the pleasure of personally introducing to you within the next week—that consideration and support which you have for so many years extended to me.

Thanking you, I beg to remain

Yours truly

C

Madam

We noticed whilst looking through our books that you have not recently favoured us with your esteemed orders.

We beg, therefore, to enclose herewith a price list and postcard, trusting to receive a continuance of your patronage, and assuring you that at all times our best attention shall be given to your commands.

We remain

Your obedient servants

D

Dear Sirs

We have to thank you for your letter of the 7th inst., and regret that you do not see your way to favour us with your enquiries for copper sheets and rods, especially as, being sole London agents for one of the best-known Sheffield firms, we are in a peculiarly good position to quote low prices. Perhaps later on, however, we may be able to approach you on this matter with better success.

Trusting to receive an order from you

We remain

Yours faithfully

E

Dear Sirs

We are in receipt of your esteemed letter of the 17th inst., with order for four rolls of cloth, but regret to say that on the terms mentioned we find it impossible to execute this. We are prepared, however, with a view to larger business, to concede you a discount of 20% and a three months' draft.

Thanking you for the support you have hitherto accorded us, and trusting still to maintain our friendly business relations.

We remain

Yours faithfully

TECHNICAL TERMS

We have already noticed that certain technical terms and specialized terminology are peculiar to particular branches of activity—*mortgage, probate,* and *tort,* for example to law; *software, chip* and *processor* to electronics; *equities, consols,* and *arbitrage* to the stock exchange; *annuity* and *actuary* to insurance; *stevedore* and *consignment* to transport; *invoice* and *overheads* to accountancy; *soprano* and *jazz* to music, while economics employs unusual terms such as *duopoly* and *oligopoly.*

The use of terms in their technical settings is not likely to cause trouble. Technical vocabularies are not, as a rule, very extensive, or, for those who need to use them, difficult to learn. More dangerous are those words that may be used in both a technical and a general sense, and care must be taken to avoid using a word in one sense when the other is intended. Any good dictionary will help you not to confuse the general sense of *property* and *considera-tion* with their technical uses in law; *market* and *value* with their technical uses in economics; *assurance* and *average* with their technical uses in insurance, and so on.

It is often possible to express a particular idea in a number of different ways. It is even possible to express technical language in non-technical form, and unless it is certain that the use of tech-nical language will be understood by one's correspondent, a message in general terms is to be preferred.

Examine the following sentences:

A trader's capital is the excess of his assets over his liabilities.
A trader ascertains his capital by deducting his liabilities from his assets.
A trader is worth the amount by which what he owns exceeds his debts to others.
By deducting what a trader owes from what he possesses we are able to ascertain his capital.

All four sentences express the same idea, but the language is different. The technical language of the accountant used in the first two sentences is replaced in the last two by terms that can easily be understood by anyone, even if they have had no training in book-keeping.

EXERCISE

Explain in non-technical language, as if for a person who knew nothing at all about business, what is meant by each of the following sentences:

A

(a) The goods will be sent by rail, carriage forward.
(b) There is a debit balance of £50 on Mr Harding's account.
(c) The gross profit for the year was £2,800.
(d) The consignment was sent on 15th February, f.o.b. Montreal.
(e) Cheques are not legal tender.
(f) Small payments are made from petty cash.
(g) A person who buys an established business must usually pay for goodwill.
(h) I have an overdraft at the bank.
(i) The society is prepared to lend money on mortgage.
(j) The goods are subject to a trade discount of 30%.

B

(a) The whole consignment is liable to an *ad valorem* duty of 15%.
(b) We understand that the goods will be consigned carriage forward.
(c) Any dispute arising out of this contract will be referred to arbitration.
(d) We should like you to make a settlement monthly.
(e) We shall consult the creditors as to the fairest means of liquidating their claims.
(f) The agenda includes the items "Matters arising".
(g) I am enclosing proposal form and premium, and shall be glad to receive the policy.
(h) The contract price of £20,000 includes £5,000 for goodwill.
(i) After the first 5,000 copies we are prepared to allow a royalty of 15%.
(j) Generally speaking, any kind of security may be dealt in on the Stock Exchange.

C

(a) As there was a trunk delay we decided to wire you.
(b) We hope to effect a mortgage on the new premises.
(c) The buyers have assumed the whole of our assets and book debts.

(d) An auditor prefers to obtain the certificate of balance direct from the bank.

(e) We hope to be able to discharge our liabilities as they mature.

(f) We agree to indemnify you for agency expenses reasonably and necessarily incurred.

(g) Your account is now overdue, and we hope you will send us a remittance by return.

(h) Our quotations are all subject to the fluctuations of the market.

(i) Please send us details of your terms of settlement.

(j) The multiple shop is a method of appealing to the customer wherever he may be.

CHAPTER EIGHT

The Art of Business Writing

Of all those arts in which the wise excel,
Nature's chief masterpiece is writing well.
Duke of Buckingham (1648–1721): *Essay on Poetry*

THE APPROACH TO GOOD WRITING

The increasing complexities associated with modern developments in science, transport and technology impose new demands for ever higher standards of clear, exact and readily-
understood expression.

The grammatical structure of sentences, punctuation and
spelling are all essential elements in good writing, but they do no
more than provide the tools for the job. Good writing goes far
beyond mere ability to handle the technicalities of language.
The whole purpose of writing, like the whole purpose of language, is to transfer thoughts, ideas and feelings from one mind
to another.

The well-written business letter has three points of focus—the
writer, the message and the reader. As the writer you must have
a clear idea of what you are going to say, and then express
yourself not only with unmistakable clearness, but in such a way
that your message is received and understood in the spirit in
which you send it. You must keep in mind that you are dealing
not only with a situation but also with a person. Writing a letter
does not call for depth of learning, but it does require the ability
to collect and classify facts and to present them in a form that
interests the reader, captures his attention, wins his approval
and gets him to take the action you want him to take.

Not every topic your letters have to deal with has inherently
interesting qualities, but there is no good reason to confine
yourself to the kind of language that is flat and uninspiring and
which your reader finds depressingly dull and monotonous.
With the necessary trouble you can turn a routine business letter
into an interesting and lively piece of business prose. Take the
following letter from a manufacturer of gardening equipment:

Dear Sir

We think you will be interested to know about our new 35cm "Green-sward" motor lawnmower, the cost of which is £115. Customers who are using this machine have expressed complete satisfaction with its performance. It is made of best quality materials and carries a twelve-month guarantee.

We should be pleased to arrange for our representative to call on you with one of these machines and to give you a demonstration.

Yours faithfully

This letter does nothing to arouse the reader's interest in the new machine or to create a wish to have it. Now compare the letter with the following:

Dear Sir

As our representative passed through Marlborough on his way to Swindon earlier this week, he noticed two of your groundsmen cutting your lawns with hand-powered machines. We can understand the preference for this type of machine of the groundsman who is particular about his lawns and does not like to see the damage to first-class turf sometimes caused by power-driven machines.

We have recently put on the market an improved version of our well-known 35cm power Model 60. The improved Model 60A is of the same high quality as the Model 60, with the added advantage of a new precision-type six-blade cutter, which we guarantee does not in any way cause damage to the finest quality lawn.

Although the price of the new model is rather more than three times that of corresponding hand-powered machines, the additional cost is easily covered by savings in wages. In fact, one of our customers informs us that since buying two of the new machines four months ago he has been able to reduce his ground staff by half, with an annual saving of several hundred pounds in wages.

If you would like to have independent first-hand information about the performance of our new model we will put you in touch with this customer, who would be pleased to answer any questions about it. Alternatively, or in addition, we would arrange for Mr L. Elphick, our representative for the West of England, to call on you at your convenience to give you a demonstration without obligation of any kind whatsoever. The model carries our usual three-month guarantee, but properly used and maintained would give you at least ten years' excellent trouble-free service.

Yours faithfully

In this letter the manufacturer goes to some trouble to show his interest in his correspondent's needs and brings his letter to life by giving it a personal and homely touch. The letter is much more likely to gain interest and win an order than the colourless letter it replaces. On pp. 197–8 you will find another example showing how interest can be written into business letters that deal with matters of a purely routine kind.

Successful business letter-writing is largely a matter of caring: caring about the accuracy of what you write; caring about the impression you create of your firm and of yourself as its representative; caring about being of service to your reader; and caring about the satisfaction you yourself get from knowing that you have done a worthwhile job. The letter you write is more than a routine chore; it is an expression of your personality. It discloses the kind of person you are, and reveals your understanding of your reader's needs and the sincerity of your efforts to help him.

It cannot be stressed too much that the great merit of all business writing is to be clear—to be quite clear about what you want to say and to express yourself so lucidly that your reader cannot fail to grasp your meaning without trouble. He may not agree with what you say, but at least he will know and understand what you say. And so, write plainly. Follow the suggestions made earlier to use short simple words except where longer words are more appropriate. Write forcefully and acquire that warmth of tone which results from using active rather than passive verbs. For example:

Instead of	*Say*
It is understood	I (We) understand
The goods will be delivered next week	We will deliver the goods next week
The mistake is regretted	We regret the mistake
Sale of the goods is proving difficult	We are finding it difficult to sell the goods
Prompt settlement of your account is requested	We ask you to settle your account promptly

The rule, discussed in Chapter Three, to use mainly the shorter sentence applies also to the paragraph. For business letters the short paragraph is better than the long; it has a less forbidding look and makes for easier reading. Provide each new thought with its own paragraph and make sure that each paragraph leads naturally into the one that follows. It may be appropriate to introduce new paragraphs with such connectives as

In addition, Nevertheless, In short, or *On the other hand.* Connectives such as these are useful and sometimes necessary to give cohesion and a sense of movement to your letter and help it to read smoothly. But connectives must not be used to excess, otherwise they give your letter a fussy flavour. As a rule, you will find it better to frame your sentences in ways that keep extraneous words and phrases of this sort to a minimum.

IMAGINATION IN LETTER WRITING

A business letter does not call for the eloquent language of the novelist or poet. What it does call for is language that is accurate, clear, sincere and concise. But it need not be pedestrian and dull. With a little imagination this is something you can avoid by thinking of your reader and his probable reaction to the sort of approach you make and the kind of language you use. Writing imaginatively cannot be taught by any formal process, but a good deal can be learned from studying good examples. Well-written sales letters provide great scope for imaginative writing. In Chapter Fifteen you will find some useful examples, and also many more in the author's *Model Business Letters.** Even experienced writers are not always original. Churchill, with his notable gift of language, was not averse to imitation. His wartime "blood, toil, tears and sweat" did no more than echo Garibaldi, the Italian patriot, and his declared policy "to make war" was no more than an echo of Clemenceau's *"Je fais la guerre"* (I make war).

Imagination in letter-writing consists in presenting what is ordinary and routine in a way that makes it attractive and interesting. It finds expression through the use of accurate and illuminating words in presenting ideas. It can be practised by looking up in Roget's *Thesaurus of English Words and Phrases* or some other dictionary of English synonyms, the wide choices of words that mean the same thing but with varying shades of strength and effectiveness. The main purpose of a dictionary is to explain what words mean, that is the ideas they stand for. The purpose of the *Thesaurus* is precisely the reverse. It first states the idea and then lists the words by which it may be expressed. The idea of *justice* as a human right may, for example, be expressed by *equity, fairness, fair play, impartiality, reasonableness* and

* Macdonald & Evans (3rd edn.), 1982.

propriety. Similarly, *book* may be expressed by *publication, volume, manual, brochure, journal, magazine, periodical,* and so with most other words.

By suitable choice of words from those available you can lighten and enliven your writing with the necessary touch of imagination. Imagination is also needed to know what your correspondent is like, if you don't know already; what position he occupies in his firm; what he is interested in; and how he is likely to react to what you have to tell him. It is important to remember that when you write or dictate a letter you enter into a personal relationship with your correspondent. He and you are human beings "talking things over". You must address him with courtesy, sincerity and in a spirit of friendly warmth. A few moments well spent in thinking what you are going to say, how you are going to say it, and the kind of person you are going to say it to will help to lift your letters above the routine run-of-the-mill class and blow away the cobwebs of dull monotonous writing with a breath of good fresh air.

EXERCISE

Reconstruct the following letters in good English, correcting any faults in style:

A

Dear Sirs

We are favoured with yours of yesterday, from which we are pleased to learn that you duly received our quotations for freight, etc. on the Gas Plant for Gisborne, and are hoping to be able to give us instructions regarding the forwarding of this parcel.

With regard to the question of insurance, we have to point out that the rate mentioned as quoted by your own regular shippers, namely 65p, is the same as that quoted by us in our telegram. We trust that this explanation will enable you to fix up through us, in which case you may rest assured that your interests will receive our most careful attention.

We are, dear sirs
Yours faithfully

B

Dear Sir

With reference to your request that we shall in future send your goods per passenger train, cheap rate, we have to state that before the railway authorities will accept parcels on such terms they require us to sign a document making ourselves responsible for any loss or damage in transit.

This, of course, we cannot possibly consent to do, the carriers and the railways being the agents of the consignee and not ours. You might, however, make a special arrangement with the authorities at your end, in which case please advise us.

Trusting that this explanation will be satisfactory, and assuring you of our best services at all times.

We remain
Faithfully yours

C

Dear Sirs

With reference to your letter dated 29th ult., in which you ask to be relieved of your contract for the supply of hand-made nails, we beg to say that we regret the mistake you have made, and, under the circumstances, are willing to pay, in addition to the price agreed upon, half the extra cost of the hand-made over the machine-made article.

Please signify your acceptance of this offer at your earliest convenience.

Yours faithfully

THE QUALITIES OF GOOD WRITING

In the ordinary course of your work in an office you will not usually be expected to write at length on particular topics unless you are making a report on some situation. Nevertheless, practice in writing compositions and essays on a variety of subjects will help you to develop the facility of expression you will find useful when you come to write or dictate letters.

The secret of good writing, whether it is a piece of composition, a report or a business letter, lies in a ready and suitable choice of words with a sense of form and style. Grammatical structure, supported by good habits of punctuation, will help you to develop a sense of form; reading, supported by regular practice in writing, will widen the range of your vocabulary, strengthen the certainty with which you choose words, and help you to cultivate a sense of style.

To be good, any piece of writing must satisfy three conditions:

(a) It must reveal the writer's ability to express himself in good English.

(b) It must have a clear purpose; in other words it must have some particular message to convey.

(c) It must have form, that is to say it must have unity and proportion and be well arranged.

Good English
Of all forms of composition, letter-writing is the most common, and to the writing of a good letter good English is indispensable. As defined by Sir Ernest Gowers, good English is English that is readily understood by the reader. In business letters especially you must be able to say all that is necessary in the fewest possible words. You will need a working knowledge of grammar, a good command of vocabulary and a critical appreciation of what is good in form and style. In brief, you will need to write grammatically, clearly, concisely and in good taste.

A clear purpose
However skilful you may be in your command of language, however cultivated your style, your first need as a writer is to have something to say and to say it in a way your reader understands, otherwise your writing, though it may be good in other respects, will remain for him a dull and lifeless collection of words and sentences.

Like the weaving of threads into a piece of cloth, the weaving of words and sentences into a piece of finished writing is a process of manufacture, and as with other manufacturing processes raw material is needed. As a writer, whether of articles, or of reports, or of business letters, your raw material consists of your thoughts, the ideas you hold and the information you are able to gather from outside sources—from books, magazines, journals and newspapers, and by observation and enquiry.

Form
Having gathered your information you must now set down your thoughts on paper. Before you attempt to write it will pay you to spend a few moments thinking out what you want to say. Jot down your thoughts as they come, never mind in what order, and when you have finished go through them striking out what is not needed. Then, of what remains, group together ideas that are related and arrange the groups in the order in which you propose to present them. This will help you to avoid unnecessary repetition and to produce a straightforward, logically arranged piece of work. To prepare in this way will have a marked effect upon the quality of your writing. It is as relevant to an important business letter as it is to any other piece of written composition.

EXERCISES

1. Write compositions on the following subjects, making use of the out-lines given and including any ideas of your own:

A

The self-service store

(a) *Definition:*
   A modern development
   Shop organization

(b) *Advantages to owner:*
   Economy in staff
   Impromptu buying by customers

(c) *Advantages to customer:*
   Goods on display and priced
   Personal choice
   Reminder of needs
   Quick service
   Cleanliness—foodstuffs wrapped

(d) *Disadvantages to owner:*
   Wrapping and price labelling
   Pilfering

(e) *Disadvantages to customer:*
   Temptation to buy
   Impersonal service
   Absence of credit
   No delivery service

(f) *Future of such stores*

B

The Post Office and the business-man

(a) *History:*
   Before 1840
   Rowland Hill's reforms

(b) *A public corporation:*
   A monopoly
   Profit-making

(c) *Services rendered:*
   Postal
   Remittance facilities
   Savings bank
   Miscellaneous services

(d) *Conclusion:*
     A valuable national service
     Indispensable to business-man

C

Transport in the Twentieth Century

(a) *A glance backward:*
     Comparison with eighteenth century,
     Effects of steam engine in nineteenth, and of
     Internal combustion engine and
     Improved roads in twentieth.

(b) *Forms of transport:*
     Road, rail, canal, sea, air.

(c) *Competition in transport:*
     Road *v.* rail,
     Rail and sea *v.* air,
     Effects of competition on efficiency and cost.

(d) *The services of transport:*
     Economic, social and personal,
     Speed, comparative safety, luxurious travel.

(e) *Effects of transport:*
     Improved standard of living,
     Created a shrinking world,
     Foreign travel.

2. Write not more than 200 words on one of these subjects:

(a) Outline the principal difficulties facing immigrants to your country.

(b) Can young people usefully take an active part in the government and administration of their school or college?

(c) Do television or radio programmes really influence the behaviour of young people?

(d) Are we justified in keeping alive people who are incurably sick and in pain?

(e) Do you favour censorship of books, plays and films?   *(LCCI)*

THE END-PRODUCT

The framework of ideas you have built up in the way suggested in the preceding section must now be clothed in words. If you are writing an article or a report develop your theme, or if you are writing an important letter develop your message, paragraph by paragraph, making sure that each paragraph deals with its own topic and leads naturally to the next. Be careful to keep a sense of proportion, avoiding the temptation to write at length on any particular point merely because it specially interests you, or because you have special knowledge of it. Follow your prepared plan and devote to each point the amount of space its importance merits.

The opening paragraph

In general composition the opening paragraph should be in the form of an introduction. It must be impressive enough to capture the interest of the reader and strike the keynote of the subject so that he knows what to expect. The following is the introduction used in an article on "The Award of Damages at Law":

"The average layman is prone to feel that 'the law is an ass', but that is only because he is often quite ignorant of the general principles that guide the courts, whose decisions, admittedly, may sometimes seem unreasonable, or even inconsistent."

This paragraph prepares the way for a defence of the apparent inconsistencies associated with the award of damages for breach of contract, the subject with which the article deals.

The following, a quotation, is shorter and was used to introduce an article on "The Art of Examining":

"Examinations are formidable even to the best prepared, for the greatest fool may ask more than the wisest man can answer."

In his introduction to *In Search of England,* H. V. Morton opens with a paragraph consisting of only one line:

"This is a record of a motor journey through England."

Although differing in length and substance these opening paragraphs have a common purpose—to arouse interest and to prepare the reader for what is to follow.

In business letters it is just as important in the opening paragraph to arouse interest as it is in any other piece of writing. If your letter is in reply to one you have received you can count upon its being read, but if it is not—if for example it is a sales circular or a letter making an unsolicited offer—there is every chance that it may not be read unless in the opening paragraph you succeed in arousing your correspondent's interest. The purpose of the opening paragraph of letters of this kind is to arouse curiosity, and the body of the letter to satisfy it.

It has long been the fashion to start reply business letters with such phrases as *In reply to* or *In answer to your letter*; *With reference to your letter*; *Referring* or *Replying to your letter*, and so on. There is nothing wrong with these and similar openings except that they are monotonously dull—worn threadbare from over-use. You can avoid them by going straight to the point; you wouldn't be writing your letter if you weren't replying to one. But if you feel a reference to the letter you are answering is needed, a little ingenuity will enable you to give your reply a better send-off. Try beginning your letter in one of the following ways:

Express thanks:

Thank you for your letter of . . .

We acknowledge with thanks your letter of . . .

I have studied with interest the literature you sent me with your letter of . . .

Express pleasure or regret:

I was glad to receive your letter of . . .

We welcome your enquiry of . . .

We were both surprised and pleased to receive your letter of . . .

I wish to say at once how pleased we were to receive your letter of . . .

We very much regret to learn from your letter of . . .

We were sorry to learn from your letter of . . . .

I am sorry not to have been able to reply sooner to your letter of . . .

Show that some action has been taken:

On receiving your letter of 10th March I telephoned our head office.

I have made enquiries about the cost of the repairs you mention in your letter of . . .

I immediately passed to the manufacturers the complaint you made in your letter of . . .

Ask or answer a question:

Before I can deal with your letter of . . . I shall need to know . . .

You are right in assuming that the price mentioned in your letter of . . . is subject to a discount of . . .

Here are some more examples:

Fashionable	*Better*
In reply to your request of ... we have much pleasure in enclosing our catalogue.	It gives us great pleasure to enclose the catalogue for which you asked in your letter of ...
In answer to your enquiry of ... concerning Mr Harris, I am able (*or* pleased, *or* sorry) to inform you (*or worse still,* I have, *or* beg, to inform you) that I have known him since ...	Mr Harris, about whom you enquire in your letter of ..., has been known to me since ...
With reference to your order of ..., we have sent the goods to you by passenger train.	The goods which you ordered on ... have been sent to you by passenger train.
Referring to your advertisement in this morning's *Daily Telegraph*, I wish to apply for the post of short-hand-typist.	I wish to apply for the post of shorthand-typist advertised in this morning's *Daily Telegraph*.

Your letter may not, of course, be a reply to another, but may be taking the initiative in seeking or giving information, making a request, or promoting a sale. In any event, the same rule applies—you must give it an interesting send-off, otherwise it will not get the attention you want it to have; it may not even be read beyond the first paragraph. Direct your opening to the reader's personal interest, and thus prompt him to read on to find out more. His interest may be that of being important, doing good, making money, saving time, keeping fit and so on. But whatever it is, address your appeal to it. There is a type of opening for every occasion. Here are just a few:

An opening seeking advice:

It is sometimes said that the highest compliment one can pay a person is to ask him for advice, and we are writing now to ask for yours on a problem that has worried us for some time. (*Appeals to self-importance.*)

An opening requesting help:

Have you ever stopped to think what it is to be blind; what it means not to see your loved ones, to watch television or read a book? There are many like this, and they need your help. (*Appeals to sentiment.*)

An opening promoting a sale:

Wise men learn from the experience of others. Would you like to learn from ours and cut your laundry bills by half? Then read what follows. (*Appeals to money-saving.*)

These openings are again all widely different; but they have one thing in common—they are directed to the personal interest of the reader.

The closing paragraph

In a piece of general composition the last paragraph is no less important than the first. Like the first paragraph it should not be too long. A brief summing up, an apt quotation, a quick look into the future, and so on will often provide a satisfactory finish.

Like any other piece of composition, a business letter must have an effective close. This does not mean that every letter must have a closing paragraph, but it does mean that the letter must end on a natural note. The well-planned letter that has followed a logical sequence, for example, brings itself to a natural close, and to add to it may well weaken rather than strengthen its force.

Often, however, a closing paragraph is needed. The type of close will depend upon the type of letter it is. If you are answering a request for something you cannot do you will explain why you cannot do it, and express regret; if you are acknowledging an order you will express thanks for the chance to be of service; if you are applying for a post you will hope for an interview; and if you are trying to sell you will invite an order, send a representative, arrange a demonstration, or do whatever seems to be called for. The ways of closing a letter are as numerous as the different purposes that letters serve.

The paragraph may consist, on the one hand, of nothing more than a simple and graceful exit, as where *Any visit you care to make to our showrooms will be very welcome*, or, on the other hand, of a strong inducement to act, as where *The special discount now offered can be allowed only on orders placed by January 31st. After that date full catalogue prices will be charged.*

There is one kind of ending you must always avoid, and that is the old-fashioned ending beginning with a participle, as *Trusting to hear from you, Thanking you for your trouble, Hoping you will place an order,* and so on. Such endings are relics of a past letter-writing age; they lack definiteness, mean nothing and serve no useful purpose. Finish your letters with a direct statement that means something—a statement that forms an essential part of the letter and is worthy of the room it takes up. Otherwise, you will become involved in meaningless jargon that merely wastes time. Thus:

> Looking forward to hearing from you soon,
> We are

is much better written as

> We look forward to hearing from you soon,
> Yours faithfully

and

> Thanking you for your interest,
> We remain

could well become

> We thank you for your interest.
> Yours faithfully

The following are some examples of suitable closing paragraphs used in correspondence:

Acknowledging an order that cannot be met (and assuming the reason has already been explained):

We are indeed sorry we cannot on this occasion supply the kind of material you need, but enclose a book of samples showing our full range of fabrics, and hope you will give us the chance to be of assistance another time.

Acknowledging an order that can be met:

We thank you for your order and are arranging to send the crockery by British Road Services tomorrow. We hope you will be pleased with it, and look forward to further orders from you.

Getting an order:

We have no wish to rush you into a decision, but as repeat orders are constantly coming in, and as our stocks are very limited, we strongly urge you to place an order at once. The completion and return of the enclosed card is all that is necessary.

Applying for a post:

When you have considered my qualifications and heard from my referees I hope you will grant me an interview and give me an opportunity to prove that, if appointed, I would give you complete satisfaction.

Giving a testimonial:

We are glad to be of help, but ask you to ensure that the information we have given you is treated as strictly confidential.

Rejecting a request for better terms:

We would welcome you as one of our customers and, despite our being unable to offer you a lower price, still hope you will give us the opportunity to be of assistance.

Answering a complaint:

We very much regret having given you any cause to complain, and assure you that we shall do all we can to put matters right.

Revision

The writing of the final paragraph of a composition or a letter does not complete your task. You must now look through what you have written, and if necessary revise it. You must be on the alert for errors of grammar, spelling and punctuation, or a faulty sentence that might have crept in. It is better that you rather than your reader should detect mistakes of this sort. Read through each sentence critically, and if you find any faults correct them clearly. If your corrections are to a business letter you have no choice but to retype it.

EXERCISES

1. The following opening paragraphs are taken from business letters. Avoiding as far as possible the traditional openings, and making any other improvements, rewrite or type them. You may think it necessary to use more than one sentence:

(a) *From a letter relating to a reference:*
We should esteem it a favour if you would kindly let us know by return whether Mr James Smith, who has applied to us for a post as warehouseman, was in fact formerly employed by you, and if so whether you found him satisfactory.

(b) *From the reference given:*
In answer to yours of yesterday's date, we have to say that Mr James Smith was in our employ about eighteen months and was, much to our regret, discharged last Saturday owing to slackness of work.

(c) *From a reminder concerning a quotation:*
We beg to refer to our quotation of 27th April for six "Carnegie" chain drives complete, and shall be glad to hear whether you have yet come to a decision regarding the installation of these transmissions.

(d) *From a letter regretting inability to supply goods ordered:*
In reply to your postcard re Tarentella tomatoes, we have to say that at the moment it is impossible to give you another fifteen cases.

(e) *From a letter cancelling an order:*
If you will refer to our order No. 762, given into your hands on 26th October last, you will find that delivery of the goods was required on or before 1st December. We are therefore cancelling the order.

2. Write or type final paragraphs to letters suitable in the circumstances outlined below:

(a) You are the owner of a drapery store that has recently been damaged by fire and are preparing a circular to your customers. Draft a suitable final paragraph explaining that there are many attractive bargains in the salvaged stock, and invite the customers to visit the shop to take advantage of them.

(b) A customer has written to complain of incivility and inattention when he visited your stores. Draft a conciliatory final paragraph regretting the circumstances and hoping for continued custom.

(c) You find yourself unable to settle an account for goods supplied. Your supplier has already given you one extension of credit, and you now ask for a further extension. Prepare a suitable final paragraph. You expect to be able to settle the account by the end of next month.

(d) Stewart Harrison has bought a haulage contractor's business. He prepares a circular announcing a change in the name of the firm, but does not propose to make any change in the policy of the business. Write or type a final paragraph asking former customers to continue to do their business with the new firm.

(e) A small fire has occurred at your shop premises and you write to the insurance company giving details of the circumstances and the extent of damage. You are very anxious that the premises should be restored in good time before Christmas, but cannot arrange for this until the insurance company settle with you. Draft a suitable final paragraph stressing the urgency.

FAULTS TO AVOID

Whether you are writing a piece of general composition or a business letter, monotony, extravagant language, hackneyed expressions and circumlocution are all faults to be avoided.

Monotony
As one writer has put it, "monotony in a letter is like a paralysing frost". Variety is as necessary to any piece of writing as it is to an attractive garden. The monotony born of sameness certainly has a chilling effect and may well kill any interest the reader might

otherwise have had. You can avoid it by using some of the devices dealt with in Chapter Three—by varying the length and form of your sentences, mixing longer sentences with short and loose with periodic, by changing normal word order and by variety of expression.

Extravagant language

The need to avoid exaggeration was referred to in Chapter Six. Guard also against the inflated kind of language known as bombast. Write simply and naturally rather than elaborately and artificially. Accept the following as your guiding lights:

(a) Reject the high-falutin phrase that so often litters our writing especially in business letters.

(b) Choose the simple word rather than the elaborate that means the same thing, preferring *sent* to *forwarded*, *use* to *utilize*, and *ask* to *request* (p. 65)

(c) Use adverbs sparingly, keeping them for those occasions when they add something to the sense (p. 68)

(d) Reserve adjectives for making your meaning more exact, and eye with suspicion those which merely serve for emphasis. Refer by all means to a *real diamond*, but be chary about referring to a *real danger* or a *real difficulty* (p. 67).

(e) Avoid needless prepositional phrases and abstractions (p. 69).

(f) Avoid tautology (p. 76).

All these are snares for the careless writer.

Hackneyed expressions

Avoid above all the use of slang expressions and be on your guard against clichés, jargon and quotations that have become threadbare from over-use (pp. 99–101). Be fresh and original.

No two people think or write alike. Each has, or should have, his own style. This will vary not only with himself but also with the subject. A person writing a letter to a friend adopts a style that is homely; a lawyer to a client, a style that is legalistic and precise; a business-man to a customer, a style that is direct and clear. For each different occasion there is a separate style.

Circumlocution

And finally, don't waste words; write to the point. Express your thoughts in direct, preferably short, simple statements, and arrange them in well-organized order. To use more words than are necessary is justified only when they add to the meaning. *I am of the opinion that* ... is merely a roundabout way of saying *I think that* ... ; but if you wish to emphasize that you have given the matter serious thought you can quite justifiably say *It is my considered opinion that* ... and so suggest that you do not wish to discuss it any further.

When tempted to litter your sentences with conjunctions like *and, but, consequently* and *however*, try a full stop instead. This will help to keep your sentences short and make it easier for your reader to grasp their meaning. He may quite naturally feel annoyed if he has to read a sentence twice before he can understand it.

EXERCISES

1. Reconstruct the following letters in good English, correcting any faults in style:

A

Gentlemen

In reply to yours of yesterday's date, we very much regret the delay in executing the balance of your esteemed order of the 8th inst., which has not been entirely our own fault. There has been, as you are aware, a great difficulty within the last two months in getting adequate supplies of the raw material. The panicky state of the market has now, however, subsided, and we have been able to lay in a stock of material sufficient to execute all outstanding orders. We fully appreciate your position in the matter and will do our very utmost to despatch the goods before the 20th, if possible.

Apologizing for the inconvenience that the delay in despatch has caused you.

We remain
Yours faithfully

B

Laundry trade circular

Madam

In thanking you for your valuable and much esteemed patronage in the past, permit us to inform you that we have recently rebuilt and greatly enlarged the whole of our business premises.

The Dry Cleaning, and Carpet Beating and Renovating Departments have been largely increased, and all orders can now be executed in the best manner at short notice. Carpets cleaned by the recently installed Renovating Machine have all the dust extracted and the colours brightened as when new.

All orders and commands entrusted to our care receive personal attention, and customers can depend upon promptness and careful execution of their wishes.

If you are desirous of any further information we shall be pleased to wait upon you and give you all particulars.

Hoping we may be favoured with your commands, which shall at all times have our utmost attention.

We are Madam
Your obedient servants

C

Dear Sir

Re your letter of 3rd inst. we unfortunately find ourselves in a position in which we are unable to let you have typewriters. They have been in short supply, of which you cannot fail to be aware, as a result of a prolonged strike at the supplier's factory.

Although we are not in a position to furnish you with new machines, we have a goodish supply of second-hand machines, which we will be delighted to show you if you could make it your way to give us a call.

May we respectfully hope that if you are not interested in second-hand machines you will favour us with a repetition of your order for new machines at a later date?

Yours truly

2. The tone of the following letters is not likely to build good will. Set them out in more friendly and considerate language.

A

Complaint to manufacturer re bedspreads

10 July 19..

Dear Sir

We are compelled to express surprise and disappointment at the way in which you have fulfilled our order for six dozen candlewick bedspreads. The samples you sent us proved to be most misleading. Neither in texture nor in shades do the bedspreads delivered conform to the samples against which we placed our order. Moreover, we must remind you that delivery was made in two instalments, the first of which was a week and the second a fortnight late. These late deliveries caused us a good deal of inconvenience and some loss of custom, and we certainly feel that we ought to have had some explanation of them from you.

This is the first order we have placed with you and, unless you are prepared to make a satisfactory allowance for the quality of the bedspreads supplied and for the late delivery, it will also be our last.

Yours faithfully

B

Manufacturer's reply

13 July 19..

Dear Sir

We are replying to your letter of 10th July. We are very surprised that you have any complaint concerning the quality of the bedspreads supplied. Both in texture and in colour they are strictly in accordance with the samples we sent you, and to convince you of this we are returning the samples against which you placed your order. We would ask you to compare them carefully with the bedspreads supplied. You will then see that we have made no mistake.

We accept your complaint regarding late delivery. The delay was due to a breakdown of our main finishing machine. This unfortunately held up production for several days. If when placing your order you had made it clear that prompt delivery was important we should most certainly have notified you of the position in which the breakdown had placed us.

Yours faithfully

CHAPTER NINE

Punctuation

The pipe, with solemn interposing puff,
Makes half a sentence at a time enough;
The dozing sages drop the drowsy strain,
Then pause, and puff—and speak, and pause again.

William Cowper: *Conversation*

THE NEED FOR PUNCTUATION

Punctuation is used in writing to do for the reader what pauses and inflexion of voice do for the listener—it helps to make meaning clear. It does no more and no less. It consists of a series of stops or symbols inserted to mark off words from one another, either to emphasize them or to show their grammatical relationship. In business letter-writing the symbols used to denote pauses (the full stop, the semicolon and the comma) are by far the most important for without them the writer could not make his meaning clear.

The basic rules for punctuation are very simple:

(a) A paragraph marks off a group of sentences that deal with the same subject-matter.

(b) A full stop marks the end of a sentence.

(c) A semicolon marks a pause somewhat shorter than the full stop.

(d) A comma marks only the shortest of pauses.

Punctuation marks are signposts for the reader and, since the multiplication of signposts can be more embarrassing than helpful, we must use no more than are necessary to clarify meaning and save our reader the annoyance of having to read a passage twice to grasp its meaning. Sensible punctuation is thus not only a matter of necessity but also a matter of courtesy.

It is often said that no two people punctuate alike. This is broadly true because the rules of punctuation are not so hard and fast that they leave no room for the exercise of personal taste. Punctuation is, indeed, very much a matter of combined taste and common sense, though there are certain underlying principles every writer must observe if he is to be clearly understood without difficulty. Generally speaking, the better the construction of a sentence, the fewer stops needed to make its meaning clear. The best constructed sentence is in fact that from which all punctuation marks could be removed without in any way impairing the meaning of what is written or the ease with which it is understood.

The following is a rather lengthy sentence, but its meaning is perfectly clear and readily understood without any help from punctuation:

> Contracts for the sale of goods are governed not only by a number of statutes dating from 1893 to the present time but also by the rules of common law except where these rules are inconsistent with the provisions of the statutes.

Even so, the insertion of commas to indicate pauses after *the present time* and *common law* would probably make the reader's task somewhat easier.

But without punctuation some passages would be almost unintelligible, while others might convey meanings very different from those intended. Consider the following:

> I learned from the reputation and remembrance of my father modesty and a manly character from my mother piety and bene-
> ficence and abstinence and further simplicity in my way of living.

A first reading of this unpunctuated passage conveys little or nothing of its meaning because there is nothing to show how the words should be grouped. But its meaning becomes perfectly clear with the insertion of the appropriate signs:

> I learned from the reputation and remembrance of my father, modesty and a manly character; from my mother, piety and bene-
> ficence and abstinence; and further, simplicity in my way of living.
>   (Marcus Aurelius: *Meditations*)

Now consider the respective effects on the following sentences of first omitting punctuation marks and then inserting them:

> The manager said his assistant is quite mistaken.
>   (Here, it is the assistant who is mistaken.)
> The manager, said his assistant, is quite mistaken.
>   (It is now the manager who is mistaken.)

And again:

> I've just had a rise of £5 more than I expected.
>   (i.e. the rise was more than £5)

> I've just had a rise of £5—more than I expected.
>   (i.e. the rise was for £5 exactly.)

These examples show that punctuation plays an important part not only in making reading easier, but also in making meaning clearer.

Nevertheless, a sentence that depends upon punctuation for its meaning is a bad, and possibly dangerous, sentence. After all, the purpose of punctuation is not to alter meaning but to make meaning easier to understand.

THE FULL STOP

With sentences

It is not easy to give practical guidance on the use of the full stop. It is of course used to mark the end of a sentence, but where one writer would close a sentence, another would delay the closure by adding some further thought. For example:

> The demand for cotton textiles in Africa has recently shown a marked increase. We are convinced that there is here a considerable market waiting to be developed.

This extract consisting of two sentences could very well have been written as one by omitting the full stop after *marked increase* and substituting the conjunction *and*.

With abbreviations

The full stop is also used to mark abbreviations (*Esq.*, *m.p.h.*, *C.O.D.*), though it is now established practice to omit it from abbreviations consisting of single letters that make pronounceable words, called *acronyms* (*NALGO, NATO, ERNIE*). Full stops are never used after letters that make up an acronym. There is also a growing practice to omit the full stop from unpronounceable letter combinations (*BBC, HMSO, GCE*) and other well-known and readily identified abbreviations (*encl, etc, viz*), especially from abbreviations that retain the first and last letters of the full word (*Mr, Messrs, Dr*).

The full stop is not used after forms that may appear to be, but which are not, abbreviations (*£, 3rd, 4to, 8vo*). Note that the abbreviation *p* (representing new pence), like the £ sterling sign, is treated as a symbol not requiring the full stop.

EXERCISES

1. First read through the following letter and decide the points at which each sentence ends; then copy the letter, inserting full stops and capitals as necessary:

Dear Sir

Thank you for your quotation of 26th March I notice that the Formafelt for which you quote is only half the width of the carpets I believe you mentioned that it was double width when we called to see you if this is so then I accept your quotation.

I think I told you that central heating was to be installed and until this work is finished it will not be possible for you to lay the carpets before then I shall be visiting St. Annes and will call and see you in the meantime I should be glad if you would put the work in hand so that there may be no delay once central heating is installed.

Yours faithfully

2. Type or write out in full the following abbreviations, frequently found in business letters:

(a) encl, Co, per pro, MS, EC2;
(b) HP, etc, viz, 4to, e.g.;
(c) a.m., COD, E & OE, fob, PS;
(d) Ltd. cif, pro tem, NB, PTO;
(e) Esq, Messrs, fcp, mph, do

3. Give the recognized forms of abbreviation for the folowing, inserting full stops where necessary:

(a) octavo, steamship, that is, manuscripts, kilowatts;
(b) inches, yards, pounds, ounces, hundredweight;
(c) Buckinghamshire, Cambridgeshire, Hertfordshire, Middlesex, Leicestershire;
(d) Northamptonshire, Nottinghamshire, Oxfordshire, North Yorkshire, Worcestershire;
(e) Lancashire, Bedfordshire, Lincolnshire, Wiltshire, Hampshire.

THE COMMA

Use with subject and predicate
The relationship between the subject of a sentence and its verb is a close one and as a rule they must not be separated by punctuation marks:

Our failure to send the goods to you last Friday as promised in our letter of 17th September, was due to the illness of our driver.

(The comma after *September* breaks the connection between subject and predicate and is wrongly used.)

But if the subject is a lengthy one, or consists of a series with separating commas, a comma may be inserted at the end of the subject to mark the pause that would take place if the sentence were spoken:

Goods subject to import quota restrictions or to import licensing which are exported to this country without the requisite permit or licence having first been obtained, are liable to seizure upon arrival. (*Lengthy subject*)

The choice of a good site, the employment of suitable labour, attractive display of the goods for sale, and the courteous treatment of customers, are all important factors making for success in business. (*Multiple subject*)

Use with relative clauses

Relative clauses, i.e. clauses introduced by relative pronouns (*who, which, that,* etc.), fall into two main classes:

(*a*) *Defining clauses* serving to define or qualify some noun or pronoun in some other clause. Clauses of this kind perform the function of an adjective and *must not be separated by a comma* from the word they qualify and to which they are therefore closely related:

The postman *who delivers our letters* retires next week.
We did not receive until yesterday the cheque *which* (or *that*) *you sent us last week.*

Each of these two sentences makes only one statement, the clauses in italics serving to explain *which postman* and *which cheque.*

(*b*) *Main* (or *non-defining*) *clauses* making separate and independent statements. Clauses of this kind are separated from each other by a comma:

I met our postman, *who said he had been ill.*
We enclose a receipt for your cheque, *which we received yesterday.*

In these two examples the clauses in italics play no part in explaining *which postman*, or *which cheque*, but make separate statements of their own.

You should have no difficulty in distinguishing between the defining clause, which serves as an adjective, and the non-defining clause, which is a main clause grammatically independent of the clause with which it appears, if you remember that the defining clause always answers the question *which?*

Other uses

(a) To mark off the separate adjectives qualifying a noun:

She is a competent secretary.
She is a competent, hard-working, trustworthy secretary.

If the latter sentence had read *She is a competent, hard-working and trustworthy secretary* the comma after *hard-working* could be omitted. It is also common practice to omit the comma where the noun is preceded by only two adjectives:

She is a competent hard-working secretary.

(b) To mark off the separate items in a list or series:

The invoice, bill of lading, certificate of insurance and bill of exchange have been sent to you by air mail.

(c) To mark off the separate main clauses in a sentence (except where the clauses are very short):

We did not realize payment was overdue, otherwise we would have sent you a cheque.

but

If you will call tomorrow you can have your cheque (where the sentence consists of two short clauses).

(d) To mark off adverbs and adverbial phrases at the beginning of or within a sentence:

Unfortunately, I could not be present.
We shall, *in the circumstances,* do our best to be present.

In cases such as these there is a modern tendency to omit the commas, except where the adverbial phrase is lengthy, or where the omitted comma would cause uncertainty in reading:

However the decision goes we shall accept it.

but

However, the decision is one we have no choice but to accept.

(e) To mark off a parenthesis, i.e. an explanatory expression or "aside" without which the sentence would still be grammatically complete:

Maurice Shaw, *our local bank manager,* was appointed treasurer.

Open and closed punctuation

The main purpose of punctuation is to make meaning clear. But many of the commas and some of the full-stops still used by some writers in business letters serve no useful purpose and do nothing for the reader. They represent a conventional or "closed" style of punctuation that has now largely given way to a modern "open" style that omits all non-essential commas outside the body of the letter—from the date, the inside name and address, and after the salutation and complimentary closure:

(a) 10 February 19..
(b) Mr. R. H. Hudson M.B.E., M.A.
(c) Acorn Electrical Co. Ltd.
(d) Southport
    Lancs.
(e) Dear Sir
(f) Yours faithfully

In the foregoing examples the full-stops traditionally used to mark abbreviations are retained, but in its *Manual for Civil Service Typists* the Civil Service Department recommends also the omission of full-stops marking abbreviations and would type:

(a) 10 February 19..
(b) Mr R H Hudson MBE MA
(c) Acorn Electrical Co Ltd
(d) Southport
    Lancs
(e) Dear Sir
(f) Yours faithfully

The practice of marking abbreviations with a full-stop is of long standing and there is much to be said for retaining it in the body of a letter, where *am* (morning), *eg* (for example), *for* (free on rail), *in* (inches), *ie* (that is) and other short cuts might not be immediately recognized as abbreviations by some readers.

Introductory references

Whether or not the "closed" or the "open" style of punctuation is adopted, introductory references in the body of a letter are always marked off by a comma:

Confirming our phone message of this morning, ...
Replying to your letter of yesterday, ...

Numbers

To assist the eye commas are inserted in large numbers to mark off the figures of thousands and millions.

£36,350   32,436,834

EXERCISES

1. Remembering the close grammatical relationship between the subject of a sentence and its verb, write out or type the following sentences, removing commas where you think they are wrongly inserted and inserting them where you think they are wrongly omitted:

(a) The practice of allowing trade discounts to customers other than those who are genuine retail shopkeepers, is not one we can recommend.

(b) It is just possible that the advice posted at the close of business on 6th July, missed the last collection.

(c) The late arrival of the goods, the inferior quality of some of them, and the damage sustained by a large number of them as a result of faulty packing, are all matters we are bound to take into account when we place future orders.

(d) The question of compensation for the damage caused by prolonged exposure to the weather, has not yet been decided.

(e) Particulars of his age, his education and professional qualifications, and his business experience, have been noted.

2. The following include both defining and non-defining clauses. Copy the sentences, inserting commas where you think they are necessary to give the meaning intended:

(a) All orders which are entrusted to us receive careful attention.

(b) The order for two dozen pairs of blankets which was received yesterday has already been dealt with.

(c) The business carried on by us in Gracechurch Street has now been taken over by Messrs Paulden & Co. who will transfer it to their own well-known premises opposite.

(d) The traveller who called this morning represents H. Roberts & Co.

(e) Our new managing director whom I first met in Rhodesia takes over at the beginning of next month.

(f) The man whom you met just now is the master of S.S. *Victoria*.

(g) We regret we shall be unable to meet our acceptance for £185 which matures at the end of this month.

(h) Please pay any warehouse charges that may have accrued and debit our account.

(i) The matter will be considered at the end of March when the year's accounts are prepared.

(j) He is longing for the day when he can retire.

3. Write out or type the following, inserting only essential commas:

A

The Secretary
Macdonald & Evans Ltd.
Publishers
Estover Road
Plymouth PL6 7PZ

Dear Sir

In reply to your enquiry of 10th October I am pleased to be able to inform you that 500 copies of *A History of Red Tape* by Craig have been sent to your Southend warehouse today.

Yours faithfully

B

Messrs Anderson Johnson & Co.
25 Woodstock Street
Sunderland SR6 8AR

Dear Sirs

Confirming my telephone message this morning I give below the estimated cost of the work to be carried out at your factory in Carpenter Road:
    External painting £2460
    Extension to existing warehouse £10000
    Installation of central heating in the office block £1250
Upon receiving your instructions we will proceed with the work immediately.

Yours truly
for Reginald Harris & Co. Ltd.
R. WATKINS
Secretary

THE SEMICOLON

The semicolon is partly comma and partly full stop; it lies between the two and may replace either. It tends to be neglected in business correspondence and could be used to greater advantage than it is. It is used as follows:

(a) To mark off separate items not linked by conjunctions when commas by themselves would not provide the required emphasis:

We do not condemn the civil servant who looks for a safe job; the teacher who looks for a pension; the barrister who looks for a high return; nor must we condemn the businessman who looks for good profits.

(b) To mark off separate statements linked by conjunctions when it is desired to emphasize some explanation, contrast, etc.:

In the circumstances you mention a discount will be allowed; but future payments will be required in full.

(c) To mark off separate statements that contain commas of their own:

If we receive supplies from the manufacturers, we will see that the goods are sent at once; but, because of the transport strike, I doubt whether they will reach you in time.

EXERCISES

1. Copy the following sentences, inserting semicolons (and where necessary, commas) at appropriate points:

(a) It happened at a time when the firm had very little working capital when exports were falling and when skilled labour was difficult to get.

(b) We are able to supply a ledger containing 400 pages ruled as follows:

250 pages with two accounts or sections 100 pages with three sections 50 pages with six sections.

(c) The Government as usual claims that the nation's affairs are running smoothly the Opposition on the other hand maintains that we are on the brink of disaster.

(d) We are prepared to pay you a fixed salary of £2,000 a year in addition we shall allow you a commission of 5% on all orders introduced by you.

(e) There are signs of prosperity everywhere farmers were never so well off manufacturers' books are bulging with orders the roads and railways are blocked with traffic and the public are spending as never before.

2. Punctuate the following paragraph replacing words by figures where customary and introducing an appropriate semicolon. Explain concisely the use of this semicolon.

A fifteen per cent dividend would cost with profits tax some thirty-one thousand pounds earnings after tax for the year to september thirtieth last were over three times that figure net assets at september thirtieth were four hundred and forty-five thousand pounds.

(RSA)

THE COLON

The colon was formerly much used to denote pauses in very long sentences, but with the modern preference for short sentences in both business letters and other forms of writing it is no longer used for this purpose. For all practical purposes it now has only two functions:

(a) *To mark the relationship between two sentences* too closely connected in thought to justify a full stop:

Mr Davis will be calling this afternoon: be sure to let me know as soon as he arrives. (*Marks close relationship*)
Some were well satisfied with the results: others were very disappointed. (*Marks strong contrast*)

(b) *To mark the introduction of something that follows*, such as a quotation (especially if lengthy), a list or enumeration (particularly after such expressions as *namely, thus as follows*), or an explanation:

Opening the conference, the Chairman said: ... (*A quotation*)
The course includes the following subjects: shorthand, typewriting, English and secretarial practice. (*An enumeration*)
She lived only for two things: her home and her husband. (*An explanation*)

EXERCISE

Copy the following sentences, inserting colons, semicolons and commas at appropriate points:

(a) The section of the syllabus on finance includes the following the various means of payment the Bank of England including its main functions the British banking and currency systems including the cheque system a detailed study of the cheque itself and the remittance facilities of the Post Office.

(b) We have today despatched the following by British Road Services 20 reams lined A5 paper 15 reams plain A4 paper I gross packets each 110 × 220 mm envelopes ½ gross boxes large paper clips.

(c) We are able to offer you the property at a very reasonable figure namely £1,500 yearly for ten years and thereafter at £1,400 yearly.

(d) There are several things you should do before you attempt to type back your shorthand notes first read through them carefully and correct any obvious grammatical errors insert the punctuation signs you propose to use and finally check doubtful spellings.

(e) He was a chairman who inspired confidence to listen to him was to feel that here was a man of tremendous character.

THE PARENTHESIS

Parenthesis is an "aside" in the form of an explanation or other additional information, inserted into a sentence that is logically and grammatically complete without it. The term is also used to signify the round brackets sometimes used to mark the aside. Parentheses vary from the mild and barely noticeable phrase in apposition (e.g. Mr Brown, *our chairman*, has retired) to that which consists of a complete break in the writer's thinking. For the strongly-marked parenthesis either brackets or dashes may be used; for the less strongly marked, commas are usually sufficient, except where the sentence contains other commas and those marking the parenthesis do not stand out clearly enough:

> Mr Trevor Brooks, our Director of Music, will address the meeting.

In this sentence the commas enclosing the phrase in apposition stand out clearly enough.

> The wages offered are high—much higher than those offered for similar work elsewhere—and we hope you will accept them.

The parenthesis here represents a fairly strong break, requiring either brackets or dashes, the choice being largely a matter of taste.

> We invite your attention (see price-list enclosed) to some exceptional bargains.

This parenthesis consists of a completely separate sentence and because it marks a very strong break is most suitably marked by brackets.

Representing as they do a break in the writer's thoughts, parentheses make the reader's thinking that much more difficult, particularly if the parenthesis is lengthy:

> Our prices (which have not been increased for over twelve months despite increases in the cost of labour and raw materials) compare favourably with those of our competitors.

The parenthesis here keeps the reader waiting too long for the predicate that completes the main statement. The point the parenthesis makes would be put much better in a sentence of its own.

As a safeguard against mistakes sums of money expressed in figures in important business documents are repeated in words placed inside round brackets:

> For the property you inspected this morning the owner is asking £10,590 (Ten thousand five hundred and ninety pounds).

THE DASH

Besides its use as an alternative to parentheses the dash (a longer form of the hyphen) is used to bring together several subjects belonging to the same verb:

> Interest in work, tact, good manners, loyalty, respect for authority and consideration for others—these are qualities we should all seek to develop.

Where, as in the above and the following example, multiple subjects are numerous it is helpful to introduce the delayed predicate by using such pronouns as *these, those* and *all*:

> Furniture, carpets and linos, kitchen utensils and electrical appliances— *all* were included in the sale.

The dash may also be used instead of the colon to introduce an explanation:

> A well-written business letter has three points of focus—the writer, the message and the reader.

EXERCISE

Copy the following sentences, inserting dashes, parentheses and commas as may be necessary:

(a) The quality of the coal now in stock is very good much better than we have had for some time and we hope you will like it.

(b) The traveller left at two o'clock for I am afraid I have forgotten where.

(c) We are pleased to quote you for electrical fittings see pages 27–35 of catalogue enclosed any of which we can supply immediately we receive your order.

(d) We have been informed and we have every reason to believe that supplies of the dictionary are likely to run out within six months.

(e) Our method or lack of method of spelling may be absurd but it is now fixed at least until the efforts of our spelling reformers meet with success.

THE HYPHEN

The primary function of the hyphen or short dash is to join two or more words to make one with a meaning of its own, but not all authorities are agreed upon what is correct usage. The following summarizes its main uses:

(a) To form compound nouns by combining an adjective with its noun:

subject-matter, sister-in-law, St Annes-on-Sea

There is a strong modern tendency to dispense with the hyphen and many words formerly hyphenated are now consolidated:

today, tomorrow, handbook, textbook, stocktaking

The current retention of the hyphen in such words as *time-table hold-up, take-over* marks an intermediate stage in the development of language from complete separation of adjective and noun in the first place to ultimate complete union. Many common words now written with the hyphen will no doubt come to be written without it.

(b) To form compound adjectives:

a *world-wide* organization, an *air-tight* container, a *break-even* chart, a *razor-like* edge, the *above-mentioned* facts, an *up-to-date* catalogue, a *balance-of-payments* crisis.

As with compound nouns there is a strong, and desirable, tendency to dispense with the hyphen in frequently-occurring compounds:

a *lifelong* friend, a *lukewarm* reception, a *fireproof* curtain, the *goodwill* of a business, a *housemaster*.

A hypen is used between an adverb and its adjective only when the adjective is a participle (past or present) used attributively; not when used predicatively:

a very good effort, a most unusual effect, a pretty shrewd person	Normal (no hyphen)
a well-earned rest, a well-known person, an oft-repeated phrase, a never-ending task	Attributive use with participle
a rest well earned, a person well known a phrase oft repeated, a task never ending	Predicative use with participle (no hyphen)

(c) To join numbers from 21 to 99 and also fractional parts:

twenty-five, thirty-first, four-and-twenty, three-quarters, five-eighths

(d) After certain prefixes, especially when it is necessary to indicate pronunciation of two separate vowels, or to distinguish between words similarly spelt:

ante-natal, extra-mural, post-war

co-education, pre-eminent, pre-estimate

re-cover (recover), re-creation (recreation) re-form (reform), re-sign (resign)

(e) To mark division of words at line-endings:

Feb-ruary, Frus-trate, accom-plish, micro-scope, con-soli-date, particu-larly

EXERCISE

Write out, or type, the following sentences, inserting hyphens and other necessary punctuation marks:

(a) Seven and twenty years have passed since he entered the company's service as an office boy.

(b) It was agreed that Mr Herbert Spencer should be coopted to the Finance Subcommittee.

(c) The subject matter of the contract will not be made known until after the meeting.

(d) We have pleasure in sending you an up to date list of our range of card index cabinets.

(e) The principal's secretary is a refined and well spoken girl and an excellent shorthand typist.

THE APOSTROPHE

The apostrophe or raised comma is used as follows:

(a) To mark omitted letters, as in *five o'clock* (of the clock), *B'ham* (Birmingham), and in such colloquial expressions as *don't* (do not), *can't* (can not), *it's* (it is, or it has). Colloquial language, as the term suggests, is the language of common conversation. It should not be used in formal business correspondence.

(b) To signify ownership or possession. The apostrophe then takes an added "*s*", except when the possessive plural itself ends in "*s*".

the *company's* registered office, the *secretary's* staff, the *member's* car, the *typist's* desk.

but

both *companies'* profits, the Chartered *Accountants'* Institute, the *typists'* department.

The possessive form is not used for inanimate things, i.e. non-living objects. Thus, we cannot write *unemployment's effects* (for the *effects of unemployment*), the *experiment's success* (for the *success of the experiment*), or *within the regulation's scope* (for the *scope of the regulations*).

(c) To give possessive form to certain words that are not in fact possessive:

a month's wages, three months' notice, a day's journey, ten days' supplies

There is, however, a growing tendency to omit the apostrophe in such cases.

EXERCISES

1. Write down, or type, the possessive plural forms of the following nouns:

(a) jury, lawyer, cashier, lady, family;
(b) secretary, manager, man-servant, Lord Mayor, shorthand-writer.

2. Copy the following sentences, inserting apostrophes and other necessary punctuation marks:

(a) The Boards decision regarding the purchase of Bartons bakery will be made known later.
(b) The companys new offices overlook St Jamess Park the typists department being to the front of the building.
(c) My pension becomes payable in two weeks time and my wifes in a months time.
(d) Members subscriptions to the Ratepayers Association are due in three months time.
(e) The activities of building societies are regulated by the Building Societies Act 1972 operations in the insurance market by the Lloyds Act 1972 telecommunications by the Telecommunications Act 1984.

INVERTED COMMAS

The so-called inverted commas marking quotations may be used either singly (' ') or doubly (" "). The former is recommended by Fowler* for all uses except quotations that appear within other quotations. Some publishers, however, prefer to use double quotes first, with single quotes for quotes within quotes. (This is the practice adopted in the examples which follow.) Inverted commas have three uses:

(a) To mark direct speech, i.e. the actual words of the speaker or writer:

*H. W. Fowler: *Modern English Usage*, OUP (2nd edn.), 1965, p. 591.

The Chairman said: "I welcome you to this our twenty-fifth annual conference."
One member described the proposals as "intolerable"; another described them as "mean".

Direct speech in business correspondence is rare and what is said about it here can be of little more than academic interest to those who write or type business letters. They would not use direct speech; they would convert it into indirect or reported speech. The first of the above examples would then become:

The Chairman said he welcomed us to the twenty-fifth annual conference.

When a quotation appears within another, that is when the speaker himself quotes what another has said or written, single inverted commas would be used to mark the inside quotation:

He asked me: "Did the Chairman say, 'the meeting is adjourned', or not?"

And so against Fowler's advice, you use double inverted commas as your normal quotation marks, then for inside quotations you would have to use single. Of these two methods the one advocated by Fowler has the advantage of giving greater prominence to the inside quotation.
You will notice that in the above examples the words quoted have been introduced by a colon. Some writers would have preferred a comma. Whether to use a colon or a comma is a matter of personal taste; there are no rules, but the practice among writers, and it is a sound one, is to use the colon to introduce lengthy quotations and to reserve the comma for short ones.
It is a much-debated question whether normal punctuation marks should be placed inside or outside quotation marks. Because it is simpler and saves trouble many printers and publishers place them inside irrespective of how they stand in relation to the words quoted. But it is more logical and grammatically correct to keep all punctuation marks in the places to which they belong in the quoted passage, and this is now the practice of many good publishers, illustrated in the following examples:

Example 1
We are uncertain about the effects of this discovery.

When quoted, this becomes:

"We are uncertain", he said, "about the effects of this discovery."

(Since there is no comma in the original statement, the comma in the quoted passage belongs, not to *uncertain* but to *he said*. It is therefore placed *outside* the quotation mark. The full stop at the end belongs to the quotation and is therefore placed *inside* the final quotation mark.)

Example 2

Why did you say, "I am too busy"?

(Here, the question mark forms no part of the quoted statement *I am too busy*. It is therefore placed *outside* the quotation mark.)

Example 3

He asked me, "How do you account for late delivery?"

(In this example the question mark is placed *inside* the quotation mark because it belongs to the question that is quoted.)

(b) To mark titles of books, plays, names of ships, etc.

The "Queen Elizabeth" will sail tomorrow.
I will meet you at the "Crooked Billet".

(c) To mark words and phrases used in a special sense

Because I don't like pop music I'm regarded as a "square".

It is the "Rolls-Royce" of the bicycle world.

The "carrot-and-stick" measures introduced are designed to reduce the present massive fuel bill (i.e. measures combining persuasion with threats).

THE QUESTION MARK

Like inverted commas the question mark is concerned with direct speech and is rarely used in business writing. The question mark replaces the full stop after questions put in the actual words of the questioner:

When will you be making the new appointment? (*Direct question*)

but:

I asked him when he would be making the new appointment. (*Indirect question*)

Nor is the question mark used after polite requests made in question form as they frequently are in business correspondence:

Will you please complete and return the enclosed form.
Would you be good enough to reply not later than next Thursday.

THE EXCLAMATION MARK

Exclamation marks are rarely used in business correspondence. They denote surprise or some other emotion, and business letters are concerned with facts, not with emotions.

The use of exclamation marks is confined to what are recognized as exclamations. These include:

(a) Words and phrases used as interjections:

Splendid! Really! Well done! Good heavens!

(b) Exclamatory sentences (with *What* and *How*):

What a thing to say! What an excellent result! How I longed for morning!

The exclamation mark also has other uses, but we need not concern ourselves with them here.

SUMMARY

The sole purpose of punctuation is to help the reader to grasp the meaning of a passage speedily and with certainty. Punctuation marks should be kept to the minimum needed to make meaning clear. If you find it necessary to use an extravagantly large number of punctuation marks you may take it as an almost certain indication that your letter needs rewording.

EXERCISES

1. Explain how the meaning of each of the following sentences would be changed if the commas were removed:

(a) The workers, who had completed their task in the allotted time, were granted a bonus.
(b) The statement, I believe, was made by the man in the dark suit.
(c) Why did you ask, John?

2. Write notes to explain the reasons for the punctuation used in the following passage:

What reasons prompted such a traveller, after so much mental debate, so to choose his travelling companions? There was as much room elsewhere; there was a corner to be had next door; the air in that compartment was not more fresh than that in a dozen other compartments. If, then, it was not superior comfort that drew him to that particular compartment, the cause of his coming into it must rest in the occupants themselves. (*London GCE*)

3. Type or write out the following letters, inserting necessary punctuation marks:

A

Dear Sirs

I was educated at King's College School where I obtained GCEs in six subjects since leaving school last summer I have attended shorthand and typewriting classes and in these subjects have now attained speeds of 100 and 40 w.p.m. respectively I am very anxious to get into a merchant's office and should my application be successful I would do my best to give you satisfaction.

Yours respectfully

B

Dear Mr Jameson

As you will see from the enclosed circular I have entered into partnership with Mr Arthur Waugh and in consequence shall not be making my regular monthly call on you in future I feel sure however that you will extend to my successor Mr Thomas Holding the consideration and support which you have for so many years given to me.

Yours sincerely

C

Dear Sirs

We thank you for your enquiry of yesterday and are pleased to enclose samples of our printing papers you do not mention the price or indicate the quality of poster papers you require but we hope you will find something suitable among the enclosed samples we can guarantee all these as being quite suitable for poster work and look forward to your placing an order with us.

Yours faithfully

D

Dear Sirs

You will no doubt remember that you acted for me last December in the purchase of the property at No. 1 Margate Road St Annes I recently received a demand note for payment of rates in respect of this property and upon enquiry am informed that the amount claimed namely £94 is for the period 5th April to 7th December last and that it should have been allowed to me upon completion of the purchase.

I am enclosing the demand note and also my correspondence with the local authority and since the borough treasurer is apparently looking to me for payment of the amount should be obliged if you would arrange for the necessary adjustment to be made in your completion statement.

Yours faithfully

E

Dear Mr Baxter

Since writing to you on 19th March about central heating for the bungalow at Frinton I have visited Cranes in London and seen their range of domestic boilers I did so because I think you mentioned that it was a Crane boiler which you proposed to install.

I am enclosing a leaflet giving particulars of the three sizes of "Cavendish" boiler supplied by Cranes for domestic purposes it seems to me that the No. 4 is the one that would be needed for the number and size of radiators we have in mind I should be obliged if you would give me your opinion on this point and also inform me whether the tiled recess in the kitchen would be deep enough to take the No. 4 size.

Yours truly

CHAPTER TEN

Spelling

It is a pity that Chawcer, who had geneyus, was so unedicated; he's the wus speller I know of.

Artemus Ward

SPELLING AND BUSINESS

It has sometimes been suggested that spelling is unimportant and irrelevant; that it is not the mechanical accuracy of what is written that matters, but rather the creativity that lies in uninhibited self-expression. It has even been suggested that good spelling, punctuation and grammatical sentence construction are hindrances rather than aids to effective communication. This philosophy in matters of written expression may be all very well for the literary craftsman primarily concerned to present his subject in vivid, imaginative and attractive language, who regards spelling and grammatical niceties as tiresome and even unnecessary tools of writing. But this is a philosophy that has no place in business writing. A secretary may not have all the personal qualities her employer thinks she should have, but it can hardly be denied that he is entitled to expect her at least to be able to spell.

A more detailed treatment of spelling than that which follows is not possible in a book on business correspondence, but attention to a few simple rules would rid us of many errors of the commoner sort. This is not to suggest that English spelling is controlled by any tidy set of rules. On the contrary, English spelling seems to be notoriously illogical. It offers numerous loopholes for error, mainly because English is a language derived from many sources. It also suffers from the drawback of a restricted alphabet that provides only twenty-six letters to represent over forty different sounds.

Weakness in spelling is not confined to those who have not had the benefit of a good education. Even the well-educated are often uncertain about spelling and find it necessary to seek regular help from their dictionaries. Among the commoner uncertainties we may cite the following:

153

(a) **Whether a word takes single or double consonants**
e.g. benefited, fulfil, pavilion
harass, install, paraffin, questionnaire

(b) **Whether a word takes "ie" or "ei"**
e.g. mischievous, relief, siege
forfeit, leisure, seize

(c) **Whether a word ends in "-ance" or "-ence"**
e.g. acceptance, perseverance, tolerance
audience, conference, preference

(d) **Whether a word ends in "-ant" or "-ent"**
e.g. dependant (noun), covenant, relevant
dependent (verb), competent, different

(e) **Whether a word ends in "-able" or "ible"**
e.g. indispensable, passable, taxable
convertible, discernible, permissible.

Much bad spelling is due to carelessness. We all know the difference between *their* and *there*, *to* and *too*, *as* and *has*, and between *its* and *it's*. Yet, how often do these and other simple mistakes creep into the letters we write!

To spell well you need to think about words clearly and to pronounce them carefully—to think of them, not as a jumble of letters but as groups of syllables. Split up into syllables the longest words become as easy to spell as the short ones: *in-stru-men-tal-i-ty* then gives no more trouble than, say, *trans-port*.

And so, the first rule of good spelling is—*pronounce carefully*. It will help you to avoid many very common errors. For example:

affi-davit	not *affa-*	*gramo*-phone	not *grama-*
ancill-*ary*	not -*iary*	imper-*ative*	not -*itive*
assim-*ilate*	not -*ulate*	*land*-scape	not *lan-*
auxil-*iary*	not -*ary*	liter-*ature*	not -*ture*
aud*ible*	not -*able*	*minia*-ture	not *mina-*
bank-*ruptcy*	not -*rupcy*	mischie-*vous*	not -*vious*
contempo-*rary*	not -*ry*	*mono*-logue	not *mona-*
defi-*nite*	not -*nate*	*symp*-tom	not *sym-*
feas-*ible*	not -*able*	*sur*-prise	not *su-*
Feb-*ruary*	not -*uary*	*temp*-tation	not *tem-*
govern-ment	not *gover-*	ultima-*tum*	not -*tim*

The following are some of the more general rules of spelling, but all are open to exceptions that need to be learned:

ie and ei

The general rule here is "*i* before *e* except after *c*", but only when the sound is that of long *ee*, as in *feel*:

brief, field, relieve (*ee* sound)
ceiling, conceive, receive (after *c*)
neither, reign, Leicester (where the sound is not *ee*)

Exceptions: counterfeit, seize, and some proper names, including Keith, Leigh-on-Sea, O'Neill, Sheila.

Endings in *ll* and *l*

Some words ending in *ll* drop one of the *l*'s in compounds:

all but almost, already, always
full ⎱
fill ⎰ but fulsome, careful, handful, fulfil
till but until
well but welcome, welfare

NOTE: *all right* (two words—never *alright*)

Conversely, words ending in single *l* preceded by a short vowel double the *l*:

equal, equally, equalling
total, totalled, totalling
travel, traveller, travelling

Exception: paralleled

Stressed final syllables

When the only or final syllable contains a short stressed vowel, the final consonant is doubled before a vowel suffix to preserve the stress of the syllable:

begin, beginning; bid, bidder; fit, fitted; occur, occurred

but:

benefit, benefited ⎫
debit, debited ⎬ where the stress falls on the first, not on the final
profit, profitable ⎭ syllable of the original words.

Endings in silent *e*

The general rule is to drop the *e* before a vowel (except where it is needed to preserve the soft *c* or *g*, as in *noticeable*, *peaceable*, and *manageable*) but to retain it before a consonant, e.g.

blame   blaming   blameworthy
care   caring   carefree
value   valuable   valueless

and similarly with debatable, movable, ratable and salable, though the *Oxford English Dictionary* retains the silent *e* in these and similar words. Usage, however, tends to follow the general rule for omission of the *e* and is supported by Fowler.* Following the above general rule such words as *acknowledg(e)ment* and *judg(e)ment* would retain the *e* of the primary word, and this is the preferred spelling of the *OED*. But there is a strong modern tendency to omit the *e* and to write *acknowledgment, abridgment, judgment* and *lodgment*. Choice between these and the other alternatives mentioned is a matter of individual taste.

Endings with related forms

It is sometimes difficult to know which of the two endings *-able, -ible*; *-cial, -tial*; *-city, -sity*; *-sion, -tion* is correct. The correct choice may often be deduced from the spelling of the final syllable of the root word (e.g. *terminate*) or some other word derived from the root (e.g. *permissive* from *permit*; *resident* from *reside*):

terminate	and therefore terminable
permissive	and therefore permissible
commerce	and therefore commercial
resident	and therefore residential
scarce	and therefore scarcity
universe	and therefore university
possess	and therefore possession
appreciate	and therefore appreciation

NOTE: *divide, exclude, provide* and other words ending with the *d* sound take *-sion*: divi*sion*, exclu*sion*, provi*sion*, etc.

Words with alternative spellings

-ise or *-ize*

On the question whether such words as *organize* and *specialize* should be spelt *-ise* or *-ize* authorities differ. It is standard practice among printers to use *-ise*, but the *OED* recommends the *-ize* spellings for suffixes because the suffix originates in either Latin or Greek, both of which use z. The *-ize* spelling is also used by *The Times*, the *Encyclopaedia Britannica* and the Cambridge University Press. For words in which the final syllable is not a suffix but part of the primary word the correct spelling is *-ise* as in *advertise, comprise, enterprise, exercise, revise* and *supervise*. With other words it is better to follow the modern practice set by the above authorities and to use *-ize* in all cases where dictionaries give *-ise* and *-ize* alternatives.

---

* H. W. Fowler: *Modern English Usage*, OUP (2nd edn.), 1965, p. 376.

Miscellaneous words

There are a number of other words with alternative spellings. The following is a list of some frequently used in business writing. The preferred spellings according to Fowler (*op. cit.*) are those in the first column.

by-law	bye-law	guild	gild
carcass	carcase	install	instal
connexion	connection*	instil	instill
dispatch	despatch*	manilla	manila
employee	employe	moneyed	monied
enquire	inquire	net	nett
(to ask a question)	(to investigate)	reflection	reflexion
enrole	enroll	show	shew
gram	gramme	wagon	waggon
grey	gray		

Plurals of nouns

General rule

Add -*s* or -*es* to the singular:

> cheques, customs, records, telegrams, sizes,
> gases, stresses, boxes, dishes, matches

-y endings

Nouns ending in -*y preceded by a consonant* take the plural -*ies*:

> currency, currencies; delivery, deliveries;
> faculty, faculties; policy, policies.

but:

> alloy, alloys
> holiday, holidays } where -*y* is preceded by a vowel.
> journey, journeys
> money, moneys

-o endings

Most nouns ending in -*o preceded by a consonant* take the plural -*oes*:

> cargo, cargoes; hero, heroes; tomato, tomatoes

but:

> portfolios
> ratios } where -*o* is preceded by a vowel.
> studios

*(Usage favours the latter spelling.)

-f and -fe endings

Nouns ending in *-f* or *-fe* usually take the plural *-ves*:

knife, knives; loaf, loaves; thief, thieves.

but there are many exceptions:

beliefs, proofs, briefs, reliefs.

You will do well to remember that there are exceptions to most rules of spelling and to take special note of words that form their plurals in ways other than those stated above.

Foreign words

Some adopted foreign words take the forms of their original language:

agendum, agenda; phenomenon, phenomena; tableau, tableaux.

For other foreign words the tendency is to use the English *-s* or *-es*, especially for the popular use of words that are also used in a formal or scientific context:

Singular	Plural (in formal use)	Plural (in popular use)
appendix	appendices	appendixes
bureau	bureaux	bureaus
formula	formulae	formulas
index	indices	indexes
plateau	plateaux	plateaus

HOW TO IMPROVE SPELLING

We have already referred to careless pronunciation as a cause of poor spelling. Another and more influential cause is careless and superficial reading, due partly to pressures from other forms of recreation and entertainment. Good spelling is largely a matter of visual imagery. Whether your spelling is good or bad depends largely on the way you read. If you read with keen critical interest you form mental pictures of the printed words, whereas superficial reading leaves you with no more than blurred impressions.

If your spelling is weak there are several things you can do to improve it:

(a) The first step is to read carefully and critically.

(b) The second is to pronounce words carefully.

(c) The third is to keep a notebook and in it write the correct forms of all words you misspell or find it necessary to look up.

(d) The fourth is systematic revision of the words in your notebook. In fact the value of your notebook is proportionate to the extent to which you use it in this way. Get someone to dictate the words to you in groups of, say, ten and then check your spellings.

(e) The final step is to use the words when opportunities arise and so consolidate what you have learned.

WORDS TO WATCH

In the following lists you will find many of the words most commonly misspelt. You might do worse than make those in the first list the starting-point for your own personal list.

Words to make quite sure of

accommodate	disappear	privilege
address	embarrass	
argument	exceedingly	procedure
beginning		quarter
benefited	February	receive
	fulfil	recommend
business	governor	referred
committee	gramophone	
comparative	harass	separate
convenient		success
correspondence	interrupt	transferred
	necessary	until
definite	occurred	Wednesday
develop	omitted	

Words commonly confused

accept, except	current, currant
advice, advise	decease, disease
affect, effect	dependant, dependent
alternate, alternative	device, devise
biannual, biennial	draft, draught
canvas, canvass	dying, dyeing
check, cheque	elicit, illicit
compliment, complement	emigrate, immigrate
continuous, continual	eminent, imminent
council, counsel	ensure, insure

envelop, envelope
faint, feint
licence, license
lightening, lightning
personal, personnel

practice, practise
principal, principle
prophecy, prophesy
stationary, stationery
their, there

Other words used in business and frequently misspelt

For the benefit of students who wish to memorize them these words are arranged in groups of ten.

abbreviate
abridge
absenteeism
accede
accelerate
accentuate
accessible
accessory
accompany
accomplish

accountant
accrue
accumulate
achieve
achievement
acknowledge
acoustics
acquaint
acquiesce
acquire

across
adhesive
adjacent
adjourn
adjudicator
adjusting
admissible
adolescent
advantageous
advisable

adviser
advisory
aerial
affidavit
aggrieved

agreeable
allege
alleviate
allocate
allotment

allotted
amateur
ambassador
ambitious
amicable
analysis
anniversary
announce
annul
anonymous

anticipate
antique
anxious
appalling
apparent
appetite
appreciate
apprentice
appropriate
architect

article
artificial
ascertain
assessor
assimilate
association
assurance
attitude
attorney

audible

audience
auditor
auxiliary
bankruptcy
barrister
believe
beneficial
biased (or biassed)
bicycle
borough

boycott
budget
bulletin
buoyant
bureau
calendar
campaign
cancellation
canvass (to solicit)
carriage

casualty
catalogue
ceiling
centre
centring
century
chaotic
cheque (a document)
cipher
circuit

clientele
collaborate
collateral

colleague
college
collusion
colour
commemorate
commission
commissionaire

competent
comprehension
concede
conceivable
concurrence
conductor
confident
connoisseur
conscientious
conscious

consensus
convenience
conveyance
corroborate
counsel (an adviser)
courtesy
creditor
criticism
curriculum
customary

deceit
decipher
deferred
deficit
demurrage
descendant
difference
different
disappoint
disapproval

discernible
discipline
discoloration
dissent (to disagree)
doubtful
draught (air)
dubious
duplicator

efficiency
eighteenth

eligible
eliminate
emergency
encourage
encyclopaedia
endeavour
endorsement
enormous
ephemeral
eradicate

erroneous
escalator
etiquette
evenness
eventually
evidence
exaggerate
excellent
exception
excessive

excise
excite
exercise
exhibit
expedite
expenditure
expense
facsimile
fallacy
fascinate

fatigue
feasible
financial
flotation
foreign
forfeit
fortuitous
freight
frequency
fullness

gauge

glossary
governor
gradient
grammar
gramophone
grievous
guarantee
guest
guilty

honorary
honourable
hygiene
illegal
illegible
illicit
immediately
immersion
immigrate
imminent

imperative
impromptu
incentive
inconvenience
incredible
indefensible
indelible
indemnify
independence
indispensable

infallible
inference
infinite
innovation
insolvent
installation
instalment
intelligible
interrupt
irregular

irrelevant
issuing
jeweller
journal
labelled

lacquer
leisure
liaison
libellous
licensed

liquidator
maintenance
mannequin
manoeuvre
manufacturer
marriage
marvellous
mathematics
Mediterranean
memorandum

metre (measurement)
miniature
misapprehension
miscellaneous
necessitate
necessity
negotiate
neighbourhood
neutral
nuisance

numerical
obsession
occasion
occurrence
occurring
omission
paraffin
parallel
parliament
pavilion

perceptible
perceive
permissible
permitting
persuade
persuasion
plausible
possession
precede

predecessor

preference
preferring
prejudice
preparation
procedure
procession
programme
proprietary
proprietor
psychology

pursue
queue
questionnaire
quorum
receivable
receipt
recipe
reciprocate
recurrence
reducible

redundant
referring
refrigerator
regrettable
reimburse
remittance
rendezvous
repudiate
rescind
residential

resistible
resources
retaliate
retrievable
revenue
review (to re-examine)
rhythm
salary
schedule
secede

secondary
segregate

seize
series
signatory
sinecure
skilful
spontaneous
stencilling
stevedore

storage
stupefy
subtle
suburb
successful
summarize
superannuation
superintendent
supersede
supervisor

surprise
susceptible
suing
symptom
synonymous
synopsis
tacitly
tariff
technique
television

temperature
temporary
temptation
tenacious
terrify
territory
thermometer
thoroughly
tidily
tidiness

tobacco
tolerant
totally
tragedy
transferable

transitory   unique   vehicle
traveller   unmistakable   verticle
trial   unnecessary   wholly
typical   unveil   wrench
ultimatum   usable   yield

WORD DIVISION

Rules for division

It is the practice in typewriting to divide words at the end of lines to avoid an uneven right-hand margin. Divisions should be made according to etymology (the way in which words originate and are built up) as in *atmo-sphere, bio-graphy, inter-act, memorandum, port-folio, post-age*; but where etymological structure is not obvious, divisions should correspond as nearly as possible to the way in which words are pronounced. This may be taken as a general guide, but you will find the following notes helpful:

(a) *The new syllable should begin with a consonant,* except where this would affect the way in which the preceding syllable is pronounced:

    cata-logue, credi-tor, furni-ture, pro-gramme

but:

    hon-orary, prep-aration, prop-erty, sched-ule

(b) *Words are divided after a prefix or before a suffix,* except when the prefix or suffix comprises only two letters:

    dis-appoint, mis-understand, trans-action, under-estimate, outlandish, correspond-ence, dictat-ing, endorse-ment, value-less

but:

    recon-sider (not re-consider), bene-fited (not benefit-ed)

because it is regarded as bad practice to have a separation of only two letters.

(c) *Words with double or treble consonants* divide between two consonants or after the first of three:

    accom-modate, bar-rister, deb-ris, travel-ling
    accom-plish, cen-tring, frus-trate, unem-ployed

NOTE: Letters forming a single sound are never divided:

    tele-*ph*one, para-*ph*rase, thorou*gh*-ness, ma*tch*-less, de*bt*-or

(d) Compound words divide at the point where the elements combine to form the compound:

hand-writing, head-master, stock-taking, work-man

Words not divided
(a) One-syllable words:

blacked, cheque, straight, thought

(b) Proper names:

Emily, Robinson, Marlborough, St Vincent

(c) Words already hyphenated (except at the hyphen):

audio-typist, dining-room, post-mortem, subject-matter

(d) Dates: Day, month and, if possible, year must all appear together on the same line:

30th December 1975

(e) Foreign words:

garçon (French for *boy*); autobahn (German for *dual carriageway*)

EXERCISES

1. Type, or write out, the opposites of the following words, by adding a prefix to each:

(a) colour	resolute	legal	human	entangle
(b) mortal	limited	redeemable	measurable	relevant
(c) necessary	numerable	similar	mortal	rational
(d) service	resistible	material	logical	noticed

2. Complete the following words by inserting *ie* or *ei* as may be required in the blank spaces, and check the results with your dictionary:

(a) gr..vous	rec..pt	dec..ve	misch..f	n..ther
(b) w..rd	s..ze	fr..nd	Mad..ra	counterf..t
(c) n..ghbour	l..sure	h..ght	fr..ght	K..th

3. Type, or write out, the following words, inserting the correct number of *l*'s in the spaces shown by the dots:

(a) a.most	du.ness	doubtfu.	forete.	a.together
(b) reca.	unti.	a.though	ski.fu.	spoonfu.
(c) we.being	we.fare	a.ways	we.come	a.ocate
(d) chi.blain	enro.ment	insta.ment	i.ness	disti.

4. Complete the following words by inserting the appropriate single or double letters; then use your dictionary to check them:

(a) begi(n)ing envelo(p)ing admi(s)ion   trave(l)er   refi(l)
(b) occu(r)ed enro(l)   benefi(t)ed   we(l)fare   foresta(l)
(c) sti(l)ness cance(l)ed   remi(t)ance   transfe(r)ed unti(l)
(d) fu(l)fi(l) omi(t)ing   a(l)ready   refe(r)ing   insta(l)ment
(e) debi(t)ed acqui(t)ed   mode(l)ing   diffe(r)ed   doubtfu(l)

5. Some only of the following words are spelt incorrectly. Type or write out the incorrectly spelt words with the necessary corrections, then use your dictionary to check them:

(a) achievment outrageous useable   endorsment   abridgment
(b) agreeing   blameable valueing   chargable   pavement
(c) valuless   debateable knowledg-   commence-   likeable
                          eable   ment
(d) moveing   servicable desireous   arguement   grieveous

6. Complete the following words by the addition of *i* or *y* as may be necessary; then use your dictionary to check them:

(a) accompan.ment stead.ness suppl.ing rel.able happ.ness
(b) accompan.ing injur.ous magnif.er env.able cop.ist
(c) betra.al   suppl.er   anno.ance satisf.ed da.ly
(d) angr.ly   enjo.ment ga.ety   ga.ly   bus.ness

7. Add the correct suffixes *-able*, or *-ible* to the following words, making any changes necessary to give the correct spelling:

(a) advise   admit   excuse   digest   endure
(b) permit   compare   access   rely   resist
(c) pity   exhaust   excite   defence   notice
(d) response dispense reverse   move   justify

8. Add the correct suffixes *-ance* or *-ence* to the following words, making any changes necessary to give the correct spellings:

(a) continue concur   excel   infer   depend
(b) remember endure   abound   exist   hinder
(c) occur   correspond further   ignore   persist
(d) insist   refer   prefer   persevere recur

9. Complete the following words by adding the correct suffixes from those indicated:

(a) *-ant, -ent*
    compet.nt independ.nt intoler.nt promin.nt relev.nt
(b) *-cial, -tial*
    commer.ial substan.ial finan.ial ini.ial   espe.ial
(c) *-city, -sity*
    inten.ity publi.ity   capa.ity genero.ity univer.ity

(d) *-sion, -tion*

quota.ion   exclu.ion   inten.ion   excep.ion   deci.ion

(e) *-cle, -cal*

musi ...   criti ...   vehi ...   periodi ...   specta ...

10. Complete the spellings of the following words; then use your dictionary to check them:

(a) compar.tive   acco.odate   misce.aneous   defin.te
(b) benefi.ed   Feb.ary   nec.ary   gov.nor
(c) permiss.ble   tempo.ry   proc.dure   assim.late
(d) sep.rate   gram.phone   We.esday   carr.ge
(e) super.ede   g.rantee   maint.nance   insta.ation

11. Type or rewrite the following, correcting all spelling mistakes:

In business it is neccessary to render acounts accuratley. A small mistake may lead to considrable work for the firm's employees. Allways cheque and recheque your columns before makeing the final entry in ink. Remember that clear figures are allways helpfull. Don't allow one line of figures to get confused with another; seperate each line. You shoud see that each entry in the ledger has a corrisponding reciept.

12. Write out the following passage, spelling all words correctly, and putting in any commas and full stops you think necessary:

When the axident ocured to my bicicle I was releived to reckerlect that it was gaurented for to years as this period of time had not then past I had every exspectashun of haveing my bicicle compleatly overhorled without my inkuring any expens as you will redily beleive I siezed the opertunity imediataly and fortunatly was sucesful in my claim.

(RSA, Elem.)

13. Ten of the following words are spelt correctly, and ten incorrectly. Pick out the latter and write these down with the correct spelling.

gramaphone   proffessor   sincerly   business   prisioner
ridiculous   omission   successful   expierience   suprised
village   completly   pursuit   carriage   recommend
comparative   dectective   develop   bycicle   athelete

(RSA, Elem.)

USE OF CAPITALS

General rule

Apart from certain well-known and generally accepted rules the use of initial capital letters is very largely governed by what a person feels to be most fitting. The word *I* is always written with a capital letter:

Alice and *I* will call tomorrow.

It is well known that initial capitals are used as follows:

(a) For the first word in a sentence, and always following a full stop:

Thank you for your enquiry of 12th October. We enclose the required catalogue and price-list.

(b) For proper names, i.e. the names of persons, places, streets, buildings, etc. and for adjectives derived from them:

Mr Gilbert Hardman
Grosvenor House
Silverthorn Street
Marlborough

He is an old Etonian and a Lancastrian by birth.

There seems to be a modern tendency to use small letters for such words as *street, road, avenue* appearing in addresses, but as they form part of a title there is no good reason for rejecting initial capitals.

Some words that originated as proper names are no longer associated with their origins and take small letters:

brussels sprouts, gum arabic, venetian blind, wellington boots

(c) For the days and months, for the names of special days and festivals, but not for the names of the seasons:

Our traveller will call on the first *Wednesday* in *December*.
Easter Day, Remembrance Sunday

but:

I shall not return until late *spring* or early *summer*.

(d) For the important words in descriptive titles, titles of publications, plays, etc.

The Importance of Loyalty
Head of the Science Department
Have you seen *Arsenic and Old Lace*?

(e) For the first word in a direct quotation:

I said, "At what time did he phone?"

In business correspondence

Initial capitals are used in correspondence as follows:

(a) *For the salutation*, and the first words only in the complimentary close:

Dear Sir (or Madam)   *(Salutation)*

We are dear sirs
Yours faithfully   *(Complimentary close)*

(b) *For the important words in official titles of institutions*, and for courtesy and similar titles:

The institute of Chartered Secretaries and Administrators
The London Chamber of Commerce and Industry
Address the letter to Professor S. Montague, care of Messrs Hatton, Brooks & Co.

But when such terms as *institute, university, college* and *department* are used in a general sense and do not refer to a particular institution small letters are used. This applies also to such titles as *professor, headmaster, vicar* and *chairman* when they are used in a general sense. In other words, *use a capital for the particular and a small for the general*:

The *College* (referring to some particular college) in every way fulfils the function of a modern *college* of education.
The *Headmaster* (meaning the head of a particular school) is as good a *headmaster* as one could wish for.

(c) *For numerical sequences:*

Invoice 562,   Paragraph 20,   Chapter 7,   Grade IV

(d) *For the first word of a resolution:*

Resolved, *That* future meetings be held monthly.

A final word—to use initial capitals excessively is to be pompous, and if you are in doubt whether a word should or should not have an initial capital, err on the side of modesty and use a small letter.

EXERCISES

1. Rewrite the following passage, inserting punctuation marks and capitals where necessary:

what you believe in a lot of make-up at work are you really serious when you suggest that mascara is not out of place in the office it may be all right with evening dress and jewellery but after all your office is neither a ballroom nor a stage dressing room remember that you are a typist and not a cover girl or a film star.

2. Rewrite the following passage, inserting the necessary capitals and punctuation:

did you buy anything in italy asked the customs official just a few small items answered mrs harrison i didnt buy anything of much value may I examine your case please asked the official certainly said the lady but youll find nothing in it of any importance

3. Type or write out the following passages, capitalizing and punctuating as necessary:

A

from the daily telegraph

private secretary required by the central electricity generating board for a principal assistant clerk in the planning department salary £6,000–£7,000 per annum modern offices near London bridge and waterloo stations staff restaurant permanent pensionable appointment candidates should be competent shorthand typists of good education applications stating age qualifications experience present position and salary to the appointments officer 24–30 holborn london ec1 not later than 4th april

B

messrs fennel & co 25 burlington avenue maidstone kent

gentlemen

in answer to your advertisement in todays times for a foreign correspondence clerk i wish to offer my services

I was born of english parents in paris and have passed several years of my life in mannheim and cologne and can speak and write both french and german with fluency i also have a fairly good knowledge of spanish

i am 32 years old and for the past four years have been correspondence clerk to messrs saurel et cie of 31 mincing lane ec3 who have extensive foreign connections especially with france and germany during the whole time i was employed by them i was in charge of continental correspondence

if my application is successful i shall do my very best to please you

yours respectfully
james mahon

C

messrs m power & sons 16–20 abbots crescent sunderland

dear sirs

i am writing to inform you that owing to the death of my friend and partner mr william morris i have taken into partnership mr robert constance late of messrs rowbotham & co 19 renfield street glasgow and with his cooperation will carry on this business under the style of

smithson & constance

all accounts of the late firm of smithson & morris will be settled by mr constance and me

thank you for the support you have given us in the past and trusting to maintain our friendly business relations

yours faithfully
r. l. smithson

PART II

BUSINESS CORRESPONDENCE

CHAPTER ELEVEN

The Business Letter

True ease in writing comes from art, not chance,
As those move easiest who have learn'd to dance.
A. Pope: *Essay on Criticism*

A firm's correspondence is often enough the principal means, and sometimes the only means, by which business relations with the outside world are established. It is therefore of the utmost importance that letters sent out should create a good impression. If they are to do this they must be attractively displayed, and unblemished by errors in grammar, punctuation, and spelling. High standards in correspondence suggest high standards of service generally, and a well-typed letter on attractive notepaper may well pave the way to an important business connection.

WRITE NATURALLY

Of all forms of composition, letter-writing is probably the most free and the most agreeable. When you are asked to write a formal composition on a given subject you may fumble for ideas that come all too unwillingly. Not so with letter-writing, which is really "a piece of conversation by post". You would not be writing the letter unless you had something to say, and the nearer what you have to say approaches the level of good conversation, the better the letter is likely to be. Indeed, one test of a good letter is to ask yourself whether the message as written could be read over the phone and still sound natural. If it could, then the letter is probably a good one. Would you say over the phone, *I have received your communication of the 15th*, or *I am in receipt of yours of the 15th, for which I thank you?* Of course you would not. Then why say it in a letter? Why not write quite simply, *Thank you for your letter of the 15th* which is what you would say over the phone and which says the same thing much better. For the business letter the style of writing required is the plain, straightforward kind of English you would use in normal good conversation with a comparative stranger. Once you begin to think of a letter as a literary effort you cease to write naturally.

When writing a business letter you may approach your task in any one of three ways.

(a) You may write in the first person singular if you hold a position of authority, since you are then reporting your personal actions and opinions:

I am sorry to learn from your letter of the 10th that some of the records supplied to your Order No. 572 were damaged when they reached you. In the circumstances you mention I will certainly arrange for replacement of those damaged.

(b) You may write in the first person plural if you hold a subordinate position. By associating yourself in this way with your firm as a whole you give your letter a semblance of authority:

We are sorry to learn from your letter of the 10th that some of the records supplied to your Order No. 572 were damaged when they reached you. In the circumstances you mention we are arranging to replace those damaged.

(c) You may adopt the impersonal approach:

The fact that some of the records supplied to your Order No. 572 were damaged when they reached you is regretted. In the circumstances you mention arrangements are being made to replace those damaged.

As explained in Chapter One, this impersonal approach produces a style of writing that is cold and aloof. It lacks the warm and friendly tone that helps to create good business relations. For this reason, the personal style in writing is generally to be preferred, but provided you don't hop about indiscriminately between singular and plural there is no good reason why the different styles may not be mixed:

We are sorry to learn from your letter of the 10th that some of the records supplied to your Order No. 572 were damaged when they reached you (*1st person plural*). In the circumstances you mention arrangements are being made to replace those damaged (*Impersonal*).

You may also quite properly use the first person singular when referring to your own actions and opinions, moving over to the other two styles when you refer in your letter to matters that concern your firm as a whole:

Dear Sir

I am sorry we cannot send you immediately the catalogue and price-list you ask for in your letter of 12th October (*1st person singular*). Supplies are expected from the printers in two weeks' time (*Impersonal*), and as soon as we receive them we will send you a copy (*1st person plural*).

Yours faithfully

PERSONAL AND BUSINESS LETTERS

Letters, broadly speaking, fall into two classes—personal letters and business letters. Business letters are concerned not only with industrial and commercial life, but also with the business side of personal life—with house purchase; maintenance of property; employment of home-help services; insurance of property, staff and against third-party risks; income tax; purchases for personal and household use; applications for employment, and so on. Personal letters are concerned with family matters, friendships and social engagements and other arrangements of a purely personal sort.

But the distinction between personal letters and business letters is not pronounced; it amounts to little more than this: that more often than not a business letter plays a specific part in a transaction; it is written to achieve a definite purpose and often gives rise to legal obligations. The essential thing about the personal letter is that the language used needs to be flowing and homely, like the piece of familiar conversation it is intended to be. But the business letter calls for language that is precise and a tone that is more formal and dignified than that of the personal letter. It calls, in other words, for a different style, and above all, for clearness and accuracy. The personal letter, on the other hand, invites a colloquial style that is unsuited to the business letter.

For business letters the typewriter is used and copies of outgoing letters are taken and filed for the record. Although the typewriter is now being used more and more generally for personal letters, there is no denying that the handwritten letter is more intimate and personal and, somehow, warmer and more sincere. It is therefore better for short personal letters to be handwritten, especially letters of thanks, congratulation, sympathy and condolence.

Apart from the foregoing, personal letters and business letters do not differ in any essential way. Both call for good English, though some people have the idea that because a business letter must be business-like it calls for a special kind of English, hedged about with all sorts of meaningless expressions such as *I have to inform you* and *We beg to acknowledge*. Such language is both unnecessary and undesirable.

Business letters in turn fall into two classes—routine letters and letters calling for special care. The former are stereotyped, follow a conventional pattern and are often left to the typist. The latter relate to matters involving special knowledge, or requiring logical presentation of facts to ensure clarity, or careful wording to ensure the right tone. Some of them may be drafted by the typist from verbal instructions or short dictated notes. Others may be important enough to require dictation either from a prepared plan, or even from a dictated longhand draft.

It is a popular but greatly mistaken belief that communication by letter is cheaper than communication by telephone especially over long distances, but modern costings show that to dictate, type and post a letter can be a very expensive business. It may sometimes be cheaper to telephone over trunk routes than to send a letter; it is certainly quicker and may be more effective since the correspondent's reaction by phone is immediately known. It is estimated that the average cost of a letter by a shorthand-typist who produces twenty letters a day on a wage of £100 a week is over 60p, and to this must be added the cost of the dictation, the cost of stationery and postage, and a proportion of overheads. The cost of these additional services would more than double the figure mentioned. The special merit of the written over the verbal message is that it is capable of greater precision and provides a record for reference.

EXPRESSIONS TO AVOID

In business letters terms peculiar to the business world must sometimes be used, but such terms have precise meanings that are accepted and understood by those who use them. They clarify rather than obscure the message conveyed. Terms such as *c.i.f.* (meaning that the price quoted covers not only the cost of the goods themselves but also the cost of their insurance and transport), *E. & O.E.* (meaning that the seller reserves the right to correct any errors contained in the invoice), and similar terms are part of the technical language of business, but except for these, the ordinary language of everyday life is all the business letter needs—the ordinary language of good conversation is good enough. Avoid as far as possible words such as *herewith, aforesaid, furthermore, whereas, undermentioned,* and *inasmuch*; they are out of place in a business letter, and should be reserved for the legal documents to which they properly belong.

Avoid, too, the use of commercialese, with its *valued favours, esteemed enquiries,* and *enclosures herewith.* Used in this way *valued* and *esteemed* are quite meaningless; they are relics of an age when the accepted style of business letter-writing was very different from what we regard today as good business writing.

THE NEED TO BE BRIEF

A good business letter is one that expresses the writer's thoughts clearly, in simple language, and in as few words as possible. In a personal letter brevity may be mistaken for rudeness, but in a business letter to be brief is to be business-like. Never write more than you need to make your meaning clear. You must, of course, be polite, but when you have said all there is to say, bring your letter to a close. Do not, in an attempt to provide an effective close, add flowery and meaningless phrases, of which *Thanking you in anticipation* is probably the arch offender. There need be nothing rude about a plain, straightforward statement, though if it is one likely to prove disappointing to your correspondent, explain why the position is as you state. If, for example, you are unable to supply on time the goods you promised by a certain date, at least explain why, if only to protect your goodwill. Besides, such an explanation is no more than common courtesy.

The advice "Be brief" must be accepted with caution. Never seek for brevity at the expense of clearness, or carry it to the point that it gives rise to further correspondence, thus wasting instead of saving time. Where there is much to be said a long letter will be inevitable, but in the saying you can achieve brevity by choosing words wisely and shunning all unnecessary words and phrases.

Businessmen have many letters to read, and naturally wish to gain their information without waste of time. They welcome the kind of letter that is clear, crisp and to the point, that tells them what they want to know without forcing them through a maze of long-winded sentences and phrases to find it. But, on the other hand, the directness associated with brevity must never be confused with curtness. Be brief by all means, but never curt.

The following is an example of tedious wordiness:

Dear Sir

We are in receipt of your letter of the 20th instant, and have pleasure in informing you that the order you have placed with us will receive our best attention, and that the twelve electric blankets you require will be sent to you as soon as we are in a position to supply them.

We are, however, very sorry to say that our stock of these blankets is at the moment very depleted, and owing to the prolonged cold weather and the resulting demand we have been informed by the makers that they are unlikely to be able to supply us with a further stock for another ten days or so.

We are extremely sorry not to be able to satisfy your requirements immediately, but we assure you that we always do everything we possibly can to see that your orders are met promptly. Should you find yourself unable to obtain elsewhere the blankets you need, or if you are able to wait for them until the end of the month, you will perhaps be good enough to inform us.

Once again expressing our regret at being unable to fulfil your order on this occasion with our usual promptness, and trusting you will continue to favour us with your continued custom.

We remain
Yours truly

What are the essential points in this letter?

(a) that due to the prolonged cold weather, the demand for electric blankets has been exceptional;
(b) that further supplies are expected in ten days' time;
(c) that if the order is allowed to stand, prompt delivery will then be made;
(d) regret that delivery cannot be made at once.

Here is the same letter rewritten. It says in a much more business-like way all that needs to be said, and in about half the length:

Dear Sir

We thank you for your order of 20th January, but very much regret that, because of the exceptional demand for electric blankets due to the prolonged cold spell, we are at present out of stock of the make you ordered. The manufacturers, however, have promised us a further supply by the end of this month, and if you could wait until then we would ensure the prompt delivery of the twelve you need.

We are indeed sorry that we cannot meet your present order immediately.

Yours truly

True brevity consists in saying only what needs to be said, and in avoiding tedious and unnecessary detail. It does not mean saying less than the occasion demands, but it does mean not saying more.

Nor is brevity to be achieved at the expense of good English. *Yours of the 5th to hand* is both brief and clear, but it is not good English; it is not even a sentence. Although *I have received your letter of the 5th* is longer by two words, it is at least good English and is therefore to be preferred. Good English, like clearness, must never by sacrificed to brevity.

STUDY YOUR CORRESPONDENT

The main reasons for writing a business letter are to establish a business relationship without personal contact and to provide a record for subsequent reference. There is also a less obvious reason—that of creating in the mind of the receiver a good impression of the writer's firm, and also of the writer himself as an efficient person eager to be of service. In Chapter One we referred to the need to look at things from the reader's angle, in other words to "stand in the reader's shoes". We must sense his feelings and anticipate his reactions and, having done this, write what we have to say in the spirit in which we want it to be received. We must ask ourselves, "What would be my reaction to this or that?", "How should I feel about it?" Not until we have done this can we begin to think of the best way to say what we want to say.

Remember that some people are very sensitive to criticism and be careful to avoid, for example, the implied criticism in such expressions as *"Thank you for your undated letter concerning ..."* and *"Please get in touch with us again if you do not understand the instructions."* Say instead: *"We have just received your letter concerning ...", "Please let us know if you feel we can be of any further help."*

Business, we know, deals with goods and services rather than with people, but even so, every business transaction depends in the last resort upon the decision of some person. When writing, then, look at your message through the eyes of your correspondent; imagine yourself to be the reader rather than the writer and try to sense the sort of reaction your message is likely to set up. It isn't difficult to do this, for when we write, "I hope to *come* to your meeting" we should write "*go* to your meeting" to be strictly correct. We speak of *coming* rather than *going* only because we are looking at the matter from our correspondent's point of view.

To fulfil its purpose your letter must be "*you* centred" and directed to the reader's interests. It must adopt the *you* rather than the *I* or *we* attitude; your reader is much more interested in what you have to say than he is in you.

This ability to adapt himself to the point of view and outlook of his correspondent is the outstanding quality of a good letter-writer, and a good letter will always be written with the reader's reactions in mind. This does not mean that you must necessarily accept your correspondent's views, but it does mean that you must so express your own as not to cause ill-feeling or offence.

The letter in the first column on page 179 is a reply sent by a wholesaler to a retail customer who owed him £270. The customer has sent a cheque for £50 on account, explaining that he was having difficulty in collecting amounts due to him from his own customers. He confidently expects to be able to settle his account in full by the end of next month, and hopes that in the meantime the wholesaler will supply the further goods now ordered.

The tone of the wholesaler's reply is unfriendly. It is likely to cause resentment, especially as the retailer has explained that he expects to settle his account in full very soon.

In the second column the wholesaler's reply is rewritten in terms that pay more regard to the retailer's probable reactions and are less likely to cause offence.

GENERAL ADVICE—A SUMMARY

We cannot do better than conclude this section by summarizing some of the advice given by Sir Ernest Gowers* to officals who have letters to answer. We are indebted to Her Majesty's Stationery Office for permission to use the passages quoted.

---

* *Plain Words* (HMSO), 1948, pp. 14–22.

The reply sent	*The reply suggested*
Dear Sir	Dear Mr............
Your letter of the 3rd inst., with cheque for £50 on account, is to hand.	Thank you for your letter of the 3rd enclosing your cheque for £50 on account.
We note what you say as to the difficulty you experience in collecting, but we are compelled to remark that we do not think you are treating us with the consideration we have a right to expect.	We are sorry to learn that you are having difficulty in collecting amounts due to you from your own customers, but at the same time do not feel that we should be expected to carry the burden of this.
It is true that small remittances have been forwarded from time to time, but the debit balance against you has been steadily increasing during the past twelve months until it now stands at the considerable total of £270.	We value the payments you have made from time to time and your efforts to reduce the amount of your account with us, but we are concerned that the outstanding balance should have steadily increased during the past year to the now considerable sum of £270.
Having regard to the many years during which you have been a customer of this house and the, generally speaking, satisfactory character of your account we are reluctant to resort to harsh measures.	Because of your long connection with us and the generally satisfactory state of your account we have no wish to press you unduly, especially as you hope to be able to settle your account in full by the end of the month.
We must, however, insist that the existing balance shall be cleared off by regular instalments of, say, £50 per month, the first instalment to reach us by the 15th instant, and that in the meantime you shall pay cash for all further goods, we allowing you an extra 2½% discount in lieu of credit.	Should you not be able to do this we feel it not unreasonable to ask you to clear it by monthly payments of, say, £50, commencing on the 15th of this month. In the meantime we shall be happy to supply further goods on a cash basis, and to allow you an extra 2½% discount in lieu of credit.
We shall be glad to hear by return that you agree to this arrangement, as otherwise we shall have no alternative but definitely to close your account and place the matter in other hands.	We shall be glad to learn that you agree to the arrangement suggested, since we sincerely wish to avoid either closing your account or placing the matter in other hands.
Yours faithfully	Yours sincerely

Answer the question

Study your correspondent's letter carefully and be sure you
know what he is asking before you attempt to reply. It is frustrating to receive only some of the information asked for.

> "Adapt the atmosphere of your letter to suit that of his. If he is rude,
> be specially courteous. It he is muddle-headed, be specially lucid. If
> he is pig-headed, be patient. If he is helpful, be appreciative. If
> he convicts you of a mistake, acknowledge it freely and even with
> gratitude."

Write naturally

Avoid formality if you can. Try to write in a tone that is natural
and friendly. To shed formality may not be easy, for "the old
style still shackles the new". Even so, you must try. It is still the
fashion to start off with *In reply to your letter*—an opening that
often leads to awkward constructions. It is a phrase you would
not think of using when replying to a friend, nor is it always
necessary to use it in a business letter.

> "Do not think it necessary", writes Sir Ernest, "always to begin by a
> reference to your correspondent's letter; use your judgment. See if
> it will not do to give your letter a heading and then go straight to the
> point without any frills. ... If you cannot make the opening *In reply to
> your letter* run on naturally, but feel bound to begin with a reference
> to the letter you are answering, make it a complete sentence, as for
> instance: *I have looked into the question of so-and-so about which you wrote
> to me on such-and-such a date,* or *I am writing in reply to your letter of* ...
> The difficulties created by the need to live up to the words *In reply to
> your letter* ... are responsible for half the icicles that so often strike a
> chill to the heart of the readers of letters of this type."

If however you feel you must begin with *In reply to your letter*
make sure that you introduce the next part of the sentences with
the pronoun *I* or *We*. You cannot say *In reply to your letter, the
goods you ordered have been sent today,* since it establishes a wrong
relationship between the opening phrase *In reply to* and *goods,*
the subject of the sentence. It is *you* and not *the goods* who are
replying to the letter.

Avoid wordiness

Choose words with care and use them with economy; be as brief
as clearness and courtesy permit.

> "Use no more words than are necessary to do the job. Superfluous
> words waste your time and official paper, tire your reader and
> obscure your meaning. There is no need, for instance, to begin each

paragraph with phrases like *I am further to point out, I would also add,* ... Go straight to what you have to say."

Prefer the short sentence

In the interests of clearness prefer the short sentence to the long.

"Keep your sentences short. This will help both you to think clearly and your correspondent to take your meaning. If you find you have slipped into long ones, split them up."

Avoid commercialese

Avoid the type of commercial expressions fashionable at the beginning of the century, and which with some writers still persist.

"Avoid commercialese expressions such as *same* as a pronoun ('I have received your letter and thank you for same'), *re your letter to hand, beg to inform, party* (for person) and *enclosed please find.* ... Some of our mentors would include *ult., inst.,* and *prox.* in this ban, and there is no conceivable reason for preferring them to the name of the month, which has the advantage over them of conveying an immediate and certain meaning."

Choose the simple word

Prefer the simple word to the more unusual. It is more likely to be shorter and will certainly convey the message more clearly.

"Of words with meanings equally precise choose the common one rather than the less common. ... Do no say *advert* for *refer;* or *state, inform* or *acquaint* when you might use the words *say* or *tell;* or *regarding, respecting, concerning* or *in relation to* when what you mean is *about.* ... Do not say *thereof, thereto, therein* or *thereunder;* use the preposition with the appropriate pronoun—*of it, to it,* etc."

Although the advice in *Plain Words* was written for civil servants, it applies equally to the business-man.

Be precise

Use expressions with precise meanings. When acknowledging a letter, refer to it by date, subject and reference number (if any). When referring to dates mention the month by name and avoid using *instant* or *inst.* (for the present month) *ultimo* or *ulto.* (for the past month) and *proximo* or *prox.* (for the next month). Say, *Thank you for your letter of 25th October concerning.* ... If information you are seeking is needed urgently, say, *Please let me know at once* and not *as soon as possible.* Never *acknowledge receipt of a favour,* but state precisely what you have received—a *letter,* or better still, an *enquiry,* a *quotation,* an *order,* or whatever you have received.

Avoid also using such vague expressions as *considerable quantity, reasonable price, appreciable rise* and, instead, state the quantity, the price and the extent of the rise.

EXERCISES

1. Rearrange the following extracts from letters so as to make what improvements you consider to be necessary:

A

(a) Replying to your enquiry of the 5th inst., the quotation we sent you only relates to goods ordered during this month.

(b) Our traveller will pay you a call on Monday next with samples of our goods for the coming season, when we trust you will favour us with an order.

(c) All communications should be addressed to the secretary of the company, when they will receive prompt attention.

(d) Your esteemed letter of the 4th inst. duly received, and I read with much pleasure your account of your interview with our traveller.

(e) I have to acknowledge receipt of your authorization and have duly registered same.

(f) In reply to your enquiry of yesterday, the external decoration of the house is expected to be completed by the end of this week.

(g) I have to inform you that the goods arrived this morning, and would also add that we are very pleased with same.

(h) We are in receipt of your postcard of the 3rd inst. and beg to inform you that the samples of artificial silk were dispatched to you yesterday.

(i) We duly received and thank you for your enquiry of the 17th inst. and have pleasure in quoting you for the charcoal as follows.

(j) We beg to enclose herewith a price-list, trusting to receive a continuance of your patronage and assuring you that, at all times, our best attention shall be given to your commands.

B

(a) We acknowledge receipt of your letter of yesterday's date, and note that you are in a position to supply the timber we require.

(b) We should be glad if you will telex us Friday afternoon your lowest price for flooring tiles.

(c) Replying to your favour of the 15th inst., we beg to enclose draft proposal from our contractors.

(d) We beg to confirm acceptance of your offer of 300 tons of "Sunbrite" fuel.

(e) We have much pleasure in handing you herewith a booklet entitled *Everything Electrical*, wherein you will find brief descriptions of the many articles we supply.

(f) In the matter of price we believe that our figures will, as formerly, show to our advantage when compared with those of any other maker.

(g) We have great pleasure in advising you that, on and after the 1st prox., Mr Walter Barton, the eldest son of our senior partner, will be admitted a member of the firm.

(h) I beg to inform you that, owing to the decease of my friend and partner, Mr William Morris, I have taken into partnership Mr Robert Anderson, late of Emberson & Co., Glasgow.

(i) In thanking you for your valuable and much esteemed patronage in the past, permit us to inform you that we have recently acquired more extensive premises.

(j) I have to inform you that the registered offices of this company have been removed to more central premises at 140 Long Acre WC2E, to which all communications should in future be addressed.

2. The following is a reply to a letter from a customer regretting his inability to settle his account, the reason given being the small demand for goods recommended as a good selling line by the supplier's traveller. Reconstruct it so as to improve its tone as you think necessary:

Dear Sir

We beg to acknowledge receipt of yours of yesterday's date, in which you intimate that you are unable to make a settlement just now, but hope to remit part of it in a week or two. This is not satisfactory. Far from the goods being slow-selling, we have had from dealers in your town no less than fourteen repeat orders, some of them for large amounts. We cannot but think that had you actively pushed the sale of our goods you would long ago have exhausted your stock. Anyhow, it is hardly fair that you should expect us to suffer from your own failure; and, though we have no desire unduly to press you for payment, we must ask you to remit us the whole amount due, on or before the 16th of next month.

Yours faithfully

3. The following is a rude and angry letter sent to a firm of heating engineers who failed to complete a central-heating installation by the promised date. Replace the letter by one more suitable and more courteous, stressing the inconvenience to which you are being put and pressing for early completion of the work:

Dear Sir

I have received your letter explaining why you did not complete the installation of the central heating by the date promised. I am afraid I am not at all satisfied with the reasons you give for the delay; they sound very much like excuses and are not in the least convincing.

I now wonder whether, when you promised to complete the work by 9th May, you really felt you could do so. Your later promise to recommence work on the installation you have also failed to keep, nor have I received the courtesy of an explanation why. It is evident that the promises you make are not to be relied upon.

My only concern now is to get the installation finished and in working order as soon as possible, and I now hope you will do something about it. I propose to give you another ten days in which to complete the work, and if by that time you haven't done so I shall take it out of your hands and arrange for it to be completed by another contractor.

Yours faithfully

4. The following is an exact copy of a letter received from a firm of office-equipment suppliers. Correct its many faults:

Dear Sirs

Order No. 9238

We are in receipt of your letter dated the 11th inst. and note your remarks. We are very concerned at the complaint you have made, and wish to offer our sincere apologises.

We would point out that we sell quite a number of these stools during the course of the year, and a complaint such as this has never arisen before, and we have taken this matter up with the works very severely, and trust that we will be able to advise you of there explanation of this defect in the near future.

However, we hope to be able to despatch to you within the next few days, eight new sets of rubber feet, and trust that this will solve your problem.

Apologising once again for the inconvenience caused and assuring you of our best attention at all times.

Yours faithfully

5. Reconstruct the following letter, arranging the various ideas in such order and using such language as will make the reader's task easier:

Dear Sir

I am now in a position to advise you that the builder has committed himself to the completion of the central heating installation and other work by the second week in May at our new bungalow at No. 14 Basildon Avenue, Cleveleys. I wrote to you earlier on the subject on 1st April last.

The situation of the various radiators has now been agreed with the builder, and also the towel rail in the bathroom, and these will affect of course the cutting out of the carpets you are providing us with, and I will advise you directly when the position makes it possible for us to have them laid.

The material for the curtains is a metre and a half in width, and if you will advise me as to what length of material will be necessary I will arrange to acquire the material for them. The pattern consists of stars. It is repeated at intervals of about five centimetres. It is a close one. We also desire to make use of the same material for the pelmets. I take it that you will be in a position to furnish the necessary linings for the curtains. We shall require them, that is the curtains, to fall below the window sills to approximately the levels of the radiator tops. The radiator in the front bedroom will approximate to 60cm high from the floor. In the lounge it will be 50cm. We shall be able to acquire a suitable material for the curtains in London. The actual making and fitting are matters than can be given consideration subsequent to our moving in. It is our wish that they should be arranged on runners in such a manner that it will be possible to draw and close them by cord from one end. The runners should preferably be plastic rather than brass.

I hope you will be able to do the needful.

Yours truly

6. Imagine that while away from home you have lost an umbrella, raincoat, or other accessory. You think you may have left it in a shop which you visited. Write to the manager asking him if it has been found there. (RSA)

7. Write a letter to a friend recommending a certain secretarial course which you yourself have taken, giving some particulars about the course, and referring to the benefits you have derived from it.

8. You have recently bought a new typewriter, but it is not giving you satisfaction.

(a) Write a letter to the makers, giving reasons for your dissatisfaction, and asking them to send a representative to call on you.

(b) Prepare the reply of the maker to the foregoing letter, expressing his confidence in the machine, and stating that he is arranging for a representative to call to examine the machine and advise you about its use and care.

9. Imagine that you have just taken over a well-known and popular fabric stores, the services of whose staff you will be retaining. Prepare a suitable circular letter to be sent to the stores' former customers, notifying the change of ownership and inviting continued custom.

10. A fire has taken place in one of the departments of a large general stores of which you are manager.

Draft and set out in proper form a circular letter to be sent to the stores' customers, notifying that the department will be temporarily closed, and that a certain amount of stock, slightly damaged, will later be on sale in other departments. It is hoped to re-open the department in about three weeks' time with entirely new stock.

11. Mr Abel Whitehead, Office Manager, Wilkinson, Sons & Co Ltd is interested in a new "Ajax" duplicating machine which he has seen advertised in *Office Magazine*. The magazine contains a long and complimentary article on the machine. He instructs his secretary to write to the manufacturers asking them to arrange for one of their representatives to phone and make an appointment to demonstrate the machine. There is a prospect of an order for several of these machines if the demonstration proves satisfactory.

As Mr Whitehead's secretary write, or type, the letter for him to sign.

12. The secretary of an engineering firm talks to his secretary as follows:

"During last July Anderson & Sykes Ltd installed central heating in the new offices, but the system isn't at all satisfactory. For one thing the radiators don't warm up as they should, nor does the thermostatic control seem to be functioning. Ask them to come along as soon as they can to check the installation thoroughly and make whatever adjustments may be necessary. I want to be quite sure that the system is in full working order before winter sets in. Write a courteous letter to them. I will sign it myself."

13. Write one of the following letters:

(a) From a manufacturer to a customer who has used his own vans to return certain goods supplied in excess of his order. As from the manufacturer, apologise for the inconvenience caused to the customer and suggest that he submits a claim for the expense incurred in returning the goods. Tell him that the amount will be credited to him in his next account.

(b) From the secretary of a firm that uses the services of an office-cleaning agency. For some weeks past the firm's offices have not been cleaned properly, and after writing a letter of complaint you find that it was sent to the wrong agency. Write a letter of apology for the mistake.

14. Write one of the following letters:

(a) To a customer who is slow in settling his accounts. He is a valued customer and you don't want to offend him. Inform him that your own commitments are based on an expectation of prompt payment from your customers and appeal to him for co-operation so that you may conduct your own financial arrangements on a sound basis.

(b) A customer complains that you have not credited him with the value of damaged goods which he claims he returned to you five weeks ago. Reply to his letter and inform him that you have no trace of the goods having been received and ask him for further details, including particulars of the goods, the date on which they were returned, by what method, and to whom they were delivered.

15. Write one of the following letters:

(a) From a textile manufacturer to a customer whose orders in recent months have tended to fall off. Invite his attention to some new fabrics that are selling well in other towns and hope he will be interested. Mention that on orders received before the end of next month a special discount of 5 per cent will be allowed on these fabrics in addition to the normal trade discount. Stress the importance of prompt ordering as present demand for the fabrics is heavy.

(b) From the secretary of a company to the manager of a fashionable restaurant, where he wishes to make arrangements for a centenary dinner-dance for his firm's employees and their guests. His letter contains full particulars of the requirements as to date, time, approximate numbers and food, and enquires about cost. It also asks for suggestions that would help to make the occasion a memorable one.

APPLYING FOR A POST

If you are still at school or college you will one day be applying for a job. The following may help you.

First, and most important of all, you must have the qualifications needed. The best letter in the world will not make up for lack of experience or ability. But if you really believe that you can competently handle the job, then go ahead and apply.

How to apply

You may make your application in either of two ways. You may write a letter and with it enclose a résumé (a c.v.) of your experience and background or you may write a comprehensive letter containing all the information you need to give. The former arrangement has two merits to commend it. First, the letter you write gives you a chance to reveal something of your personality and of your attitude to work; secondly, the résumé provides a ready means of referring to factual details. Your prospective employer will appreciate both.

The covering letter

To serve its purpose your letter must be something more than a mere covering letter forwarding an enclosure. You must not neglect the opportunity it affords to show your ability to write a good business letter, and to stress those aspects of your qualifications most likely to be of special interest. You must express yourself concisely, yet attractively. Your letter must be correctly addressed, sensibly punctuated, and properly spelt. It must be business-like in appearance, that is to say well arranged, and not written or typed on paper that is more suitable for social than for business purposes. Use plain, good quality white paper of either quarto or international A4 size, with matching envelope. Your letter will be half judged before it is even read, and the slightest failure in any of these matters may be enough to seal your fate at once; carefully prepared, however, it may put you in the lead even before the interview takes place.

If the post you are applying for includes typing as part of the work your application should certainly be typed, and signed *in ink*. Even if the work does not include typing, it is advisable to type the letter unless you are asked to apply in your own handwriting, or the post is one of a purely clerical or book-keeping nature. Not only is a typed application business-like, but it also makes for easy reading, and an employer handling fifty or more applications will naturally welcome anything that makes his task easier. Moreover, a well-typed application attracts attention and creates a favourable first impression. Even so, many employers still like to see a specimen of candidates' handwriting, and if your application consists of a covering letter with a résumé, and if the covering letter is short, it should be handwritten and the résumé typed.

What to include
If you are asked to write to a Box number, address your letter to "The Advertiser, Box No. ...". You can then quite logically start your letter with the salutation "Dear Sir". Confine yourself to information in which the advertiser is likely to be interested and do not include particulars of minor examination successes in subjects that have no bearing on the post applied for, but on the other hand, give details of your training and of your highest successes in relevant subjects.

Testimonials are of little practical value since candidates submit only testimonials that are favourable, and so they are rarely asked for nowadays. But if they are, do not send the originals since they may not be returned; send copies only and take the originals with you should you be called for interview.

The terms of your letter must be specific. General statements such as "*I am an experienced typist*" and "*I have been employed by Lamb & Co. for three years*" do not help an employer very much. Give him details of your ability to type—mention your typing speed and the kind of work you have been engaged on. He will then know what to expect from you. Likewise, in the matter of references do not say, "*I am able to provide references, if required*", but give the names and addresses of persons who are willing to speak for you, having, of course, first obtained their consent. Mention also the capacities in which they have known you.

It is from your résumé that an employer will be able to assess what you can do now. But he may be more interested in the kind of person you are and in how you are likely to develop in the next five or ten years, or more. He can best judge this from the way in which you enlarge on the details given in your résumé. That is why your letter is important. If you think it will help, enclose a photograph, but let it be small and business-like.

Planning the letter

Bear in mind what is said in Chapter Twelve about planning a lette. Your application letter is, after all, the first important business letter you will write, and it is well worth while to spend time and care on it. It is a letter in which you are trying to sell your services, in much the same way as a sales representative sells the products of his firm. It must therefore be attractive, persuasive, and convincing, but always truthful and straightforward. Never make claims you cannot justify, but by all means show a proper appreciation of your qualifications and say, "I can", rather than, "I think I can".

Figure 1 gives an example of an application letter, but it is intended only as a guide and not for imitation. Never copy someone else's letter, but be original and write your own. It is *your* personality, *your* attitude to work, and *your* outlook on life in which the employer is interested.

Remember, too, that yours is probably only one of many applications. You must therefore make it stand out from the rest. Stress what you can offer that is different in kind or degree from what other candidates can probably offer—a second language for instance. Give it an interesting send-off. Phrases such as *"With reference to your advertisement in ..."* and *"I am writing to apply for the post of ..."* are overworked and make tedious reading for anyone faced with a profusion of them. Try to start your letter with something a little more interesting.

For example:

Immediately I saw your advertisement in ... for a private secretary I felt it was just the kind of post for which I have the qualifications and for which I have been looking for some time.

Visualize the kind of work the new post involves or, better still, find it out if you can and then stress any qualifications you may have for that sort of work. If, for example, attendance at meetings and preparation of reports on them is involved, make an

26 Gordon Road
CHINGFORD E4 6AT

15 May 19..

The Personnel Manager
Leyland & Bailey Ltd
Nelson Works
CLAPTON E5 2QA

Dear Sir

I feel I have the necessary qualifications and experience needed for the
position of private secretary to your managing director, advertised in the
Daily Telegraph.

When I left Woodford County High School at eighteen it was intended that I
should go to University College, London, to read modern languages, but owing
to my father's death I was unable to accept the place offered. I then
decided to train for secretarial work and, as you will see from the résumé
enclosed, successfully completed a two-year course at the Bedford Secretarial
College.

My first post, with Babcock, Harris & Co., called for high standards of care
and accuracy in shorthand and typewriting, often in conditions of urgency.
This experience has been most valuable. I left college with speeds of
150 and 50 words a minute in shorthand and typewriting respectively, and
these speeds I have at least maintained.

As personal secretary to the managing director of Reliance Cables I regularly
attend and make reports on meetings and interviews, receive callers and, in
his absence, make minor decisions and deal with much of his correspondence
on my own initiative. I also make detailed arrangements connected with his
attendance at conferences, both in this country and overseas, and deal with
many of his personal matters such as payment of accounts, renewal of licences
etc.

The kind of work in which your company is engaged particularly interests me,
and I welcome especially the opportunity it would afford to use languages.
Having spent much time on the Continent I speak and write French and German
well and hold G.C.E. passes at 'A' level in both.

Enclosed are copies of testimonials by Mr. S. Astins, C.B.E. and Canon J.
Bardeley. These, and the references given in the résumé will I feel sure
vouch for my ability to get on well with people and to work happily and
efficiently. I like responsibility, enjoy the challenge of new situations,
and derive much pleasure from improving my abilities and from helping others
to improve theirs.

I hope I may be granted an interview, when I can explain my qualifications
more fully.

Yours faithfully

Miss Jean Carson

Fig. 1. *Letter of application.*
The letter must be well arranged and business-like in appearance.

important selling point of any experience you may have had in this field.

Show that you are genuinely interested in the post offered, and avoid suggesting an overwhelming interest in yourself by cramming your letter with questions about salary, superannuation, sick pay and holidays. The purpose of your letter is to get an interview and these are matters you can suitably discuss at the interview, if you get one; if you do not get an interview they cannot concern you. Unless asked to do so, make no mention of salary, except perhaps to say that it is a purely secondary consideration. Should the advertisement ask you to state a salary, deal with the matter tactfully. You can do so in a number of ways:

> Say you are prepared to accept any salary which the firm ordinarily pays for the type of work;

OR,

> if you are not prepared to move except for more money, mention your present salary and say you hope there would be some improvement on this;

OR,

> if you wish to be more precise, find out what is normally paid by other firms and then suggest a range—say, £5,000 to £5,500 rather than a specific figure.

A little flexibility of this kind will probably help you.

The résumé

The résumé will provide your personal details and a summary of your qualifications. It must therefore be thought about and prepared with care. Since it is the source from which you will select the items you wish to stress, it must, of course, be prepared before you write your letter.

It must be attractively set out. The items summarized must consist only of bare facts, and be classified and grouped under concise headings in a way that makes for quick and easy reference (*see* Figure 2).

You will include facts about your education, examination successes, training and special qualifications, present and previous employment, with dates. Personal details will include your age (or date of birth), whether you are single or married, the number of children, your health, outside interests, and so on. Particulars of persons to whom reference may be made should be

```
                    APPLICATION BY JEAN CARSON

                26 Gordon Road  Chingford  E4 6AT
                    (Telephone:  01-524-3546)


                      PERSONAL DETAILS

Age: 26; Single                    Special Interests: Music, languages
Health: Excellent                  Activities: Hockey, golf, swimming
Photograph: Enclosed

                        EDUCATION

Woodford County High School, 19.. to 19..  G.C.E. 'O' level 7 passes
                                                  'A' level 3 passes

Bedford Secretarial College, W1Y 2EB, 19.. to 19..  Secretarial Diploma

  (a) Subjects studied:

        English        Secretrial Duties      Accounts
        Shorthand      Commercial Mathematics  French
        Typewriting    Current Affairs         German

  (b) Practical Training:

        Typewriters (all standard   Duplicators (Gestetner,
           makes, including            Roneo, Banda)
           electronic)              Dictation machines
        Telephone switchboard          (Dictaphone, Emidicta)

  (c) Special awards:

        Royal Society of Arts:  Silver medal for Shorthand. 150 w.p.m.
        Governors' prize for first place in College examination

  (d) Activities:

        Member. Students' Union Committee
        Vice-captain. Hockey, first team

                      BUSINESS EXPERIENCE

Shorthand-typist                    Secretary to Managing Director
Babcock, Harris & Co                Reliance Cables
Solicitors                          Vicarage Road
                                    Leyton E10 9BN
60 Kingsway WC2B 6HG                (April 19.. to present)
(September 19.. to March 19..)

                         REFERENCES

  Dr R G Davies, Principal, Bedford Secretarial College W1Y 2EB
  Mr W Harris, Partner, Babcock, Harris & Co, 60 Kingsway, WC2B 6HG
  Mr W J Godfrey, OBE, Managing Director, Reliance Cables,
                          Vicarage Road, Leyton E10 9BN
```

Fig. 2. *Résumé of qualifications.*
The items summarized must consist only of bare facts, and
be grouped for quick and easy reference.

given at the end; two or three are usually enough. The reference of a person leaving school will usually be to the head. An applicant with business experience should refer to present or previous employers.

Courtesty requires that names and referees should be given only after you have requested and obtained permission. It will enable referees to reply to enquiries more helpfully if you have given them some details of the post for which you apply.

Ten Commandments

1. Remember that the immediate purpose of your letter is not to get the job, but to get an interview.

2. Prepare your application to stand out from the rest; make sure it is of good appearance—well typed and attractively set out. You will have many competitors.

3. Don't make exaggerated claims, or over-use the "I". "Modesty will serve you better than conceit."

4. Avoid writing a starchy letter; write sincerely and in a friendly tone, but without familiarity.

5. Avoid discussing salary, except to say that it is a secondary consideration.

6. Don't suggest you are applying for the job because you are dissatisfied with your present one.

7. Don't suggest that you find your present work boring; on the contrary, make it quite clear that you enjoy it.

8. Make your covering letter informative; not too long, but to the point.

9. Give the details in a carefully planned résumé.

10. After the interview write appreciating the courtesy shown; you will create a good impression by doing so.

EXERCISES

1. On 25th April James Loeber applies for the position of Cashier/ Book-keeper advertised in the *Evening News* by J. Wilmot & Sons, Bankside Mill, Darlington. Applicants are required to state salary. The person appointed would be responsible for handling cash and for keeping all books of account. Loeber is 27, holds an RSA certificate for advanced book-keeping, and has had ten years office experience with three different firms, from two of which he encloses copies of testimonials. Write a suitable letter of application.

2. From the Situations Vacant column of any newspaper select a vacancy for which you consider yourself qualified, and write a letter of application.

3. Write letters of application in answer to the following advertisements:

(a) Clerk, 17–20, wanted for invoicing. Must be rapid and accurate with figures. Previous experience desirable, but not essential. Address full particulars, age, salary, etc. Box 321, *Daily Telegraph*, Fleet Street, EC4N 5AB.

(b) Private Secretary required for Sales Manager. Must be expert shorthand-typist, with good education. Good appearnace and personality essential. Experience in similar post desirable. Apply R. Thomas & Arnold Ltd., Willow Bank, Leeds LS11 2QA.

4. Write a letter of application for a post, just advertised, as sales assistant in the household equipment department of a large local store. You are interested in prospects of promotion and pension scheme. Deal with these matters tactfully.

5. Answer the following advertisement:

Experienced shorthand-typist required for local solicitor's office. Must be able to work without supervision and on own initiative. Write, stating age, education, experience, and salary required, to C. Hindley & Co., 25–27 Pendleton Street, Manchester M4 3QP

6. Write a suitable reply from an eligible reader of the following press advertisement and attach a brief summary of her career:

SECRETARY/SHORTHAND-TYPIST required by international group. Good shorthand and typing speeds and working knowledge of Spanish. Hours 9–5, 4 weeks' hols. Age, sal., experience and other material details. Box 542 *Daily Telegraph*, Fleet Street, EC4N 5AB.

7. Write a letter of application in answer to the following advertisement:

Well-educated private secretary required by managing director of large firm of constructional engineers. Applicants must be between 25–35 years of age, with good shorthand and typing speeds, and a working knowledge of French and German. Must have initiative and personality. Write to personnel manager, Hardwick & Long Ltd., Victoria Buildings, Liverpool L5 3TN.

8. Write a letter of application for the post of Private Secretary of a professional institution. Give details of your experience and qualifications.   (*ICSA Pt. 1*)

CHAPTER TWELVE

Planning the Letter

There are three classes of writers: those who think before they write; those who think while they are writing; and those who think after they have written.

B. L. K. Henderson: *The English Way*

There are four main reasons for writing business letters:

(a) to provide a convenient and inexpensive means of communication without personal contact;

(b) to seek or to give information;

(c) to furnish evidence of transactions entered into;

(d) to provide a record for future reference.

There is also an important incidental purpose—that of building goodwill by creating in the mind of the reader an impression of the writer's organization as one that is efficient, reliable and anxious to be of service.

If letters are to fulfil these requirements effectively, hasty composition will not do. Letters must be carefully thought out and planned.

First consider what you want your letter to do. Is it to seek or give information or advice, to promote a sale, to get an interview, to remedy a grievance, or merely to create good will? Think of the person you are writing to. What sort of a person is he? What does he hope or expect to get from me, and what sort of reception is he likely to give my letter? Not until you have answered these and similar questions can you say what should be said in the way most likely to achieve the result you are after.

The need for the writer to put himself in the shoes of his reader has already been referred to. No letter can be completely successful unless the writer adopts this attitude of looking at the matter from the reader's angle. The temptation to think about ourselves and our own problems is always great, but the most effective letters are those which concentrate on the needs and interests of the reader and take into account *his* problems and *his* convenience. We cannot dispense with the *I* and the *We* when we write letters, but we can emphasize the *You* and the *Yours*.

THE RIGHT TONE

Although much business is done by telephone or through personal contact, the business letter is by far the most widely used means of communication. Telephone and private conversations that lead to a business deal must usually be confirmed to prevent misunderstanding and to provide a record of the deal. Often enough, too, correspondence is the sole means by which contact with customers is maintained, and the customer's impression of the firm he is dealing with is that created by the tone and standard of its correspondence. To cultivate the art of good letter-writing is therefore well worth while.

There is a certain grace in language called "tone", which is the mark of an educated person. If ignored it may warrant a charge of aggressiveness, tactlessness, curtness or even discourtesy. The tone of a letter reflects the spirit in which the writer projects his message to the reader. The letter must establish rapport with the reader and be accepted favourably by him if the message is to be effective and evoke the response which the writer is seeking. Good tone in correspondence creates its own psychological impact and does much to foster that sense of tolerance and considerateness which makes for happy personal relations. In business such relations are important, and the power to say what has to be said in an effective, finished and even graceful way is a cardinal part of the art of business letter-writing.

The following letters illustrate the importance of tone even in routine business letters:

Dear Sir

On 17th October last we ordered fifty copies of *Business Correspondence and Reports* by L. Henson and stressed the importance of delivery by 31st October at the latest. The books have not been delivered and there has been no acknowledgment of our order.

Please look into the matter at once and let me know when you expect to fulfil the order.

Yours faithfully

The commanding tone of the above letter and the suggestion, implicit in the wording of the message, that the supplier is at fault are hardly calculated to put him in a co-operative mood. It may well be that an acknowledgment of the order was sent and has gone astray and that the goods, despatched on time, have been delayed en route. Now compare the above letter with the improved tone of the following:

Dear Sir

On 17th October last we placed with you an order for fifty copies of *Business Correspondence and Reports* by L. Henson, stressing the importance of delivery by 31st October.

At the time of writing we have not received the books, nor have we received an acknowledgment of our order. Delay in receiving the books is creating difficulties and I shall be glad if you will please look into the matter as one of urgency and let me know when we may expect to receive them.

Yours faithfully

Behind every letter lies a purpose, and a letter is good only if it achieves its purpose. It cannot do so unless the writer is himself clear about his aims, and writes in terms that leave no doubt of his intention in the reader's mind. To this end he must first ask himself, "What is my object in writing this letter; what do I hope to achieve by it?" Then observing an orderly arrangement he must include all relevent information and write in language that is unmistakably clear and to the point. The tone of his letter, too, must be right. He must consider the way in which he wants to influence his reader and express himself accordingly. The tone he adopts must suit both the occasion and the purpose—persuasive, apologetic, conciliatory, friendly, firm and so on. However good in other respects, a letter written in the wrong tone may produce an effect very different from that intended.

The following is an example of the all-too-frequent dull, routine type of business letter. It is an answer to a request by a dealer for a catalogue and price-list of sewing machines; yet the writer failed to seize the opportunity it presented to write an effective sales letter:

Dear Sir

Your enquiry of 15th instant to hand. Enclosed you will find the catalogue and price-list asked for, and I trust you will find them satisfactory.

We are able to meet promptly any orders you may place with us, and feel sure you will be satisfied with the type and quality of our machines.

Yours truly

Here is the same letter written from the standpoint of the manufacturer who realizes the sales-promotion value of his letter:

Dear Sir

Thank you for your enquiry of 15th February. The catalogue and price-list for which you ask are enclosed. The catalogue is our latest, and in its preparation we have spared neither trouble nor expense to make it both attractive and informative. It is profusely illustrated and we believe it contains everything a dealer like yourself will wish to know about our unusually wide range of sewing machines before placing an order. Inside the front cover you will find particulars of our trade discounts.

We know there are cheaper machines than ours on the market; nevertheless our annual output exceeds by some thousands that of all our competitors combined, a fact that indicates the preference of the public for machines of quality.

May we suggest that the next time you come to Manchester you should allow us to show you over our factory, where you would see for yourself the high quality of materials and workmanship put into our machines. It would also enable you to become acquainted with all that is new and up to date in sewing-machine manufacture, and to return with interesting and useful information for your customers.

If we can be of service to you in any way you may rest assured of our interest and help if you care to use it.

Yours truly

This letter as rewritten is not stereotyped in form, but is original and friendly. The writer aims to interest his reader, to create in him a feeling of confidence and win his consideration and friendship—and ultimately his custom.

EXERCISES

1. The following letter is cold and over-emphasizes the *We* at the expense of the *You* attitude. Revise the tone of the letter to show that you are pleased to receive the enquiry, that you have a real interest in the enquirer's problem, and that you wish to be helpful.

Dear Madam

We have received your enquiry about a new typewriter and enclose leaflets which we think give a good idea of the range of makes we can supply. When you have studied the leaflets you may need more information before making a decision. If so, we suggest that you call at our showroom to enable us to demonstrate the various makes of machine we have in stock. We could then give you any further information you may need.

We look forward to hearing from you again.

Yours faithfully

2. The tone of the following letter is hardly courteous. Make what improvements you think are necessary.

Dear Sirs

Referring to your letter of 4th March, we think you must be mistaken when you say you sent us a cheque on 3rd January for the amount then owing on your account. We have no trace of receiving the cheque, and it is most unlikely that we have made any mistake because we have a very reliable method of dealing with inward remittances. Moreover, your letter of 3rd January makes no mention of an enclosed cheque. Surely you would have mentioned the cheque had you enclosed it.

I am afraid we cannot accept your claim that the amount owing has been paid and must ask you to look further into the matter at your end. We expect you to settle your account without further delay.

Yours faithfully

3. The following letter has been sent by an agency superintendent to a client who is dissatisfied with the terms of the policy issued to him. Its tone is aggressive and likely to cause resentment. Recast the letter in conciliatory terms.

Dear Sir

Your letter of 20th April has been passed to me by our agent, Mr L. A. Brazier. I cannot agree that you were misled into taking out the policy. You will remember that I was with Mr Brazier when the terms of the policy were explained to you. All your questions were dealt with in detail, and at the time you expressed yourself satisfied with the answers given. It surprises me that a businessman of your standing should have misunderstood the terms of the policy. You had every opportunity to examine them thoroughly before committing yourself to them.

The terms of the policies issued by my company are among the best obtainable, and I am sure that if you compare them with those offered by other companies you will find that you have no cause to be dissatisfied. In my experience you are the only client from whom we have had a complaint.

Yours faithfully

4. The exaggerated tone of the following circular is likely to fail in its purpose to convince prospective customers. Draft the circular in more reasonable and convincing language.

Dear Sir

Don't forget to visit the most amazing sale ever held. Next week we shall be offering a tremendous number of truly astounding bargains, which you couldn't possibly get anywhere else.

Your present chance to acquire a truly magnificent radio or television set at an incredibly low and unrepeatable price is absolutely un-rivalled, and what is more you will never have another like it. No other store has ever offered anything at all comparable with the stupendous bargains that are now yours for the asking. Don't delay for a moment, or you will miss an opportunity unique in the history of selling.

Yours

5. The tone of the following reply to an applicant for a secretarial post is impersonal and pompous. Write the letter on a more friendly note.

Dear Madam

This letter is to acknowledge your application for the post of private secretary to our sales director. A perusal of your application gave the impression that you have the qualifications and experience necessary to fill the post satisfactorily. Consideration of applications received from other applicants, however, showed that while their qualifica-tions were in no respect superior to your own, their experience was of a kind more likely to be suited to the company's present require-ments. It is therefore with regret that I have to inform you that your present application has not been successful. I am, however, to ex-press the hope that this decision will not deter you from applying for appointment to any similar post that may be advertised in the future.

Yours faithfully

6. Would you agree that the tone of the following letters is satis-factory? If not, reconstruct the letters to give them what you consider to be better tone and style.

A

Complaint concerning delivery

18 March 19..

Dear Sirs

The four electric blankets which we ordered a month ago were not delivered at the beginning of this week as promised. When we placed the order we made it quite clear that delivery by the promised date was most important. If at that time you had any doubt about your ability to keep your promise we feel the proper course would have been to advise us.

Unfortunately, this is not the first time you have failed to keep your promises, and we have now reached the stage when we feel compelled to point out that you cannot expect us to continue business with you on these lines much longer.

When you receive this letter we hope you will send the blankets immediately and take steps to ensure that any future orders we may send you are dealt with promptly.

Yours faithfully

B

Reply to above complaint

20 March 19..

Dear Sirs

We were quite surprised to receive your letter of 18th March. You are quite mistaken about the promised date of delivery, which was the 23rd and not the 13th of March as you state. Nor do we accept your suggestion that earlier promises of delivery have not been kept, except for one occasion last December, when bad road conditions made delivery impossible.

The blankets are being sent to you by passenger train today.

Yours faithfully

THE NEED FOR PLANNING

Planning is as necessary for a business letter as it is for a social event or a demonstration. Whenever you have attended a social function that has run smoothly you may be sure that its details had been carefully thought out beforehand. And have you ever attended a cookery demonstration that has not been carefully planned—where the mixing bowl was not there or one of the ingredients was missing? This is the sort of thing that may well happen to a business letter that has not been planned. Information needed may not have been sought, or information sought may not have been given. In either case there is inconvenience and possibly annoyance, and at least one more letter is needed to put matters right.

To plan a successful letter you must do three things:

(a) You must assemble the relevant facts.

(b) You must select the right approach.

(c) You must be clear about what you want to say, and prepare a plan.

ASSEMBLING THE FACTS

The plan of a letter will differ with the kind of letter you are writing, but whatever the kind of letter, you must first know the facts about it. You must know to whom you are writing and consider how he is likely to think and feel about what you write.

If you are writing for a company you must know what the company's policy is. You must be in possession of all the information that affects the matter in hand—previous correspondence, prices, qualities, dates of delivery and so on. And you must know the circumstances that give rise to the letter. You must know why it is necessary, and how you can fulfil the need for it. If, for example, your letter is one in answer to a complaint, you must know the exact nature of the complaint, whether or not it is justified, and, if justified, who is responsible, and what steps can be taken to right matters. Only when you know these things can you write a letter that will satisfy the complainer. If you are planning an enquiry you must know exactly what information is needed so that you can ask the kind of questions that will bring all the information you want, and not merely some of it. If you are writing about an outstanding debt you must know how much the customer owes, how long it has been owing, what it is owing for, and whether he is a customer worth keeping on your books. If your letter is a reply to one received you must read carefully what your correspondent has to say or to ask about, and make sure you deal with all his points.

SELECTING THE RIGHT APPROACH

If your letter is to have the right tone it must start on the right note. The opening paragraph must be right. If, notwithstanding the suggestions on p. 180, you decide to begin your letter, *In reply to* ... be careful to follow it with *I* or *We*. You may not, for example, write, *In reply to your letter,* YOU *will be sorry* to learn ... Your correspondent is not replying to his own letter. Nor, worse still, may you write, *In reply to your letter,* OUR WAREHOUSE *was burnt to the ground.* If you do, your correspondent will be surprised that his innocent enquiry should have had such a disastrous consequence.

Depending on the type of letter, the opening may be any one of three kinds—direct, indirect or persuasive.

The direct approach

This approach calls for an opening that goes straight to the point, with no preamble or explanatory introduction. It would be used, for example, in a letter enquiring about the supply of goods and in the reply sent. The direct approach is in fact appropriate wherever information is sought or given. The following are examples:

Request for samples

Will you please send us samples and prices of the best notepapers you can offer of the following kinds:

Supply of samples

In reply to your enquiry of yesterday, we are pleased to enclose samples of notepapers of the following kinds:

or better still:

We are pleased to enclose samples of notepapers about which you asked in your letter of yesterday. They are as follows:

Request for quotation

Please quote your lowest price for 10 tonnes of Westmorland stone suitable for rockery work, including delivery at the above address.

Quotation

Replying to your letter of . . . we shall be pleased to supply 10 tonnes of best quality Westmorland stone suitable for rockery work at £16 a tonne, delivered to your address.

The indirect approach

The indirect approach consists of an opening paragraph that makes use of explanatory or other prefatory matter before making the main statement. It is appropriate whenever there is unpleasant or disappointing news to be conveyed. The preliminaries prepare the way for the unwelcome news to be conveyed. This approach should always be used where a request cannot be granted or an order cannot be met, or in any other circumstances likely to cause disappointment to the receiver. Its purpose is to prepare him for what is coming and to temper the blow when it does come. The following are examples:

Publisher's rejection of MS

I am grateful for the opportunity you gave me to examine your MS on *The Law of Contract*. I read it with interest and was impressed by the care and thoroughness with which the subject had been treated, but as we have recently published a book on the same subject, and as your MS covers much the same ground, I am sorry we cannot accept it for publication.

This is a much more appropriate opening than:

I am sorry we cannot accept your MS for publication because ...

It is kinder to the feelings of the author, who is bound to be deeply disappointed at the rejection of his MS, since it represents much trouble and hard work on his part.

Letter declining liability for loss

When we received your letter of 23rd November we sent a representative to inspect and report on the damage caused by the recent fire in your warehouse. He has now submitted his report, which confirms your claim that the damage is extensive. He states, however, that a large proportion of the stock damaged or destroyed was either obsolescent or obsolete. We therefore regret that we cannot accept as a fair estimate of the loss the figure of £15,000 mentioned in your letter, a figure that is based on the original cost of the goods.

EXERCISE

Remembering the importance of a right approach to letter-writing, draft a suitable opening paragraph for each of the situations outlined below. (*Note:* Only opening paragraphs are needed.)

A

(a) The manager of the Clarence Hotel, Didsbury, writes to a firm of heating engineers explaining his wish to install central heating in his thirty-bedroom hotel, and seeks advice on relative merits of different types, and costs.

(b) An office equipment manufacturer who has a number of new designs which he proposes to exhibit at the forthcoming Business Efficiency Exhibition writes to a large insurance company in an effort to gain their interest.

(c) The heating engineers referred to in (a) reply to the letter from the manager giving him details of different systems. They need to inspect the premises before they can quote, and seek the necessary permission.

(d) A customer has written to enquire about the supply of high-class stationery. Reply to this, sending him a brochure containing samples. Include prices and mention discount terms allowed on contracts of not less than one year.

(e) Orders from an old customer have tended to become less and less frequent. Write enquiring why. Hope that dissatisfaction is not the reason. If it is you would like to have details.

B

(a) You are proposing to place an order for 100 pairs of ladies' suède gloves in various shades and sizes. Write to a manufacturer who has been recommended to you. You require such details as qualities, colours, prices and delivery date.

(b) Write thanking an important customer for a large order. You are pleased at the confidence in you which his order suggests, and promise careful attention.

(c) A customer has ordered 150 pairs of house slippers of your manufacture. You cannot fulfil the order by the date mentioned. Give an imagined reason for this.

(d) You have received an order for goods you no longer stock. Write regretting inability to supply, and explain why.

(e) Write referring to a customer's order. Tell him the goods asked for cannot be delivered on time, and give an imagined reason.

The persuasive approach

This is the approach to use when you wish to sell a product or to convert the reader to your way of thinking. Its essential aim is to arouse interest. This is done in the opening paragraph. Somehow or other this paragraph must appeal to the reader's interest in himself or in matters that concern him. Most people are interested in saving time or expense, in their health, personal appearance and prospects of advancement. These are rational interests. People also have emotional interests such as fear, pride, display and social prestige. The opening paragraph should be addressed to the particular interest that you feel will encourage the reader to want to know more about the proposal you are making.

Persuasion is based largely upon your knowledge of your reader's needs and feelings. The persuasive approach is appropriate to what is termed the sales letter, a letter that is which aims at selling a product or an idea. Such letters frequently take the form of circulars, and the expense of time and money involved in distributing your letter widely in large numbers makes it all the more necessary for it to be just right for the occasion. To succeed in its aim your letter must accomplish four things. It must gain attention, arouse interest, create a desire for the thing or idea you are selling, and finally it must prompt the reader to

take whatever action you are recommending—to visit your
showroom, see a representative, send for a sample or make a
purchase. Once you have managed to arouse interest, you need
not worry about attention; it will be there.

In a sales letter the opening paragraph is vital; it will deter-
mine whether the letter continues to be read or finds its way
unceremoniously into the waste-paper bin. If it arouses curiosity
so much the better. This may be done by offering something
new, such as the first domestic washing-machine, or something
old in a new guise, such as a tuner/amplifier with quadrophonic
sound. You then continue by showing how the product can
benefit the reader, following it up by evidence of its efficiency
and good value. Your letter needs to convey the assurance that
what you say about your product is true and that the claims you
make for it can be relied upon. Then finally, to evoke from your
reader the action you want him to take, you make it easy for him
to take it, e.g. by providing a prepaid-postage card or envelope.

The following are examples of paragraphs likely to arouse
interest:

An appeal to financial gain

Can you say that you have an expert knowledge of conditions in
thirty foreign countries, and that your information concerning trade
opportunities abroad is completely reliable and up to date? If not, we
can perhaps help you. We have representatives in thirty different
countries who regularly supply us with reports on current market
conditions. They are working for you, to provide you with the information you need to increase your exports.

An opening like this will catch the interest of a manufacturer
who is seeking outlets for his products and, if followed by some
details of the kind of information the reports contain and a
statement that the reports will be supplied regularly on payment
of a small subscription, it holds out the promise of a successful
sales letter.

Most people would like to be able to speak well, but many lack
the confidence to try. An opening paragraph such as the following is likely to do all that is needed to get the letter read:

An appeal to self-esteem

Are you nervous when asked to propose a vote of thanks, to take the
chair at a meeting, to join in a discussion, or make a speech? Then
you are one of the people for whom this letter has been written.

An opening such as the following would almost certainly
arouse interest and urge the reader to find out more:

An appeal to money-saving

If you are looking for a means of cutting your domestic fuel costs by 20% you should read the following:

If the letter then goes on to explain that the fuel-saving effected over a period of two years would be enough to pay for a permanent system of roof insulation that would save five times its cost over the next ten years the reader is given a strong incentive to act.

EXERCISE

Remembering the special importance of the right approach in sales and similar letters, draft an opening paragraph for each of the following:

A

(a) As a local school outfitter you write persuasively to parents of pupils drawing attention to your wide range of clothing for all school purposes.

(b) Take any advertisement from a newspaper or magazine and use it as a basis for the opening paragraph of a sales letter.

(c) Just out is a publication entitled *Everyman's Lawyer*, written in everyday language. The contents cover an extensive field, including house purchase, hire purchase, pensions, traffic laws, insurance, employment, neighbours, wills and many other aspects of everyday life. As publisher prepare the opening paragraph of a circular letter to be sent to addresses taken from a telephone directory.

(d) Imagine you are the manufacturer of "Shampfloor", a floor cleaner that eliminates all stooping, mopping and scrubbing. Draft the opening paragraph of a letter to be circulated to housewives.

(e) The Excelsia Teleprinter Company is preparing a circular letter for business houses. The printed word can now bridge time and distance; no more mistakes, delays or extravagant costs. Draft a persuasive first paragraph.

B

(a) You are principal of a commercial college and have prepared a questionnaire to find out what qualifications are needed for successful secretarial work. You wish businessmen to whom it is to be sent to complete it and return it promptly. Write the opening paragraph of a covering letter.

(b) The committee of a charitable organization concerned with the welfare of old people have decided to solicit donations from local businessmen and instruct their secretary to prepare a circular letter.

(c) Imagine you are a builder with six £60,000 bungalows for sale in a fashionable seaside town. They are ultra-modern, in pleasant

semi-rural surroundings, and have excellent shopping and transport facilities. Write the first paragraph of a letter to a person who is about to move into the town.

(d) You have been appointed as secretary of the committee responsible for organizing a bazaar to provide funds for your parish church. It is decided to approach local tradesmen, in the first place by letter, for gifts of articles to be sold at the bazaar. Draft the first paragraph of the letter you would send.

(e) Assume you have recently taken over a business that specializes in the sale of LP records but which is in poor shape because of the unsatisfactory service given by the previous owner. You have completely reorganized the business and greatly improved its stock, are well qualified to advise on purchases, and guarantee to obtain records not in stock within twenty-four hours of order. Draft the first paragraph of a circular to be distributed to local householders, soliciting their custom.

PREPARING THE PLAN

When you write a letter try to imagine you are talking to the person you are writing to. Put yourself in his place and try to imagine the sort of questions he might ask. Then go ahead and write your letter, dealing with all the points you think he might have put had you been in conversation with him. Give him all the information he is likely to want, simply, clearly and without trimmings. The simpler the message, the clearer it is likely to be. Think about what you want to say before you begin to write and not while you are writing, or worse still, after you have written. Jot down the points you wish to make as they come to you; never mind the order. Then rearrange them in logical sequence so that your message reads naturally and fluently. This will make it all the easier for your reader to understand. Suppose, for example, your letter is one of complaint that certain work promised for a specified date has not been completed. Then the logical sequence of the points for your letter would be:

(a) a reference to the promise made;
(b) the fact that the promise has not been kept;
(c) that you are inconvenienced in consequence;
(d) a request to complete the work without further delay.

If the letter is short or routine this sort of planning may be unnecessary. But many business letters are not short or routine, and because of their importance need to be thought about and planned before they are written or dictated. If you are one of those who dictate letters it will save time for the typist if you run through your morning's correspondence before calling her in, and jot down either in the margins or on separate slips the points you propose to make. Having done this, number the points in the order in which you propose to dictate them. As a practised dictator you will then have no difficulty in saying at once what you want to say in the order in which you have thought it best to say it. Your letters will be all the better for this. Moreover, dictation that might have occupied an hour will have been disposed of in half the time.

If you are one of those still learning to write business letters you will have ideas of course, but they will need to be worked out. You will need to plan your letters until, like the practised dictator, you can manage with a few odd notes as reminders. You must first have a clear mental picture of the letter you wish to write, its purpose, the propositions you wish to make, or the questions you wish to ask. In a word, you must be quite clear about what you want to say before you begin to write. If the purpose of the letter is not clear in your own mind you cannot expect it to be clear in your reader's.

To clear your mind you will need to prepare a plan as a foundation and a framework for what you want to say. It really means that you have to begin writing your letter before you start it. A few minutes devoted to thinking out what you are going to say and how you are going to say it will help to prevent your letter from being routine and monotonous, give it individuality and character, and make it more effective.

Your written plan need not be elaborate. It is no more than a tool to help you to write your letter, and nobody but yourself is going to see it. You can write it in the margin or on the back of the letter you are answering, or sketch it out on a piece of scrap paper. Besides clarifying your ideas, the plan will help to prevent important details from being overlooked; it will also make the actual writing of the letter easier.

The first step, then, in writing a business letter is *to think*. Ask yourself these questions:

(a) What is the purpose of my letter; what do I want it to do?

(b) What sort of person am I writing to, and how can I make my letter interest him?

(c) What are the points I want to put to him?

(d) What is the best point for a first paragraph to attract his attention and arouse his interest?

(e) What can I do to make my letter sound natural and friendly; if he were sitting on the opposite side of my desk how would I say what I am wanting to say now?

DRAFTING THE LETTER

If your letter is an important one it may be necessary to prepare a draft. Don't depend on starting your letter with *Dear Sir* in the hope that the greeting will inspire you. It won't. First think out what to say and set it down in rough draft form, point by point. This in the end will save time you would otherwise waste in making one attempt after another until a satisfactory letter emerges.

No-one but yourself need ever see your draft, so don't worry if at first reading it doesn't sound well. The important thing is to get your thoughts down on paper. Never mind if they are not in the right order, or if your sentences are not phrased in the best way. You can do the polishing-up later. Then read your draft through, imagining yourself to be the reader of the letter and not the writer. If possible, read it through aloud. Many business letters, or parts of them, are at some time or other read at meetings or over the phone to someone who has to be told or consulted.

As you read through your draft ask yourself such questions as the following:

(a) Can I shorten my letter without in any way detracting from its clarity, e.g. by deleting unnecessary words or condensing wordy phrases? In the sentence, *A knowledge of German is an essential condition of the appointment, and a knowledge of French would be a distinct asset*, the words *essential* and *distinct* add nothing to the meanings of the words they qualify and should be left out. The following sentences could both be shortened by using the single words in brackets to replace the phrases in italics:

> The attitude of our competitors *in relation to* (towards) our activities is unreasonable.
> Rates of pay vary *in relation to* (with) length of service.

In the sentence, "*I would point out that* we cannot extend the offer beyond the end of this month" the words in italics should be omitted as mere padding.

(b) Does my letter contain any expressions so badly phrased as to give offence? I am too busy to see you tomorrow is good plain English, but it is also blunt to the point of being rude. It would be much better and less hurtful to say, *I regret I cannot make an appointment to see you tomorrow.*

(c) Have I made any claim I cannot make good, or said anything that could be taken as libellous? If, for example, you complain about the standard of service provided or the quality of goods

supplied, you have every right to say, *I am far from satisfied with* (or *I do not accept*) *your explanation,* and *Your advertisement is grossly misleading,* but you cannot say, *Your representative is grossly incompetent,* or *You knowingly misled me* without laying yourself open to a legal action for defamation.

A well-thought-out letter is likely to be shorter and more to the point than one not previously thought out. And there is more life in a short well-thought-out letter than in a wordy long one.

To help you to plan letters of your own some examples follow.

Plan 1: Report on an examination
The candidates entered by a school for a certain examination have done badly and the examiner has been asked for a special report on their work.

As the examiner you will first jot down, *as they occur to you,* the points you propose to make. When you feel you have covered them all you will arrange them in logical sequence as the basis for your letter.

Rough jottings
1. Enquiry
2. Summary of results
3. English
4. Presentation
5. Handwriting
6. Spelling
7. Untidiness
8. Grammar
9. Individual questions
10. More interest in English
11. More time needed
12. Many candidates unsuitable

Prepared plan
1. Refer to enquiry.
2. Summarize school's results and compare with general results.
3. Take each question and comment on candidates' performance.
4. Poor English standards:
    (a) bad presentation— handwriting poor; work untidy,
    (b) bad spelling—examples
    (c) bad grammar—examples.
5. Suggestions;
    (a) don't submit candidates obviously unsuitable;
    (b) more interest needed in English aspect of work;
    (c) is enough time being given to subject?

Plan 2: Reply to enquiry about bicycles
A retailer has sent an enquiry to a bicycle manufacturer. He wants information about models, prices, delivery dates and conditions and guarantees. Here is the plan for the reply:

Rough jottings	Prepared plan
1. Thank	1. Thank for enquiry.
2. Summary of models	2. Enclose price list.
3. Guarantee	3. Details of charges for extras— gear case, colour enamelling, accessories.
4. Reputation for quality	
5. Assure satisfaction— testimonials	4. Summary of models, with details of gearing, size and weight.
6. Delivery	
7. Price-list	5. Two-year guarantee on each machine.
8. Extras	
9. Trade terms	6. Good stock available— immediate delivery.
10. Payment terms	7. Trade terms: 30% off list.
11. Anticipate order	8. Terms of payment: 2d% monthly.
	9. Reputation for high quality.
	10. Assurance of satisfaction— buyers' testimonials.
	11. Look forward to order and hope for mutually profitable trade connection.

Plan 3: A sales letter

Insulaglass Ltd. prepare a circular letter for distribution to occupiers of new property in a good-class residential area. Their circular is based on the following plan:

Rough jottings	Prepared plan
1. Heat loss	1. Insulation can reduce fuel costs by as much as 45%.
2. Insulation and fuel costs	
3. How Insulaglass works	2. Explain nature of heat losses:
4. Facts and figures	(a) with conventional heating, house colder;
5. Reasons for superiority	
6. Testimonials	(b) with central heating, fuel costs higher, since thermostat controls temperature.
7. Easy to lay	
8. Durability	
9. More warmth and comfort	3. How Insulaglass works (diagrams to show air circulation).
10. Enclose reply card	
11. Price reduction on prompt orders	4. More warmth, more comfort; entire house warmer.
	5. Reasons for superiority of Insulaglass.
	6. A thoroughly tested material (give facts and figures).
	7. Testimony from previous customers.

8. Explain how to lay—easy.
9. Its hygienic and durable prop-
   erties.
10. Complete enclosed card; rep-
    resentative will call and
    give estimate; no obligation.
11. 5% reduction on all orders
    placed before end of July.

The foregoing plans are somewhat elaborately drawn. In business, or even in the classroom, something less detailed may be all
that is needed. Nevertheless, they demonstrate an important
general principle which, if followed, should help you in your
business letter-writing, especially when you come to write letters
that are lengthy or important.

To write an important letter without first preparing a plan is
like sending a company of soldiers on parade without a leader
and expecting them to shuffle themselves into position in readiness for inspection.

FORM LETTERS

It is inevitable that in every business there should be much correspondence that is routine. Many of the letters sent out fall into
patterns; basically they say very much the same thing. Routine
enquiries and requests for catalogues and other specific information
can frequently be met by the same type of letter. The same phrases
constantly recur. Repeatedly to dictate the same letter or phrase-
ology would be a waste of time. Once experience has shown the
kind of matters that constantly recur, many firms prepare standard
or form letters and paragraphs for use as occasion demands.
Some firms use dozens of them, and from a selection of standard
paragraphs often find it possible to make up complete letters.

Since these standard letters and forms are intended for use
over and over again, they must naturally be prepared with
special care. Copies are made and numbered and placed in a
Form Book, and either classified or indexed, or both. At least two
identical Form Books must be in use, one by the dictator and one
by the typist. The dictator is then able to instruct his typist to
send, say, letter No. 5 or letter No. 12. Or he may instruct her to
build up a letter by beginning with, say, form paragraph No. 5
followed by paragraph No. 10, followed possibly by a dictated
paragraph to cover some point not touched on by any of the
standard paragraphs in the Form Book.

In composite letters made up in this way from standard paragraphs transition from one paragraph to the next may sometimes be abrupt. Transitions can be made to run smoothly by slight alterations of wording, particularly in the opening sentences of new paragraphs. This is something that can usually be left to the typist if she is capable.

A reliable system of form letters and paragraphs saves valuable time, and if the prototypes have been well prepared ensures a uniformly high standard of letter-writing. The system, on the other hand, is not without dangers, since a wrongly chosen letter or paragraph may easily cause confusion. There is a danger, too, that letters and paragraphs may not be kept up to date to meet changing conditions, or where possible improved.

Form letters may also consist of a pre-printed supply of letter forms with blank spaces for the inclusion of variable items of information—reference numbers, correspondents' names and addresses, dates and sums of money. Against the gain of time saved by using pre-printed form letters for conveying information must be set the loss of personal touch which individual letters would provide. It is a loss that must be carefully weighed when the introduction of printed form letters is being considered.

This drawback does not apply to documents prepared by word-processing apparatus, where forms and letters stored in the "memory" can be merged with names and addresses and other variable items of information to produce documents that appear to have been typed individually.

CIRCULAR LETTERS

Circular letters are used when it is wished to supply the same information to a number of people—to members of societies, ratepayers, a firm's employees and its customers, and so on. More often than not circulars are sales promotion letters. Like advertisements in newspapers and magazines they are addressed to many, but more usually they are sent only to selected readers who are likely to be interested by virtue of social class, age or connection with some particular trade or profession. Because of their wide circulation they need to be drafted with care. Names and addresses can be obtained from many different sources. These include specialized directories and society membership lists. There are also agencies that specialize in compiling classified lists of the kind useful to advertisers of different types of product or service, e.g. drugs for doctors and pharmacists, kitchen equipment for hotels and boarding houses, and translation services for exporters.

Since circular letters are unsolicited, recipients have no particular interest in your message. You must therefore keep your letters as short as possible and capture interest in the opening paragraph, otherwise the recipient's reaction will be "just another circular" and he may well throw it away without bothering to read it. Give your letter an interesting look and make it as "personal" as you can, observing the following guidelines.

(a) *Print your letters, preferably in imitation type,* using good quality paper with an attractively-designed letter-head. They are then much more likely to arouse interest and be read than duplicated letters on cheap paper. A well-produced letter attractively presented has a favourable psychological effect that more than compensates for the relatively small addition to overall cost.

(b) *Seal them in their envelopes.* The mere fact that a letter is under sealed cover arouses momentary curiosity and helps to create interest from the start.

(c) *Invest them with a personal touch.* Give your message a conversational style and a friendly tone, and address recipients by their names if you know them. *Dear Mr Jennings* is much more friendly than *Dear Reader, Dear Subscriber, Dear Householder, Dear Customer,* though these salutations are certainly better than the formal *Dear Sir* or *Dear Madam.*

You can strengthen the personal touch even more by using word-processing equipment for inserting recipients' names and addresses, and even more by signing the letters individually, or if this is not possible by signing in facsimile.

The impression of personal interest is also strengthened if, in the body of your letter, you adopt the more personal *you* in preference to such general expressions as *our customers, our clients, everyone* and *anyyone.* For example:

Instead of	Say
Our customers will appreciate	*You* will appreciate
We are pleased to inform our clients	We are pleased to inform *you*
Everyone will be interested to learn	*You* will be interested to learn
Anyone visiting our store knows	If *you* visit our store *you* will know

EXERCISES

1. Each of the following outlines includes rough jottings for a letter. Delete unnecessary repetitions (each outline includes at least one), and arrange the remaining items to form a connected plan for a letter.

(a) The manager of an insurance company replies to an enquiry from a person who wishes to insure his personal effects during a four-month tour abroad.

(i) Proposal form is basis of contract	(v) Premium covers all clothing
(ii) Enclose proposal form	(vi) Separate policy required for valuables
(iii) Premium covers "baggage" only	(vii) Contingencies covered by policy—specify
(iv) Time short—return proposal form at once	(viii) Thank for enquiry
	(ix) Quote premium

(b) You are proposing to have the exterior of your house painted, and write to a decorator.

(i) Best-quality paint required	(vii) Metalwork black, woodwork cream
(ii) Property bought recently	(viii) Burn off before painting
(iii) Estimate wanted	(ix) Priming and two coats
(iv) Address of property	(x) When can work begin?
(v) Moving in on 1st May	(xi) Early completion wanted
(vi) Work to be completed by then	

(c) You have decided to apply for a post as private secretary to the managing director of an engineering firm.

(i) Reference to advertisement	(vi) Examinations passed
(ii) Hope for interview	(vii) Testimonials and references
(iii) Details of education	(viii) Outside interests
(iv) Age	(ix) Speeds
(v) Qualifications	(x) Promise loyal service

(d) As secretary of an organization formed to aid the blind you are called upon by your committee to circularize local residents and organizations for support.

(i) Predicament of the blind	(vii) Lack of social life
(ii) Imagine yourself blind	(viii) Donations of gifts and money needed
(iii) Special needs of the blind	(ix) Wireless sets especially wanted
(iv) Invite into your homes	(x) Deserve sympathy
(v) Buy articles they make	
(vi) Home visitors needed	

(e) An agency firm in Brazil, offering their services to a British manufacturer, stress the excellent openings for trade in that country and apply for a sole agency.

(i) Good opportunities in Brazil	(vii) Already represent other manufacturers
(ii) Advertising campaign would be productive	(viii) Suggest 10% agency commission
(iii) We have centralized showrooms	
(iv) We have branches in all parts of country	(ix) Action must follow any advertising campaign
(v) Our reputation is high	(x) Give references
(vi) Look forward to appointment	(xi) We have special knowledge of local conditions
	(xii) Can offer first-class facilities.

2. Suppose you are preparing to write the following letters. Adopting an imaginative treatment, first jot down items suitable for inclusion, and then rearrange them in the form of a connected plan. (You are not required to write the letters.)

(a) As a retailer of footwear in a high-class residential area write to one of your suppliers. Tell him you wish to make a striking window display for Christmas, and ask if he can provide you with special display equipment for the purpose. Mention the benefits likely to accrue to him, and ask about charges.

(b) As personnel manager of a large firm write to a firm of caterers asking them to quote for a works' dinner, the first to be held. State where, number of guests, etc., and ask for specimen menus and charges, excluding wines. The information is wanted for a social committee meeting in seven days' time. You want dinner to be a great success.

(c) As the supplier referred to in (a) above reply that you can supply the equipment needed, carriage both ways to be paid by retailer. Alternative displays are available for windows of different sizes. Window-light plant can also be supplied for a weekly rental of £20. Ten days' notice required for supply of either display equipment or lighting plant. Display could be arranged by supplier's staff for a charge of £25–£35.

(d) As a manufacturer of cotton goods thank one of your customers for his order. State when delivery will be made, and how. Tactfully suggest you would like early payment. Hope for further business. Enclose invoice.

(e) One of your customers has complained that curtains supplied are inferior and not in accordance with samples. Reply, expressing regret. Add that some mistake on your part seems to have been made, and that you are arranging to send a representative. Promise to remedy any faults and offer a generous allowance if goods are retained. Point out tactfully that order was not very clear and that you exercised discretion in making the selection.

3. You are secretary of a rapidly expanding company and your directors have agreed to your appointing an assistant secretary to help you. Having interviewed several applicants you have seen one to whom you are prepared to offer the appointment.

Draft the letter you would send him telling him of your decision and explaining what his duties would be.

4. Your directors have decided to appoint an accountant to be responsible for all matters connected with the firm's internal finance. On their behalf you are required to write to the selected candidate stating:

(a) the duties he will be required to carry out;
(b) two matters to which he must pay special attention in so far as the cashier's work is concerned.

Making any assumptions you may consider appropriate, write the letter you would send.

5. Two employees are leaving your company.

One is being dismissed as redundant;
The other is leaving by his own choice.

The managing director wishes to thank the two employees for their services and asks you to draft two separate letters.   (*LCCI Priv. Sec. Dip.*)

6. (a) Last January a firm of publishers placed an order with printers for 5,000 copies of *English for Business Studies* by L. Hamilton on the understanding that an initial delivery of 2,000 copies would be made not later than the end of July. It is now mid-August and no books have been received, nor has any explanation of the delay. Write the letter you would send to the printers.

(b) The cause of the delay in delivery of the books at (a) is a fire at the printer's factory. It severely damaged the machines, but these have now been replaced and the printers fully expect to be able to make an initial delivery of 1,000 copies by the end of August, the balance to follow not later than the end of September. Write to the publishers explaining the position and conveying your regrets and apologies.

7. Write a letter in reply to a request from a radio and television dealer to be appointed sole distributor in his town for your products. Inform him that you sympathize with his request but cannot grant it because it is important for you as manufacturer to increase sales by using as many outlets as possible. Express to the dealer the hope that he will place orders and allow his name to be included in your list of approved dealers.

8. A customer has sent you an order and requested a special discount because of the size and importance of the order. Write a tactful letter giving reasons why you cannot grant the discount asked for.

9. Write *one* of the following:

(a) A letter to the editor of a newspaper protesting against the wilful damage occasioned by youthful visitors to your local park.

(b) A letter to the secretary of a local charitable organization who has asked if it may open an account with your bank. Your reply should give him full instructions on the procedure.

10. A married friend of yours with two young children has recently moved into your town and, having applied to the local housing authority for tenancy of a council house, asks you to write to the housing manager supporting his application. You know the housing manager well. Write the letter you would send him.

CHAPTER THIRTEEN

Form and Mechanical Structure I

The heavens themselves, the planets, and this centre
Observe degree, priority, and place,
Insisture, course, proportion, season, form,
Office, and custom, in all line of order.

Shakespeare: *Troilus and Cressida*

DISPLAYING THE LETTER

Although formality in business letter-writing is rapidly giving way to a less conventional and more friendly style, the layout, or mechanical structure of the letter as it is called, still follows a more or less set pattern determined by custom and not resulting from any deliberate plan. Choice of layout is a matter of individual taste, and while departures from customary form may not be wrong, they may reflect to the disadvantage of those who indulge in them, in much the same way as peculiarities of dress and conduct reflect upon those who practice them. There may be successful exceptions to the rule, but even so, it is better to follow established practice, which is convenient if only because it provides a standard to which the business world has become accustomed, and therefore avoids confusion and waste of time for both sender and receiver.

Good form in letter-writing, like good form in any other activity, comes from making correct practice habitual. It is a good plan to adopt one form of layout and to stick to it. The Civil Service and some business firms prescribe the layout to be used in all their letters.

Because the business letter is now nearly always typed, make a point of studying the style and layout of good models. Among those included in Chapter Twenty-three you will find some that conform to the generally accepted British pattern as well as some that depart from it.

Letter-headed paper and continuation sheets should be

ordered together so that they match. Matching envelopes should also be used. The watermark indicates which side of the paper is the face side, and which the reverse side. All letters should be typed on the face side, if only because of the grain, which makes for neat erasing. The reverse sides of letters are sometimes used for the carbon copies of replies sent, an arrangement that not only economizes in paper and filing space, but also ensures that letters and their replies are kept together.

For most business letters, whatever their length, A4 size paper measuring 210×297 mm (approx. $8\frac{1}{4} \times 11\frac{3}{4}$ in.) is now used, though some firms continue to use quarto-size stationery (*see* p. 289). Whereabouts on the sheet typing should begin depends upon the length of the letter and is a matter of experience. The aim should be to centre the typescript on the page. For long letters, the date and inside name and address must be typed closer to the printed heading than for short letters. If the letter is very short it may be necessary to begin lower down and to shorten the typing line in addition so as to produce a balanced effect. A common fault is to make the margins too narrow and this gives the letter a very unprofessional look. A left-hand margin of about 3cm is normal, with a right-hand margin of corresponding width and a somewhat wider margin at the foot of the sheet. The effect is to frame typescript with a white surround in much the same way as a picture is displayed within its frame. Careful word-division at line-endings will minimize the inevitable raggedness of the right-hand margin and give it a smoother uniformity. By using certain types of machine, including word-processing typewriters, it is possible to justify right-hand margins so that all lines of type are of the same length (*see* p. 378).

Single line-spacing gives a letter an appearance of compactness and is usual for both long and short letters, though double line-spacing is preferred by some for very short letters. But for either single or double line-spacing, typing of the message begins two or three clear line-spacings below the salutation.

Basically, there are two main patterns of layout—the modern blocked style (Fig. 3) and the conventional indented or fully displayed (Fig. 4).

Blocked letter style

The practice of displaying letters in the blocked style saves typing time and is now firmly estalished. Its outstanding feature is the commencement of all typing lines, including those for the date, inside name and address, salutation, subheadings and complimentary close at the left-hand margin of the paper. The loss of clarity occasioned by the absence of indentations may be made good by increasing the number of separate line-spacings between paragraphs from two to three as in Fig. 3.

With this style it is customary to use "open" punctuation, the style of punctuation that omits all but essential punctuation marks outside the body of the letter, e.g. from the inside name and address, the salutation and the complimentary close. This again saves typing time, since it restricts punctuation to its essential purpose of making meaning clear.

Indented letter style

This style takes in the first line of each paragraph of the letter, usually five spaces for pica type, and six for elite, though deeper indentations are sometimes preferred. Use of the blocked style for the inside name and address helps to give the letter a tidy appearance (Fig. 4).

The effect of indenting is to throw into relief the thought-form of the letter and this helps the reader. Traditionally, such items as headings, complimentary closures and designations are centred in relation to the length of the typing line and full, ie. "closed", punctuation is used throughout (*see* p. 138). Criticism of the indented style is that it involves much extra work, especially where a word-processing typewriter is not used.

Semi-blocked letter style

The blocked style suffers from the disadvantage that placement of the date and reference data on the left-hand side of the paper causes inconvenience when particular letters are required from the files. Because of this, many businesses prefer to modify the blocked style by placing date and reference data on the extreme right of the paper, thus making particular letters more readily identifiable in the filing system.

Other variations of the blocked style are sometimes adopted and create a particular form of "House-style", for example placement of the complimentary close and designation of signatory in blocked form in the middle of the typing line (Fig. 5).

The style of display adopted is determined by personal taste or by a firm's preferred house-style, but whichever style is used the business letter consists of seven parts.

(*a*) the letter-head;
(*b*) the reference and date;
(*c*) the inside name and address;

Macdonald & Evans

Estover, Plymouth PL6 7PZ
Telephone Plymouth (0752) 705251
Telegraphic address MACEVANS Plymouth
Telex 45635

RBN/FM   10 January 19..

Mr R W Jackson OBE MA
108 Kingsway
ROCHDALE Lancs
OL16 4UX

Dear Mr Jackson

Revision of Catalogue

We are preparing a revised edition of our Professional and Business Studies
Catalogue. I enclose a copy of the current issue and should be glad if you
would check to ensure that all your books are included and that the
Appendix correctly summarizes their syllabus coverage.

It would be most helpful too, if you would check the classification symbols
indicating the class of reader each of your books is designed to serve.
Classification has proved to be of great help not only to lecturers and
students in selecting books. but also to booksellers themselves.

I look forward to receiving from you details of any necessary alterations
for the reprint as soon as you can let me have them - if possible, please
not later than the end of this month.

Yours sincerely
for MACDONALD & EVANS (Publications) LTD

Roy B North
Director

Encl

Macdonald & Evans Ltd Directors R B North M A Chairman M W Bevans F C A W D J Argent A L Rowers F C A (non-executive) Registered in England Number 488368
Macdonald & Evans Publications Ltd Directors R B North M A Chairman M W Bevans F C A W D J Argent W D Antrobus A L Rowers F C A (non-executive) Registered in England Number 590426
Macdonald & Evans Distribution Services Ltd Directors R B North M A Chairman M W Bevans F C A W D J Argent A L Rowers F C A (non-executive) Registered in England Number 1253538

Fig. 3.   *Blocked form of layout.*

This is the style recommended for use in Civil Service Departments
(*Manual for Civil Service Departments*, HMSO 1974). It is now used by
most large business houses.

Macdonald & Evans

Estover, Plymouth PL6 7PZ
Telephone Plymouth (0752) 705251
Telegraphic address MACEVANS Plymouth
Telex 45635

GBD/FM   4th April. 19..

R. Jameson. Esq., B.Com., A.C.A.
25 Silverthorn Gardens.
BATH, Somerset
BA2 9AN

Dear Mr. Jameson,

A few days ago I wrote to Mr. R. Faulkner, a well-known chartered
accountant in the City, inviting him to read a manuscript on <u>Accounts for
Beginners</u> and advise us on its suitability for publication. He has
replied that he cannot help us because of pressure of work, but he has very
kindly suggested that you might be able to do so.

The manuscript is the work of Mr. F. Baron, a commercial teacher in
one of the London technical colleges. We are attracted by it, and think it
would make a book likely to appeal to the more progressive teacher of
Accounts, as it presents a quite new approach to the teaching of the subject.

We should be very glad if you could read the manuscript and send us a
report on it. We would of course pay an appropriate fee, the amount of
which we could perhaps discuss when you have seen the manuscript.

We look forward to hearing that you can undertake the work for us.

            Yours sincerely.
      for MACDONALD & EVANS (Publications) LTD

            G. B. Davis
            Managing Director

Fig. 4. *Conventional layout of a business letter.*

Some people regard this as the most attractive of all letter-styles. The
indented paragraphs make for easy reading, while the blocked inside
name and address gives an added tidiness to the left-hand margin.

Macdonald & Evans

Estover, Plymouth PL6 7PZ
Telephone Plymouth (0752) 705251
Telegraphic address. MACEVANS Plymouth
Telex 45635

Your ref: KM/fh

13 September 19..

The Principal
Ridgeway Business College
Chingford
London E4 9HD

Dear Mr Graham

The English Way

We are surprised to learn from your letter of the 11th that the fifty
copies of the above title ordered by you on 12th August have not reached
you. We received your order on the 14th and, as our stock records showed
the books to be available, passed it to our warehouse staff the same day.

We phoned the warehouse manager this morning and he confirms that the books
were collected by British Rail on the 22nd for delivery to you.

We very much regret the delayed delivery and the inconvenience it is
causing you and have taken the matter up with the railway authorities at
this end. We will phone you as soon as we have any information about the
consignment. Meanwhile, may we suggest that you make similar enquiries at
your end.

Yours sincerely
for Macdonald & Evans

L Jameson
Director

Fig. 5. *Semi-blocked form of layout.*
Placement of the date on the right simplifies retrieval of filed papers.

(d) the salutation;
(e) the message;
(f) the subscription or complimentary close;
(g) the writer's signature and designation.

A common fault is to type the letter too high on the paper. It should be neither too high nor too low, but nicely placed to preserve an appearance of balance and dignity. Another fault is to leave too little space for the signature. For this, not less than 4cm should be allowed between the complimentary close and the writer's designation. However faultless a business letter may be in matter, style and tone, it will not only create a bad impression but also weaken its effect if it is not attractively displayed.

EXERCISES

1. Type the following letter, using the letter-style illustrated in the facsimile letter in Fig. 4, with open punctuation.

INCORPORATED SOCIETY OF SALES MANAGERS

Clarendon House Bedford Square LONDON WC1N 3HY

Today's date and Ref. JGG/EH

Mr E Arnold 16 Wellington Road BEXHILL-ON-SEA TN39 3DT

Dear Mr Arnold, At the beginning of last month you asked to see a copy of the examination paper in Commercial Law as approved by the Examinations Committee, and I am now enclosing one. I hope you will agree that it comprises a representative selection from the proposed questions that you submitted. (New paragraph.) Regarding Question 14 on Commercial Associations, members of the Committee felt that we should try to find an alternative case to that of *Salomon* v. *Salomon & Co.*, which appears in most textbooks on Commercial Law, and which in consequence would be easily recognized by candidates. (New paragraph.) The inclusion of a less well-known case than *Salomon's* would add greatly to the value of the question, and I should therefore be glad if you would kindly propose an alternative, and let me have it if you can during the next week or so. Yours sincerely, Secretary

2. To what special points would you pay attention when arranging to display a typed letter on headed paper?

3. As secretary of the Excelsior Secretarial College, Britannia Court, Liverpool L3 9HJ, you are required to inform suppliers that as from 1st January next the College proposes to settle all its accounts through the credit-transfer system. Express the hope that suppliers will be willing to accept payment in this way, and explain that advice notes giving particulars of payments you instruct your bank to make will be sent to

them. To ensure that credits are transferred correctly you will need to know the names and addresses of the banks at which suppliers keep their accounts.

Draft and type a suitable letter, and address a copy to Mr J. Clarkson, 15 Ansdell Road, Christchurch, Hants, BH23 4PA.

4. Type the letter given in altered typescript below, as you would in business, ready for signature. Adopt indented layout.

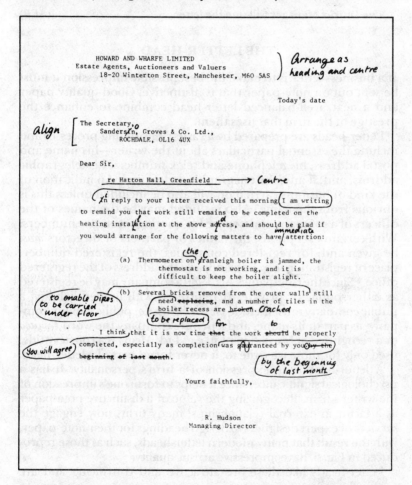

5. Compose and type a letter from the following notes:

The District Manager of Brown. Cox & Thomas Ltd. is writing to a client, M. J. Dixon, of 28 Fitzjohn's Road, Leeds, to confirm that their foreman, Mr Arnold, will call on July 20th at 2 p.m. to inspect

Mr Dixon's house and give an estimate for alterations and decorations. He asks Mr Dixon to write before that date to give the general outline of the alterations he has in mind, the period when the premises would be vacant for the workmen, and the longest period which Brown, Cox & Thomas could have for the work. These points are likely to affect the estimate as considerable alterations carried out in a limited time mean increased costs.

The District Manager will sign the letter.   (*AEB*)

THE LETTER-HEAD

If a business letter is to make the best possible impression it must be sent out on note-paper that is distinctive. Good-quality paper and a neat, well-balanced letter-head combine to enhance the prestige of the firm that uses them.

Letter-heads are prepared by a variety of printing processes and include the essential particulars about the writer—his name and postal address, his telephone and telex numbers, his telegraphic address, and, if any, the telegraphic codes used. An indication of the kind of business carried on will also be included unless this is obvious from the name. Also included may be the names of the officers of a company and a space for quoting reference numbers. With certain exceptions, the names of partners or directors *must* be given and, for registered companies, the registered number, place of registration (e.g. England) and the address of the registered office.* Since the Companies Act 1980 a company may be registered as either public or private. If registered with limited liability, a public company must include *plc* (or *PLC*), i.e. public liability company, as part of its name, and a private company the word *Limited* or a recognized abbreviation of it, e.g. Ltd. *Messrs* is a courtesy title, used only for those we write to; it never forms part of a letter-head.

A letter-head is an expression of a firm's personality. It has a psychological significance, since it helps to form one's impression of the writer's firm. Recognizing the value of a distinctive note-paper as a factor in external relationships, many firms now engage the services of expert designers to design headings for their note-paper, with the result that many modern letter-heads, such as those reproduced in Fig. 6, have impressive artistic quality.

Letter-heads like these are attractive and convincing and are

---

*Names of partners must be included where a firm's title does not include the true names of all the partners (s.18, Registration of Business Names Act 1916). No company may state in any form the name of any of its directors in a business letter, except in the text or as a signatory, unless it states in legible characters the Christian name, or initials, and surname of every director of the company (s.201 Companies Act, 1981).

(a)

Curran
Careers
Centre

Curran House
Regency Place
London W1 2BJ
01-661 1472

(b)

W **Welbeck Constructional**
Engineering Company

P.O. BOX 731   72-76 CANAL STREET, BOLTON, LANCS.
TEL 0204 93765   BL1 3AU

(c)

Charles Kempster

Furniture Repairer and Restorer
The Old Forge Broad Lane Richmond Surrey RI6 3BZ
01-823 7325

(a) This heading is in die-stamped relief, printed black on white. Its appearance is plain, but attractive and business-like.

(b) This attractive heading makes use of two colours in die-stamped relief. The letter W is die-stamped in gold, while the remainder of the heading is die-stamped in blue, on white paper.

(c) This heading is printed in two colours by offset lithography. The trader's name is printed in deep orange and the rest of the printing is in black. The paper used is white.

Fig. 6.   *Modern letter-heads.*

Letter-heads like these are attractive and convincing. A distinctive note-paper adds little to the overall cost of correspondence.

relatively inexpensive. In a brochure issued by the British Stationery Council under the title of *Behind the Symbol* the cost of the average business letter is analysed. Whereas dictation and typing account for an estimated 72 per cent of this cost, headed paper accounts for less than 9 per cent. A distinctive note-paper adds little to the overall cost of a firm's correspondence.

More and more firms are discovering the advantages of what is termed "house-style", that is a standard design, similar to that reproduced in Fig. 7, for use not only on note-paper but also on publications, products, vehicles, and in fact on any of the innumerable items capable of giving outward and visible expression to a firm's personality. One famous example is used by the electrical group EMI who together with HMV, one of its associated companies, continues to display on some of its products the symbol of a dog listening to "His Master's Voice" on an old-fashioned gramophone.

THE DATE

The date should be typed three or four line-spacings below the letter-head and, when used with the indented form of layout, so placed to the right that the last figure serves as a guide for line-endings in the body of the letter, though other placements are now accepted. It should always be typed in full and never abbreviated, such as by shortening of the name of the month (e.g. *Nov.* for *November*). Traditionally, the figure for the day is followed by *st, nd, rd*, or *th* (e.g. *10th February*), but as they are not essential there is a growing practice to omit these letters, particularly with the modern fully-blocked form of layout (e.g. *10 February*). There is, however, no merit in departing from the practice of typing dates as they are pronounced.

Never give the date in figures (e.g. *10/2/19–5*); it could easily be confusing, for instance in correspondence with the United States, where it is the practice to write dates in the order of month, day and year. The English practice, which follows the order of day, month and year, is a logically unassailable sequence and is the order that should always be adopted, thus:

10 February 19..

The practice sometimes adopted of printing 'Date as Postmark" as part of the letter-head is one to avoid. It causes inconvenience and creates difficulties that increase with time, since neither the letter nor the carbon copy bears any indication of its age. Even with postcards, the practice may cause trouble if the postmark is not clearly legible.

Reference codings are dealt with on p. 249

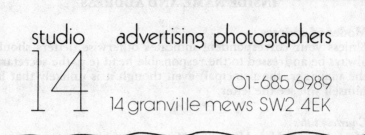

Fig. 7.   *A typical house-style.*

Constant reiteration of a good basic theme is an essential element of
effective publicity. The idea of a house style is a logical extension of this
principle.

INSIDE NAME AND ADDRESS

Modes of address

Unless your correspondent indicates otherwise, letters should always be addressed to the responsible head (e.g. the secretary, the manager, the principal) even though it is unlikely that he himself will see the letter.

Courtesy titles

Mr (or *Esq.*), *Mrs*, *Miss*, and *Messrs* are the ordinary courtesy titles used for addressing correspondents. *Esquire* was originally a title of honour borne by persons of gentle birth who attended on a knight. According to the *Oxford Dictionary* the title is now legally restricted to certain classes of persons (e.g. eldest sons of knights, and also judges, JPs, and barristers). There are some who continue to use *Esq.* instead of *Mr* in business correspondence as a courtesy to all who are regarded as gentlemen, and it is customary to use *Esq.* when addressing men with letters after their names, e.g. W. C. Hall Esq. BSc. but except in the special cases mentioned, *Mr* is the more appropriate mode of address for general use. *Mr* is the preferred form in the United States and is always necessary when forenames or initials are not known (e.g. *Mr Carlton* and not *Carlton Esq.*) *Mr* is also used in letters to minors. *Mr* and *Esq.* are alternative forms and it is wrong to use both. We must not, for example, write *Mr W. Brown Esq.*

Should *Esq.* be used with *Sen.* or *Jun.* its logical position is after and not before, but it makes for greater clarity if it is put before.

Messrs (abbreviated from the French *Messieurs*) is used as the plural of *Mr*, but as opinions concerning its use differ, it is considered more fully in the next chapter. *Mmes* (abbreviated from the French *Mesdames*) is used as the plural of *Mrs*. To distinguish it phonetically from *Mrs* the form of address used for two or more spinsters is *The Misses:*

The Misses Alice and Gertrude Brooks

A married woman should be addressed by her husband's name or initials, if known, and not by her own; if her husband's name or initials are not known her surname only should be used. For example, Muriel Jones, the wife of Harold Jones, should be addressed as *Mrs H.*(or *Mrs Harold*) *Jones*, or *Mrs Jones*, and not *Mrs M. Jones*. A widow, on the other hand, should be addressed by her own Christian name or initials. Where it is not known whether a woman addressed is married or single *Ms* or

M/s has recently crept into use as an alternative for both *Mrs* and *Miss*, but it is not yet in sufficiently general use to warrant its recommendation as an acceptable alternative. When in doubt use *Miss* rather than *Mrs* since many married women in business and the professions often prefer to be known by their maiden names. Should there be doubt about the sex of the person addressed, use *Mr* as most business and professional correspondents are men.

Titles of rank

Where a person holds a special title, such as *Doctor, Professor, Colonel, Sir,* and *Reverend,* he is addressed by his special title which displaces the ordinary titles *Mr* and *Esq.*:

> Dr H. Mason (*or alternatively* H. Mason Esq. DSc)
> Professor A. Wardle
> Colonel S. Mellowdew
> Sir Thomas Marsden
> The Rev. W. Ryan

The title *Sir* signifies a knighthood and is followed by the full Christian name or forename by which the knight wishes to be known. He is therefore addressed as *Sir Thomas* and not *Sir T.* Similarly with the title *Dame,* the rank equivalent to knighthood conferred on a woman, the Christian name is used:

> Dame Margot Fonteyn

As a rule only one title is used, but there are exceptions:

> ADMIRAL SIR James Barker
> THE RT HON. SIR Winston S. Churchill
> THE REV. MR Ryan (*but only where the ecclesiastic's initials are not known; otherwise* THE REV. W. Ryan)

The ceremonious forms of address used for persons of title and rank are found in any good Year Book or Dictionary. A list of the more usual is given in Appendix B.

Addressing reply letters

A letter sent in reply to another must always be addressed to correspond with the signature of the recipient. If he has written signing himself *Frank W. Baron,* it is courteous to observe his preference and to address your reply to *Frank W.* and not to *F. W.* Baron. Always be most careful never to mis-spell his name or to use his initials wrongly. Never guess at his signature, but if necessary verify it from whatever source you can, even if to do so means phoning his secretary. A name mis-spelt may easily cause irritation and create an unfavourable reaction to your letter. Care with the apostrophe is necessary, because some names omit it where it should be included, e.g. *Barclays Bank Ltd.*, *Railway Passengers Assurance Co.*, but *King's College*, London, *Queens' College*, Cambridge (founded by two queens).

Similarly, when addressing a company or firm do so using the full title; these titles have a legal significance. If, for example, you are writing to *Howard Collinson & Co.* address the firm in that way and not as *H. Collinson & Co.*

Many business houses request that all correspondence be addressed "*To the Secretary*" or in some other way, and not to individuals. The request should be respected, otherwise in the absence of the person addressed your letter may remain unopened.

Matters of layout
In ordinary business letters the preferred position for the correspondent's name and address is the upper left-hand side of the sheet, three or more line-spacings below the line of the date, depending on the length of the letter, which should be well placed on the sheet. If "window" envelopes are used the position for the name and address will, of course, be fixed and is usually indicated by guide marks. In official correspondence the inside name and address is sometimes placed in the lower left-hand position—of the first sheet if there is more than one. Of the two arrangements, the upper left-hand position is the more convenient: letters are more readily handled, and the bottom left-hand position remains free for the inclusion of a reference to enclosures.

For obvious reasons the *Post Office Guide* recommends that the name of the post town should appear on envelopes in block capitals, and a similar use of capitals for the inside address is now generally adopted. The county name in lower-case characters follows the town name on the same line, though on the envelope it is more helpful to the Post Office if the county name appears on a separate line.

It is the usual practice to type the inside name and address in blocked paragraph form in alignment with the left-hand margin of the letter. This helps to give the letter a tidy appearance.

Orders, decorations, etc.
Most persons entitled to letters after their names like their qualifications (e.g. *BSc*) and decorations (e.g. *MBE*) to be mentioned.

When they are included, it is important to arrange the letters in order of their status.

Orders, decorations and Crown appointments precede degrees and other qualifications, in the sequence shown below:

(a) Orders (starting with the highest). A higher class of an Order (e.g. a Knighthood) precedes a lower class of a more senior Order (e.g. a Companionship):

KCMG, CB, OBE

(b) Decorations (starting with the highest):

VC, DSO, MC, MM, TD

(c) Crown Appointments (offices to which the holders have been appointed by the Crown):

PC, QC, JP

(d) University degrees (starting with the lowest):

BSc, MSc, PhD, DSc

(e) Professional qualifications:

ACA, AMIMechE, FSCT

(f) Letters denoting professions:

RN, RAF, MP

Here is an example:

L. F. Urmston Esq. OBE MC JP MA

If a person is entitled to several sets of letters it is sufficient to use only one or two of the most important. It is usual, for example, to include letters representing orders and decorations, but, except for doctors'degrees (*PhD, DSc, MD,* etc.), not other qualifications, unless a person is being addressed in his professional capacity. If you write to a chartered accountant about an audit you will include his accountancy qualification, *ACA* or *FCA*, but not if you write to him on a matter unconnected with his profession.

THE SALUTATION

The salutation is the complimentary greeting with which the writer opens his letter. The particular form used depends upon the writer's relationship with his correspondent. To some extent it settles the form of the complimentary close; the two must always be in keeping.

For ordinary business purposes *Dear Sir* (or *Dear Madam* for both single and married women) is used for addressing one person, and *Dear Sirs* (or *Mesdames*) for addressing two or more, as where a letter is addressed to a firm, i.e. a partnership.

There is a growing feeling that we should drop this ancient and stereotyped *Dear*, but modern thought in this country has not yet advanced far enough to shed it in favour of such openings as *Thank you very much, Mrs Jones, for your letter of 28th March*, or *Since receiving your letter, Mr Chapman, I have tried to get the information you want.*

The following are other forms of salutation in use:

Sir	Being much more formal than *Dear Sir*, this form is more appropriate to official correspondence (e.g. with government departments), and to letters addressed to superiors (e.g. by an applicant for a post), than to ordinary business correspondence, where it is now rarely used. *Sirs*, as the plural of *Sir*, should never be used.
Gentlemen	Like *Sir* this is a formal mode of address now mostly reserved for official correspondence and for letters addressed to bodies such as councils, boards and committees. The abbreviation *Gents.* is in very bad taste and must never be used.
Madam	Again, like *Sir*, this is a formal kind of salutation not usually met with in business.
My Dear Sir	This again is more formal than *Dear Sir* and, like *Sir*, is now rarely used in business letters.
Dear Mr Shaw	This more familiar greeting may be used where the correspondents are personally known to each other, or where the writer wishes to establish a relationship of friendly equality between himself and his correspondent. It is used also by concerns that aim to foster the "personal touch" as a matter of business policy. The use of personal names in business correspondence should not go beyond this.

	These forms, in the order given, stand for increasing degrees of familiarity. They should be used only in correspondence of a personal nature between friends or others who are well known to each other.
My Dear Mr Shaw Dear Shaw My Dear Shaw	Only where a writer holds a more important position than that of his correspondent should he address him by surname only, as this implies superior status or at least equal status on the writer's part.
Dear William	This greeting is used only with relatives or others with whom the most friendly relationship exists.
My Dear William	This greeting introduces a note of affection, and is the most intimate of them all.

Whatever its form, the salutation always appears on a line by itself, conventionally three line-spacings below the inside name and address.

Judging by complaints and correspondence in the Press, there is a growing carelessness in regard to names, especially titles. An Air Vice-Marshal understandably objects to being addressed as Air Vice Marshal, which suggests that he is in some way connected with evil-doing. Again, titles such as Admiral, General, Colonel and Commander are a recognition of eminence or distinction in a profession, and it is a sound rule not to abbreviate them, not even when they form part of the inside address or appear on the envelope. In any case, names and titles must always be set out in full when used in the salutation. We may, for example, address ourselves to *Mr Wm. M. Paterson*, but must greet him as *Dear William*, and not *Dear Wm*. Similarly, we may perhaps write to *Col S. Mellowdew*, but must greet him as *Dear Colonel*.

When the correspondent is unknown, and may be either a man or a woman, e.g. a firm's welfare officer, the form *Dear Sir* should be used. In general circulars, but not in any other circumstances, the form *Dear Sir, or Madam* may be used, though with certain circulars it is better to take the trouble to prepare two separate letters, one addressed *Dear Sir* and the other *Dear Madam*. This does represent at least an attempt to do the job befittingly and makes the circular a little less impersonal than it would be otherwise.

In testimonials and other letters intended for general use "To whom it may concern" is a suitable salutation.

Salutions are not used for postcards, departmental letters,

office memoranda, and communications which, like formal invitations, are written in the third person.

EXERCISES

1. Arrange in correct order the items included in each of the following. Then type them correctly as if on headed paper. Pay attention to
setting out and the correct use of titles.

(a) 10/23/19..
Galvin Wm MA JP CBE
Harold Court, No. 14
Reading Berks RG1 2HX

(b) 31/8/19..
Sales Mngr
Hbt. Mallory
F J Mallory & Sons Ltd
Bridge St 32–36
Broxbourne Herts EN10 7DH

(c) 1/9/19..
Margaret Greaves the wife of Harold Greaves
St Albans Herts EN7 4ST
Clifton Dve 32

(d) Oct 22/19..
Dr Harold Cliffe DSc MP OBE
Director (Managing)
Cliffe Laboratories Ltd
Hesketh St
Romford Essex RM1 4EF

(e) 3/22/19..
Lord Chorlton CMG JP MD
Privy Councillor
The Towers
Malvern Worcs WR14 3AT

2. Type in proper form, with open punctuation, the inside name and
address for each of the following. Use the appropriate salutation.

(a) Harold W. Manders, 32 Marine Drive, Ilford, Essex 1G4 5BN has
written to you. He is an Officer of the Order of the British Empire, a
Knight of the Order of the Bath, and a Doctor of Science. Having met
him several times, address him personally.

(b) The Secretary, J. Harrap & Sons. Harraps are a limited company
with their registered office at 67–69 Quadrant Arcade, Longhope,
Glos., GL17 0PD. Address the secretary in his official capacity.

(c) Write to J. B. Lawrence at the County Hall, Preston, Lancs. PR1 3HJ.

Mr Lawrence is the Chief Education Officer of the Lancashire Education Committee, and is an Officer of the Order of the British Empire. Addresss him as if you were Chairman of the Education Committee.

(d) John G. Black, Quartermaster-General's Department, War Office, Whitehall, London, SW1P 4LN. He is a Major-General, a Commander of the Order of the Bath, and a Knight of the Order of the British Empire. He has also been awarded the DSO and the VC.

(e) The Rector at the Rectory, Rochdale, Lancs. OL16 4UX. His name is R. Sharples, and he is a Bachelor of Divinity and Master of Arts, Oxford. He served in the Second World War as a chaplain and was awarded the Military Cross. He has recently been made a Canon of Salisbury Cathedral.

CHAPTER FOURTEEN

Form and Mechanical Structure II

Set all things in their own peculiar place,
And know that order is the greatest grace.

Dryden

THE BODY OF THE LETTER

The foregoing matters are the formalities of business letter-writing. They are no more than ancillary to the main purpose of the letter, which is, of course, to convey a message. This message should follow an arrangement that makes the reader's task as easy as possible. To this end you must take care not only to set out your letters attractively and with unmistakable clearness but also to express them in terms your reader can readily understand.

Much has been said in earlier chapters about the need to write letters in language that is easily understood. The following are no more than reminders:

(*a*) Write simply, clearly, courteously, grammatically, and to the point.

(*b*) Paragraph correctly, confining each paragraph to one topic.

(*c*) Avoid stereotyped phrases and commercialese.

If there has been previous correspondence the place to refer to it is in the opening paragraph. The paragraphs that follow will contain further details, and the closing paragraph a statement of your intentions, hopes, or expectations concerning the next step.

If you decide to start your closing paragraph with a participle, be careful to add *I am, We are*, or some similar expression beginning with a pronoun, otherwise you will commit the common fault of the unrelated participle (*see* p. 60). *Hoping to hear from you* not followed by *I* or *We* is quite wrong. It is better to avoid the participial closure if you can and to say quite simply, for example, *I hope to hear from you soon.* It is, and sounds, much better.

THE SUBSCRIPTION, OR COMPLIMENTARY CLOSE

The complimentary close is merely a polite way of ending a letter. Just as the use of *Dear Sir,* etc., is purely conventional, so is the use of *Yours faithfully, Yours truly,* and similar expressions. Neither salutation nor closure can be logically defended. Is our correspondent as dear to us as our salutation suggests, and is the faithfulness in our complimentary close a really true expression of our reliability? There is nothing faithful about a failure to deliver goods on time, or true about a mistake in sending the wrong goods; yet the letters explaining these things would be signed *faithfully* or *truly.* Used in this way the terms are meaningless; nevertheless, convention imposes these fashions on us, and for the time being we must accept them, always bearing in mind that the expressions used must be appropriate to the occasion, and that salutation and closure must be in keeping. A list of salutations arranged with their appropriate closures is given below.

Salutation	Suitable closure	Comment on closure
Dear Sir(s) Dear Madam Mesdames	Yours faithfully	This is the standard closure for business letters. Like all other complimentary terms, it must always be typed in full, and never as *ffly.*
	Yours very faithfully	This form of closure should never be used.
Dear Sir(s) Dear Madam Mesdames	Yours truly	Now somewhat old-fashioned and little used in business. Being a little less formal than *Yours faithfully* it is sometimes used between persons acquainted with each other, or where a personal relationship exists, as with solicitors, bankers, and doctors.

Salutation	Suitable closure	Comment on closure
Dear Sir My Dear Sir Dear Madam My Dear Madam	} Yours very truly	Expresses rather more feeling than *Yours truly*, and would be suitably used, for example, when acknowledging a favour.
Sir Gentlemen Madam Mesdames	} Yours respectfully	Appropriate only in letters to superiors, but is now no longer fashionable and is best avoided.
Sir Gentlemen Madam Mesdames	I am, Sir (etc.) Yours obediently OR I am, Sir (etc.) Your obedient servant	Except in the Civil Service this form of closure has now disappeared. Nor is it now often used in the Civil Service, having been replaced by the standard form *Yours faithfully*.
Dear Mr Shaw	Yours sincerely	For private letters between persons known to each other, though it has now become fashionable in business between persons well known to each other, or where there is a wish to shed formality and establish a warmer and more personal note in the letter. Indeed, when the salutation mentions the addressee by name, *Yours sincerely* is now the preferred closure.
Dear Mr Shaw My Dear Mr Shaw	} Yours very sincerely	Expresses a little warmer feeling than *Yours sincerely*. (As when refusing a request without wishing to cause offence.)

Dear Trevor	Sincerely	Less formal than *yours sincerely*. Used only between close friends.
Dear Janet	Kind regards	Gives the letter a friendly personal touch. Used between persons well known to each other.
Dear Shaw My Dear Shaw Dear William	} Yours ever As ever	Used between close friends.
Dear William My Dear William	} Yours affectionately	Used between intimate friends.

Avoid the following:

(a) Inverted forms like *Faithfully, Truly* or *Sincerely yours*, or *Cordially yours* (common in the United States). They are somewhat forced and artificial.

(b) Yours, etc. To use this form of closure is in bad taste.

(c) I (We) remain. The closures in the above table serve all occasions.

In order to convey an impression of personal interest a writer will sometimes instruct his typist to omit both salutation and complimentary close from the typing so that he can insert them in his own handwriting. In such cases care is needed to leave enough space for the handwritten insertions, and to see that the information is added to the office copy before it is filed.

If the complimentary close is connected with the last sentence in the body of the letter, as in: *Hoping to hear from you soon, We are, Yours faithfully*, the sentence must be given a paragraph of its own.

> Hoping to hear from you soon
> We are
> Yours faithfully

With the blocked form of layout (*see* Fig. 3), the complimentary close, the name of the firm or company, and the writer's designation or title of office all begin at the left-hand typing margin (*see* Fig. 8(*a*)).

In conventional (indented) layout (*see* Fig. 4) the complimentary close may occupy either of two positions in relation to the typing line:

(a) Towards the right, starting at the middle of the typing line, e.g. at 40 on the scale with pica type, and margins at 10 and 70; or at 45 on the scale with élite type, and margins at 10 and 80 (*see* Fig. 8(*b*).

(b) In the middle, in which case the words are typed to fall evenly on each side of the middle of the typing line (*see* Fig. 8(*c*).

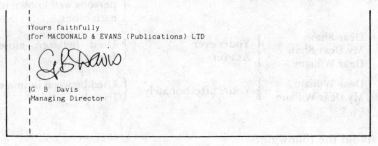

(a) Blocked.
This fully blocked style is that favoured by the Civil Service and most business organizations today.

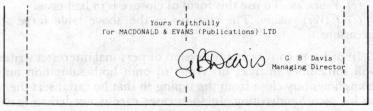

(b) Indented.
This is the style of closure to use with the indented form of inside name and address. It helps you to give the letter an appearance of balance.

(c) Centred.
Some like to use this centred style of closure with the blocked form of inside name and address as an alternative to the indented style illustrated in (*b*).

Fig. 8. *Alternative styles of complimentary close.*

The name of the firm or company, if included, is centred on the line immediately following the complimentary close. Note that only the first word of the complimentary close takes a capital letter. The designation, or title of office, is typed as shown in the examples namely several spaces to the right of middle in example *(b)*, and in the middle in example *(c)*.

Five line-spacings will usually leave enough room for the writer's signature, but it may be necessary to allow more if the signature is a bold one.

The complimentary close must never be separated from the substance of a letter by being carried to a separate sheet. If through faulty judgment this becomes necessary the letter must be scrapped and retyped, with some portion of the subject-matter carried over to the next sheet (*see* p. 405).

Like the salutation, the complimentary close is omitted from postcards, formal invitations, branch and departmental letters, and office memoranda.

THE SIGNATURE

Need for consistency

The signature is the signed name or mark of the person writing the letter or that of the firm he represents. It is written in ink immediately below the complimentary close. Because a signature is the distinguishing mark of the one who uses it, the same style must always be adopted. For example, *M A Webb*, *Maurice A Webb*, *M Arthur Webb*, *Maurice Webb*, and *Arthur Webb* must not be used indiscriminately for the same person. If your correspondent signs as *M A Webb* you must address him as such.

Illegible signatures

An illegible signature is not, as some suppose, an indication of high office; rather it is an indication of inconsiderateness and bad manners. Nevertheless, many modern signatures are illegible and it is now common practice to type the name of the signer above his designation if he has one. The actual signature is then placed immediately above:

Maurice Shaw
Personnel Manager

The signature as written and the signature as typed must correspond exactly. Thus, in the above example the written signature must be *Maurice Shaw* and not *M Shaw*.

It should never be necessary for typists to have to repeat the signature in type, but the practice has now become so firmly established that it is adopted even where signatures are quite legible, and it is unlikely that any general improvement in writing signatures will now change it. The only justification for the practice is that it avoids the embarrassment and annoyance that sometimes result from a misreading of badly written signatures.

Incorporated bodies

An official signing for a registered company or other incorporated body adds to his signature the title of the office he holds and, notwithstanding the use of headed paper, frequently repeats above his signature the name of the organization for which he signs; if his letter is written in the plural *we*, he must do so. The Secretary of a company may, for example, be found to sign in any of the following ways:

Yours faithfully

F A Howard

F A Howard
Secretary

Yours faithfully
WHARFE & HUGHES LTD

F A Howard

F A Howard
Secretary

Yours faithfully
for WHARFE & HUGHES LTD

F A Howard

F A Howard
Secretary

Yours faithfully
on behalf of WHARFE & HUGHES LTD

F A Howard

F A Howard
Secretary

Partnerships

The correct signature of a partner signing for his firm is that of the name of the firm, without the addition of his own name or initials:

Hopkins, Wright & Co

"Per pro." signatures

Strictly speaking, only a partner is entitled to sign the name of his firm, but for convenience authority to sign is often given to a responsible employee (e.g. by a firm of solicitors to their managing clerk) by a document known as a power of attorney, though the authority to sign may also arise from custom. In either case the attorney, or agent, as the authorized signatory is called, signs *per procurationem*, or *per pro.*, sometimes further abbreviated to *p. pro.*, or even *p.p.*, as follows:

per pro Hopkins, Wright & Co

J. Bell

An employee with no special authority to bind the firm should not sign *per pro.*, but as follows:

Hopkins, Wright & Co   for Hopkins, Wright & Co

OR

per J. Bell   *J. Bell*

Authority to sign *per pro.* is also sometimes given to the officials of public companies, but if it is clear that the person signing is an authorized agent of the company, as where the degree of authority is indicated by the title of the office held (e.g. Works Manager), *per pro.* is unnecessary.

Women's signatures

To ensure that she is correctly addressed in any reply a woman writing to a stranger should indicate whether she is married or single. She may do so in the following ways:

If married   (a) *(Mrs.) Alice Brooks*

                    (b) *Alice Brooks*
                        Mrs Alice Brooks

                    (c) *Alice Brooks*
                        Mrs John H Brooks

If single   (a) *(Miss) Dora Ward*

                    (b) *Dora Ward*
                        Miss Dora Ward

If instead of her Christian name or names she uses initials she should indicate her status and sign:

(Miss) J. E. Anderson

or

J E Anderson

Miss J E Anderson

If she fails to show her status she must not take offence if, being married, she is mistakenly addressed as *Miss*, which is the usual form of address for women in business. Socially, a married woman takes her husband's Christian names or initials, but in business normally takes her own, as do widows and women who are divorced. Some married women in business choose to be known by their maiden names when they sign and are of course addressed as *Miss*.

There is a tendency for women in business not to disclose whether they are married or single. They would then be addressed as explained on pp. 232–3.

Signatures by proxy
If a person writes and is required to sign a letter for someone else, this would be indicated as follows:

W S Harris

for Marketing Director

or if the letter is signed for a superior:

W S Harris

for A H Brooks
Marketing Director

Private secretaries
A private or personal secretary will sometimes write and sign letters for her employer, in which case she will sign:

Yours faithfully,

(miss) C. Buckley

Secretary to Mr A Seddon

Facsimile signatures

Never sign your letters with a rubber stamp. A letter that is worth writing is surely worth reading through by the person responsible for it, and to sign it in addition is but the work of a moment. To send out an individual letter "signed" with a stamp is as discourteous as it is unnecessary—discourteous because it suggests that the reader is not important enough to warrant the personal touch of an original signature; unnecessary because the time saved is negligible. If you *must* have a rubber stamp see that it bears a printed and not a facsimile signature, and reserve it for copies for the files, or sent "For information".

Even for circular letters a rubber stamp is not justified. If a personal signature on a printed circular is not possible your printer for a small sum will provide a block with a good facsimile, or if the circular is stencilled the signature can be cut on the stencil.

SOME FURTHER POINTS

Reference numbers

Most letter-heads provide for reference letters and numbers.

When one firm writes to another each will give a reference, and these are marked *Our ref:* and *Your ref:* to avoid confusion.

In a fully-blocked layout references are usually placed immediately above the date. In the indented form of layout, to give a balanced effect, they are usually placed at the left-hand margin on the same line as the date. Sometimes a rectangle or other space is provided for them in the printed heading.

The reference may take a variety of forms. It may serve, for example, to identify either the department and section of a department from which the letter was written:

```
Our ref:  Dep. A/5

Your ref:  Dep. C
```

or the particular file in which the correspondence is to be found:

```
Our ref:  W.2357

Your ref:  542
```

Quite commonly, and especially in small offices, the reference consists of no more than the initials of the person dictating the letter followed by those of the typist: The typist's initials are sometimes typed in lower-case letters:

```
Our ref:  LGB/WW

Your ref: JDM/jc
```

a simple method that enables responsibility for a particular letter to be identified with the person who dictated it. Note the complete absence of full stops.

Some firms make use of references printed in pairs on small gummed labels, perforated and usually coloured:

A	B
Please Quote in any future Correspondence	PLEASE ATTACH THIS PART TO YOUR REPLY
T/GA/49198	T/GA/49198

Each business house adopts its own method of quoting references, but whatever the method the purpose is the same—to enable replies to be linked with previous correspondence and to find their way quickly to the appropriate official or department. Failure to quote a given reference causes inconvenience and is rightly regarded as discourtesy.

"For the attention of ..."
This phrase is used where the writer of a letter addressed to an organization wishes to direct it to a particular official. It forms no part of the letter and is therefore typed two line-spacings *above* the salutation, is underscored and should be aligned with the left-hand margin (unless the blocked style is not used, in which case it should be centred over the body of the letter):

```
The Secretary
Anderson Construction Co Ltd
Phoenix Works
ENFIELD  Middx


For the attention of Mr T Blumson

Dear Sir
```

Not being a sentence, this heading does not take a full stop.

Subject headings

Main headings

Often useful as a time-saver is the practice of including at the head of a letter a short title announcing the subject-matter, especially where correspondence is considerable. A heading will be appropriate:

(a) if one has already been used by your correspondent, in which case your reply should carry the same heading;

(b) if you are beginning a correspondence likely to lead to a number of letters on the same subject.

The heading belongs to the letter and so is typed two line-spacings *below* the salutation, is underscored and should be aligned with the left-hand margin (unless the blocked style is not used, in which case it should be centred over the body of the letter).

As the heading is not a sentence it does not take a full stop.

```
          Dear Sir

          Insulation of Bungalow
```

or

```
          Dear Sir

          Your Order No. 5346
```

For your correspondent headings such as these serve much the same purpose as the "For attention" heading, enabling him to see at a glance what the letter is about and to pass it immediately to the department or official concerned. For you as writer it saves the trouble of having to read, or at least partly read, every letter when referring to your files.

Paragraph headings

Whether a letter dealing with more than one subject should be given paragraph numbers or headings is a matter of judgment. Give them by all means if it is likely to make future reference easier or to minimize the risk of points being overlooked, but not otherwise.

Either block capitals or underscored lower-case characters may be used.

```
Dear Sir

Thank you for your letter of 5th April. I am now writing to confirm the
telephone call I made to you this morning to proceed with all the work
for which you quoted.

CENTRAL HEATING   Since you are satisfied that the boiler and radiators
specified will provide an efficient system I shall be glad if you will
proceed with the work as follows:

     (a)  The existing boiler to be replaced by a Glow-worm automatic
     gas-fired boiler, Model 75, in cream.

     (b)  Seven "Duplex" or similar flat-type radiators to be fitted
     under windows of three downstairs and two upstairs rooms, and in
     hall and kitchen, sizes to be as specified in your letter.

ROOF INSULATION   I have changed my mind about the insulation of the
roof, and would now like this to be done at the quoted cost of £95.  It
is understood that "Insulaglass" will be used.

Having had good reports on your standards of work, may I say I am glad
you can undertake the work referred to above.  My only regret is that it
cannot now be finished in time for Easter.

Yours faithfully
```

Paragraph headings may be useful, but it is better to confine each letter to one subject if possible, because:

(a) different subjects may need attention by different departments or different persons;

(b) filing complications may arise where a number of unrelated subjects are dealt with in the same letter.

CHECKING THE LETTER

Before a letter leaves the premises it should be checked for the accuracy of its contents, the correctness of its expression, and for its general suitability, which must be tested against questions such as the following:

(a) Is its appearance attractive; is it well laid out?

(b) Is it correctly spelt and properly punctuated?

(c) Does it include all the information needed or asked for, and is the information given correct?

(d) Does it include all the enclosures referred to; in other words, is it complete?

(e) Will it be readily understood by the reader?

(f) Is the general tone right, and is the letter likely to create the impression intended?

If the answer to all these questions is "Yes", then the letter may safely be sent.

A final word. Avoid adding a PS (i.e. a *post scriptum*, or post-script) to your letter. The PS may suggest that you failed to plan your letter before you wrote it or dictated it.

EXERCISES

1. Set down complimentary closures appropriate to the salutations in Exercise 2 on pp. 238–9. In some cases more than one closure would be appropriate.

2. Distinguish between a signature *per pro.* and a signature by proxy. Give one example of each.

3. What purposes are served by reference numbers in correspondence? Give an example of: *(a)* a departmental reference; *(b)* a file reference; and *(c)* a dictator's reference, and explain the data on which you have based your reference in each case.

4. Type the following, taking care to set them out exactly as you would in a letter:

(a) Show how you would prepare a business letter for signature by R. G. Dawson (an illegible writer), Personnel Manager of the Abbotsford Motor Co Ltd, including the company's name.

(b) As managing clerk of Howard, Fisher & Co, Solicitors, you have been authorized by power of attorney to sign for your firm. Sign for the firm with any name of your choice.

(c) Sign as for *(b)*, but without having been given authority by power of attorney.

(d) Using any name you care to choose, sign a letter as personal assistant to Mr R Rushbrook, Sales Manager of the Dawson Engineering Co Ltd.

(e) Sign as if you were the wife of J F Steele.

5. Type the following as they should be set out in a letter:

(a) On 15th June you write addressing The Secretary, Paul Smith & Carter Ltd, 27 Riverside Close, Birmingham B3 1AD. You want your letter to be passed to Mr F Winton.

(b) The Sales Manager of Edwards & Blake Ltd, Crighton Works, Manchester M1 3FJ, writes giving you particulars of a billiards table for

your firm's social club. On 5th August you write back. Give your letter a suitable heading.

(c) On behalf of your firm you write on 4th October to the District Superintendent of the Excellent Insurance Co Ltd informing him that a fire has damaged your premises, and that you wish to make a claim under Policy No. 1,235,647. Give your letter a suitable heading.

6. First read the following letter, then type it in blocked form, giving it an appropriate subject heading. Use open punctuation.

> 1 Margate Road,
> St Annes on Sea,
> Lancs. FY8 3EG
> Jan. 6/19..

The Circulating Manager,
Caxton Publishing Co. Ltd.
24–26 Victoria Street.
LONDON, SW1H 0ET

Dear Sir,

On 4th December last I wrote informing you that I had changed my address from Chingford London to the above. I have now received a copy of *Monthly Letter* for December sent to my old address as well as a further copy of the same issue sent to my present address.

I am returning the two envelopes in which I received the copies and hope this letter will now enable you to adjust your records.

> Yours faithfully,

7. Type the following letter setting it out in blocked form. Give each paragraph a suitable subject heading, and prepare the letter for signature by J Hargreaves, General Manager, Albert & Roche Ltd.

> Today's date

The Secretary,
Kerr & Winterton Ltd,
24–28 Mincing Lane,
LONDON, EC3A 7PP

Dear Sir

We are pleased to send you the attached quotation in reply to your enquiry of yesterday.

The prices of cocoa have fallen in recent weeks owing to a slackening in demand. We have just received 1,000 bags from Costa Rica and because of the supplier's favourable terms are able to offer them to you at the specially low price quoted.

Owing to heavy demand for Madras rice the price has risen considerably since the beginning of the month and is likely to rise still further. We have a limited stock of this rice and if you place an order hope we shall not have to disappoint you.

Sales of coffee have slackened considerably during the past month and prices in consequence have fallen heavily. We have on hand a good stock of most varieties and think you will agree that the quoted prices are very attractive. As demand is expected to improve in the near future these prices are likely to rise.

Owing to the generally slack state of the market just now we consider that the present is a very favourable time for buying and we suggest that you place your order with us immediately.

Yours faithfully,

8. Your employer wishes to send out 1,000 letters, with a facsimile signature, on headed notepaper, to look as nearly as possible like individually typed letters. How would you propose to deal with this?

(*RSA*)

XIV TERM AND MEMORANDUM LETTERING
and prices in consequence have fallen sharply. We have on hand a
good stock of must ... ...

CHAPTER FIFTEEN

The Kinds of Business Letter

Since truth and constancy are vain,
Since neither love nor sense of pain,
Nor force of reason can persuade,
Then let example be obeyed.
George Granville: *To Myra*

CLASSIFICATION

It is convenient to classify business letters according to tone and
structure as follows:

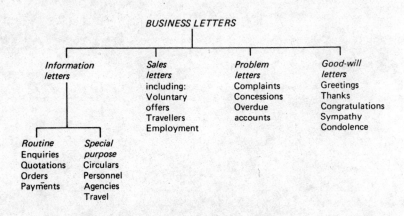

BUSINESS LETTERS

| Information letters | Sales letters including: Voluntary offers Travellers Employment | Problem letters Complaints Concessions Overdue accounts | Good-will letters Greetings Thanks Congratulations Sympathy Condolence |

| Routine Enquiries Quotations Orders Payments | Special purpose Circulars Personnel Agencies Travel |

Information letters
Information letters are letters aimed primarily at seeking or
giving information. They include enquiries and replies; quotations, estimates, tenders and acknowledgments; and letters relating to accounts. Many of these letters are routine in the sense
that they follow a familiar, and sometimes even an identical,
pattern that constantly recurs. Another type of information

letter is that concerned with matters requiring special investigation, or involving policy or adjustments to meet unusual circumstances. But whether routine or special, information letters are all alike in that they are free from any suggestion of the "reader resistance" associated with sales letters or with letters concerning complaints and concessions, for in all letters of this type there is an element of persuasion whereby one party tries to convert the other to his way of thinking.

It is a cardinal rule of all business letter-writing that the opening paragraph or paragraphs should establish *rapport*, a sympathetic relation as it were, with the reader. In information letters this relationship is best achieved by coming to the point at once, details and other supporting information being reserved for subsequent paragraphs. To state at the outset what is required, or to give information that has been sought, is to show regard for the reader's time and convenience: he finds it helpful to know immediately what the letter is all about. Some examples of this direct approach will be found on p. 203.

Sales letters

But with sales letters a different approach is called for since there is a natural resistance to letters aimed at persuading people to place an order or take some other suggested form of action. Somehow this resistance must be overcome. To begin a sales letter with a statement of its purpose or of the price at which goods or services are on offer has the effect of fanning reader resistance. We need to begin by thinking about the person to whom we are writing. A barrister studies his opponent's case just as sharply as he does his own client's; a football manager studies the tactics of the opposing team and analyses the individual qualities of its members. And so, in all sales letter-writing we must begin by studying our reader's interests and ask ourselves how he is likely to be affected by what we say. First and foremost our opening paragraph must establish *rapport* by arousing interest and so create a willingness, even a desire, to know more about what we are trying to sell. Then and only then can we enter into a profitable discussion of the goods or services we want our reader to buy. Therefore, in letters where sales resistance presents itself, or is likely to do so, the opening paragraph must be given special care if the message that follows is to have a fair chance of at least being read. The type of approach required is the persuasive, already discussed and illustrated on pp. 205–6.

Problem letters

Problem letters are letters in situations where the reader's interests are in some way in conflict with the writer's, as where complaints are made, concessions sought or payment of accounts is overdue. Like the sales letter, letters of this kind call for an indirect approach. If the letter is one conveying unwelcome news, refusing a request or disclaiming liability for a loss, the reader is sure to be disappointed and the way for his disappointment must be prepared by a suitable opening paragraph. Use of this type of approach is illustrated in the two letters on p. 204.

In face-to face confrontations gestures, facial expressions and tone of voice all help to form the listener's impression, to influence his thinking and to condition his reactions. But the written word has no such linguistic aids and the reader is affected solely by the way in which words are used and by the tone adopted.

In Chapter Twelve mention was made that the tone of a letter must suit both the occasion and the purpose; if it does not, then the effect upon the reader may be very different from what the writer intended. Consequently, problem letters must be written with restraint and show a proper regard for the reader's point of view. In letters of this kind it helps if we use passive rather than active verb constructions. A verb is active when the subject of the verb performs the action (e.g. *She posted the letter*); it is passive when the subject suffers the action (e.g. *The letter was posted by her*). Passive verbs are for the most part impersonal and so have a mellowing effect on what is said. For example:

Active construction	*Passive construction*
You made an error in calculating the discount.	An error was made (*or* There was an error) in calculating the discount.
You did not enclose the cheque with your letter.	The cheque was not enclosed with your letter.
You appear to have misunderstood our terms of payment	Our terms of payment appear to have been misunderstood.

Problem letters should always be answered promptly. If you cannot do what the writer asks tell him what you can do and close your letter in a way that leaves the door open for further correspondence, if further correspondence is likely to help.

Good-will letters

Most business letters have two objectives: to promote a particular transaction and to build good will. Every business letter should be a good-will letter in the sense that it aims to create or maintain good feeling based on a mutually beneficial business relationship. But there are some letters written for the sole purpose of building good will. They include letters of thanks or appreciation to new customers for first orders, to existing customers for specially large orders or regular promptness in settling accounts. Also included are letters to employees for difficult jobs well done. There is no obligation to write letters of this kind; their writers could despatch the goods, issue receipts or accept the work done without any further acknowledgment and there end the matter. But to send voluntary expressions of gratitude or sympathy gives pleasure to those who receive them and makes for happy working relationships.

Good-will letters take a variety of forms and each has its own characteristics depending on the circumstances to which it applies. Besides letters expressing thanks or appreciation, there are letters of congratulation, letters of welcome, letters of condolence and of sympathy in times of illness or trouble. While they naturally differ in form these letters have one quality in common—they are written to show genuine interest in the reader. They can be as brief and simple as you wish, but they should express what you feel in terms that are warm and sincere. Sincerity is indeed by far their most important quality. A formal letter written because the writer feels it is expected of him and therefore must be sent does not give the pleasure it should. Make sure, then, that your good-will letters have an unmistakable ring of sincerity to them. This is much easier to do if you write at an early stage while you are feeling grateful and appreciative or sympathetic than if you leave it till the emotion has cooled. One can judge the success of the good-will letter by asking oneself "Does the letter sound sincere and is it the sort of letter I myself would be happy to receive?" One person cannot suggest to another the precise wording for letters of the kind discussed since the essence of sincerity is to express one's feelings in one's own way, but later in this chapter you will find examples of good-will letters that may help to point the way.

ESSENTIAL QUALITIES

If you work in an office or are hoping to do so, you must learn to write business letters that put you yourself and your firm in the best possible light. No sensible businessman would for long tolerate a tactless or untidy salesman, yet business letters—a firm's "silent salesmen"—sometimes reflect little or no credit on those who send them. Such letters can do more harm than good by destroying the very confidence and good will they seek to create. What, then, are the qualities of a good business letter? Foremost of all, it must achieve its aim; the tone and spirit in which it is written must find acceptance with the reader. But to be a good letter it must do more; it must accomplish its mission in a way that commends itself to the reader and leaves him with a favourable impression both of the writer and of his firm. To do this it must possess certain intrinsic qualities: it must use language that is clear and free from faults of grammar and mis-spellings; it must be well typed on good quality stationery and have an attractive look. In a word, it must not merely do the job it was designed for but must do it in a way that leaves a good impression and creates good will.

Over the years the business letter has developed certain conventions of form and structure. These have been discussed in the two preceding chapters. Most businessmen, however, leave such matters to their secretaries and typists, whose attitudes are largely shaped by their training and experience.

SPECIMEN LETTERS

The rest of this chapter is devoted to letters offered as examples in the modern English style illustrating the accepted principles of good business writing as applied to a somewhat limited range of transactions. Readers wishing to make a closer study of the business letter in a more comprehensive range of transactions are referred to the author's *Model Business Letters**, which contains over six hundred specimen letters classified and grouped for reference according to subject-matter.

Enquiries and replies
When making an enquiry begin by stating simply, clearly and concisely what it is you want. It helps your correspondent to know at once what your enquiry is all about. Say no more than needs to be said and then finish.

A routine enquiry
Enquiries should be answered promptly—on the same day as they are received if possible.

*Macdonald & Evans (3rd edn.), 1982.

25 October 19..

Dear Sirs

We understand that you are manufacturers of polyester-cotton bed-sheets
and pillow cases and should be obliged if you would send us particulars
of the sizes and colours in which these are available. We should also
like to see samples of the materials used and to have details of the
terms on which you could supply quantities of about 500 sheets and 1,000
pillow cases.

Provided quality and price are satisfactory, we would expect to place
regular orders for fairly large quantities.

Yours faithfully

   In the following reply the manufacturer is careful to give all
the information asked for and at the same time takes the opportunity to draw attention to the high quality and wide range of his
manufactures:

Manufacturer's reply

Dear Sirs

We were pleased to receive your enquiry of 25th October and, as requested,
enclose samples of the poly-cotton materials used in the manufacture of
our bed-sheets and pillow cases. When you examine the samples we think
you will agree that they represent material of the very highest quality.

From this material we also manufacture a wide range of other items in
which we feel you may be interested. You will find them fully illustrated
in the catalogue we are taking the opportunity to enclose.

The bed-sheets and pillow cases are available in blue, pink, lilac and
white, in sizes and at the prices stated in the list enclosed. From
these prices we would allow you a trade discount of 40 per cent on
orders for the quantities you mention, with an additional discount of 2½
per cent for payment within one month of invoice.

These terms are exceptionally favourable and we very much look forward to
the pleasure of receiving an order from you.

Yours faithfully

If the enquiry contains a number of separate questions it will help your correspondent if you either tabulate your questions, or put each one in a paragraph of its own. The separate questions stand out even more clearly if they are numbered serially, as in the following example.

A tabulated enquiry

10 February 19..

The Regional Gas Board

Dear Sirs

I am considering conversion of the central heating system at the above address from solid fuel to gas and should be glad if you would answer the following questions and send me any other information that will help me to decide.

(1) The present system is fired by a No. 4 Crane "Cavendish" solid-fuel boiler. What would be the cost, including fixing, of replacing this by a suitable gas-fired boiler, complete with automatic clock control?

(2) The premises are not at present gas-connected. What would be the charge if any, for laying the necessary service pipe and mixing and connecting a meter?

(3) The present installation includes six radiators and towel rail. What would be the estimated annual running costs of a gas-operated system?

(4) What facilities are available for periodic servicing of a converted system. and on what terms?

Yours faithfully

The following reply is considerate and helpful. It tells the enquirer in the plainest terms just what he wants to know, and the offer to send a representative is evidence of a genuine desire to be helpful.

Tabulated reply to enquiry

Dear Sir

We welcome your enquiry concerning conversion of your central-heating system and enclose a copy of a recently published brochure on Gas in the Home. For efficiency and convenience and economy of operation. central heating is superior to all other forms. and we are confident that the facts and figures in the brochure will convince you of this.

Answers to the questions you raise are as follows:

(1) We could replace your existing "Cavendish" boiler with a "Glow-worm Model 75" at a cost of £920. including clock control to give automatic operation of the system at pre-determined times.

(2) No charge would be made either for laying the service pipe or for supplying and installing the Board's standard credit meter.

(3) Our current tariff provides for a fixed standing charge of £9.20 per quarter and a charge of £35.20 per therm of gas consumed. For the installation you describe, and assuming the system to be in operation for 12 hours a day in average weather conditions for 30 weeks in the year the cost would be in the region of £350 a year, depending on the setting of the. thermostatic control.

(4) The installation would be guaranteed for twelve months. From the end of this period the Board operates an optional servicing and maintenance scheme for an annual charge of £23.00.

We hope the foregoing will give you the information you need, but if you would like further details we shall be happy to arrange for Mr T R Pugh. our representative for your area, to call on you on a day and at a time convenient to you.

Yours faithfully

Quotations

When asking for a quotation state exactly what it is you want, giving necessary details. In particular, be careful to make clear whether or not the price is to include delivery. Failure to do this may lead to subsequent serious disagreement with the supplier.

A satisfactory quotation is one which, like the following:

(a) expresses thanks for the enquiry;
(b) states clearly what the quoted prices cover (e.g. packing, carriage and insurance);
(c) mentions the period for which the quotation is valid (particularly important in times of inflation);
(d) gives an undertaking as to date of delivery.

Request for quotation

12 October 19..

Dear Sirs

Please send us patterns and quote prices for supply of your waterproof serges suitable for suitings.

We use large quantities of serge and. provided qualities and prices are right, would expect to place fairly substantial orders with you at regular intervals. In particular. we are at present looking for an inexpensive military serge suitable for army and navy contract work.

Your quoted prices should be for settlement of accounts for cash and should cover cost of delivery to our address.

Yours faithfully

Reply quotation

15 October 19..

Dear Sirs

Thank you for your enquiry of 12th October. We have today sent you by parcel post pastterns of our waterproof serges. and are pleased to quote for them as follows:

Black, fast dye	£22.50 a metre
Blue, best indigo dye	23.84 a metre
Mixtures, as per patterns	21.30 a metre
Military serges from	13.60 a metre

These prices include delivery to your address and are valid for one month from the date of this letter.

All serges are 1½m wide, supplied in 50m lengths. They are guaranteed un-shrinkable and non-fading and, except for the military serges, are made of pure wool. We can especially recommend our quality of military serges at £16.20.

The international reputation enjoyed by our serges testifies to their high quality. We have been manufacturing them for the past twenty years and can now claim to produce a cloth that no competitor has yet succeeded in producing at anything like the prices quoted. We hold good stocks from which we can deliver within three weeks of receiving order and. if required. can usually supply special shades within five weeks.

The prices quoted are for quantities of five or more 50m pieces of each separate serge ordered. For smaller quantities the above-quoted prices should be increased by 3 per cent. Our terms of payment are 2½ per cent one month.

We hope you will find our prices satisfactory and look forward to the pleasure of an order from you.

Yours faithfully

Orders
The use of serially numbered printed order forms facilitates reference; it also ensures that all essential information is given.
   Orders placed by letter should:

(a) give full details and quote catalogue numbers, if any;
(b) give full directions for forwarding (e.g. date of delivery, mode of transport, and whether *carriage paid* or *carriage forward*);
(c) confirm the agreed terms of payment.

Where the order is for two or more items these should be tabulated; it lessens the chance of items being overlooked. Orders by telephone should be confirmed in writing.

An order for cloth

<pre>
                                              19 October 19..

Dear Sirs

We thank you for your quotation of 15th October enclosing patterns of
your serges. We find both qualities and prices satisfactory and,
confirming my telephone conversation with your Mr Baxter this morning,
I am pleased to place a first order with you for the following serges
at the prices and on the terms quoted:

             Quantity   Item   Price
            (50 m pcs.)   (per pc.)

                6   Black serge   £1,125.00
               12   Blue serge   1,192.00
                5   Serge, pattern 24   1,065.00
                5   Serge, pattern 37   680.00

Above prices to include delivery by rail, with a cash-payment discount
of 2½ per cent.

We place the order on the understanding that the goods will be despatched
to reach us not later than 15th November.

Yours faithfully
</pre>

If the order is a "first" order it should be acknowledged by a letter welcoming the new customer and expressing pleasure at receiving it.

Acknowledgment of order

<pre>
We are writing to say how pleased we were to receive your order of
19th October and to welcome you as one of our customers.

We can supply from stock all the serges ordered and are arranging to send
them next week by British Rail. We feel sure you will be well satisfied
with the goods; at their prices they represent exceptional value.
</pre>

Besides serges we supply a wide range of other manufactured cloths, including fine worsteds, tweeds and gaberdines and enclose a copy of our current price-list. Should you be interested in any of these cloths we shall be glad to send you patterns.

We hope that our handling of this first order with us will lead to further business between us and mark the beginning of a mutually satisfactory working relationship.

Yours faithfully

Circular letters

There are occasions when it becomes necessary to give the same information to a number of people. This is done by circular letter. Circular letters are extensively used in sales promotion and for notifying important developments in a business. Because circulars are mass produced the original must be drafted with special care. It is important to catch the reader's interest at the outset. This is done in the first paragraph. Also important is to create the impression of personal touch, by inserting names and addresses of recipients and by using the second person *you* in preference to such impersonal expressions as *our customers, our readers, everyone* and *anyone*.

Removal to new premises

Dear Sir

The steadily growing demand for our products has made necessary an early move to new and larger premises. We have been fortunate in acquiring a particularly good site on the industrial trading estate, Trafford Park, Manchester.

The new site is served by excellent transport facilities by road and rail, and will enable deliveries to be made promptly. It also provides scope for greatly increased output and better methods of production that will improve still further the quality of our products. The move will be completed by 1st July next and as from that date all our manufacturing operations will be carried on at Trafford Park.

We take this opportunity to thank you for your custom (not our customers for their custom) in the past and hope that the improvements in service which we confidently expect to be able to offer you (not our customers) will lead to even more business between us.

Yours faithfully

Disposal of a business

Dear Mr Edwards

It is with regret that I write to inform you of my decision to retire from business on account of continued ill-health. As from 1st March next the factory and equipment at Harlow, but not the stock, will be taken over by Messrs Jordon & Co of Chingford, Essex.

Existing stock will be sold in lots at the factory at greatly reduced prices for cash, and with this letter I enclose a list of the items to be disposed of. It may be that some of them will interest you. If so, may I suggest that you visit the factory during the week commencing 17th February, when I shall be available to receive offers. Especially during the first few days you should find some unbelieveably good bargains.

I have always been grateful for your custom and have appreciated our friendly business relationship during many years. I shall look forward to meeting you again, this time for a final transaction. Should you not call, I take this opportunity to thank you for many past orders and to wish you continued and increasing prosperity in the future.

Yours sincerely

Agencies

Manufacturers seeking to develop their markets investigate closely the qualifications, experience, business connections and reliability of prospective agents, and also the extent to which they may hold other agencies. For suppliers seeking suitable agents abroad there are useful sources of information, more particularly the Overseas Trade Division of the Department of Trade and Industry, the consular services, the chambers of commerce and the banks' overseas branches.

Agency terms are sometimes agreed in correspondence between the parties, but where business is likely to be on a large scale a formal agency agreement is desirable. Sometimes the initial approach is made by the firm seeking an agency, as in the following letter.

Application for agency

Dear Sirs

Having learned that you are looking for a reliable firm with good connections in the hardware trade to represent you in the North of England we are writing to offer you our services.

For some years we have acted as agents for Messrs Nelson and Hughes of Walthamstow, but in the reorganization following their recent registration as a public limited company, they have decided to set up branches of their own in Manchester and Leeds. Since they no longer need our services we are now free to offer them to you.

Having already had experience in marketing products similar to your own we are familiar with customers' needs and are confident we could develop a worthwhile market for you. We have well-equipped showrooms in Manchester, Preston and Newcastle and an experienced sales staff, who make regular calls on customers in their respective areas.

We should appreciate your letting us know very soon whether our offer interests you. If it does, then I would suggest an early meeting with Mr J Hopkinson, our marketing director, who would call on you at your convenience to discuss details of an arrangement agreeable to both of us.

Yours faithfully

A commission agent differs from an ordinary agent in that he does not establish a contractual relationship between his principal and third parties, but buys and sells in his own name, receiving a commission for his services. Commission agents are common in foreign trade, and when they guarantee payment for the goods supplied are known as *del credere* agents.

When seeking an agency the applicant will stress two things:

(*a*) the opportunities in the market in which he or his firm operates;

(*b*) the advantages he or his firm can offer.

Application from commission agent

Dear Sirs

Over a period of fifteen years I have established a well-developed sales organization in Kenya and am represented by an experienced sales staff in various parts of the country. Their recent reports suggest that there is a promising potential demand for cameras and other photographic equipment. I understand that you are not at present directly represented in Kenya and am writing to offer my services as commission agent.

I have first-class business connections throughout the country and there is every indication that your products, with their reputation for high quality and reasonable prices, would find a profitable market here. Provided we could agree upon satisfactory terms, I would be prepared to guarantee payment of all accounts due on orders placed through me.

You will of course wish to have information about me and for this I refer you to Nylon Fabrics Ltd, 8 John Street, London, WC1N 2HY, for whom I have held the sole agency in Kenya for the past six years, and also the Midminster Bank, Nairobi.

I firmly believe that an agency for marketing your products in Kenya would be of considerable benefit to both of us, and look forward to learning that you are interested in my proposal. I am sure we could come to a satisfactory arrangement as to terms.

Yours faithfully

Sales letters

The essence of the sales letter is persuasion. To be a good sales letter it must do all of the following:

(a) Attract attention, by opening with a striking paragraph (e.g. a question, a challenging statement, or an anecdote).

(b) Arouse interest, by making an appeal to some buying motive (e.g. health, personal appearance, economy, fear, future prospects).

(c) Create desire for the product or service being offered.

(d) Carry conviction, by supporting the claims made, giving guarantees, providing evidence of tests, etc.

(e) Induce action, by persuading the reader to do what you want him to do (e.g. seek further information, visit your showroom, place an order).

In purchasing almost any sort of commodity the buyer has a choice between what you are offering and what others are selling. You must therefore show him that what you are offering possesses some special quality that makes it superior to the products or services being sold by others, and persuade him that he needs it. Some examples of the use of persuasion in sales letter-writing are included at pp. 206–7.

The action you wish your reader to take must be made as easy for him as possible, as by asking him to return a prepaid reply card, or to complete and return a simple form.

A typical sales circular (an appeal to comfort)

Dear Reader

Skirts get longer, skirts get shorter, but one thing that will never go out of fashion is keeping warm in winter time. After all, keeping warm is no more than common-sense and you can keep warm in the home for the rest of your life for as little as it costs to take the family on holiday for a fortnight.

You have electric fires or coal fires, of course, but they warm only certain rooms. Think of the comfort you and your family would enjoy living in a house that is warm all over all the year round - just as warm as you want it at the mere turn of a knob.

Can you think of a better gift to your family? You can give them this by installing central heating. "Which system?", you ask. "Why, gas of course", because it has all the advantages of its rivals and is cheaper to run. Equipped with one of our "Warmomatic" gas-fired boilers your central heating will do the job as efficiently as any other thermostat-controlled system on the market and at lower cost. The enclosed brochure will convince you of the reasons why.

Some of your friends and neighbours are sure to using the "Warmomatic".
Ask them about it before you make up your mind or, if you prefer, fill
in the enclosed prepaid reply card and we will arrange for our
Mr R Singleton, our representative for your area, to call to give you
further details and, if you would like it, an estimate of the cost of
installation. You are under no obligation whatsoever. Just state a
date and time.

Yours faithfully

Voluntary offers

Voluntary offers are a form of sales letter. They have the same
objective and often take the form of offers of free samples,
goods on approval, special discounts and so on. Where such
offers are frequent they may create a sense of annoyance and as
sales resistance is then particularly strong the offer must win the
reader's interest at once, otherwise your letter will quickly dis-
appear into the waste-paper bin.

Offer of a demonstration

Dear Mrs Rayliss

If you haven't yet invested in a dishwasher, we think you will like to
know about our new "Olympus" - the latest addition to our range of time-
and labour-saving household equipment.

The "Olympus" is much more than a washer of dishes. With its piping-hot-
water washing and hot clean-air drying it washes and dries pans, glass,
china and cutlery quicker and more hygienically than is possible by
hand. Powerful jets of fresh hot water from a triple-level spray system
wash every plate and pan thoroughly, hygenically - and quietly. A
built-in water softener rinses everything to a brilliant sparkle. Built
as it is for quiet efficiency the new "Olympus" represents an entirely
new order in luxury kitchen equipment.

We especially invite you to the exhibition to see our display on
Stand No 42. I enclose two admission tickets and look forward to
meeting you there, where I hope you will allow me to demonstrate to you
this latest and best of all dishwashers.

Yours sincerely

Complaints

Making complaints is never a pleasant business, but when a
complaint is necessary it should be made with tact and restraint
if it is not to impair future business relations. Plan your letter of
complaint as follows:

(a) Regret the need to complain.

(b) State clearly your reasons for complaining, ask for an
explanation and explain what adjustment you seek.

(c) Refer to the inconvenience caused and suggest how matters could be put right.

(d) Conclude by expressing confidence in the expectation of a favourable and helpful reply.

The following is a courteous letter of complaint sent to a local postmaster. It is confined to the facts, with a request for an unsatisfactory situation to be put right. (All names used in both complaint and reply are fictitious.)

Letter of complaint

30 March 19..

The Postmaster

Dear Sir

I am sorry there should be cause to complain about the collection service in my locality.

At 7.00 p.m. last night I went to post an urgent letter at the nearby pillar-box at the Victoria Road sub-office. Although collection times displayed on the box showed the day's last collection to be 7.30 p.m., the next-collection disc indicated No. 1 - presumably for the following day's first collection.

In view of the urgency of my letter I walked to the next nearest pillar-box at Ripon Road to find the collection disc again indicating No. 1. I then tried two other boxes, one outside the sub-office on Union Street and the other in Park Drive, only to meet with a similar situation there. I eventually posted my letter at the head post office in Melton Road, at 7.30 precisely by the post office clock, and hopefully assume it was dealt with that night. Only at Ripon Road pillar-box did the disc correctly show the next-collection time, the official last collection from there being 5.30 p.m.

A situation where collection discs displayed on pillar-boxes do not fall within the pattern of the officially displayed collection times is both confusing and annoying and I am sure you will wish to take the action needed to put matters right. In particular, I should be grateful if you would confirm actual collection times from the Victoria Road pillar-box as I make regular and frequent use of this service, sometimes as last night for urgent correspondence connected with my business.

Yours faithfully

You should acknowledge at once any complaint you receive, and if the complaint is justfied admit it readily, express your regret and undertake to put matters right. If you are unable to meet your complainant's demands, explain the reasons carefully and sympathetically. If the complaint is unreasonable point this out in a way that does not give offence. A sympathetic tone will go far to retain good will.

The above letter was promptly acknowledged, and rightly, by a "Receiving attention" card, and a week later the postmaster sent the following reply. It is concise and to the point and does all that is necessary. The added touch of informality in the salutation and complimentary close imparts a warm and friendly tone that suggests the writer's sincerity.

Reply to complaint

Dear Mr Davidson

Further to your letter of 30th March concerning early collections from
certain letter boxes, I have now completed my enquiries and find as
follows:

Ripon Road Box Park Drive Box	These boxes have their last collec- tions at 5.30 p.m.
Victoria Road Box Union Street Box	These boxes should not have been cleared before 7.30 p.m. and I have taken the matter up with the drivers concerned

I am very sorry indeed that our failure to deal correctly with the
collections at Victoria Road and Union Street caused you so much
unnecessary trouble, and we shall do everything we can to ensure that it
does not happen again.

Yours sincerely

Concessions

Letters replying to requests for special terms, credit or other concessions must be handled tactfully and with care if they are to avoid giving offence or losing customers. When a request is refused, reasons for the refusal should be given.

Letter refusing special terms

Dear Sirs

We are, sorry to learn from your letter of 12th October that you find our
quotation for Nimrod cream sherry too high.

We have carefully considered your request for a special discount and,
bearing in mind the large amount of business you have placed with us
recently, would be very happy to grant your request. But unfortunately
there are difficulties. Despite the rise in costs due to the fall in
the exchange value of sterling, the recent increases in duty on imported
wines and the continued rise in overheads, our quoted price was a
specially low price. We feel that a study of current market prices would
convince you of this.

Our quotation provided for only the narrowest of margins and any further
cut in price would leave us with little or no profit. I am therefore
sorry to inform you that circumstances do not permit us to allow the
special discount you ask for.

I hope you will appreciate our position and that we may still look
forward to receiving the order for which we quoted.

Yours faithfully

If the request is for credit that you cannot grant, tactfully
explain the reason and say in what circumstances you might
possibly grant it.

Letter refusing to extend credit

Dear Sir

We were pleased to receive your order of 15th April for a further supply
of transistor sets, but as the balance of your account now stands at
over £750, we hope you will be able to reduce it before we grant credit
for further supplies.

We fully realize how difficult conditions are just now. We ourselves
have many commitments of our own and I am sure you will understand when
I say we can meet them only if our many customers keep their accounts
within reasonable limits. We would therefore be grateful if you could
send us your cheque for say, half the amount you owe us. We could then
arrange to supply the goods you now ask for and charge them to your
account.

Yours faithfully

Overdue accounts

Letters seeking payment of overdue accounts can very easily
give offence. They call for the utmost tact and restraint. In the
first instance, it is wise not to send a letter, but to send instead a
statement of account marked "Second application", "Account
overdue", etc. If it is necessary to send several reminders the
first letter, preferably printed, should make a short, formal
request for payment. The second will be typed and somewhat
firmer in tone, and if a third is necessary it will usually be
reasonable to say that steps will be taken to secure payment.

Final request for payment

Dear Sirs

We find it hard to understand why we have not heard from you in answer
to our two letters of 10th and 24th March reminding you of the amount
still owing on your December statement. It is very disappointing not
to have received from you at least an explanation of the reason for non-
payment, all the more so because of our past satisfactory dealings over
several years.

We are anxious to avoid taking any steps from which your credit and
reputation might suffer, and have decided to give you a further fourteen
days in which either to settle our account or at least to offer a
satisfactory explanation. Failing this, I am afraid we have no choice
but to consider what further steps to take to obtain payment.

Yours faithfully

Good-will letters

Good-will letters are letters that need not be written unless one
chooses to write them to build good personal relationships. Businessmen everywhere take the opportunity to build good will by
sending letters of congratulation to mark success in some particular field—a promotion, the award of an honour, and so on—
or letters of sympathy when the occasion arises. Letters of this
kind should be brief and to the point. Writing the letter is in
itself a gesture of good will, to which words can add very little. In
fact, to use too many words may well spoil the effect.

The personal good-will touch can also be built into the ordinary business letter, as in the final short paragraph of the following letter.

Business letter with a good-will touch

Dear Mr Harrison

English for Commerce

You will be glad to know that sales of the above title have got off to
a very good start, and as stocks are already running low we are arranging
for a reprint early in the New Year.

Because of serious delays within the printing industry at the present
time, we are anxious to put our reprint programme for next year in hand
as soon as possible. We should therefore be glad if you would let us
have very soon a note of any amendments you may wish to make to the
present text.

My warm regards and best wishes.

Yours sincerely

Note: An alternative and more extended personal greeting might have been as follows:

I was delighted to learn of your recent appointment as principal of the
Fylde College of Further Education, and send you my warm congratulations.

Business letters written in a cordial and friendly tone, reflecting concern for the reader's interests, also create good will and make for happy working relationships.

Business letter with a friendly tone

Dear Sir

We were very happy to receive your enquiry of 26th April and by separate
post are sending you a copy of our latest illustrated catalogue, and
also samples of some of our newest fabrics.

Unfortunately, we cannot send you a full range, but Mr George Eastham,
our sales representative for your area, will be in Harrogate next week
and will gladly call on you and show you fabrics not represented in the
parcel we are sending you.

If there is any other way in which you feel we can be of service, you
may rest assured of our interest and help if you care to use it. We look
forward to hearing from you again.

Yours faithfully

Letters of thanks and appreciation always give pleasure to those who receive them and so help to build good will. Businessmen have many opportunities for letters of this kind; thanks, for example, for first orders, particularly large orders, prompt settlement of accounts, advice given, services rendered, and so on.

Letter of thanks

Dear Mr Goodier

I am writing to you personally just to say how very much I appreciate the
warm welcome you extended to our Mr Wardle when he visited your town
last week.

The help and advice you gave him, and the introductions you arranged for
him, have resulted in a number of very valuable business contracts and I
should like you to know how very grateful I am for all you have done to
make them possible.

I realize the value of time to a busy executive like you and this makes
me all the more appreciative of the time you so generously gave to
Mr Wardle.

Yours sincerely

EXERCISES

1. As secretary of a firm of dealers in electrical household appliances write to the Welling Electrical Co. Ltd., Swindon, asking for particulars, including prices, of their various models of the "Thermomaster" dishwasher exhibited at the recent trade fair in Birmingham. If details and prices are satisfactory you expect to find a good market for these dishwashers.

2. Using imaginary details write a letter in reply to the enquiry in Question 1. In your reply draw attention to other electrical household appliances of which your firm are distributors and which you think would interest the enquirer.

3. You have received an order for a Model 65 electric lawn mower. Having just sold your last mower of this model you cannot meet the order for another two months, but can strongly recommend a different though rather more expensive model, which you can supply from stock. Write a suitable letter to your customer explaining this.

4. Because of temporary financial difficulties you find you cannot settle the account of one of your suppliers. Write to him explaining your difficulty and asking for six weeks' extension of credit.

5. You are secretary to a firm manufacturing modern office equipment. Using imaginary details write a circular letter to be sent to important retailers, drawing attention to some of your latest products and offering a special discount on orders placed within the next month.

6. As manufacturers and exporters of photographic equipment write to an overseas customer who has placed a substantial order for cameras informing him that you will be unable to keep the promised delivery date, much of your stock having been destroyed in a warehouse fire. You hope, however, to ship the consignment within four weeks of the originally promised delivery date.

7. Your firm wishes to appoint an agent to sell its well-known waterproof textiles in South Africa. The Overseas Trade Division of the Department of Trade and Industry has given you the name of a reliable distributor. Write to him offering him the agency and stating terms.

8. Your office telephone has been out of order for three days. You reported the fault immediately you discovered it, but it has not yet been attended to and you are being seriously inconvenienced in consequence. Write a tactful letter of complaint to your telephone manager asking for the service to be restored without delay.

9. Your firm has a valuable overseas customer who usually settles his accounts promptly by banker's draft. He has failed to settle his latest account, payment of which is now two months overdue, nor has he offered any explanation. Bearing in mind that you are anxious to retain his custom write drawing his attention to the unpaid account and requesting early settlement.

10. As secretary of a charitable or benevolent organization, write a letter to a new contributor thanking him for his donation and indicating how it will be used.

11. You are retiring after twenty-five years as managing director of a business that has established a reputation for friendly personal attention. Draft a farewell letter to your regular customers; include appropriate comments about your successor.

12. Your employers, manufacturers of kitchen utensils, have received complaints that the handles of some of their saucepans are not heat-resistant as claimed. In some instances the material used has cracked. An investigation has shown that this defect is confined to one particular batch. At the time of production, supply difficulties necessitated the substitution of a material slightly different from the usual one.

Write a suitable apologetic explanatory letter to the aggrieved customers. In your letter you should:

(a) assure them that the defect is not dangerous;
(b) offer immediate free replacement of goods, all charges paid;
(c) thank them for writing about the complaint;
(d) explain the cause of the problem.

(LCCI Jnr Sec Cert)

CHAPTER SIXTEEN

Miscellanea

It is consequently my degrading duty to serve this upstart as First
Lord of the Treasury, Lord Chief Justice, Commander-in-Chief,
Lord High Admiral, Master of the Buckhounds, Groom of the Back
Stairs, Archbishop of Titipu, and Lord Mayor, both acting and elect,
all rolled into one.

Sir W. S. Gilbert: *The Mikado*

THE USE OF "MESSRS"

Messrs as a courtesy title is the plural of *Mr*. Strictly therefore its
use in the plural is appropriate only when *Mr* (or *Esq.*) would be
used in the singular. But there are some difficulties in applying
this rule, and these are now considered.

In addressing partnerships
When we address a firm, i.e. a partnership, no difficulty arises,
since we are in fact addressing the partners themselves. The
partners *are* the firm. When they die, or any of them, the
firm dies with them. Therefore, whether a firm adopts the title
Bardell & Pickwick or *Bardell & Co* makes no difference to the
manner of addressing it—*Messrs* is used in both cases. But if
Bardell & Pickwick decide to call themselves by such impersonal
names as *Arcadia Electrical Co.* or *Pest Extermination Co.* it would
not be very sensible to address them by an essentially personal
expression such as *Messrs*. Recognizing this, custom prescribes
the rule that firms are addressed as *Messrs* only when the firm's
name includes a personal element, and not even then if the
name itself includes a courtesy title or the word *The* (e.g. *Sir Ivor
Marsh & Sons, The Benjamin Metal Co*).

In addressing incorporated bodies
When, however, we come to address incorporated bodies such as
limited companies opinions on the use of *Messrs* differ. For a
long time commercial and secretarial textbooks consistently
taught that these bodies should be addressed in the same way as
partnerships; but not many people now accept this.

(a) Some take the view that, since incorporated bodies are mere artificial creations of the law, they exist only on paper, and can no more reply to a letter than can the pillar-box in which it is posted. It is manifestly absurd, they claim, to address these impersonal bodies as if they were persons, by using *Messrs*, or *Dear Sirs*, or even to address them at all.

(b) Others who continue to use *Messrs* do so on the ground that an incorporated body cannot exist without members, and that in addressing it one is indirectly addressing its members.

Thus, the use or non-use of *Messrs* in addressing an incorporated body like a limited company is very much a matter of opinion. If we adopt the first view the use of *Messrs* is definitely taboo, and so is the use of *Dear Sirs*. We must address ourselves to John Brown & Co. Ltd.—nothing more and nothing less—and begin our letter without any salutation into the bargain.

If, however, we adopt the second view we find ourselves floundering in such monstrosities as *Messrs British Road Services* and *Messrs Reliance Garage Ltd.*

The fact that a limited company or other incorporated body cannot logically be addressed except through an agent provides a way out of the dilemma. Apart from logic, there is a probable gain in efficiency if we address correspondence direct to the company's representative for whom it is intended—the managing director, the personnel officer, the sales manager and so on. In such a case we *specify* the company but do not *address* it; the company's title becomes part of the address in much the same way as the name of the street or town. In all such instances *Messrs* may therefore be omitted without creating any sense of discourtesy. If we cannot know which of the company's officers will deal with our letter, we should address it to *"The Secretary"*, since by the Companies Acts every registered company must have one.

Recommended practice
For firms (i.e. partnerships)

(a) Use *Messrs* only with titles that contain a personal name not qualified by one of the exceptions referred to below:

Messrs J. Harvey & Co.   *(Personal)*

but

Ajax Electrical Co.   *(Impersonal)*

(b) Omit *Messrs*

(i) when an individual of the firm is addressed:

> Mr J. Simpson
> Lloyd Harris & Co.

(ii) when the personal name already carries a title:

> Sir James Murphy & Co.

(iii) when the personal name begins with *The*:

> The Robinson Furniture Co.

For incorporated bodies

Never use *Messrs* when addressing an incorporated body, whether incorporated by Act of Parliament. by charter or by registration under the Companies Acts, Address correspondence to the particular officer concerned or, if he is not known, to "The Secretary".

The Public Relations Officer	*(statutory*
Port of London Authority	*corporation)*
The Chief Cashier	*(A chartered*
Bank of England	*corporation)*
The Secretary	*(A registered*
E. Collins & Co. Ltd.	*company)*

ENCLOSURES AND COPIES

To send a letter without its enclosures is an act of carelessness amounting to discourtesy. To receive a letter "enclosing" much-wanted information that is not there is frustrating and a genuine cause for annoyance. Responsibility for making sure that enclosures referred to are in fact enclosed is the typist's, if she makes up the post, otherwise that of the post clerk.

Neither has time to read through all letters to make sure they are complete, and some device is clearly needed to show at a glance when letters have enclosures. There are several ways of doing this:

(*a*) by fixing a coloured adhesive "Enclosure" label to the letter, usually in the top or bottom left-hand position;

(*b*) by typing in the bottom left-hand portion of the letter the abbreviation *Enc*, followed or preceded by a figure indicating the number of enclosures, if there is more than one;

(c) by a horizontal line, a solidus (/), or a series of dots, typed or written, in the left-hand margin of the letter immediately opposite the lines that mention the enclosures.

Of these methods, the first, with its coloured label, provides the most striking signal, but it does no more than show that one enclosure, or more, is needed. It does nothing to show whether there is only one, or two, or three, or whereabouts in the letter they are referred to. It thus becomes necessary to read the letter through.

The second is the method in popular business use. Though less striking than the first, it is superior in that it shows the number of enclosures at a glance. When this method is used the indication *2 Enc* or *Enc (2)*, etc., is placed in the bottom left-hand portion of the letter, two line-spacings below the designation and in alignment with the left-hand margin.

The third, and most effective method of all, is one used by some government departments. It shows at a glance not only the number of enclosures but also the points in the letter at which they are referred to, thus enabling the nature as well as the number of enclosures to be speedily checked. An objection to the method is the appearance of untidiness it gives to the left-hand margin of the letter.

It is an excellent plan to attach enclosures to their letters before correspondence is sent in for signature, unless the enclosures are bulky; they should then be placed in their envelopes. In this way enclosures are less likely to be overlooked in the rush at the end of the day.

When copies of a letter are taken for distribution to interested parties, it is customary to indicate this at the foot of the letter in the left-hand corner by adding *Copies to*, or more commonly *cc* (copies circulated to), followed by the names of the parties.

STAMPED, ADDRESSED ENVELOPES

Whether or not to enclose a stamped, addressed envelope with a letter seeking a reply is largely a matter of common sense. As a rule, a reply envelope is unnecessary, except as follows:

(a) where your correspondent has indicated the need for one, as when theatre bookings are made by post;

(b) where you seek information as a favour, as where an author writes to a firm of publishers for permission to quote from one of their books—you are, after all, putting your correspondent to

some trouble, and you would not wish to put him to expense as well.

A reply envelope is unnecessary, for example, with a request to a manufacturer for particulars of his prices, since the information sought is provided, not as a favour, but in the normal course of a business transaction from which the manufacturer stands to benefit.

ADDRESSING ENVELOPES

The three important requirements of envelope addressing are accuracy, clearness, and good appearance, in that order. The paper used for the envelope should, of course, match exactly the paper used for the letter-head.

To copy the inside name and address from a letter may be a simple matter, but it is an important one. Few things cause more annoyance than letters returned undelivered through being incompletely or wrongly addressed. Non-delivery of an urgent letter may also have serious consequences. In a recent year the Post Office returned to their senders approximately seventy million undelivered letters. They deal with five million wrongly addressed letters every day, though most of these they are able to deliver.*

A sender who feels that his letter might go astray and remain undelivered should write his name and address on the back of the envelope.

Some firms adopt the practice of having their names and addresses printed on their envelopes, either inconspicuously on the front or better still on the flap. The practice is an excellent one, and if universally adopted would help to ensure the speedy return of letters not delivered. It would also save much of the time now spent by Post Office officials in dealing with undelivered mail. The practice, moreover, has useful publicity value. Inland letters that cannot be delivered for any reason are automatically returned to their senders. If the sender's name and address appears on the outside of the envelope the letter is returned unopened, but where these particulars are not given the letter will be opened and then returned. These arrangements for the return of undelivered mail apply equally to letters charged at first-class and second-class rates. No charge for the service is made to the sender.

* Public Relations Department, Post Office

Undelivered letters that cannot be returned to their senders are destroyed.

Post Office rules

To assist speedy delivery the Post Office concentrates mail on certain *post towns*, each of which serves as a clearing-point for a particular district. These towns are key points of the postal system and are specially chosen for their accessibility. A provincial postal address may therefore include the name of a post town with which the addressee has little connection, and in some cases an official postal address may bear the name of a neighbouring county instead of the county in which the addressee lives. The official postal address of Staines in *Surrey*, for example, is Staines, *Middlesex*.

The *Post Office Guide*, copies of which may be bought at any post office, gives detailed information on envelope addressing, with examples, and some useful suggestions to ensure speedy delivery, including the following.

(a) Write or type the name and address in the lower part of the envelope, beginning at least 4 cm from the top so as to leave ample space for stamps and postmark. If set too high name and address are liable to be obliterated by the postmark.

(b) Use your correspondent's full address, including the post town followed by the county name and postcode. The county name is especially important when the destination is not well known, and is essential where there is more than one town of the same name (e.g. *Newport*, of which there are five in the United Kingdom). The county name may, however, be omitted from addresses in cities and certain large towns (e.g. *Birmingham, Cardiff, Edinburgh*) and from towns that give the names of their counties (e.g. *Buckingham, Nottingham, York*).

(c) Write or type the name of the post town in block capitals and the county name in full, unless it is one of those included in the following list of abbreviations recognized and approved by the Post Office:

Beds	for Bedfordshire
Berks	for Berkshire
Bucks	for Buckinghamshire
Cambs	for Cambridgeshire
Co. Derry	for Co. Londonderry
Co. Durham	for County Durham
E. Sussex	for East Sussex
Glam	for Glamorgan

Glos	for Gloucestershire
Hants	for Hampshire
Herts	for Hertfordshire
Lancs	for Lancashire
Leics	for Leicestershire
Lincs	for Lincolnshire
M. Glamorgan	for Mid Glamorgan
Middx	for Middlesex
N. Yorkshire	for North Yorkshire
Northants	for Northamptonshire
Northd	for Northumberland
Notts	for Nottinghamshire
Oxon	for Oxfordshire
S. Humberside	for South Humberside
Staffs	for Staffordshire
W. Yorkshire	for West Yorkshire
Wilts	for Wiltshire
Worcs	for Worcestershire

(d) Write or type the postcode in block capitals, without punctuation. Show it as the final item in the address on a line by itself. If a separate line is not possible the postcode may share the last line (usually the county) provided an adequate gap (two to six spaces) is left between name and code. Alternatively, the post town and the county name may appear on the same line and the postcode on a separate line.

(e) For addresses in the Irish Republic, after post town and county name, add the words IRISH REPUBLIC in block capitals as the final line of the address. There is no post-code.

(f) For postal packets to be called for, write or type the words *Post Restante* or (*To be called for*) on the next line below the addressee's name. Packets of any kind to be called for may, as a rule, be addressed to any post office except a town sub-office. The service is provided solely for the convenience of travellers.

(g) If the postcodes for London and Glasgow are not known, include the letters and numbers of the postal districts (e.g. LONDON EC4; GLASGOW SW2), and after certain other cities and large towns, their postal district numbers (e.g. MANCHESTER 5).

(h) When sending a parcel, place the address *on the parcel itself* as a label may become detached, and include your own name and address *both inside the parcel and on the cover*, in case the wrapping gets damaged, or the parcel cannot be delivered.

To avoid delay and mistakes in delivery the methods of address illustrated in Fig. 9 are recommended by the Post Office.

The *Post Office Guide* includes full details for addressing members of HM Forces and places outside the United Kingdom.

Post Office "don'ts"

(a) Don't use the name of the house instead of the number. If the house bears a number the name is unnecessary.

(b) Don't use the name of the county town for the name of the county (e.g. DURHAM for Co. Durham).

(c) Don't use the words *Local, By* or *Near* as part of the address, except where the words form part of the place-name (e.g. *Stanton by Dale*). Used with the name of the town these words are redundant, and a letter addressed *Local* without the name of the town may well go astray and remain undelivered.

(d) Don't use the abbreviated addresses registered for telegrams.

(e) Don't type anything on an envelope below the level of the line used for the postcode.

Some further suggestions

(a) Type the envelopes when you type your letters; to wait till the letters are signed may create bustle at the end of the day and lead to mistakes.

(b) There is as yet no settled pattern for addressing envelopes—the blocked form with single line-spacing and the indented form with double line-spacing are both in general use. The blocked form is the one most often adopted for the plates and stencils used with addressing machines. If the indented form is used indentations should be about five or ten spaces depending on the length of the lines in the address. For large envelopes the indented form is the more suitable.

(c) Type your correspondent's name exactly as he uses it himself, and be sure to spell it correctly. To fail in this is to be discourteous as well as careless. If he signs himself *James Bent* address him as *Mr James Bent* and not as *Mr J. Bent*.

(d) Don't use *No.* before street numbers, but include it when using a Post Office Box Number, thus: *PO Box No. . . . (followed by the postal address)*.

(e) Type words such as *Street, Road, Avenue* in full.

(f) Mark an envelope *Confidential* rather than *Personal*, unless your letter is intended for your correspondent in his purely private capacity. In the absence of your correspondent a *Personal* letter will remain unopened, but one marked *Confidential* will be dealt with by his deputy. Keep the word well clear of the address in the top left-hand corner, where it is likely to be spotted by

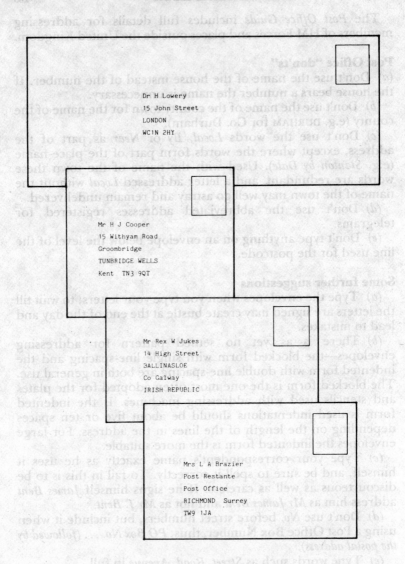

Dr H Lowery
15 John Street
LONDON
WC1N 2HY

Mr H J Cooper
15 Withyam Road
Groombridge
TUNBRIDGE WELLS
Kent TN3 9QT

Mr Rex W Jukes
14 High Street
BALLINASLOE
Co Galway
IRISH REPUBLIC

Mrs L A Brazier
Post Restante
Post Office
RICHMOND Surrey
TW9 1JA

Fig. 9.   *Methods of addressing envelopes.*
(*a*)   A standard form of address.
(*b*)   An address with combined county name and postcode.
(*c*)   An Irish Republic address.
(*d*)   A Post Restante address.

anyone opening the post. To avoid obliteration by the postmark type the words *Confidential* and *Personal* at least 4 cm from the top edge of the envelope. They should also be displayed prominently at the head of the letter itself.

(*g*) When using "window" envelopes type the name and address carefully in the correct position; this will usually be marked in some way to help you.

(*h*) Submit your typed envelope to an independent check, e.g. from your correspondent's letter if the one you are sending is in reply to another.

(*i*) Use envelopes within the Post Office Preferred (POP) range of sizes to assist mechanical sorting (*see* p. 292).

Postcoding

The system of postcoding introduced in the early 1970s is a condensed system of address information enabling letters to be machine coded and then sorted electronically at each stage of their journey right down to the stage of street delivery. *RM2 4EF* is a typical code. Each code is in two parts. The first or outward half consists of one or more letters followed by a number. In the foregoing example the letters *RM* identify the post town (Romford, *Essex*) and the figure *2* a particular district in Romford. The second or inward half of the code, *4EF* in this example, consists of a figure followed by two letters. The figure represents a geographical sector, while the letters identify the street, or part of a street, or even a particular address if that address receives a large amount of mail (normally more than twenty letters by the day's first delivery).

To enable the various sorting machines to "read" the postcode it is converted by an operator at a coding desk into two rows of phosphorescent dots marked across the envelope at the office of departure. The bottom row represents the outward half of the postcode and the top row the inward half. A sorting machine then "reads" the outward half and directs letters to the destination post town, where another machine "reads" the inward half and distributes the letters already sorted to the appropriate delivery postman.

For the efficient working of the system and to avoid delay in the delivery of letters, postcodes must be included in addresses on envelopes. To ensure that postcodes are used correctly firms now include them in their letter headings.

The Post Office issues directories of addresses for each postcode area.

THE USE OF "OHMS"

There are some who have the impression that, when addressing a government department, they may mark their envelopes "OHMS" and omit payment of postage. Others have the impression that this practice is permissible only with letters addressed to the headquarters of government departments, e.g. to government departments in London.

The matter is governed by an instruction issued by HM Treasury. This states quite clearly that postage on all letters and packets addressed by members of the public to government departments should be prepaid by the senders. It is therefore quite wrong to write to any government official or department without first stamping the letter in the ordinary way.

It is, however, customary for government departments who are in correspondence with members of the public to enclose an *Official Paid* cover or label in cases where a reply is required, as, for example, with requests for payment of income tax.

EXERCISES

1. In what circumstances would you omit *Messrs* from an address?
2. What are the Post Office requirements concerning the use on envelopes of:

   (a) display;
   (b) names of Post Towns;
   (c) county names;
   (d) *London*, and postal districts;
   (e) *To be called for*?

3. (a) When would you abbreviate a county name forming part of an address?

   (b) Type the following list in two-column form, using the approved abbreviated forms for those which may be shortened. Then check your list with the *Post Office Guide*.

Bedfordshire	Leicestershire
Cambridgeshire	Mid Glamorgan
Cheshire	Nottinghamshire
County Durham	Oxfordshire
County Londonderry	Staffordshire
Dorset	Suffolk
Gloucestershire	Worcestershire
Hampshire	

4. In the course of your day's duties you require to write letters to the

addresses given below. Show: *(i)* the salutation and complimentary close you would use in each case; *(ii)* how you would address the envelope. (Use imaginary addresses where necessary.)

(a) a close friend who has asked you to address him at the Post Office, Forest Road, Leyton, London E11.

(b) a limited company whose title includes a personal name;

(c) a firm (i.e. a partnership) of solicitors;

(d) an electrician for an estimate for work to be done;

(e) your local Medical Officer of Health;

(f) the Vicar of your parish, asking for a donation;

(g) two ladies carrying on business as hair stylists under the name of *Jeanette*;

(h) your local Member of Parliament, who is a member of the Privy Council;

(i) R. W. Bamford, your national health insurance doctor;

(j) the head of your technical or commercial college (as a former student).

PAPER AND ENVELOPE SIZES

Paper sizes

Some twenty or more basic paper sizes have been in use in Britain for a considerable time. It is from these that the smaller sizes are cut, resulting in a great variety of paper sizes for business documents of all kinds. These basic sizes originated haphazardly, each mill making paper of a size to suit its own facilities.

From the multiplicity of paper sizes in use throughout the world, with all its inconvenience and expense, has emerged an international system of standardized sizes. The system is already in use in many overseas countries and was accepted by the British Standards Institution in 1959. It was adopted by the British Government in 1967. It provides only three basic sizes, known as A, B and C, designed for use as follows:

Size A   For general printing, including stationery
Size B   For posters, etc.
Size C   For envelopes used with A-size stationery

The A series for use in business is now in regular use by British government departments and by a growing number of British business houses, including some of the country's largest companies.

The A-size series are somewhat larger than standard British paper sizes with which they compare as follows:

International A series	*Standard British*
A5 148 × 210 mm (approx. 5⅞ × 8¼ in.)	5 × 8 in. Large post octavo
A4 210 × 297 mm (approx. 8¼ × 11¾in.)	8 × 10 in. Large post quarto
A3 297 × 420 mm (approx. 11¾ × 16½ in.)	8 × 13 in. Foolscap folio

Figure 10 shows how the various sizes in the A series are related. A1 is twice the size of A2; A2 is twice the size of A3; and so on. Sizes A3, A4 and A5 are the sizes normally used for business letters.

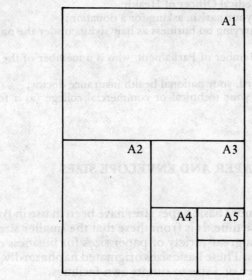

Fig. 10. *International paper sizes.*

Envelope sizes

International size envelopes are slightly larger than their British counterparts. They are prepared from basic size C paper and compare with standard British envelopes as illustrated in Fig. 11.

Methods of folding

There is a right and a wrong way to fold letters, based on the simple principle "as few creases as possible". Careless folding can easily spoil the appearance of a well-typed and attractively-displayed letter.

Folding methods vary with the size of notepaper and matching envelopes used, but, observing the general principle, they are the same for both British and international size stationery. Used with the smaller of the two international size envelopes illustrated in Fig. 12 a sheet of A5 paper is folded once across its

Standard British envelopes

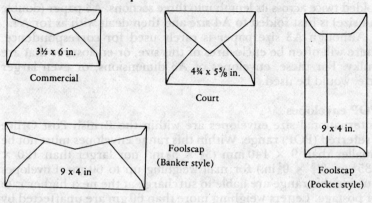

3½ x 6 in.
Commercial

4¾ x 5⅝ in.
Court

9 x 4 in.

Foolscap
(Banker style)

9 x 4 in

Foolscap
(Pocket style)

International size envelopes

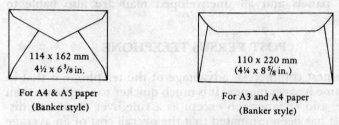

114 x 162 mm
4½ x 6³/₈ in.

For A4 & A5 paper
(Banker style)

110 x 220 mm
(4¼ x 8⅝ in.)

For A3 and A4 paper
(Banker style)

Fig. 11. *Envelope sizes.*

These sizes are all within the Post Office Preferred (POP) range and are those commonly used in business. International size envelopes are also available in the pocket style.

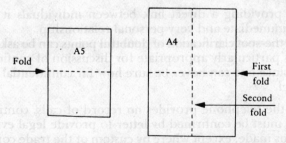

A5

Fold

A4

First
fold

Second
fold

Fig. 12. *Folding international size paper.*

length. A4 paper (double A5 size) is folded first to A5 size and then once more across the middle as in Fig. 12.

Used with the larger international size envelope, A4 paper is folded twice across its length into three sections. A3 paper (double A4 size) is first folded to A4 size and then dealt with as for A4.

Although A3 size paper is rarely used for correspondence, there will often be enclosures of this size, or enclosures that are bulky. For these, envelopes of A3 dimensions, or even larger size, would be used.

POP envelopes

International size envelopes are within the British Post Office Preferred (POP) range. Within this range envelopes must not be smaller than 9 × 140 mm (3½ × 5½ in.) nor larger than 120 × 235 mm (4¾ × 9½ in.) for mail weighing up to 60 gm. Envelopes outside this range are liable to surcharge at the next higher rate of postage. Letters weighing more than 60 gm are unaffected by choice of envelope size. Envelopes with uncovered cut-out address panels and all unenveloped mail are also liable to surcharge.

POST VERSUS TELEPHONE

The greatest commercial advantage of the telephone is that in saving time it saves money. It is much quicker to telephone than to write, and cheaper too except as a rule over trunk-call distances. It has been estimated that the overall cost of an average business letter is at least ten times that of a local call. Trunk calls, however, are expensive and unless there is urgency are not normally used where correspondence serves equally well. Besides speedy communication the telephone can claim the following advantages.

(a) By providing a direct link between individuals it establishes an immediate and very personal relationship.

(b) On-the-spot clarification of doubtful points can be asked for.

(c) It is particularly appropriate for discussion of confidential matters, since one can never be sure how far confidential letters may travel.

But as the telephone provides no record of calls, contractual messages must be confirmed by letter to provide legal evidence of bargains made, except where by custom of the trade contracts agreed upon are binding in honour, as for example Stock Exchange and Lloyd's insurance contracts, or other contracts in which the motto "My word is my bond" is recognized and adopted.

EXERCISES

1. What general principle would you observe in folding letters for the post, and why is the principle important?

2. (a) What are the dimensions of: (i) quarto and foolscap paper; and (ii) commercial and foolscap envelopes?

(b) How would you fold quarto paper for use with: (i) a commercial; and (ii) a foolscap envelope?

3. (a) You have just taken over a well-known and popular hardware stores, the services of whose staff you will be retaining. Draft and set out in proper form a circular to be sent to one of the firm's former customers, notifying the change of ownership and inviting continued custom.

(b) Address an envelope to an imaginary customer and place the letter in it.

4. (a) Imagine you are Secretary of the Clifton Printing Co. Ltd., Clarendon Road, Birmingham B15 3DL, and that you have received a letter dated 15th June from W. Aldred & Co. Ltd., Publishers, Garstang Road, Preston PR1 2BA, complaining that the supply of 1,500 copies of *Modern Business Correspondence* by R. W. Jukes, ordered last January and promised by you for the end of April, have not yet been received.

A fire in your printing works severely damaged the printing machinery and is the cause of the delay, but the machinery has now been replaced and you are hoping to deliver the full quantity of the books by the end of July.

Taking care to set out your reply in proper form and using today's date, write to the publishers explaining the position and conveying your regrets and apologies. Sign the letter, using any name you care to choose.

(b) Prepare the letter for post, as in Q.3 (b).

5. (a) "Brian Jameson, who was offered the job of research chemist, has now turned it down. It is nearly two months ago now. Harold Gardiner was a close runner-up. Ask him if he is still interested, and if so to phone me for an appointment to come and see me—the sooner the better. We shall cover hotel and first-class travelling expenses as usual. He's an MSc, Manchester, and a PhD, London, and should be good. Sign the letter for me."

The Personnel Manager of Eric Castle & Son Ltd., Castle Mills, Romford RM1 2EG has been talking. As his secretary write a suitable letter. Mr Gardiner lives at 252 New Road, Newcastle upon Tyne NE2 2BL.

(b) Using a commercial envelope prepare the letter for post.

6. What are:
(a) a window envelope;
(b) a trap packet;
(c) a certificate of posting? (RSA)

CHAPTER SEVENTEEN

Telecommunication Services

I'll put a girdle round about the earth
In forty minutes.
Shakespeare: *A Midsummer Night's Dream*

Until 1981 the entire system of inland postal and telecommunication services in Britain was controlled and operated by the Post Office, but in that year responsibility for telecommunications, including telephone and telegraph services, was transferred to a newly-formed public corporation operating under the name of British Telecom.

A network of efficient communication services must at all times be available to governments, business and private persons to enable them to make the intricate arrangements connected with the political, economic and social life of a modern community.

THE TELEPHONE SYSTEM

The earliest communication system by telephone was over long-distance transmission lines, but dramatic changes took place after 1900 with the development of wireless transmission. The whole system is now supplemented by a complex satellite network in space, and today messages can be sent to and received from all parts of the world including ships at sea. There are over 6,000 telephone exchanges in operation in Britain; all are fully automatic and currently serve thirteen million subscribers. Over 50 per cent of householders now have a telephone and the number continues to grow rapidly.

Call facilities
The following are among the most important telephone services now provided.

British Telecom is converting the telephone network over a

period of years to what is termed System X. Telephone exchanges will become digital instead of electro-magnetic. This will mean a much higher quality of transmission than at present and make many additional services available to subscribers.

(a) *Subscriber trunk dialling (STD)* is available for all trunk calls. Calls are connected immediately the telephone number of the subscriber called is dialled. If the subscriber dialled lives outside the area from which the call is made, the caller must first dial the code number of the area in which the person called lives. As calls are connected they are automatically recorded on the subscriber's meter, the charge for a call being based on the duration of the call, the distance of the call and the time of day.

(b) *International Direct Dialling (IDD)* is available to all United Kingdom telephone users, who can dial direct to other users in over 100 countries. Like STD it is an all-figure system and when fully developed will enable subscribers throughout the world to dial one another direct. As for STD, calls are charged on a time-and-distance basis.

Long-distance calls can, however, be expensive. For example, the charge for a three-minute call to the USA starts from £1.61 (cheap rate at 1984 prices).

(c) *Special call facilities* include *Personal calls*, the timing of which does not start until contact with the person wanted has been made; *Fixed-time calls*, by which trunk calls can be connected at specified times booked in advance; *Prolonged trunk calls* lasting not less than two hours, or for a consecutive daily use lasting not less than 15 minutes—both at reduced rates of charge; *Alarm calls* by which telephone users can arrange to be called by the operator at any time of day or night.

(d) *Freephone service*, which enables customers, employers' representatives and others to telephone an organization without cost to themselves. It encourages customers to place orders by telephone and saves representatives and agents the trouble of using coins and claiming refunds for calls made to their employers. Organizations using the service pay a quarterly rental and a small additional charge for each call made.

(e) *Credit card facilities* are available for businessmen whose work frequently takes them away from their headquarters. Cards are obtained from local telephone sales offices and holders can make calls from any telephone, including coin boxes, and have them debited to their regular bills. To enable them to be recorded calls must be made through the operator.

(f) *Private Automatic Branch Exchanges (PABX)*. For a business with a number of telephone extensions British Telecom will arrange to install a switchboard, or PABX. The facilities include direct dialling of external calls from internal extensions, interconnection between extensions, and for internal conversations to be conducted privately while outside callers are held. Small amplifiers enabling incoming calls to be heard at a distance from the telephone can also be provided.

(g) *Teleconference.* It is now possible to arrange for meetings to be held over the telephone (or by television) by groups of people in three or more different rooms, or even buildings. Most electronic telephone systems make it possible for discussions to take place while the parties are sitting at their desks using telephone extensions.

(h) *Radiopaging* is a system which provides a person with a pocket receiver that bleeps (i.e. produces a short high-pitched note) when the person is called. If, for example, a doctor is on his visiting round his receptionist would dial the appropriate radio-paging code. The doctor would then telephone his surgery for the message. It is also possible to have a coding system so that on hearing one bleep the doctor would phone his surgery and two bleeps his hospital. Group calling is also available so that it is possible for a number of persons to be alerted by dialling only one paging number.

(i) *The telewriter* is a small machine with an electronic writing pad. When connected to a telephone it is possible for conversations to be supplemented by written text and diagrams. When one of the subscribers wishes to use the machine to make or illustrate a particular point he presses a switch and writes or draws on the pad with an electronic pencil. What is written is instantly reproduced on the telewriter at the other end. Constant interchange of conversation and writing eliminates misunderstanding, and helps clarify the discussion of details. The written text and the diagrams also serve as useful reminders of what has been discussed and the results that have been reached. Automatic answering equipment makes it possible to transmit information at times when the receiving office is unattended.

(j) *Digital* is a press-button system using a microcomputer. It comprises all the call facilities of PABX and operates at press-button speed. It can store in its memory all frequently-dialled calls and recall them as required at the press of a button. It can also store the last number dialled and reconnect the caller, thus eliminating time-wasting redialling.

(k) *Telephone directories.* No charge is made to subscribers for their home area directories, or for the London, Northern or

Midland Commercial Classified Directories to subscribers in the areas covered.

The *Yellow Pages* classified sections of the directories contain the names, addresses and telephone numbers of subscribers indexed under their trades and professions. The *Yellow Pages* are useful when a subscriber wishes to get in touch with persons and organizations engaged in some particular branch of business activity.

Using the telephone

The operator

The telephone has now become so much a part of normal everyday life that most students entering business for the first time will already be accustomed to using it. It has become an almost indispensable part of modern life, particularly so in offices where many transactions could not be carried on without it. The switchboard operator is a significant link between the firm and the outside world, and through the effect on callers of the manner of speech, and the speed, accuracy and courtesy with which calls are handled does far more to enhance or impair the good name of the firm than is often realized.

Some preliminary training is therefore desirable. It should be directed to establishing proper habits and desirable qualities in telephone usage—clear diction, unaffected and free from any trace of unpleasant accent, and a business-like and pleasant manner. Discourtesy on the telephone is more often than not the result of thoughtlessness. Any form of unnecessary delay is a form of discourtesy. The operator can help to avoid this by keeping a pad and pencil near at hand. Notes can then be taken without wasting the caller's time. The habit of speaking "with a smile in the voice" is one which should be cultivated. To smile when we speak goes far to make the voice pleasant.

Telephone etiquette

(a) Answer the phone promptly, speak clearly and announce your telephone number or the name of your firm, or both. Where it is more appropriate, give your name and department, adding *Miss* or *Mrs* if you are a woman, but not *Mr* if you are a man. The addition of "Good morning" or "Good afternoon", or "Can I help you?' creates a good first impression. Good speech habits are more than ever necessary on the telephone since interference from other lines sometimes makes even the clearest speech difficult to understand.

(b) Avoid the greeting "Hello" or "Yes?". Such greetings are discourteous as well as time-wasting, since they put your caller to the trouble of finding out who you are.

(c) Be polite, courteous and pleasant, but never familiar, and speak in a warm and friendly tone "with a smile in your voice".

(d) Avoid slang expressions such as "Hang on" (say *Hold the line please*), "OK" (say *Certainly,* or *Very good*), or "Half a mo" (say *Just a moment please*). Avoid, too, the irritating "Yep" for "Yes".

(e) Offer to ring your caller back if information is wanted that will take you some time to find, but if the caller decides to wait keep him or her aware of what is happening.

(f) If the caller states that he or she wants to speak to a particular person, repeat the name of the person calling, and if the caller has not already identified himself, ask "Who is calling please?". If there is likely to be any delay, ask him to hold the line (Please hold the line Mr/Mrs/Miss . . .).

(g) If you cannot deal with the caller and must transfer the call to a colleague, explain to your colleague the nature of the call. It wastes the caller's time and tries his patience if he has to repeat a question he has already asked or information he has already given.

(h) When speaking on an imperfect line do not shout, but speak more slowly and with greater deliberation. Shouting causes distortion and makes matters worse.

(i) Treat with strict confidence matters you overhear on the telephone. Your duty in this is as confidential as the private secretary's in dealing with her employer's correspondence.

(j) When making a call check and make sure that you are connected to the organization you want, and then ask to be put through to the person or extension you want. (Please put me through to Mr . . ., or to Extension . . .)

Economy and the telephone
It is estimated that the overall cost of an average business letter is not less than about 60p. For local services the telephone is therefore cheaper and wherever possible is recommended unless a written record of the transaction is necessary for future reference or as evidence in the event of legal proceedings. Trunk calls, on the other hand, are rather expensive and unless it is a matter of urgency should not normally be used if correspondence will serve equally well.

THE TELEPRINTER SERVICE (TELEX)

The teleprinter is a universal telegraph instrument closely

resembling a typewriter in both appearance and operation and is easily operated by a competent typist. It has been described quite simply as "a machine for typing over wires". It combines the speed of the telephone with the authority of the printed word, and no confirmation of messages sent is necessary.

Private telephone and telegraph facilities of various kinds may be rented from British Telecom. These facilities provide instant communication between subscribers and their correspondents, and are operated by means of direct circuits, either by telephone or by teleprinter. British Telecom's new electronic teleprinters use microprocessors which enable messages to be stored and transmitted automatically at high speed. Should the number called be engaged the teleprinter will make further attempts.

The system

The simplest form of teleprinter service is a line connecting two teleprinters for either internal or external communication, the latter often over long distances. Every subscriber is given an answer-back code for identification purposes.

To send a message the operator dials the number of the person or organization to be contacted. When the answer-back signal is received—indicating that the receiving machine at the other end is free—the operator sends the firm's own code signal and proceeds to send the message. The message is typed on a continuous paper roll and is instantaneously reproduced in the same form on the machine at the other end of the line. To attract the attention of the receiving operator the transmitting operator can press a button marked "Bell" on the keyboard and this operates a bell or buzzer on the receiving machine.

By using either carbons or specially prepared rolls up to five or six copies of the message can be produced. Should a larger number of copies be needed the teleprinter will cut a duplicating stencil.

The teleprinter system is widely used both by British Telecom for its telemessage and telegram services and by private firms, some of which install their own teleprinters and operate them on contract from British Telecom.

Automatic transmission

Like STD telephone calls messages sent by teleprinter are charged on a time-and-distance basis, and because of the distance sometimes covered can be very costly. These costs can be cut considerably by using special equipment for transmitting messages automatically at high speed. This equipment is generally fitted to the teleprinter as an alternative to the standard equipment.

The message is typed in the normal way. This produces a typed copy of the message and at the same time punches on paper tape a series of holes corresponding to the symbols on the teleprinter keyboard. The code used is the standard teleprinter code (*see* Fig. 13). When the typed copy has been checked the punched tape is fed through the machine for automatic transmission. The receiving teleprinter can receive the message either as normal printed copy or in code on punched tape.

Combn. No.	Letters case	Figures case	Start	Code elements	Stop
1	A	—	○	●●○○○	●
2	B	?	○	●○○●●	●
3	C	:	○	○●●●○	●
4	D	Who are you?	○	●○○●○	●
5	E	3	○	●○○○○	●
6	F	Optional	○	●○●●○	●
7	G	Optional	○	○●○●●	●
8	H	Optional	○	○○●○●	●
9	I	8	○	○●●○○	●
10	J	Bell	○	●●○●○	●
11	K	(	○	●●●●○	●
12	L	)	○	○●○○●	●
13	M	.	○	○○●●●	●
14	N	,	○	○○●●○	●
15	O	9	○	○○○●●	●
16	P	0	○	○●●○●	●
17	Q	1	○	●●●○●	●
18	R	4	○	○●○●○	●
19	S	'	○	●○●○○	●
20	T	5	○	○○○○●	●
21	U	7	○	●●●○○	●
22	V	=	○	○●●●●	●
23	W	2	○	●●○○●	●
24	X	/	○	○●●○●	●
25	Y	6	○	●○●○●	●
26	Z	+	○	●○○○●	●
27	Carriage Return		○	○○○●○	●
28	Line Feed		○	○●○○○	●
29	Letters		○	●●●●●	●
30	Figures		○	●●○●●	●
31	Space		○	○○●○○	●
32	All spacing		○	○○○○○	●

Mark Element ●;   Space Element ○

Courtesy: Creed & Co. Ltd.

Fig. 13. *Standard teleprinter code.*

Letters and figures are represented by holes punched in various positions across the width of the tape. Messages are transmitted at a constant speed of 66 words a minute.

Automatic transmission has two advantages:

(a) *the high speed of transmission* (400 characters a minute) greatly reduces costs, but against this saving must be set the cost of the equipment used;

(b) *the message can be checked* for operational errors in advance of transmission.

Teleprinters with a visual display unit, similar to that of the word processor, make it possible to correct errors more easily than when the punched-tape system is used, but it sacrifices the advantages of automatic transmission.

The telex service

Telex is the name given to the teleprinter service operated and maintained by British Telecom. For an annual rental a subscriber to the service is provided with a teleprinter and a direct line to one of the fifty or more automatic Telex exchanges widely distributed throughout the country. The subscriber is given a Telex number, which is published in the Telex Directory.

Calls are made by direct subscriber dialling to all Telex subscribers in the United Kingdom and to most European Telex users. Calls to overseas subscribers who cannot be dialled directly are connected through the International Telex Exchange in London. This Exchange has access to the entire world-wide Telex network, which links over 100,000 subscribers in over fifty countries, including the United States and countries as remote as Japan and Australia.

The system provides a 24-hour service, and messages may be sent to a subscriber even though his teleprinter is unattended, provided it has not been switched off. It is thus possible to send messages at night ready to be dealt with first thing next day. All calls are charged on a time-and-distance basis.

Telex subscribers can also use the teleprinter to send messages direct to British Telecom for outward transmission. Incoming messages can also be received directly on to the subscriber's teleprinter in the same way. This arrangement allows messages to be sent and received more quickly than by the normal method, and also at any time.

DATA PROCESSING SERVICES

Datel

Datel is the name given to a separate group of communication services provided by British Telecom for transmitting data (information) over the telephone network. It involves the use of special equipment at both the transmitting and receiving ends of the line, with standardized connections for teleprinters, coding and decoding units and other forms of input/output equipment.

The system is used by banks, insurance companies and other large organizations to meet the demand for up-to-date information on matters that concern them. For example, a head office equipped with a computer may receive information by telephone, teleprinter or punched tape and feed it into the computer for processing. By this means all branches and agencies linked to the central computer have immediate access to up-to-the-minute information on items in which they may be interested. A branch bank, for example, could have immediate access to information on share prices and monetary rates of exchange prevailing at any particular time of day.

Prestel
Prestel is a viewdata service introduced in 1979 and now operated by British Telecom. The service affords access to a virtually unlimited store of computerized information provided by numerous organizations on a wide range of subjects such as up-to-date news, rail and air travel information, job vacancies, educational opportunities and welfare information. The information is displayed on a screen and is obtained by connecting either a modified television receiver, or a purpose-built terminal, over a telephone exchange line to a central computer.

The subscriber dials for information by pressing a key on a pad attached to the receiver. An information index is held in the system itself.

Until recently the system was available only for receiving information but it is now adapted for two-way transmission. In the main, current use is restricted to business firms or other organizations who require up-to-the-minute information on a wide variety of matters. The system can also be used for ordering goods and services, reserving seats on trains and aircraft, and so on.

Teletex
Teletex is a system enabling typescript messages, especially those produced by word processors, to be electronically transmitted over the telephone system. It is not to be confused with *Teletext*, which is a viewdata system for broadcasting simple graphical information in the form of text and drawings to viewers who have specially adapted television receivers.

TELEGRAPHIC SERVICES

The telegraphic services operated by British Telecom provide speedy and reliable transmission of urgent messages both inland and overseas. The services are operated by a separate department in each British Telcom area. To send a message it is necessary to telephone details to this department, or to send them by teleprinter if one is available. If the department's phone number is not known contact can be made by dialling 100 (190 in London). The operator will then make the connection. When the caller is informed of the connection, the department's operator will require the following information:

    (a) caller's name, address and phone number;

    (b) terms of the message to be telegraphed;

    (c) class of message required if other than ordinary, e.g. whether priority (urgent), in code, etc.;

    (d) if the message is to be transmitted in a language other than English, the caller must name the language.

The caller then dictates the message, including his correspondent's name and full address. To enable the caller to verify the details of the message dictated the operator will read them back for checking.

The charge for a message telegraphed abroad includes a basic standard charge which varies with the destination country, plus a charge for each word in the message, including the correspondent's name and address. The charge for the message is debited to the calling subscriber's telephone account.

Preparing a message

Because of the high cost, messages must be as short as clearness, completeness and exactness permit. Salutations and closures and all other unnecessary and unimportant words are omitted, phrases being replaced by single words or by shorter phrases where possible.

In letters	*In telegrams*
in the event of	if
in the matter of	about
make an effort	try
by means of	by
we are unable to	we cannot

Abbreviated forms of expression, sometimes called "telegraphic

English", that would be out of place in a business letter, are permissible in telegraphed messages.

In letters	*In telegrams*
We are prepared to rely on your judgment in the matter.	Prepared accept your judgment.
We are glad to say that just now the market is in a very strong position.	Present market position very strong.

It is a good plan first to draft the message in the language of ordinary correspondence, then delete unnecessary words and rephrase. Care is needed not to carry abbreviating to the point of creating uncertainty or ambiguity, otherwise money is not saved but wasted. Much can be done, however, by using words in their most effective way. For example:

Instead of :	Shoes ordered not available, *can supply in* five days. (9 words)
Say:	Shoes ordered not available, *can supply next Wednesday.* (8 words)
Instead of:	Coming tomorrow with books. (4 words)
Say:	Bringing books tomorrow. (3 words)

Inland services

The inland telegram services were withdrawn shortly after British Telecom took over telecommunications from the Post Office. They were replaced by a similar *telemessage* service.

On payment of an annual fee business firms or private persons may register with British Telecom an abbreviated telegraphic address for use by their correspondents, including correspondents from countries that admit registered addresses in telegrams to the United Kingdom. Where a business house receives large numbers of telegraphed communications this arrangement effects considerable savings for those who deal with it. The following are examples:

Full address	*Telegraphic address*
Macdonald & Evans Estover PLYMOUTH PL6 7PZ	Macevans Plymouth
J Harrap & Sons Ltd 67–69 Quadrant Arcade ROMFORD, Essex RM4 6UT	Harrapsons Romford

International services
British Telecom continue to provide a speedy and reliable
method of sending urgent messages abroad. International telegrams may be sent to most parts of the world: to ships in port, to
aircraft at airports, and to trains at railway stations abroad.

The procedure for sending telegrams abroad is similar to that
for telemessages at home, contact being made with the International Telegraph Department by dialling 100 (190 in London)
if the phone number of the Department is not known.

KINDS OF TELEGRAPHIC SERVICE

The following are some of the more important facilities available
for telegraphing information to correspondents at home and
abroad.

Open telegrams/telemessages
An open telegram (or telemessage) is one written in language
whose meaning is apparent to all, including any foreign
language written in the letters of the English alphabet.

Charges for telegrams and telemessages have risen very considerably in recent years and in the interests of economy it pays
senders to be familiar with Telecom rates and charges. The
current charge (1984), for example, for an inland telemessage is
£3 for fifty words, and £1.50 for each additional fifty words or
part.

Charges for overseas telegrams include a standard charge
which varies according to the destination country, plus a charge
of 34p for each word used, including correspondent's name and
address. The standard charge for Australia, for example, is £2.
The charge for the message is debited to the calling subscriber's
telephone account.

Priority telegrams/telemessages
For messages of exceptional urgency priority telegrams and
telemessages may be used. On payment of a supplementary fee
the message receives priority in both transmission and delivery
over messages sent at the ordinary rates.

Letter telegrams
It is sometimes necessary to send lengthy messages of a somewhat less urgent character than those sent by the ordinary
service. Such messages may be sent by letter telegram, and may

be in either plain or secret language. The facilities for this service are provided at a lower rate than for the ordinary service, and are useful where it is desired to send an urgent message that is lengthy and which, if sent by the ordinary service, especially to distant places, would be very costly.

Letter messages may be sent to most places outside Europe. They are delivered during the day following that of handing-in, but may take longer to remote places with no telegraph delivery office. The service is not available for addresses within the United Kingdom.

Press telegrams/telemessages
Press telegrams and telemessages for publication in newspapers may also be sent at reduced rates. They must be in plain language.

The service is available to most overseas countries. Information concerning rates and conditions may be obtained from the Commerce and Press Division, International Telegraph Services, London.

Code telegrams

Code sources
The need for more rapid business intercourse than that provided by letter post progressively increases with the distance of the country it is desired to reach. Yet it is for the more distant countries that telegraphic charges are highest.

Because of the high cost of sending telegrams abroad it is the practice to draw business telegrams for overseas in code. The messages can be understood only by those who have access to the particular code book from which they are compiled. Several international codes are published and extensively used. The ABC, Bentley's and Marconi's are among the best known, though many banks and business houses with foreign branches and agencies have their own private codes.

Published codes usually consist of five-letter words. The code words and the subjects under which phrases and sentences are grouped are both arranged alphabetically to facilitate reference. A reference to the *ABC Code Book*, which contains over 100,000 code words, will serve to show how a code is used. The book includes an alphabetical Index of Vocabulary containing a large number of key words, like *Buying, Correspondence, Delivery, Please, Prospectus*, and *Qualify*, with references to the numbers of the pages on which phrases and sentences relating to these subjects are grouped under their key words, as illustrated below:

EXTRACT FROM ABC CODE—SEVENTH EDITION

Code No.	Code word	Phrase
70339	QIGXI	**BUYING**
		(See *Buy*, also *Demand*, Part I)
70340	QIGYJ	Active buying
1	QIHAN	Advise buying (See *Buy*)
2	QIHBO	Advise buying at your end
3	QIHES	Apparently buying elsewhere
4	QIHGU	Apparently not buying
5	QIHIW	Are opponents buying?
6	QIHKY	Are you buying?
7	QIHMA	As to buying
8	QIHOC	At what prices are opponents buying?
9	QIHRE	At what prices are you buying?
70350	QIHUH	Avoid buying
1	QIHVI	Await buying instructions
2	QIHYL	Await your reply before buying
3	QIIAP	Before buying
4	QIIBR	Before buying further
5	QIICS	Best time for buying (See *Buy*)
6	QIIDT	Better continue buying
7	QIIEV	Better stop buying for the present
8	QIIGW	Better wait before buying
9	QIIHX	Better wait before buying more
70360	QIIJZ	Bulls are buying (See *Bulls*)

Other sections deal with numbers, quantities and prices, and provide a code word for every number, quantity or price in a number of foreign currencies.

It will be noticed that each code word is given a corresponding serial number, and that each word or number indicates a phrase or complete sentence. The use of the word rather than the number is advisable, since errors in transmission are then less likely. The code word corresponding to the phrase or sentence selected is easily obtained from its particular section and written down until the message is complete.

(b) An example

Suppose, for example, J. Fotheringill & Sons wish to send the following cablegram to The Martindale Company, Inc., Broadway, New York, USA (Telegraphic address *Marco, New York*):

At what price can you quote for 120 bales South Sea Island cotton, delivered FAS (free alongside ship) in Liverpool during second half of October?

In the section or word-group of the Code Book headed *Quote* we find that the code word given for the sentence *At what price can you quote* is KJOMO. Similar references to the appropriate word-groups provide the following code equivalents:

Word-group	Phrase or sentence	Code word
Quote	At what price can you quote	KJOMO
Numbers	120	XASAO
Bale(s)	Bales	OTDIG
Cotton	South Sea Island cotton	DLUYF
Delivered	Delivered FAS in Liverpool	EGTHA
Delivery	Delivery in second half of October	ELDOI

Thus, a message of twenty-two words in plain language is reduced to one of six words in code—a saving of sixteen words. The message for transmission would then be entered on the overseas telegram form, as follows:

MARCO   NEW YORK

  KJOMO   XASAO   OTDIG   DLUYF   EGTHA   ELDOI

                                    FOTHERINGILL

Since all code words are arranged in strict alphabetical order, starting with AACAC and ending with ZAGFA, the receiver of the code message has no difficulty in decoding it.

Firms using the published codes usually include a reference to them in their letter-heads, as they do to their telephone and telex numbers and telegraphic addresses.

Cipher telegrams

Telegrams in cipher referred to in the *Telecom Guide* appear to be those based on private or secret codes, as distinct from telegrams based on the published codes available to anyone who cares to invest in the necessary code book.

Cablegrams and radiotelegrams

Cablegrams are telegraphic messages sent by submarine cable. Radiotelegrams are messages sent by wireless telegraphy; they are used for but not restricted to the transmission of messages to ships. To many places both cable and wireless routes are available. A person sending a message to any of these places may request the type of transmission he prefers.

Like ordinary telegrams, cablegrams and radiotelegrams may be sent in either plain or secret language.

Phototelegrams

Pictures, photographs, drawings, and printed, typed or written documents may be telegraphed in facsimile from London to many places overseas. They are accepted at the more important post offices and then forwarded to London for onward telegraphic transmission. Matter for transmission must be on one side of the paper only and must be capable of being rolled. Charges vary with size of document and distance of transmission.

RULES FOR SENDING TELEGRAPHED MESSAGES

(a) Keep a copy of your message for reference.

(b) Use your correspondent's telegraphic address if he has one (you will find it on his letter-head), and add his full name and address to your office copy.

(c) Omit ordinary courtesy titles, salutations and complimentary closures, but include special titles like Sir, Admiral, Reverend.

(d) Use telegraphic English if its meaning is clear, preferring short sentences to long, and omitting all words that can be readily implied.

(e) Use the word *Stop* if it is needed to mark the end of a sentence.

(f) Express important figures in words. This may add to the cost, but it reduces the liability of error.

(g) Express words in full (e.g. *instructions*, not *instrs*; *creditor*, not Cr). To abbreviate a word saves nothing on the cost.

EXERCISES

1. What important points must you observe when preparing a telegram?

2. What is a telegraphic code? Explain and illustrate the statement that such codes are "the shorthand of telegraphic communication".

3. Give a short description of a teleprinter, and explain how the teleprinter is used.

4. Give a short account of the Telex service, mentioning its advantages.

5. Reduce each of the following messages to suitable telegraphic form:

(a) "On 15th June you sent us 500 metres of your excellent Brinylon, for which we have had a very heavy demand. As the demand is likely to increase we should be glad if you would send us a further 500 metres immediately, in assorted shades."

(b) "I am very sorry indeed that I shall not be able to see you tomorrow afternoon as arranged, owing to being called away on urgent business. I shall, however, be pleased to see you next Friday afternoon. Please let me know whether this is convenient and whether I am to expect you."

(c) "Unless your order reaches us by next Friday, 25th February, we cannot guarantee delivery until after Easter. Orders on hand are sufficient to keep us fully employed till the end of March."

(d) "I am sorry to inform you that, owing to a somewhat serious breakdown in the factory, only half your order has been forwarded. Unfortunately, we cannot deliver the rest of the order before 5th April."

(e) "I am writing to inform you that your order for 25 pairs of men's boots can be fulfilled, but as the boots will have to be specially manufactured we shall not be able to deliver them until the beginning of next month."

6. What are the advantages of using:

   (a) an "intercom" or internal telephone system;
   (b) the British Telecom Telex system?   *(RSA)*

7. Write a cable, not exceeding 25 words in length, exclusive of names and addresses, to your employer who is abroad on holiday, informing him of the following circumstances:

You received a telephone call late at night from the caretaker at the office, telling you that a water tap had been left running in an upstairs cloakroom, and that, as a result, water was running through the ceiling of your employer's office. You went at once to the offices and discovered that the water had unfortunately been dripping right on to your employer's desk, and had presumably seeped into some of the locked drawers, to which he alone held the keys. You moved the desk and tidied up as well as you could. The next morning, when you arrived at the office, you found that an area of ceiling had fallen down on to an expensive rug which had been lent to him by a client.   *(RSA)*

8. Your employer, a sales manager, has just been informed that your central warehouse has been destroyed by fire. Twenty well-known customers must be told that they will not receive any goods until your local warehouse can deliver instead. After telephoning the warehouse your employer learns that it will be ten to fourteen days before any supplies can be sent out.

Five of the customers are in a nearby large town. Prepare a telegram to be sent to the most important one, enquiring whether their order is to stand or is to be cancelled.

Indicate at the bottom of your answer two types of telegram which would be suitable to use.   *(LCCI Priv. Sec. Cert.)*

CHAPTER EIGHTEEN

The Business Report

In full, fair tide let information flow;
That evil is half-cured whose cause we know.
Charles Churchill: *Gotham*

ROUTINE AND SPECIAL REPORTS

Reports are especially important as a means of gaining and giving information. At some time or other all organizations require them. Reports in business are of many types, ranging from the informal verbal report of a telephone conversation or interview to formally written reports of considerable length. Many of these reports are *routine reports* submitted at regular intervals. Examples are reports by travellers to their sales managers, by departmental heads on the work of their departments, and reports made at committee meetings or at the annual meetings of shareholders. Reports of this kind create no special problems. Many are in fact often made on predesigned forms that cut non-essential matter to a minimum and greatly simplify the work of those who present them.

But many of the reports required in modern business are *special reports* dealing with special situations of every conceivable kind. They range from short reports that may be little more than replies to requests for up-to-date information on some special matter to reports involving prolonged enquiry and detailed investigation into matters of wide-ranging significance, requiring those who make them not only to submit details of their findings but also to make recommendations on the course of action to be taken. They may be produced by an individual, or as a result of an investigation carried out by a group or committee, in which case the actual preparation and writing of the report falls upon the secretary.

ESSENTIAL QUALITIES

Report-writing is a specialized form of communication and its cardinal merits, like those in business letter-writing, are clarity, brevity and strict accuracy.

311

Clarity

Your report must be crystal clear. Clear writing is the product of clear thinking; if you don't think clearly you can't write clearly. Your facts and the interpretation you place upon them must be carefully organized, otherwise your reader will not be able to follow what, to you, may be a clear-cut line of reasoning. The art of good report-writing resides not so much in the well-turned phrase and the nicely balanced sentence as in the orderly arrangement and presentation of ideas and in the marshalling of the arguments put forward.

Completeness and accuracy

Whether the report is routine or special, short or long, it must be both complete and accurate. A course of action based on incomplete or inaccurate information may well prove to be a costly business.

Before you can begin to write you must know exactly what is wanted and why it is wanted and then investigate everything that falls within your terms of reference, that is, within the limits of what you have been requested to do. It may be merely to provide information, or on the other hand to consider a subject and make recommendations on a course of action. If the report has not been asked for and is written on your own initiative, then you must define your own terms of reference and set out clearly the limits of your investigation. In either case you must gather your facts carefully, interpret them honestly, distinguishing clearly between what you present as facts and what you express as opinion and, whether your findings are favourable or otherwise, make certain that the evidence on which you raise your conclusions is both adequate and reliable.

Readability

Nothing that is written can be useful unless it is attractive enough to be read. Clear presentation is important of course, but it is not by itself enough. Nothing you write will get the attention you want it to have if you present it in terms that are pedestrian and dull. To use bright and colourful language adds interest to what you have to say and makes your report more readable. To say:

> Men the world over have the same basic instincts, the most important being the instinct of self-preservation.

is pedestrian and dull. It is much more colourful and more likely to catch the reader's interest if we say:

No matter what his colour, race or creed man has the same basic instincts foremost among which is the instinct to want to live.

And again:

The subject of commerce is concerned with every kind of business activity.

is a flat and uninspiring way of saying:

The subject of commerce extends over the entire field of man's business relationships.

Those who write reports have a duty to make the reader's task as interesting and as easy as possible. This will be done only if the report is carefully planned as explained in the following section and directed to the reader's present knowledge of the subject in language that is within the level of his comprehension. The writer must take into account:

(a) what the reader knows of the subject already, avoiding the risk of annoying him by needless repetition;

(b) what he needs to know in order to understand the report;

(c) the kind of language he will understand, particularly if the report deals with technical matters.

Tone

The tone for a report is more formal than that for the business letter. It is therefore customary to write in the impersonal third person, except when the report is the account of an eye-witness or is made in letter form. For example, in the more informal report in letter form we would write:

Our enquiries have included discussions with senior assistant examiners and a close scrutiny of syllabuses and past examination papers, and as a result *we are satisfied* that the syllabuses currently in use are entirely satisfactory as to both form and substance.

But in the formal type of report we should use the impersonal form of the third person and write:

Enquiries have included discussions with senior assistant examiners and a close scrutiny of syllabuses and past examination papers. *These enquiries show* that the syllabuses currently in use are entirely satisfactory as to both form and substance.

PLANNING THE REPORT

A good report calls for the most careful planning and what was said in Chapter Twelve about planning the business letter applies with even greater force to planning a report, since a report will often be a much lengthier and more complex document involving collection, assembly, selection, logical arrangement and interpretation of material from which conclusions are drawn and recommendations sometimes made.

Assembly and selection

Every report has its own special requirements, but certain sources of information are common to all and the extent to which each is used will vary with the nature of the report and the kind of information it calls for. These sources are as follows.

(a) *Recorded information* to be found in previous reports (if any), documents and files of correspondence, books and special articles in magazines and journals.

(b) *Investigated information* from such sources as questionnaires, and interviews with persons who have first-hand experience or special knowledge of the kind with which the report is concerned.

(c) *First-hand information* obtained from personal observations, and specially conducted tests and experiments.

Information obtained at first-hand is more reliable than information recorded by others or obtained from answers to questionnaires and at interviews. Information recorded by others may not always be accurate and reliable and answers obtained from questionnaires and at interviews may state as facts what may be no more than impressions formed or opinions held. Consequently, information obtained from these and other indirect sources should always be checked as far as possible.

Organization and presentation

Collecting and assembling relevant information is the foundation of all good report-writing. It is often a bigger task than the actual writing of the report. The order in which the material for the report is collected is not important; what is important is that you collect enough for the purpose in hand. When you come to collate it you may find that some of your detail is unnecessary and must be rejected and that other information may have to be supplemented and expanded. The next step is to sectionalize your findings and to give each section a defining heading. You will find it useful to break down the process and to proceed as follows.

(a) Decide on a title that makes plain the purpose of the report. This will help you to keep to the point and to reject the unnecessary.

(b) Set up some sort of filing system, using either a loose-leaf folder or card-index system, with sheets or cards appropriately headed with the titles of the sections in which you propose to classify your material.

(c) Arrange your headed sheets or cards in the order in which you propose to write them up. The order you adopt may be either chronological or psychological. In an eye-witness report— of an accident for instance—the record of events should be chronological; any other arrangement is liable to confuse the reader. But for other kinds of report a psychological arrangement in which items are recorded in order of their significance is better. It tells the reader at the outset what he most wants to know and makes the report more interesting. As in a report on a football match the reader does not want to wade through to the end before he can know the result.

(d) From the assembled material bring together related facts and ideas and write them up under their appropriate headings.

STRUCTURE OF THE REPORT

Short reports
In short reports it is customary to arrange items in the following order:

(a) terms of reference;
(b) investigation procedure adopted, i.e. an outline of the methods used to collect information;
(c) findings, i.e. the interpretation placed upon the information;
(d) conclusions drawn;
(e) recommendations, if these are required.

Detailed reports
Because of its greater length the detailed report calls for more organization if the reader is to find his way through it easily. It will often include a table of contents and a synopsis. For the lengthier type of report the following is a typical arrangement:

(a) a title page

(b) a table of contents

(c) a synopsis

(d) the body of the report, sectionalized under headings and sub-headings consisting of:

    (i)   an introduction

    (ii)   investigation methods adopted

    (iii) findings

    (iv) conclusions drawn

    (v)   recommendations

(e) acknowledgments

(f) appendixes

Title page

The title page will usually consist of a separate sheet forming the front cover of the report. The title should be brief but informative enough to show clearly what the report is about, by whom it is submitted, and the date.

```
        REPORT ON PROPOSED INSTALLATION OF AN
                AUTOMATED FILING SYSTEM


                          at


        HEAD OFFICE OF THE NATIONAL ASSURANCE CO. LTD


                          by


                 Office Consultants Ltd


                   12 October 19..
```

Table of contents

Whether a table of contents should be provided is a matter of judgment determined by the length of the report. Where a table is provided the reader can turn at once to those parts of the report that specially interest him. Except in very lengthy reports the table will usually provide all the reference help needed and render a separate index unnecessary, though it may be noted that in a table of contents items are arranged chronologically, appearing in the order presented in the report, whereas in an index they are arranged alphabetically. Moreover, an index will usually give much more detail and provide quick and easy reference to particular topics.

Synopsis
Inclusion at the beginning of the report of a synopsis summarizing the evidence and recommendations not only gives the reader a quick grasp of the substance of the report, but also makes it easier for him to follow the detailed report itself. Being already familiar with the main points he can read the report with a critical frame of mind and assess the relevance and importance of each section as bearing on the recommendations made. Although the synopsis appears at the beginning of the report, it cannot be written until the report, of which it is a summary, has been completed.

Body of the report
If a report is lengthy, its material must be arranged in sections, each with its appropriate heading or sub-heading. These headings are signposts providing points of reference for readers interested only in certain aspects of the report, and also for readers who may wish to use the report for reference in the future. For reports of any length headings and sub-headings are necessary; for short reports they are not. In very short reports they do nothing to help the reader and needlessly elaborate the text.

When diagrams are used to supplement the text each should be placed as near as possible to its textual reference and bear an identifying caption or title. So as not to interrupt the smooth flow of the narrative, references to sources of information should be given either in footnote form at the bottom of the appropriate page or in a reference section at the end of the report. For the same reason statistical evidence, tabulated data, charts, graphs, correspondence and other detailed information should be transferred to appendixes.

The *Introduction* should set out the terms of reference and state how far it has been possible to carry them out. The reader then knows what to look for and can assess and judge what he reads. This opening should be followed by a paragraph explaining the *Methods of investigation* used and the sources from which information has been obtained.

If several possible solutions emerge from the investigation, all of them must be presented in the *Findings* together with the respective advantages and disadvantages of each. If a particular solution is recommended, the reason for choosing it rather than any of the others must be justified by a full and clear explanation.

Conclusions may be given either at the end of each section of the report or, more usually, in a separate "Conclusions" section near the end, though a combination of the two methods can be very effective in very lengthy reports. Where this combination is adopted, the final conclusion takes the form of a summary of main points from the section summaries.

The *Recommendations* made will suggest the course of action to be taken and indicate the probable results. Recommendations must be based on facts and free from bias or prejudice of any kind. Personal feelings must not be allowed to enter into what should essentially be a factual, unbiased and unemotional account of an investigation.

Acknowledgments

For information included in a report, especially if the report is lengthy, the writer will draw upon a variety of sources. These will include books, articles in magazines and journals, records of investigations and experiments carried out by others, and also help given in more direct ways by firms and persons with experience and special knowledge of the matters concerned. Courtesy requires that all such help should be acknowledged, or at least that mention of it should be made. This may be done either at the beginning or at the end of the report. In a book the usual place is at the beginning, either in the Preface or, as in the present book, in a separate "Acknowledgments" section. In a report the more usual place is at the end, in a separate paragraph.

References to written or published work should give full particulars in the following order: author, title, publisher, place and date of publication, edition (if more than one), page numbers and, if known, the price, e.g.

FOWLER, H. W.: *A Dictionary of Modern English Usage*, Oxford U.P., London, 1965, 2nd edn., pp. 85–92.

This not only gives credit to the writer whose work has been used, but also enables the reader to refer to the work for further information. References of this kind will appear as footnotes. If they are numerous they should be listed to form a bibliography placed at the end of the book or report.

The following are among abbreviations that frequently appear in footnotes:

ibid. (L.) for *ibidem* meaning "in the same place". It is used to refer to a book or article mentioned in an immediately preceding footnote.

op. cit. (L.) for *opero citato* meaning "in the work cited". It is used when the book or article referred to is not in an immediately preceding footnote.

et al. (L.) for *et alibi* meaning "and elsewhere" and for *et alii* meaning "and others". It is used to avoid repeating all the names of the joint authors of a publication already referred to, e.g.

CHESHIRE et al.: The Law of Contract

sic (L.) enclosed in brackets and placed immediately after an extract or quotation means "so written" and indicates that the statement is reproduced precisely as shown, as when it includes an error of some kind.

Appendixes

Appendixes provide a convenient means of relieving the text of statistical data and other detailed information that may have little interest for some readers. Readers who find the details irrelevant are not obliged to read them. For other readers the details are readily available if they want them.

An appendix should carry an appropriate title, and if there is more than one appendix each should be designated A, B or C, etc. as in the present book.

CHECKING THE REPORT

When completed, the draft of the report should be carefully checked to make sure that the facts, and especially figures, are correctly quoted and that the language used flows easily and smoothly and is unmistakably clear. The reader is then spared the tedium of having to read any of it a second time before he can grasp its meaning.

In its completed form the report should be dated and signed by the person or persons responsible for submitting it.

FORMS OF PRESENTATION

Reports in letter form

Short reports dealing with subject-matter that is simple and straightforward are often made in letter form. So, too, are reports by consultants and others outside an organization invited to express views, make suggestions, or report on investigations to be carried out for the organization. Similarly, reports requested by a company's board of directors will usually be in letter form. Reports in this form take on the guise of business letters, in which it is helpful if the subject-matter is arranged in numbered paragraphs, as in the following example.

The Director of Education,   20th August 19..
OXBRIDGE

Dear Sir

The Teaching of Commerce

On 5th June you asked us to investigate and make recommendations on the teaching of the subject of Commerce to pupils in secondary schools administered by your Authority. This we have done and now submit the following report.

1. *Enquiries made*
Our enquiries have included discussions with heads of schools both in your area and in the areas of several other Authorities, with senior staff engaged in teaching the subject, with HM Inspectors for Commerce, and with a number of businessmen who have generously placed their extensive practical experience of commercial know-how at our disposal. Our report and recommendations take full account of the views and suggestions obtained from these various sources.

2. *The present situation*
Concerned as it is with the entire field of man's commercial relationships, Commerce covers such a vast and varied range of commercial institutions and services that, as often as not, a study of the subject leaves the pupil with a mass of uncoordinated and often ill-digested information from which he gains little or nothing that is of much value to him. He sees many parts, but never the whole. He fails to grasp the very thing his studies should give him, namely an appreciation of the nature and purpose of business activity as a whole. This is the situation as we assess it following an extensive series of visits to schools in your area, and after a careful scrutiny of the work being carried on in the Commerce classes.

3. *Future policy*
In our view the central aim of the course in Commerce should be to show how the activities of widely different commercial institutions combine to fulfil a common purpose, namely the exchange of goods and services as a means of raising living standards.

4. *Recommendations*
We therefore recommend as follows:

   (a) Teaching should be geared to achieving the overall objective of providing a balanced view of the business world.

(b) It must take account of the changes that are constantly occurring in the business world and link them with the work done in the classroom. Pupils must be persuaded to follow these changes by reading a good newspaper and also be encouraged to bring to class for discussion and explanation press cuttings related to their studies.

(c) Lecturing is not normally a suitable method of classroom teaching. Especially for young people, the technique of questioning should be freely employed in the teaching process, use being made of the pupils' own observations and of associations with relatives and friends engaged in commercial work.

(d) Questions calling for written answers serve important educational ends and should be set at regular intervals. The pupil is then *thinking* and *doing* and therefore *learning*, and the teacher is able to measure the success of his teaching.

(e) High standards of presentation in written work should be demanded and insisted upon since acceptable standards of handwriting and neatness will be required of the pupils when they take up office work.

(f) Because it encourages habits of enquiry and self-reliance, pupils should be taught to refer to sources of information and to discover things for themselves. This raises the need for a suitable and adequate supply in the school library of books on commercial topics.

(g) Educational visits to business houses, factories and exhibitions provide useful contacts with the business world and should be arranged. Properly organized and supervised they give purposeful meaning to what is taught in class.

We are unanimous in feeling that these recommendations provide a sound basis for teaching Commerce in schools of the type referred to.

Yours faithfully

Reports in tabular form

Where the material is complex and detailed the letter form of report is not suitable, and in a lengthy report it becomes necessary to adopt a tabular or schematic arrangement in which subject-matter is classified and grouped in sections under headings and sub-headings, with still further subdivisions if the material lends itself to this. Headings of equal importance should be in the same part of speech and similarly displayed in reference to such matters as centring, indentation, use of capitals and underlining. These points are illustrated in the following example of simple tabulation consisting only of headings and sub-headings.

<u>REPORT ON MAIL ORDER SELLING</u>

(1) <u>Types of Mail Order Business</u>

    (a) Manufacturers

    (b) Department stores

    (c) Warehouses

(2) <u>Causes of Rapid Growth</u>

    (a) Credit facilities

    (b) Returnable goods

    (c) Housewife agents

    (d) Customer convenience

(3) <u>Future Prospects</u>

    (a) Customer appeal

    (b) In-town transport problems

The following is an example of a more elaborate scheme, with headings arranged in five degrees of importance. Note how headings of equal importance are similarly displayed in the matters of indentation, etc. mentioned above. Note also the alternate use of numerals and letters for the different grades of heading, with upper-case roman numerals for the most important and lower-case for the least important headings.

<u>REPORT BY TREVOR BROOKS, MA, ARIBA</u>

on

<u>Proposed Alterations to Property</u>

at

<u>1 Silverless Street, Reading</u>

<u>1 CHALET BUNGALOW</u>

A <u>Lounge</u>

    (1) <u>Structural Alterations</u>

        (a) Heat insulation
        (b) Dividing partition
        (c) Fireplace
        (d) French window

```
        (2)  Electrical Work
                  (a) Power points
                  (b) Radiators:
                        (i) Number and type
                       (ii) Positions
                  (c) Lighting:
                        (i) Switch positions
                       (ii) Light positions

        (3)  Decorations
                  (a) Ceiling
                  (b) Fireplace
                  (c) Walls:
                        (i) Painting
                       (ii) Papering

   B  Kitchen

        (1)  Doors

        (2)  Serving Hatch

        (3)  Boiler
                  (a) Type
                  (b) Position


   C  Bedrooms

        (1)  Ground Floor

                  (a) Radiators
                  (b) Decorations

        (2)  First Floor

                  (a) Fitted furniture
                  (b) Radiators
                  (c) Decorations


              II OUTBUILDINGS

   A   Conservatory      These main sections are
   B   Greenhouse        suitably sub-divided
   C   Garage            and headed as above.
```

From an arrangement of this kind the reader can see at a glance what the different sections are all about. The headings are signposts enabling him to pass quickly over sections of the report that do not concern him and to concentrate on those that do. Inclusion of a Table of Contents makes his task easier still.

An alternative method that makes use of a system of numbered sections only is sometimes used in government reports:

1, 2, 3, 4 etc. for main sections;

1.1, 1.2, 1.3, 1.4 etc. for subsections;

1.2.1, 1:2.2, 1.2.3, 1.2.4, etc. for subordinate sections, or for paragraphing within the subsections.

This alternative method is sometimes used in the civil service and in local government.

Reports in paragraph form

Not all reports are long enough or detailed enough to call for five-point headings; four, or even three (the scheme for the most part adopted in the present book) are probably more usual. What is important is not so much the choice of scheme but consistent use of the scheme chosen so that headings of equal importance conform to a uniform pattern of display. For very long reports it is sometimes better to follow the simpler arrangement of numbered paragraphs grouped under section headings, the arrangement adopted in many government reports and illustrated in the following example.

BUSINESS LETTER-WRITING

The Art of Creative Writing

121   Commerce and industry are deeply involved in the art of communicating ideas. It is imperative to write letters that interest
readers, capture their attention, win their approval, and get
desired action.

122   The intelligence brought to this task by the letter-writer does not
need depth of learning, but the ability to correlate and co-ordinate
facts and present them in attractive form.

123   A letter should do in ink what an artist does in oils - pick out the
significant, the interesting, the appealing, and thus give the reader
an intelligible representation of a slice of life. No-one can teach
the art, but it may be learned.

124   When an engineer takes the trouble to find out why and how his
engine works the way it does, he is a better engineer than if he
knows only that to pull a certain lever starts the engine and to
push a button stops it. When a writer understands how his mind
works, and how the minds of other persons work, he will be in a
far better position to progress in his profession than if he
knows only how to put words together grammatically. He will cease
to be a human barrel-organ with a little list of tunes he plays
over and over again.

<u>Some Guidelines</u>

125 In writing anything from an acknowledgement of a routine report to
     the sponsoring of a revolutionary idea it is well to keep in mind
     that you are dealing not only with a situation but also with a person.
     You need to act as interpreter of this piece of business to a reader
     who views the world not only in terms of facts but also of personali-
     ties and emotions.

126 Talent in letter writing is a matter of caring; caring about the
     accuracy of what we write, caring about being of service, caring
     about the esteem in which our firm is held, caring about our personal
     reputation, caring about the satisfaction of doing a job so well
     as to make us feel good.

127 A business letter needs more than a good stenographer. She can
     repair broken grammatical constructions and put the commas in the
     right places, but she cannot supply facts, or add colour, or
     replace muddled language, or say what has to be said in a way more
     likely to appeal to the interest of the reader.

128 What is urgently needed is the personal interest of the writer in
     what he is doing. He must consider the things that concern the
     reader, his level of comprehension, his present understanding of
     the subject, any prejudices he may have, any blind spots which may
     make it difficult for him to accept what you wish to say, and the
     kind of language he will consider appropriate.

(Royal Bank of Canada: *Monthly Letter*—adapted)

THE MEMORANDUM

As defined in the *Shorter Oxford Dictionary* a memorandum is "a
note to help the memory", and in commerce as "an informal
communication, especially one on paper headed with the word
Memorandum". It is a kind of internal business letter—a written
communication between persons employed in the same organization, and often in the same department of an organization, as
where an employee with ideas and initiative wishes to submit
suggestions to his immediate superior.

The memorandum is an informal document and, unlike the
business letter, bears no inside name and address, no salutation
and no complimentary close. Handwritten memoranda are
frequently used for giving instructions and conveying routine
messages. An executive will sometimes present what he may call
a report to draw attention to some matter which he feels should
be made known. The periodical reports submitted by sales
representatives to their sales manager will also usually be in
memorandum form.

Memoranda are often written on printed forms headed in some such manner as the following, followed by the message in the body of the memorandum.

```
                            MEMORANDUM


     From ........................      Date ........................

     To ..........................      Ref .........................

                              Subject



                                        Signature ...................

     Copies to .....................
     Encl ..........................
```

It is always helpful to introduce the message with a heading briefly defining the subject. For a message in the form of a report a heading is necessary and the memorandum must be given a short title indicating exactly what the report is about. If a suitable short title cannot be found, then a short title with an amplifying sub-title is preferable to a single lengthy title. For example:

APPOINTMENT OF BRANCH MANAGER
*Report on Interviews of Candidates for the Vacancy
at Chelmsford*

Space should be provided to indicate to whom copies of the memorandum have been sent, and for a statement of any accompanying enclosures.

Some firms make use of standard memo forms pre-printed on NCR paper (i.e. *No Carbon Required*) arranged in sets of two or more according to the number of copies required. Using a three-part set in different colours the sender passes the original and one of the copies to the addressee and keeps the other for his own use. Should a reply be necessary the addressee uses the original and returns it to the sender, retaining a copy for himself. Thus, both sender and receiver now have complete copies of the original message and the reply.

For the rest, the rules that apply to report writing apply also to the memorandum.

The paper size most often used for memoranda is either octavo (British size) or A5, i.e. half A4 (International size). The memorandum is therefore suitable for only very short reports, though A4 paper may sometimes be used for longer reports.

EXERCISES

1. Imagine that the head of your college has asked for an account of the sports facilities provided by your college sports club and for your suggestions on how these facilities could be improved. Write the report you would submit to him.

2. Write an account of the course you are taking at school or college. Estimate the value of the course to you and, giving your reasons, suggest ways in which you think the course might be improved to make it more useful to you.

3. Imagine that there has been a road accident outside your school, college or place of business as a result of the large number of people leaving the building at one time. Write a short report to the principal or general manager suggesting ways in which the danger could be avoided.   (*UEI*)

4. You are the branch manager of a bank or other large business organization. A vacancy has occurred among your senior assistants. Three junior members of your branch with varied backgrounds and experience have good claims to fill it. Write a report to your area manager giving a balanced outline of the claims of the three candidates.

5. As secretary to the managing director of a company employing 250 office staff you have been asked to give your views on the following two proposals:

(*a*) that the present luncheon voucher system should be discontinued and replaced by a staff restaurant;

(*b*) that 100 junior staff at present paid weekly in cash should be paid monthly by bank transfer.

6. Write a report giving your views on one only of these two proposals.

Either

(*a*) You are a manager of a shop in a holiday resort which sells giftware. You have to send a monthly report to the head office of the group on the month's trading.

Write a report covering either the month of January or June.

Or

(*b*) An essay competition with a £100 award has been run by a college (or school). The subject is "How to control pollution". The assessors publish a report on the winning essay and its author, commenting on subject-matter and style.

Write the report.   (*LCCI*)

7. You have assisted the Company Secretary in devising a new centralized stationery stock issue system (it is a medium-sized undertaking) and he asks you to draft a memorandum to all Heads of Department stating clearly how this new system operates and the reasons for its introduction.   *(LCCI Priv. Sec. Dip.)*

8. Your company has been taken-over, but the new owners have not yet announced any decisions affecting the operation of your company. As Secretary to the Managing Director you are asked to draft a notice to all employees, which will contribute to the maintenance of good morale.
(LCCI Priv. Sec. Dip.)

9. Your employer has asked you for your confidential opinion on a proposal to introduce a typing pool. Write a short report, concentrating on the reaction you expect from departmental typists.
(LCCI Priv. Sec. Dip.)

10. Your employer has asked you to attend and report on a one-day conference with the theme "Mechanization in the Office". Prepare the report, outlining the points made both by the chief speaker and in open discussion.

11. Your college or institute has a refreshment bar open each evening of the session. Write a brief report to the principal on the first year's working. Show to what extent and how it has been a success: draw attention to any difficulties and suggest possible improvements.
(ULCI)

12. As a clerk in a personnel department, write a report on the junior clerk engaged during the past six months, noting his or her *(a)* school last attended, *(b)* educational qualifications, *(c)* bearing during interview, *(d)* attitude to work, *(e)* progress in the company. *(NCTEC)*

13. Your organisation is considering the introduction of more modern office equipment to help overcome deficiencies in internal communications and the storage and filing of correspondence. As Office Manager you are required to prepare a report to the Board setting out your recommendations on the type of equipment which should be installed to improve efficiency in either

(a) internal communications, or
(b) storage and filing of correspondence.   *(ICSA Pt.2)*

14. Your firm is thinking of producing a suggestion scheme. Write a memorandum setting down how you think such a scheme might be organised and the basic requirements which should be observed by management to ensure its success.   *(ICSA Pt.1)*

CHAPTER NINETEEN

Filing and Indexing Systems

Not chaos-like together crush'd and bruis'd.
But, as the world, harmoniously confus'd;
Where order in variety we see,
And where, tho' all things differ, all agree.
A. Pope: *Eloisa to Abelard*

THE PURPOSE OF FILING

In any business house the constant need to refer to previous correspondence is met by a filing system, that is a method of storing papers to provide a readily accessible record of past transactions. The essential qualities of such a system are reliability and accessibility; the only reason for having it at all is to be able to find papers quickly when they are wanted. A person writing a letter will often need to refer to previous correspondence to refresh his memory, or, if he is acting for someone else, to gather the threads of what has gone before.

It is a far cry from the days when correspondence was preserved on spikes and in boxes and pigeon holes, though these old-fashioned methods are still used in some small offices. In keeping with the growing complexity of modern business, filing systems and techniques have been advancing steadily during the past few years to meet the increased demands made on them. Some systems may seem elaborate and complicated, but in actual practice they are usually easy to understand and simple to operate. The original concept of filing still holds good, but the emphasis on types of equipment is shifting, the governing criteria being minimum space and maximum accessibility. Finding space is in fact one of the major problems. The following are some of the things that can be done to help:

(*a*) typing replies on the backs of incoming letters, thus saving not only filing space but also stationery;

(*b*) regular removal of temporary papers and the transfer to the archives of papers no longer in current use;

(*c*) adoption of lateral filing (*see* p. 336);

329

(d) removal and destruction of "dead" papers from the archives;

(e) microfilming archive material where records must be kept for long periods.

MERITS OF GOOD FILING

The essence of filing is to bring together in a single folder or file all papers relating to a particular person or subject; letters received are filed with those sent in reply. A file cannot be restricted to correspondence alone, but must include telexes, notes of important interviews, decisions at meetings, telephone messages, and any other matters needed to make it complete as a record of information.

A difficulty in filing results from the multiplicity of sizes of papers to be filed. Postcards, telexes, notes of telephone messages all have sizes of their own. As most correspondence is conducted on paper of quarto and A4 size, some degree of uniformity can be achieved by recording all telephone messages, notes of interviews, etc., on sheets of those sizes. It may be argued that this entails waste of paper where the record is a short one, but against this must be set the important gain from the increased efficiency of the filing system. Uniformity of size is especially important where papers remain loose in folders not provided with a clip or other fastening device.

A good filing system will have the following merits.

(a) *It will be housed in suitable equipment*—this need be neither costly nor elaborate.

(b) *It will always be up to date*—each day's correspondence will be filed first thing next day and not left to accumulate.

(c) *It will always be tidy*—each file will be clearly titled; if handwritten, in block letters; if typed, in jet-black capitals.

(d) *It will always be easy to handle*—the latest papers will be placed on top or, in vertical filing, in front, since they are the ones most likely to be needed. Non-current matter will be periodically removed and transferred to long-term storage files so that the system is not littered with unwanted material.

(e) *It will be flexible*—it will be capable of expansion or adaptation to suit changing circumstances.

Filing is an essential and vital part of any business; it affects the whole organization. An inefficient system is frustrating to everyone concerned. To the executive who has to wait for the information he wants it is irritating; to the employee who has to fumble and rummage through ill-kept papers it is time-wasting. An efficient system depends as much upon the care with which the work is carried out as upon the care with which the system has been planned. Filing is in fact too important a job to be left entirely to the mercies of unsupervised juniors. It should be done only by the person or persons authorized to do it, and no document should be filed unless it has been marked by a responsible official for filing, as by initialling.

CENTRALIZED AND DEPARTMENTAL FILING

Filing may be organized either centrally or departmentally. Whether one method or the other is adopted is often a matter of opinion. There is something to be said for both. Some large organizations prefer the centralized system based on a specialized filing office, but in most commercial offices departmental filing is preferred.

In favour of centralized filing it is claimed:

(a) that it concentrates the filing, and thus avoids divided responsibility;

(b) that related matter from all departments is brought together in one file, so that staff consulting the file will have all the information available;

(c) that it puts filing under the control of specialists and makes for efficiency;

(d) that filing is more likely to be kept up to date;

(e) that it ensures an efficient follow-up and absent-file system.

On the other hand, files are not immediately accessible when wanted, and must be sent for. In a commercial office this may be a serious drawback.

In favour of departmental filing it is claimed:

(a) that the method of filing most suited to the needs of particular departments may be adopted, e.g. geographical filing for the sales department, and alphabetical filing for the personnel department;

(b) that files are immediately available and that this saves time and raises efficiency.

Centralized filing should not be used for confidential records, such as personnel records, wages and salaries records, and other records of a personal nature.

FILING SYSTEMS

An efficient filing system must be planned to suit the needs of the organization it is to serve. Commercial offices, technical colleges, hospitals and libraries will not all use the same system. Even among institutions forming each of these groups important differences in systems will be found. Each separate application is a matter for special consideration by the organization concerned.

The provision of filing and indexing equipment is now an important industry. Systems range from the simple conventional filing and card-index cabinets to automated storage and retrieval systems of varying sizes and filing capacities. Details of the different systems available may be obtained from the many firms specializing in this field. There are also a number of good textbooks on the subject.

Documents may be filed either horizontally, i.e. flat and on top of one another, or vertically, i.e. upright and either behind one another or side by side. Horizontal filing is the earlier of the two systems but is now little used, except for documents of large size, such as maps, plans and blueprints. The disadvantages inherent in horizontal filing have led to the almost universal adoption of vertical filing for business correspondence and documents; it forms the basis of most modern filing systems.

The following are the systems in present use:

(a) horizontal filing;
(b) vertical systems;
    (i) drawer filing,
    (ii) suspension filing,
    (iii) lateral filing,
    (iv) shelf filing;
(c) microfilm filing;
(d) random access filing;
(e) automated filing.

These will now be considered in turn.

Horizontal filing

Flat or horizontal filing is the earliest of the modern systems. The well-known box file is an example, and is still useful where the amount of correspondence is small, or where there is a need to keep a particular set of papers together.

This method of filing is now little used for business correspondence, but is extensively employed by architects, engineers, and in drawing offices for storing plans, drawings, tracings, photographs, etc., in a flat position in cabinets fitted with shallow drawers about 3–5 cm deep, the drawers usually being labelled.

Drawer filing

The vertical system of filing originated in the use of the well-known filing cabinet. It marks a great advance on the earlier system of flat or horizontal filing; its capacity and therefore its range of reference is many times greater. It is easily expanded, and is easily adapted to a variety of classifications, which may be alphabetical, numerical, geographical and so on.

The equipment needed is:

(a) a cabinet with one or more containing drawers;

(b) a supply of stout manilla covers, called folders, either tabbed to take particulars of the contents of the folder or with the back slightly higher than the front;

(c) a supply of dividing guide cards, which may be tabbed either alphabetically or numerically according to the form of classification adopted.

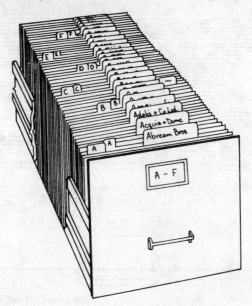

Fig. 14. *Drawer filing.*

Folders are arranged side by side in an upright position behind their respective guide cards. Named tabs make for quick and easy reference.

A separate folder is provided for each firm, subject or other heading under which papers are to be filed. The folders are placed upright in the containing drawers, alphabetically or numerically as the case may be, *behind* their appropriate guide cards (*see* Fig. 14). Papers are filed in their individual folders, in date order, with the latest paper on top, i.e. in front. Should the container drawer not be completely filled, folders are kept upright by means of an adjustable support.

With this and the other systems of vertical filing, folders need not be removed from the drawers when papers are inserted. This eliminates the risk of misplaced folders.

Suspension filing

Suspension filing is an improved form of vertical filing. The containing drawer is fitted with a metal frame from which pocket folders are suspended. The tops of these pockets are flat and take the printed or typed title strips. All titles are visible immediately the drawer is opened (*see* Fig. 15).

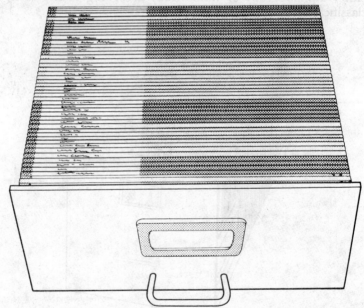

Courtesy: Roneo Vickers Ltd.

Fig. 15.   *Flat-top suspension filing.*

The flat-top title strips enable wanted files to be located at a glance, and give the drawer a neat and orderly appearance.

A folder similar to that for ordinary vertical filing is provided for each suspended pocket and is labelled to correspond with the title strip. It is in this folder and not in the suspended pocket that papers are filed. The pockets are so designed that they can be clipped together at the top to form a continuous concertina-like arrangement that makes it impossible for papers to get lost through being filed between the pockets. (*see* Fig. 16).

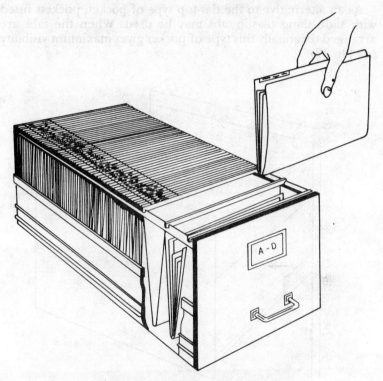

Fig. 16.   *Pockets in suspension filing.*

Folders are removed and replaced without disturbing the arrangement of the pockets.

Suspension filing has the following advantages.

(*a*) The names or numbers of files are prominently displayed, and this greatly facilitates filing.

(*b*) As each inside folder is filed in its own clearly titled pocket, it can be found immediately and replaced just as quickly, without disturbing the alphabetical or numerical arrangement of the pockets.

(c) New files can easily be added to the system in their correct sequence.

(d) The capacity of the pockets is considerable, but no matter how fully loaded pockets may be, the containing drawer always retains its neat and orderly appearance.

(e) Coloured metal signals can be clipped over the flat tops of the pockets to indicate special facts.

As an alternative to the flat-top type of pocket, pockets fitted with slide-along plastic tabs may be used. When the tabs are arranged diagonally this type of pocket gives maximum visibility (*see* Fig. 17).

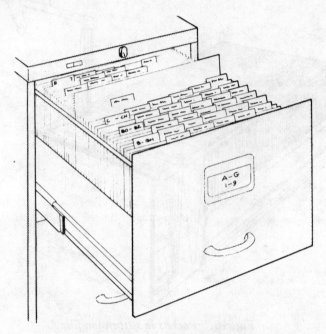

Courtesy: Roneo Vickers Ltd.

Fig. 17.   *Flexatab suspension filing.*

Slide-along tabs can be moved to positions that provide maximum visibility.

Lateral filing
Lateral filing is a variation of the suspension system described above. Files are arranged in very much the same manner as books on shelves. They are placed in interconnected concertina-like pockets similar to those used in suspension drawer-filing,

but which hang from rails laterally either in cupboards or in open shelving (*see* Fig. 18). Each file is fitted with an adjustable title holder (*see* Fig. 19).

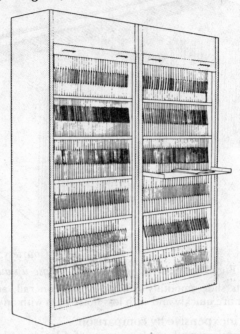

Courtesy: Roneo Vickers Ltd.

Fig. 18.   *Lateral filing.*

A "hook-on" system in which files are hung on rails extended across cupboards or between open frameworks. It is very economical of floor space and, by comparison with the drawer-suspension system, is inexpensive.

Office floor space becomes more and more expensive, and in order to make the best use of it there is a tendency to imitate the growth of the modern office building and to adopt filing systems that extend upwards instead of outwards. Lateral filing makes this possible. Its chief merit is in fact its economical use of floor space, and for this reason it is often the preferred system where accommodation is the overriding factor. Over ordinary vertical and suspension filing it has a number of advantages.

(*a*) It occupies much less space. For example, if taken to a height of only five rails it occupies less than half the amount of floor space.

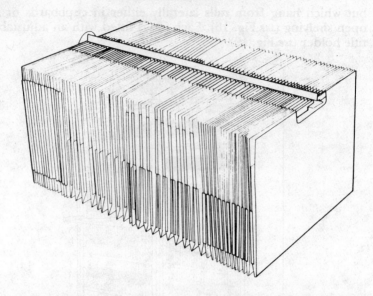

Courtesy: Shannon Ltd.

Fig. 19.   *Lateral filing section—close-up view.*

The pockets slide smoothly along the hook-on rail, and folders are extracted more quickly and with less noise than with any other system.

(b) It is inexpensive by comparison.

(c) Extraction and replacement of files is quicker and less noisy.

Shelf filing

Shelf filing is the most economical of all. Shelves can be installed up to ceiling height, and the distance between them need only be an inch wider than the folders. Pivoting dividers, which adjust automatically as the number of files increases or diminishes, hold the files at an angle and create a "vee" opening at any point where they are parted, thus making it easy to remove or replace files. Alternatively, movable dividers made of wood or metal may be used to maintain files in an upright position.

Microfilm filing

Microfilming is a method of commercial reproduction now used by many large organizations for copying documents of which permanent records are needed. The method is widely used in specialized libraries, and by banks for preserving records of customers' cheques.

To view the documents that have been microfilmed a "viewer" or "reader" is used which projects the film on to a screen. Should a copy of the filmed document be required the relevant film is processed by a "reader printer".

The great advantage of the microfilm lies in its economical use of filing space. Films are stored in canisters occupying only a small fraction of the space needed for the corresponding documents which, having been filmed, can be destroyed. The filmed documents may be indexed in such a way that reference to particular documents is as quick and easy as with a conventional filing system. But for many of its uses film needs to be divided into its separate images and filed in a more conventional manner, as by fixing the separate images permanently to special cards, or inserting them in the pockets with which the cards are sometimes provided.

The equipment required consists of a *camera*, as a rule using 35 mm film and fitted with an automatic feeding device into which documents are inserted in batches in the sequence required for filming, and a *scanner unit* for projecting the filmed documents on to a screen for subsequent reading. As the initial cost of this equipment is high, microfilm filing is justified only where records that must be kept for long periods are fairly numerous, or where normal filing or storage accommodation is not available.

Random access filing

Random access is a system of electronically controlled filing in which cards—opaque, aperture, microfilm, or transparent envelopes containing microfiche (*fiche* for short*—are edge-punched to indicate a letter code.

The equipment consists of a series of trays (each with a capacity of 2,000 cards), a push-button control panel and a coder device. The coder is activated by the control panel to edge-punch the cards for items of information represented by the code used. A record is maintained of the different codes available.

When a particular item of information is wanted the relevant code-letter keys on the control panel are depressed and all the cards containing the information are automatically ejected. The whole operation takes only a few seconds.

This system of filing has a wide range of applications, including hospital, insurance and personnel records, and documentation.

*A fiche is a rectangular sheet of microfilm about the size of a postcard. A standard A6 fiche will normally contain anything up to 100 images, but can hold more depending on the reduction ratio.

Automated filing

The simplest automated systems consist of a cabinet fitted with a large-diameter storage wheel with a capacity for up to 5,000 13×8 mm record cards and push-button operation enabling particular cards to be located and retrieved in a few seconds. More sophisticated equipment consists of two facing banks of filing containers arranged from floor to ceiling. At the touch of a button on the operator's control panel the selected container is withdrawn automatically from its allotted place on the shelving system and delivered to the operator on a movable platform. When the file or other record has been dealt with its container is returned to its original shelf position at the touch of the "Restore" button (*see* Fig. 20). A much larger version of this electronically controlled system is the Roneo-Vickers *Conserv-a-trieve*, which handles storage containers occupying the space of a large room.

Courtesy: Roneo Vickers Ltd.

Fig. 20.   *An electronically controlled storage system.*

This model selects files from two facing banks of containers at the touch of a button.

EXERCISES

1. What is the purpose of filing, and what are the essential qualities of a good filing system?

2. What is centralized filing? What advantages are claimed for it, and in what circumstances would you recommend it?

3. Explain briefly what is meant by (a) vertical filing, (b) suspended filing and (c) lateral filing, mentioning their similarities and differences.

4. What special advantages are claimed for suspended filing?

5. Explain what is meant by (a) departmental filing and (b) centralized filing. Discuss the advantages and drawbacks of these two systems.

6. You work in a firm which has grown from one department to four departments over the past year. Previously only you and your employer handled all correspondence. Now correspondence is going out from four different departments, each department keeping its own files. As a result, letters cannot easily be traced. Write a report on how you would arrange a central filing system, and what rules you would make for its use. *(RSA)*

7. What important general rules must be observed to ensure the efficient working of a filing system?

8. What factors have to be considered when a heavily-used filing system is breaking down and a new and more appropriate system has to be introduced? *(LCCI Priv. Sec. Dip.)*

9. Discuss the advantages and disadvantages of: (a) lateral filing systems; (b) suspended filing systems. *(RSA)*

10. How could you economize in the space occupied by both filing and indexing systems? *(RSA)*

METHODS OF CLASSIFICATION

Four basic methods of classifying correspondence for filing are in use: (a) alphabetical; (b) numerical and alpha-numerical; (c) geographical; and (d) the subject. Which of these methods is adopted will mainly depend upon the type and size of the organization and the nature of its work. Sometimes where filing is carried out in the departments different methods will be used within the same organization. For a sales department, for example, the geographical may be the most useful method, and for an accounts department the alphabetical, while subject filing will almost certainly play some part in the secretary's office of any organization.

Alphabetical filing

The alphabetical classification is the most commonly used of all. Even where the geographical or the subject classification is used, the arrangement of place-names and subject-names is still alphabetical.

Alphabetical filing is especially appropriate to small concerns where correspondence is not very considerable, or the number of separate folders is not numerous. It operates very simply. A folder is prepared for each person or firm dealt with and labelled with the name. The surname or other key word comes first, followed by Christian names or forenames. Folders are arranged in strict alphabetical or dictionary order and divided by and placed *behind* guide cards with tabs bearing the letters of the alphabet or some combination of them.

(a) Primary guide cards are inserted with the tab on the left-hand side of the filing drawer.

(b) Secondary guide cards are inserted with the tab in the centre of the filing drawer.

(c) Labels on individual folders are placed on the extreme right-hand of their folders.

Staff retrieving files will then cast their eye to the left to locate the primary section (e.g.*B*), then to the centre to locate the subsection (e.g. *BE, BL, BR*), and then to the right for the file wanted (e.g. *Benson, S* etc.)—*see* Fig. 21.

Incoming letters and copies of outgoing letters, notes of phone messages, etc., are all placed in their folders in date order, the latest document always on top, i.e. in front.

Placement of particular names

There is sometimes uncertainty about the placing of particular names. How, for example, are we to place names such as *A & Z Supply Co., The 99 Club, De Lacey, McAlpine* and *St Edmund*, and names including such words as *a*, and *of*, and *and*? Not all dictionaries and directories adopt the same practice in these matters, but unless your firm has its own rules you may safely adopt the following, which are widely accepted. They are the rules followed, for example, in the compilation of the *Post Office Telephone Directories*.

(a) Arrangement follows the first word. Thus:

East Ham precedes *Eastdown*, although the fifth letter of the former is later in the alphabet than the fifth letter of the latter.
Abbey National precedes *Abbeydale*.
Hall's Radio precedes *Hallam*.

Note: Surnames in the singular possessive immediately follow all similar surnames without the possessive. Thus, *Hall's Radio*

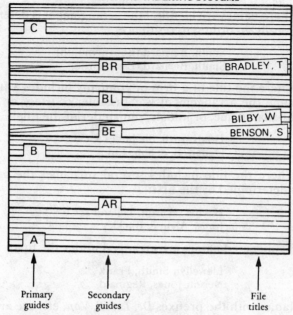

Fig. 21.   *Alphabetical filing with subdivisions.*

Folders are arranged in alphabetical order and placed *behind* the guide
cards.

follows all entries for *Hall*, and *Barton's Café* would follow *Barton,
Zechariah*. In the plural possessive the apostrophe is ignored.
Thus, *Grimes' Wharf* precedes *Grimes, William*.

(*b*) Surnames precede Christian names:

> Brooks, John H.

(*c*) Christian names and initials follow a strict alphabetical
order. *D*. precedes *D.E.*, which precedes *DOnald*, which in turn
precedes *D.R.*

> Higham, D.
> Higham, D. E.
> Higham, Donald
> Higham, D. R.

(*d*) Courtesy and other titles are ignored, and placed immediately after the surname, but do not affect the Christian-
name order:

> Hargreaves, Rev. L.
> Hargreaves, Miss L. H.
> Hargreaves, Dr Lionel

(e) Where names are identical the arrangement is determined alphabetically according to residence:

> Smith, Bernard (Bournemouth)
> Smith, Bernard (Eastbourne)

(f) Where the title of a firm or company includes a full personal name the arrangement is: Surname; courtesy or similar title; Christian name, or initials; remainder of the title:

> Holdsworth, Sir James & Co.
> Ogden, B. & Sons Ltd.

(g) Where the title includes several surnames the arrangement is determined by the first:

> Haynes, Wilson, Yelland & Co.
> Jones, Alvin & Buckley

(h) Hyphenated names are arranged under the first:

> Llewellyn-Smith, Frank
> Nelson-Jones, Reginald

(i) Names with the prefixes *De, Le, O', Van,* etc. are arranged alphabetically under their prefixes:

> De la Rue, Charles
> Le Mare, G. W. & Co. Ltd.
> O'Mahony, Patrick
> Van Dyck, Sir Anthony

(j) The abbreviated forms *M* and *Mc* for *Mac* are treated as *Mac* and the next letter in the name determines the entry:

> McAlpine, John
> MacFisheries

Note: A separate guide card labelled *Mc* or *Mac—Mc* is frequently provided and placed at the *beginning* of the *M*'s, but in the Telephone Directories *Mac* is arranged alphabetically as above. *St* for *Saint* is, however, placed after *Saint*:

> Saint Mary's Convent
> St John Ambulance Brigade

(k) The ampersand, as well as the word *and* itself, is disregarded, but is not omitted:

> Anderson and Davies Ltd.
> Anderson, Kenneth
> Anderson & Moss Ltd.

Of, on the other hand, is included and follows the normal alphabetical arrangement:

> City of Westminster College
> City Parochial Foundation, The

(*l*) When it begins a name, *The* is disregarded and is either omitted or placed at the end:

> Grayson Furniture Co.
> or
> Grayson Furniture Co., The

(*m*) Ministries and town and city councils (but not other incorporated bodies) are arranged under their key words:

> Health, Ministry of
> Westminster City Council
> but
> British Transport Commission
> National Union of Teachers, The

An exception to this rule is the *City of London Corporation*, which, in the London Telephone Directory, is entered under *C* as:

> Corporation of London

(*n*) Numbers are treated as if spelt in full:

> Niner, J. G.
> 1940 Cleaners Ltd.
> Ninette
> 90 Club
> Ning's Coffee House

(*o*) Names composed of initials without surnames are placed at the beginning of their respective letter groups:

ABC Cinemas
ASC Timber Supplies } all precede Aaron, H.
AYS Manufacturing Co.

M&B Contractors Ltd.
MBT Frozen Foods Ltd. } all precede Mabbitt, Henry G.
M/G Twin Set Co.

Subdivision of index

By separating folders into groups of convenient size, dividing guide cards show instantly the approximate position of a wanted file. This saves time in finding it.

It will not usually be convenient to file more than twenty to thirty folders, depending on their thickness, behind any one guide card, and as the number of folders grows subdivision of the groups becomes necessary. The simplest alphabetical sequence makes use of twenty-six guide cards, each labelled with a letter of the alphabet, but as groups such as *B*, *S*, and *W* expand more rapidly than others, they will probably be the first to call for subdivision. (*see* Fig. 22).

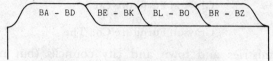

Fig. 22.   *A subdivided index.*

The diagram illustrates a simple alphabetical subdivision with only four dividing guide cards. Subdivision can be carried to any extent necessary as the filing system expands.

An analysis by HM Treasury of various government department indexes covering sixty million names shows the percentage frequency of these three initial letters to be as follows:

$$B—10.6\%; \ S—9.3\%; \ W—7.4\%$$

In other words, these three letters begin more than 27% of the names indexed. The letters I, U, and Y, on the other hand, account for only 1%.

Subdivision by vowels

A useful method of subdivision sometimes adopted is that known as the *vowel method.* Each letter of the alphabet is divided into six parts, the dividing cards being given a main letter followed by one of the five vowels and the letter *Y*, which has the force of a vowel (*see* Fig. 23).

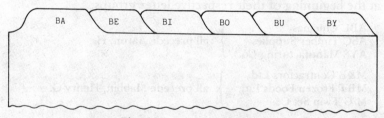

Fig. 23.   *The vowel index.*

Although not without value where folders are not very numerous, the system suffers from a number of drawbacks. It does not, for example, lend itself to further subdivision, and may also prove awkward for those who are accustomed to straight alphabetical filing.

Filing follows, the first vowel (or *Y*) to appear in the name after the initial letter:

Name	Filed under
Bradley	BA
Aspinall	AI
Byatt	BY
Unsworth	UO
Aldred	AE
Rushworth	RU

It will be noticed that the first vowel is not always the second letter in the name. Within each of the vowel subdivisions files are arranged in strict alphabetical order. The particular sub-group in which the folder is filed is thus known at a glance (*see* Fig. 24).

A	E	I	O	U	Y
Barber, G.	Bennett, R.	Bird, L.A.	Boberg, R.	Blumson, T.	Bryan, A.
Blair, H.	Brett, D.	Bridge, D.	Brooks, A.	Buckley, G.	Bryce, L.
Blake, H.J.	Brewer, A.	Brierley,K.	Brough, W.		Byles, E.
Braine, N.			Brown, T.		

Fig. 24.   *Filing within a vowel index.*

Within each vowel subdivision the arrangement of files is strictly alphabetical.

There is a small problem with names such as *Anns, Eld, Ibbs, Orr,* and *Ulph* that contain no vowel after the first letter. Such names are not numerous, and on the principle that "nothing comes before something" (e.g. *Smith* before *Smithe*), or "no vowel before a vowel", they should be placed immediately in front of the *Aa*'s, *Ea*'s, etc., i.e. immediately behind their first guide card.

Miscellaneous folders

In many cases it will be found that, in addition to regular correspondents who require individual files, there will be some with whom correspondence is so little that it would be a waste of time and money to prepare separate files for each. Although their papers may be few in number, it is just as important to find them as quickly as those of regular correspondents.

To accommodate these papers "Miscellaneous" folders are prepared, one being placed immediately behind each guide card. The front covers of these folders provide for an index to the correspondence placed in them, each correspondent being given a separate number.

Papers bearing the same number are, of course, kept together within the "Miscellaneous" folder by means of either tabbed insert sheets or insert folders, numbered in either case to correspond with the index on the front of the outer "Miscellaneous" folder (*see* Fig. 25).

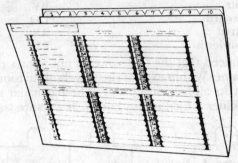

Fig. 25.   *A miscellaneous folder in vertical filing.*

The index on the outer cover of the folder illustrated is ruled for the names of thirty correspondents, but it is desirable to restrict the number of insert sheets or folders, and therefore the number of miscellaneous correspondents, to ten. Since names are indexed chronologically and not alphabetically a greater number than ten may prove inconvenient for reference.

In suspended filing a "Miscellaneous" pocket is prepared. Having a metal top of different colour from the rest of the pockets in the system, it serves the additional purpose of dividing the system into subdivisions of convenient size (*see* Fig. 26).

For each of these pockets a "Miscellaneous" folder similar to that used in ordinary vertical filing is provided.

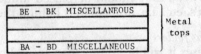

Fig. 26.   *A miscellaneous pocket in flat-top suspension filing.*

Each pocket is titled with the appropriate division of the alphabet and, having a metal top of different colour from the rest, serves not only as a "Miscellaneous" folder but also as a dividing guide.

When correspondence with a firm grows it is transferred from the "Miscellaneous" to an individual folder, and takes its normal place in the filing system.

Numerical filing
The method of filing by numbers instead of by names is generally used by firms with numerous correspondents, many of whose

names are likely to be identical or nearly so. The allocation of a distinctive number to each correspondent lessens the risk of confusing similar names. The alphabetical method is direct and automatically provides its own index, but numerical filing is indirect and a separate alphabetical index of correspondents is necessary. The number allocated to each correspondent becomes his file number. Files are arranged in numerical order and are separated by guide cards numbered in multiples of ten.

It is only from the alphabetical index that a correspondent's number can be known, and when a file is wanted the index must first be consulted. It thus takes longer to find a particular file by this method than it would by the method of direct reference possible with an alphabetical arrangement. The method has, however, a number of important advantages.

(a) Files bearing numbers are more quickly "spotted" than files bearing names.

(b) If a file is misplaced the mistake is promptly noticed.

(c) File numbers may be used as reference numbers on outgoing letters.

(d) Expansion of the system has no complications; all that is necessary is to give a new file the next number in the series and to add it at the back.

(e) The initial cost of installation may be less than that for an alphabetical system, which must at the outset provide equipment capable of dealing with the full range of the alphabet.

Alpha-numerical filing

Alpha-numerical filing is a combination of the alphabetical and numerical methods described above. It combines the exactness of the latter with the convenience of the former, and avoids the need for a *separate* card index.

Files are arranged numerically behind alphabetically arranged guide cards. In addition to its letter each guide card is numbered, and also ruled to serve the purpose of an index. The guide card, for example, covering the first division in the B section of the alphabet (say BA—BD) would be numbered B1; that covering the next division (say BE—BK) would be numbered B2, and so on. As new files are prepared for correspondents their names are entered in consecutive order in the index on the front of the appropriate guide card and numbered to correspond both with the card and with their position on it (*see* Fig. 27).

Numbers borne by the individual files can be used as references in correspondence.

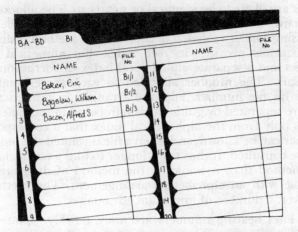

Fig. 27. *An alpha-numerical guide card.*

As new files are prepared they are entered consecutively on the guide card and numbered as shown. Filing takes place numerically behind the guide card.

Baker's file would bear the number B1/1, Bagshaw's B1/2, and so on. The files would then be placed *in numerical order* behind the B1 guide card (*see* Fig. 27).

As the arrangement of names on the guide cards is chronological and not alphabetical, a little time may be lost in finding a person's name when his file is wanted. But when the number of names on a guide card reaches the point at which it becomes difficult to spot particular names quickly, the card would be replaced by an updated version containing the names rearranged alphabetically, thus:

BACON, Alfred S.	B1/3
BAGSHAW, William	B1/2
BAKER, Eric	B1/1

The numerical arrangement of the files themselves behind the guide card would remain undisturbed.

Alpha-numerical filing is frequently found in geographical filing. Guide cards would first be prepared for the different countries or regions dealt with and arranged in alphabetical order. The names of correspondents would then be entered in the index of the appropriate guide card and a folder would be prepared for each. Each folder would then be given a number to correspond with that of the index and placed in numerical position behind its guide card.

Geographical filing

Geographical filing is an arrangement of countries, towns, or other areas in alphabetical order, with the names of correspondents arranged alphabetically within the areas to which they belong.

The method is used in offices where it is an advantage to group correspondents by territories. Basically, it is no more than a variant of the alphabetical method, though it is sometimes convenient to introduce a numerical content by giving numbers instead of names to the files of individual correspondents. (*See Alpha-numerical filing* above.)

The method is frequently found in the sales and export departments of large concerns. Where, for example, it is necessary to keep in touch through agents with customers in different parts of the world a filing classification similar to the following may be adopted:

(*a*) *into countries*, using coloured guide cards tabbed on the extreme left;

(*b*) *into towns*, using guide cards of a different colour tabbed in the centre;

(*c*) *into customers*, using folders bearing customers' names, or alternatively numbers, in which case some sort of name index would be necessary. Names or numbers would be written on the extreme right.

An organization marketing its product on an extensive scale would probably wish to divide the territory covered into clearly defined areas and to appoint a representative for each. It is unlikely that such areas would coincide with county or other recognized geographical boundaries; the determining factors would usually be density of population and sales potential. Individual territories could therefore embrace several counties, or only parts of several counties, or even only part of one county. Each separate territory would be named and a guide card prepared to correspond. Folders of individual customers would be filed either alphabetically or numerically within their relevant sections.

Where, as with an insurance company, agencies are established in towns the filing problem is simplified. All that is necessary is a guide card for each town; the folders of customers would then be filed in the section assigned to their town.

Subject filing

Filing by subjects rather than by correspondents is one of the most useful methods of storing information for quick and easy reference. It is adopted when the subject-matter is of greater interest than the identity of the correspondent. It can be used with advantage in most offices collaterally with other methods. Brochures, publicity material, catalogues, circulars, etc., can all be filed according to their subject-matter, so that when needed all available data relevant to a subject is immediately accessible.

Main headings and sub-headings are readily distinguished by the use of guide cards of different colour, suitably tabbed, main headings on the extreme left and sub-headings in some other convenient position.

.It may often be more convenient to file under subjects than under correspondents. A contractor engaged simultaneously on a number of projects, for example, may be in correspondence with government departments, local authorities, architects, surveyors, and various public undertakings. It will clearly be more convenient to file the individual personal folders under project main headings. (*see* Fig. 28).

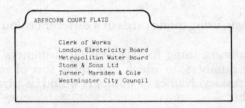

Fig. 28.   *Guide card for main subject heading.*

Folders are entered on the guide card and filed, either alphabetically or numerically, behind it. If filed numerically they would be numbered serially on the guide card.

A subject filing system that includes folders bearing the names of correspondents requires, like the numerical filing system, an alphabetical index, otherwise a person wanting a particular correspondent's file and not knowing which subject was involved would have difficulty in locating the file. In Fig. 28 for example the alphabetical card-index would immediately reveal that the file for Stone & Sons Ltd. is filed in the *Abercorn Court Flats* section.

CROSS REFERENCES

Cross-referencing is an essential part of any good filing system. It sometimes happens that a name may be filed in different ways and that staff wanting a particular file may not always look for it in the section where it is stored. A person wanting the file of the *British Transport Docks Board* may remember the title as the *Transport Docks Board*, or simply the *Docks Board* and therefore look for the file in the *T* or the *D* section of the system, when in fact the file is stored under its correct title in the *B* section. In such cases a cross-reference card (for a card-index system) or a sheet (for a folder system) should be made out and placed in the section to which persons wanting the file are likely to refer.

```
┌────────────────────────────────────────────┐
│           Cross-reference Sheet             │
│                                             │
│        TRANSPORT DOCKS BOARD                │
│                                             │
│                  see                        │
│                                             │
│        BRITISH TRANSPORT DOCKS BOARD        │
└────────────────────────────────────────────┘
```

```
┌────────────────────────────────────────────┐
│           Cross-reference Sheet             │
│                                             │
│              DOCKS BOARD                    │
│                                             │
│                  see                        │
│                                             │
│        BRITISH TRANSPORT DOCKS BOARD        │
└────────────────────────────────────────────┘
```

Cross-referencing is sometimes necessary with individual letters that may be filed equally well in more than one place. This is so especially with the method of subject filing. A letter from a contractor may, for example, refer to work on two different building sites, say *Abercorn Court* and *Priory Court*. In such an event the letter is filed in one of the two relevant folders and a copy made (a simple matter if photostat equipment is available) and filed in the other. Alternatively, a cross-reference sheet instead of a copy may be prepared and filed. The sheet must record sufficient information to enable the original letter to be found at once should it be wanted.

```
┌────────────────────────────────────────────┐
│             CROSS-REFERENCE SHEET           │
├────────────────────────────────────────────┤
│   1   Name of correspondent                 │
│   2   Date of letter                        │
│   3   A brief reference to the subject-matter│
│   4   Title of folder in which original letter is filed │
└────────────────────────────────────────────┘
```

"ABSENT" MARKERS

Not infrequently the same file is wanted when already in use by someone else. It is frustrating and annoying to go to a cabinet only to find that the file wanted, and perhaps urgently, is missing, with no indication of its whereabouts. In the search that follows time is lost and tempers are frayed.

Trouble of this kind is easily avoided by the simple expedient of leaving an *"Absent" marker* in the place from which the file has been taken. The marker may be a folder similar to those in the cabinet, but preferably of a different colour, or it may be a card of folder depth. If it is a folder a note should be placed inside stating:

(*a*) the title or number reference of the file;

(*b*) the date issued;

(*c*) the name or initials of the person to whom it has been issued.

The use of a folder has the further advantage of providing a receptacle for the receipt of papers while the file is out. If the marker is a card the above information should be written on it (*see* Fig. 29).

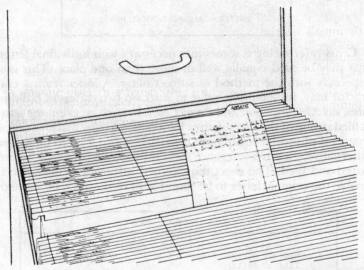

Courtesy: Roneo Vickers Ltd.

Fig. 29.   *An "absent" card.*

The use of "absent" markers provides a check on the whereabouts of borrowed files, and is an essential feature of an efficient filing system.

If the card has a simple pocket into which the slip requesting the file can be inserted, time is saved since the slip will contain all the required information.

A further method for recording borrowed files is to keep a *Files Requested Book*, headed as follows:

Date taken	File No. or Title	Taken by	Date returned

This arrangement takes up more time since it involves reference to a separate source when a file is missing, but it has the advantage that overdue borrowings can be spotted at a glance and systematically followed up. Where a *Files Requested Book* is not in use, some other form of follow-up system similar to those explained in a later section becomes necessary.

In no circumstances should a person who withdraws a file transfer it to someone else without noting the transferee's name or initials on the marker, otherwise the whole purpose of the arrangement to locate missing files is lost. This difficulty is solved if the person passing on a file completes a "passing slip" and sends it to the file registry. The filing clerk can then update the absent card. A marker must, of course, remain in the containing drawer or cabinet until the file is returned.

```
     FILE PASSING SLIP

To filing clerk

Please note:

     File No. .......
     Passed to ......
     on (date) ......

Signed ............
```

Nor should individual papers be taken from a file save in exceptional circumstances. A substitution document should then be inserted to replace the document, identifying the document and giving the name of the person who has taken it and the date.

TRANSFER OF "DEAD" PAPERS

From time to time it will become necessary to remove from
the current filing system papers, or even complete files, that
have become "dead" from age or other cause. The removed
material must not be destroyed, but transferred to the archives,
where it should be kept for as long as it is likely to be needed
for reference. After that, it should be destroyed. Document
shredders may be used. These shredders rapidly reduce
unwanted documents to paper waste, for which there may be a
use in packing goods for despatch. Some concerns adopt the
practice of destroying papers more than six years old, six
years being the period allowed by the Limitation Act 1980
for legal action on contracts other than those entered into
by deed.

A note of papers transferred should be made either in the file
from which they have been removed or, where the complete file
has been removed, on a "Transfer Record" kept in the filing
drawer. The removed papers and files should be placed in
"Transfer Storage Cases", suitably labelled (*see* Fig. 30).

Courtesy: Roneo Vickers Ltd.

Fig. 30.   *A transfer storage case.*

Filing equipment is often expensive, and only active correspondence
should be kept in the current system. "Dead" material should be placed
in storage cases and transferred to the archives.

TEN FILING COMMANDMENTS

1. Name each file clearly, either in block capitals or in jet-black typed capitals.

2. Provide a dividing guide card for every twenty to thirty folders.

3. Keep filing up to date by filing first thing each day. (A task done daily with ease becomes a burden if left.)

4. First sort filing material into order. (This saves running about from drawer to drawer. There are various types of alphabetical sorter on the market to help you.)

5. Remove all paper clips and, instead, use staples for papers that must be kept together; otherwise, single papers may become trapped and wrongly filed. Then file in date order, always placing latest papers on top, or in front.

6. Avoid removing individual papers from files, and prepare markers for all absent files.

7. Transfer correspondence from "Miscellaneous" to individual folders as soon as there is enough of it.

8. Remove "dead" material to "transfer" files (*see* Fig. 30). (Deal with a few each day; this will eliminate bulky files and spare you the tedious and irksome task of periodical weeding. At the same time note in the current file the contents of the transfer file.)

9. Keep your card index handy and up to date. (It is a most valuable friend.)

10. Remember that prompt and careful filing contributes heavily to the efficiency of your office.

FOLLOW-UP SYSTEMS

Every office needs some kind of artificial memory to remind staff of things to be done. Appointments have to be kept, meetings attended, visits made, reports submitted, and letters to which replies are outstanding followed up.

Card-index follow-up

One of the simplest forms of reminder is the ubiquitous diary; but something more elaborate is sometimes needed. Several methods are available. The most commonly used is the small card-index box with a dividing card for each month, and one for each of the thirty-one days. The thirty-one day-dividers are placed in front of the box immediately after the divider for the current month, the remaining eleven dividers being placed in month order at the back of the box (*see* Fig. 31).

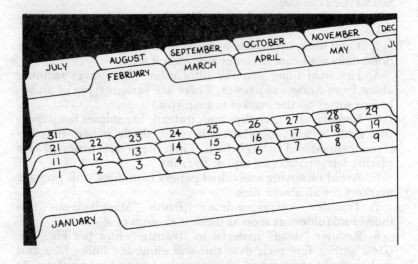

Fig. 31. *A card-index reminder system.*

The card index is one of the simplest, cheapest and most efficient devices for ensuring that matters are brought forward at the right time and not overlooked.

Suppose a particular file is to be brought forward on the 20th. The fact would be noted on a record card and the card placed behind the divider for that day, if the day falls within the current month. If it falls within some later month the card would be placed for the time being behind the divider for that month.

One of the advantages of this system is that the same card may serve for several reminders, or it may be used over and over again, as where a particular payment must be made promptly every three months. A card like Fig. 32 would be prepared. When payment has been made on 26th January the card would be placed behind the April divider in readiness for the next bring forward.

Follow-up folders
As an alternative to the card-index system a folder system may be used. Some office-equipment firms provide single-drawer follow-up filing cabinets for the purpose.

Notes are made of matters for bringing forward and filed in

```
Payment due to J Meade & Co

26/1/19..    26/4/19..    26/7/19..    26/10/19..
```

Fig. 32. *A reminder record card.*

A brief note on a card-index record card provides a safe reminder of both periodical and non-recurring items of business.

their appropriate date folders. Extra copies of outgoing letters requiring replies may also be taken and filed in the follow-up cabinet until the replies are received.

CARD INDEXES

How prepared

Card indexes serve an unlimited number of purposes and form part of the indispensable equipment of any well-run office. Their uses are by no means restricted to their services in conjunction with the numerical filing system described on p. 348. They are especially useful for anything in the nature of a register, and every commercial office should maintain a reliable register at least of the names, addresses and telephone numbe s of its correspondents.

A separate card is prepared for each person and filed in alphabetical order behind its appropriate dividing card in a containing box or drawer. When the number of cards is considerable one of the methods of alphabetical subdivision explained on pp. 345–7 may be used. Cards 153 mm×102 mm (6 in. by 4 in.) or 127 mm×77 mm (5 in. by 3 in.) are sizes commonly used. If the larger size is adopted it can be used to record much useful additional information.

Card filing-drawers may be obtained with a retaining rod on which the cards are threaded to prevent easy removal. This safeguards the alphabetical distribution of the cards. The advantages of securing cards in this way more than compensate for the little extra trouble involved in withdrawing existing cards or inserting new ones. Cards may be handwritten, but greater clarity and uniformity are obtained if they are typed. Names should be typed as high as possible on the cards, and always with a jet-black ribbon to help the eye.

Uses and advantages

Card indexes have many advantages over the older type of book index:

(a) They are convenient to handle, and form a source of quick and easy reference.

(b) They are capable of indefinite expansion.

(c) Cards may be typed instead of handwritten.

(d) Individual cards may be inserted *in their exact* places.

(e) Insertions and withdrawals do not disturb the alphabetical continuity of the index.

(f) The use of suitably tabbed dividing cards greatly facilitates reference.

(g) The number of alphabetical subdivisions can be increased as the system expands.

(h) The index does not harbour unwanted names; "dead" cards can be withdrawn and stored at the back for as long as needed.

(i) The cards can be printed and specially ruled to record any kind of information.

(j) The system can be used for many different purposes:

(i) to provide the numbers required for numerical filing (*see* p. 348);

(ii) to provide a mailing list for circulars, catalogues, etc.;

(iii) to provide detailed information about a correspondent, such as his telephone number, his postal and telegraphic addresses, terms of payment agreed upon, discounts allowed, correspondent's working hours, half-day closings, names of persons in charge of his departments, and his secretary's name, and for partnerships the partners' names. Temporary information, such as that relating to his absence through illness, travelling, or holidays, should be inserted in pencil and removed when the need for it has passed.

Visible-record systems

The visible-record system is an important development in card-indexing. It is a combination of the card index and the horizontal file. The cards are housed in flat metal trays and overlap, leaving exposed only the titles on their lower edges (*see* Fig. 33).

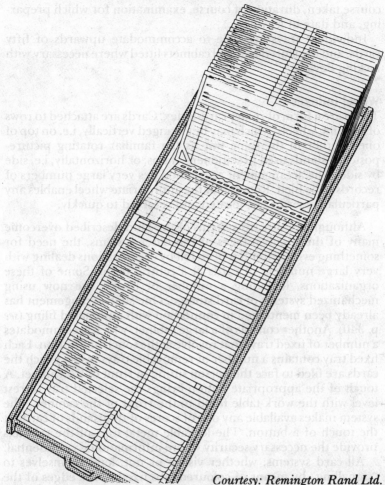

Courtesy: Remington Rand Ltd.

Fig. 33.   *A visible card-index record.*

Titles are displayed on the exposed edges of the cards, to which
coloured markers may be attached signifying items of special interest
recorded on the cards. Pivoted on their trays, cards can be handled
rapidly with no fear of disturbing their sequence.

The cards are often ruled to meet special requirements and
can receive a good deal of information. In a technical college,
for example, the system can be used to record particulars of full-
time students. A separate card may be prepared for each student and to give his name and address, date of birth, examinations passed, date of admission, department to which admitted,

course taken, duration of course, examination for which preparing, and date of leaving.

Individual trays are able to accommodate upwards of fifty cards, and are stored in metal cabinets fitted where necessary with locking devices.

Wheel indexes

These are a form of rotary card-index. Cards are attached to rows of rotating wheels, which may be arranged vertically, i.e. on top of one another in the same way as the familiar rotating picture-postcard stands used in stationers' shops, or horizontally, i.e. side by side. The arrangement accommodates very large numbers of records to be filed. Rotation of the appropriate wheel enables any particular record to be located and referred to quickly.

Although visible card systems of the kind described overcome many of the disadvantages of the older systems, the need for something even better has been felt by organizations dealing with very large numbers of cards at a central point. Some of these organizations, including a number of banks, are now using mechanized systems of card storage. One such arrangement has already been mentioned in connection with automated filing (*see* p. 340). Another consists of a large cabinet, which accommodates a number of fixed trays that revolve at the touch of a button. Each fixed tray contains a number of removable trays inside which the cards are filed to face the person sitting in front of the cabinet. A touch of the appropriate button brings the selected tray to rest level with the work-table fitted to the front of the cabinet. The system makes available any one of scores of thousands of cards at the touch of a button. The lockable metal tops of the cabinets provide the necessary security where information is confidential.

All card systems, whether visible or not, lend themselves to "signalling" by means of coloured tabs fixed to the edges of the cards to serve as reminders and for other purposes. Tabs are available in a wide range of shapes and colours.

EXERCISES

1. What is meant by alpha-numerical filing? Give an example to show how it is used.

2. Explain how, in alphabetical filing, you would deal with the following:

  (a) names with prefixes;
  (b) courtesy titles;
  (c) names beginning with *M, Mc* and *Mac*;

(d) names including *and, the* and *of*;

(e) names composed of initials only.

3. Explain when, and with an example how, "Miscellaneous" folders are used.

4. What is geographical filing, and in what circumstances would it be advantageous to use it?

5. When opening a new filing system what would influence you in your choice between alphabetical, numerical, geographical or subject methods of indexing? *(RSA)*

6. Discuss modern methods of using files. What do you consider the best method of storing:

(a) confidential staff records;

(b) large size plans? *(RSA)*

7. What arrangements would you make to keep a check on files withdrawn for use?

8. Explain, with examples, the advantages of a card index of names and addresses.

9. Make suggestions for a suitable filing system for:

(a) an accountant's office;

(b) a building contractor's office;

(c) a manufacturer with twenty sales representatives;

(d) a manufacturer with world-wide exporting interests.

10. Arrange the following names in alphabetical order:

Oundle, A. B.	Oliver, Brian
Odeon Cinema	Orme Ring Mill Ltd.
O'Reilly, F.	Ozone Private Hotel
O'Neil, T. J.	Oxford Garage, The
Oldfield, Major J. A.	Oakden, R. A.
O'Donnell, J.	Old England Hotel
Oldham Corporation	Ogg, R. O.
Oliver, B. W.	Oldroyd, F. D.
Osmond, Mrs E. M.	Olde English Cafe, Ye
Orr, R. A.	Ogmundson, F.

11. Arrange in vowel-index order the names in Question 10.

12. Discuss the uses and advantages of visible card and strip indexing systems. Place the following names of individuals, professional bodies and trading organizations in the order and form in which you would index them:

Rowland Denbigh	The Dental Supply Company
Robert Denbigh	Dennis Howard and Brothers
Denmore and Jones	Limited
Jones and Denmore	De Rosa Nurseries
The Dennison Lamp Company	*Design Weekly*
Limited	O'Donovan and Sons
Lord Denman	Derry O'Donovan
Derby Ex-service Club	De La Rue and Company Limited

13. Your present system of filing correspondence is not working efficiently. Draft a report setting out in detail the inefficiencies of the present system and recommend what should be done to remedy them.

14. You are Secretary to the Manager of a Department. Describe fully the systems you would recommend for use in his office for filing, dealing with engagements, and bringing to his notice the documents required in connection with his job.   (*LCCI Priv. Sec. Dip.*)

15. Compare the relative advantages of alphabetical and numerical filing, and explain why many companies arrange their files chronologically with the aid of an alphabetical index notwithstanding that alphabetical filing is self-indexing.

16. What method would you adopt for filing up to 150 insurance policies? Give reasons for your choice of method.

17. Your firm has acquired a small fleet of delivery vans. Your employer wishes you to set up a new card-index system which will show all details of the vehicles, monthly mileage, maintenance and repairs, and names of drivers. Advise him as to the type of equipment you wish to use. He has seen index-cards incorporating marginal punched holes to indicate certain information in place of written entries. Explain why you would, or would not, adopt this type of card.   (*RSA*)

18. Your employer has hitherto shared an office with another executive, and they have used the same files. Each has now been given his own room on the same floor, and your employer sends for you to discuss the problem of the files. What suggestions would you make?
                    (*RSA*)

19. A number of technical reference books are kept in your office for use in your department. You keep a card-index record, which is constantly consulted, of the movement of books. Design the type of card which you will use for this purpose.   (*RSA*)

20. Write short notes on alphabetical, numerical and geographical systems of filing.

21. Under what letters of the alphabet would you file the following correspondence:

James T. Smith	Harold Mowbray & Company
Charteris & Smith	Limited
Harold, Mowbray & Co. Ltd.	The British Pen Company Limited
The Borough of East Hamton	The Ministry of Security
Royal Society of Arts	Yorkminster Technical College
Miss Mary Browne-Curtis	(*RSA*)

22. (*a*) You are in charge of the mailing room in a large organization. What procedure should be adopted in order to ensure that incoming mail is dealt with efficiently? Mention the equipment to be used and also bear in mind that money is received in the Post Room and must be safeguarded.

(*b*) What should be done if a letter must be seen by more than one department?   (*NWRAC*)

CHAPTER TWENTY

Office Machine Systems I Processing Systems

And while I understand and feel
How much to them I owe,
My cheeks have often been bedew'd
With tears of thoughtful gratitude.

R. Southey: *The Scholar*

Efficiency in the office is just as important as efficiency in the factory, and efforts to improve productivity in the office have never been greater than now. Nearly every concern of any size has instituted some form of what is known as O and M, an Organization and Methods Section specially concerned with reviewing office organization and recommending improvements. Concurrently with O and M, and stimulated by it, machine systems are now in use for a greater variety of purposes, including the handling of correspondence. Office methods are changing rapidly. New machines are constantly being marketed and older-type machines improved. It therefore pays to keep in touch with modern developments, as by visits to exhibitions and office-equipment showrooms, and through a study, too, of advertisements in various trade journals.

The cost of correspondence is high and continues to rise. This cost reflects chiefly the time spent in dictating and typing letters, but it also includes the cost of equipment and stationery used, the mailing procedures adopted and office overheads. The cost of a letter is much higher than most employers realize and, except for long distances, a telephone call is usually less expensive than a letter.

More and more attention is now being given to ways in which the new business technology can help to eliminate unproductive paper-handling operations, and at the same time provide business with the information it needs. The information must be reliable, up to date and presented promptly in readily understandable form after being subjected to some degree of sorting and rearrangement.

DATA PROCESSING

What it is

Data is defined in the dictionary as "information, especially information organized for analysis or used as a basis for a decision", or "numerical information in a form suitable for processing by computer". Data processing is a term that covers the whole range of activities involved in analysing, classifying and using information to achieve a predetermined objective. Processing is as relevant to an isolated business transaction as it is to the complex operations involved in preparing a computer program. An order for four new machines for a typing pool, for example, would involve:

(a) the pool supervisor deciding as to quantity, quality and type of machine required;

(b) the supervisor sending a request to the office manager;

(c) the office manager's approving the request and passing it to his firm's buying department;

(d) the chief buyer requesting quotations from suppliers, with delivery dates;

(e) the chief buyer receiving the quotations, accepting one of them and placing order;

(f) supplier informing buyer that the machines are available and ready for delivery;

(g) preparing delivery note, delivering the machines and sending invoice to buyer;

(h) buyer checking invoice against quotation, and if it is correct, signing it and passing it to the accounts department;

(i) cashier preparing a payment voucher and drawing a cheque for the amount authorized;

(j) sending cheque, with payment voucher, to the supplier;

(k) filing duplicate payment voucher and supporting correspondence and documents;

(l) receiving and filing receipt if one has been requested. This completes the processing operation and the transaction is completed.

Even the smallest offices use some form of equipment to assist with the task of processing the data as a transaction passes through its various stages.

Processing procedures

Data (information) processing may take a variety of forms. Of the methods used in business the computer, punched cards, and word and information processors are the most commonly used. Where a computer is installed the data for processing may be fed directly into the machine as it is received, as where items of stock are bought and sold and immediate checks on the amount of stock held are required. Alternatively, data may be stored up into batches as it is received and then processed at convenient or suitable intervals. This method is used by the banks. The day's transactions at the branches are processed overnight at the bank's computer centre so that each day the branch can tell its customers of the state of their accounts as at close of business the previous day.

PUNCHED-CARD SYSTEMS

Processing method

Punched-card systems have numerous applications in business. They can handle much of the repetitive and uninteresting work involved in accounting procedures, and this they do with extraordinary rapidity. The cards are specially designed and preprinted for the purpose for which they are to be used, and include all the items on which information is likely to be needed. A typical 40-column punched card is illustrated in Fig. 34.

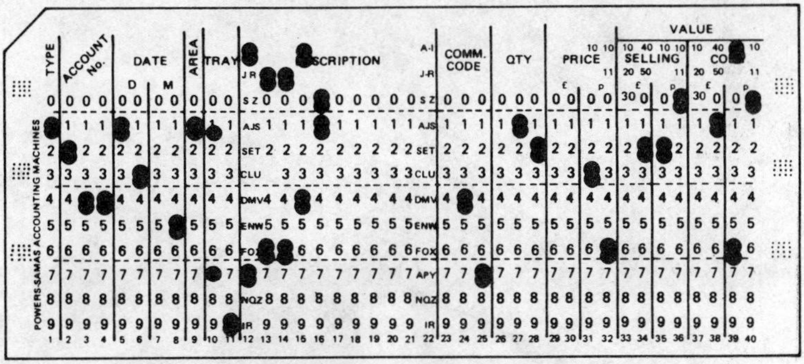

Fig. 34. *A 40-column card, punched and verified.*

The holes punched in the card represent data such as products, quantities, prices and names and addresses transferred in code form from original documents such as invoices, stock lists and other sources. Holes are punched in the appropriate columns. The cards are then sorted by machine into the sequences needed to produce the required information which is then transferred to a tabulator. Tabulators that print a whole line at a time are in common use.

Edge-punched cards

Use of the edge-punched card is an extension of the punched-card method designed to combine a card-record system with a rapid method of sorting and analysing the information recorded on the cards (*see* Fig. 35). Records of personnel, customers, etc., stock control and sales analysis are only a few of the many possible uses of the system.

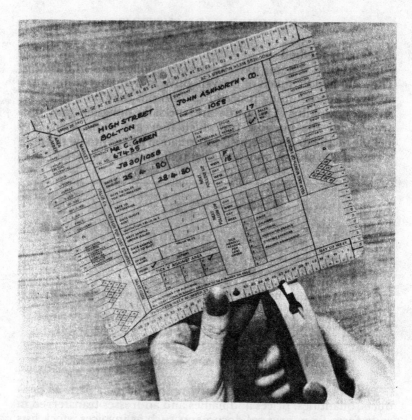

Courtesy: Kalamazoo Business Systems.

Fig. 35.　*An edge-punched card.*

Combines a card-record system with a rapid method of sorting.

The cards are individually designed for their particular purpose and pre-printed to include all the items on which information is likely to be needed. For example, an estate agent prepares a card for each of his clients seeking housing accommodation and on it records details of his client's needs, e.g. whether a flat, a bungalow or a house, and the price he is prepared to pay. The edges of the cards are divided into "fields", each representing a type of property (bungalow, house, etc.), and a price range (£25,000–£30,000 etc.). The card would be edge-punched at the relevant points indicating type of property etc., and similarly at the appropriate point in the price range stated by the client.

To provide a client with a selection of bungalows on offer at or about his stated price all that is necessary is to pass a metal rod through the hole punched in the "bungalow" field and to raise the cards, the operation being completed by passing a rod through the hole in the appropriate "price" field of the raised cards. The cards lifted by this rod are the only ones required, and all other cards fall back into their home position.

This manual method of sorting is suitable for small firms because no expensive equipment is required.

An electronically controlled system can be used where the amount of sorting justifies its adoption. Cards, designed preprinted and punched as for the manual system, are placed in a sorting unit fitted with adjustable bars which are moved into positions that coincide with the punched spaces on the card. At the press of a button a light electric vibration causes the card or cards wanted to drop slightly out of position, when they can be retrieved immediately for reference and updating (*see* Fig. 36).

ELECTRONIC PROCESSORS

The word processor
The word processor is an electronic device consisting of a typewriter keyboard, a microprocessor (a small integrated circuit), and a cathode-ray screen. The complexities and capabilities of these processors vary dramatically with the type of machine. At the lower end of the range they may be used independently as highly sophisticated electronic typewriters enabling "copy" for letters and other documents to be stored, corrected and then printed, or at the other end they may be linked with other machines, even computers, to form part of a complete information system. They operate either by being programmed or by typing on the keyboard.

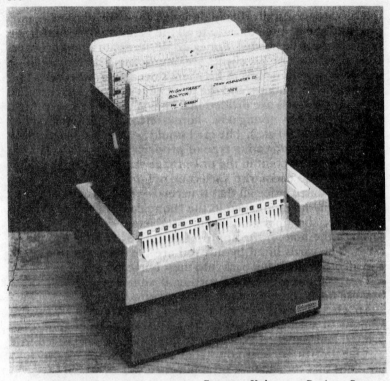

Fig. 36.   *An electric card-sorting unit (The Fact Finder).*
Adjustable bars are moved into positions that coincide with the
punched spaces on the cards.

Like the standard typewriter word processors are restricted to
dealing with text; they cannot manipulate formulae, sketches,
drawings or similar material. But they do have a number of
important distinguishing features. Most of them are capable of
the following:

   (a) Storing information. A letter for example can be recorded as
it is typed and held in the machine for later use. The "memory"
device may be in the form of a magnetic card, a cassette tape or
the disk of a microcomputer.

   (b) Editing text. Text that has been stored can be retrieved and
amended, e.g. by deleting or adding words, whole lines, sentences and even paragraphs. Text can also be transferred from
one part of a document to another. All these operations are
carried out without retyping the document.

   (c) Addressing letters. Standard letters stored in the processor

can be merged with a mailing list to produce personal letters correctly printed with names and addresses.

(d) Updating. The ease with which text can be amended makes it possible to update all kinds of records such as those relating to stock, finance and mailing lists.

The word processor is very much faster than a typewriter and also more reliable since it has fewer moving parts. It also makes possible high standards of correspondence—one of the hallmarks of an efficient business.

The information processor

The increasing demand for up-to-date and reliable information is met by an extension of the word processing system to a system of information processing in which word processing and simple computer techniques are combined and operate together in a single working unit. One such unit is the Exxon 520 information processor which, like the word processor, has storage and editing facilities (*see* Fig. 37). It has, in addition, a built-in electronic dictionary feature consisting of two distinct "dictionaries"—a look-up dictionary and a scanning dictionary. The dictionaries are activated by pressing the appropriate keys in the row above the standard typewriter keyboard. There are separate keys for adding, deleting, substituting, checking spellings and scanning.

(a) The look-up dictionary contains the correct spellings of many commonly misspelt words. It can be consulted and corrections made as typing proceeds. It is also possible to check spellings of words not included in the "commonly misspelt list". To do this the operator first types as much of the word as there is certainty about its spelling, and then presses the "Dictionary" key. This throws onto the screen the three words closest to the word or part of word that has been typed. Take, for example, the word *foreign.* If the operator types *for* and, being uncertain of the rest of the spelling, presses the "Dictionary" key, this would reveal such words as *foreground, foreign* and *foreman* from which the word required would be selected.

(b) The scanning dictionary contains some 35,000 words. It will scan a typed document automatically and stop at any word or words wrongly spelt or not included in its vocabulary. When this happens, incorrectly spelt words can if necessary be checked in the look-up dictionary and then retyped correctly.

Up to 10,000 new words can be added in combination to both these dictionaries. They can thus be expanded to include all

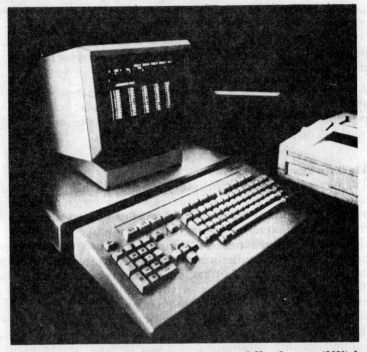

Courtesy: Exxon Office Systems (UK) Ltd.

Fig. 37.   *An information processor with printer and built-in dictionary.*

technical words and other words unique to particular types of business. Words can also be deleted if necessary.

The machine also has a built-in mathematics capability that helps to make and check calculations.

COMPUTERS

A computer has been defined as "an electronic machine that assembles, stores, correlates and otherwise processes and prints information from coded data in accordance with a predetermined program". A computer is not the complex machine it is often thought to be, but a group of machines, some mechanical and some electronic, which combine to process data (i.e. information) to produce results. It consists of five units each of which performs the function assigned to it in Fig. 38.

The *control unit* is the centre of the entire computer system. Through the *input unit* it receives its instructions, called a

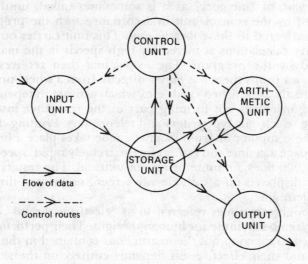

Fig. 38. *Diagram of a computer system.*

program, in the form of punched cards, punched tape (*see* Fig. 39), magnetic tape, magnetic diskette (floppy disk) or magnetic disk (hard disk), and stores them. The *input unit* receives the data to be processed, again in the form of punched tape, etc. The data is then "read" by the unit, which converts it into computer language (binary notation),* and passed on to the

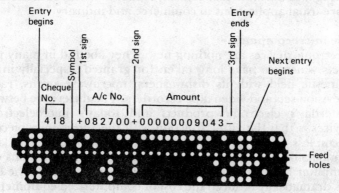

Fig. 39. *Five-track punched paper tape.*

The pattern of holes punched in each vertical row represents a number in the particular code used – in this case the binary code.

* *See* Glossary.

storage unit, or "memory" as it is sometimes called, until it is activated by the control unit in accordance with the program and transferred to the *arithmetic unit*. This unit carries out the necessary calculations at incredibly high speeds in the manner directed by the program. The *output unit* then receives the results and prints them out either directly from a wheel printer or indirectly as punched cards etc., which activate independent printing machines not forming part of the computer installation, e.g. electronic typewriters and teleprinters. Printing direct from the computer or from magnetic tape takes place a line or even a page at a time and is therefore extremely rapid, speeds of up to 1,000 lines a minute being not unusual. The results may also be displayed on a cathode ray screen, or printed directly onto microfilm.

Although sometimes referred to as "electronic brains" computers are no substitute for human thought. Their performance is limited to carrying out the instructions contained in the program, and their effectiveness depends entirely on the skill of those who prepare that program. Program preparation is therefore a highly skilled and mentally exacting task.

The computer's chief benefits have so far been to eliminate much routine clerical work, and to increase the amount of detailed information available and the speed with which it can be obtained. Computers are now regularly used to control stocks and forecast sales, and in such diverse operations as preparing payrolls, bank statements, railway timetables, newspaper typesetting and machine-tool control, to mention only some of their more usual applications in commerce and industry.

The microcomputer
Electronic devices are nothing new. They abound in many products which we have long taken for granted, especially in the domestic field with its dishwashers, microwave ovens, radio, television sets and video tape recorders. The difference between yesterday's electronic products and today's microelectronic devices is that the latter function with the *microchip*, a piece of silicon less than a cm square on which can be printed very large numbers of circuits carrying out all the essential functions of a computer but combined into a single integrated unit. The chip has dramatically reduced the cost of computerized equipment as well as the size of the machines used. It is now possible to buy for a few hundred pounds a desk-top computer that will carry out most of the standard applications of formerly much more expensive and much larger computers (*see* Fig. 40).

Courtesy: The Tandy Corporation (UK) Ltd.

Fig. 40.   *A Model 16B floppy disk-based microcomputer.*

Microcomputers and word and information processors normally use *cassettes* (tape) or *diskettes* (floppy disks) as the medium for storing prepared data. (Programs designed to handle aspects of business control not already provided for in the computer can generally be obtained from the manufacturers, e.g. programs for stock control, sales analysis, even for aligning typing margins, etc.) The diskettes are inserted into a *disk drive* which revolves at very high speeds. The capacity of the diskette varies from about 50 to 250 pages of data, but the magnetic disk, referred to as a "hard disk", has a very much greater capacity and can hold up to about 24,000 pages of A4 size paper.

The computer has already had far-reaching effects on the kind of work done by office staff and on the type of records kept. More recently, computer techniques have moved onto the stage when they can make reliable forecasts, and by their power to assess the probable financial results of different policies and schemes of capital investment have become important factors in management and control. But the computer can never replace the human mind. All it can do is to extend the power of the mind by providing information with extreme rapidity, and so enabling alternative policies and procedures to be considered and decisions taken much more rapidly than would otherwise be possible.

OFFICE AUTOMATION

The microchip used to be found only in such devices as calculators and watches but is now firmly established as a feature in large numbers of new products, and has been developed as the focal point in a wide range of automated office systems and appliances.

Business administration has come to rely more and more on the supply of up to date and reliable information, first about the business itself and then about the environment in which it has to compete. Fully computerized systems now operated by banks, building societies, insurance companies and other large organizations maintain a central reserve for storing information to which departments and branches equipped with the requisite terminal apparatus have instantaneous access.

The computerized systems operated by some banks and building societies afford good illustrations. The five hundred and fifty or so branches of the Halifax Building Society, for example, are equipped with a total of around 5,500 terminal work stations staffed by cashiers at the branch counters. The system works very simply: cashiers use their terminal keyboard to key-in details of customers' payments and withdrawals. This information is instantaneously transmitted by British Telecom circuits to Head Office, where it is checked and recorded in the customer's account. If the transaction is valid it is accepted, but if there is any question of validity, an error message appears immediately on the branch cashier's display screen and the transaction is halted. A valid transaction will immediately pass to the second part of the cashier's equipment—the printer. The cashier feeds the customer's passbook into the printer, which instantly and automatically updates the entries in the passbook by printing in it the amount of the payment or withdrawal, at the same time including accumulated interest and any other transaction not previously recorded. For withdrawals by cheque the terminal also prints the cheque. Payment or withdrawal is fully completed from beginning to end in one or two minutes.

EXERCISES

1. The advertising department in which you work is considering a big promotion campaign. A personalised standard letter is to be sent to all clients together with an updated illustrated booklet.

State two ways in which word processing could be used in the production of both the personalized standard letter and the draft copy of the booklet. *(RSA)*

2. What is meant by data processing? Give an example.

3. Write a short composition (about 150 words) explaining the ways in which the increasing mechanization of office work is likely to affect those who work in offices.

4. You have been promoted from the typing pool to be secretary to a manager who has never before had his own secretary. An additional small room has been acquired for you. It is newly decorated, but is empty. Make a list of the furniture and equipment you will need. *(RSA)*

5. *(a)* Giving reasons, state whether you agree with the suggestion that today there is a tendency towards over-mechanization in the office.

(b) What types of office machinery and equipment would you suggest for use by a company employing 100 clerical staff all housed in the same building.

6. The use of records on microfilm is expensive. Under what conditions could it be justified? Should your company decide to introduce microfilming, what equipment will be needed? *(LCCI, Priv. Sec. Cert.)*

7. With the rapidly increasing quantity of paper which now has to be stored, many firms turned to microfilm. These microfilm rolls can be cut up and made into microfiche sets.

(a) State *two* factors which would have to be considered before changing over to microfiche/microfilm.

(b) What would be the advantages to your firm of this change?

(c) What equipment would have to be purchased? *(NWRAC)*

CHAPTER TWENTY-ONE

Office Machine Systems II Typing and Reproducing Services

Pray, Madam, do not put up your hair with all those letters. I find
I must keep copies.   Witwood

THE TYPEWRITER

There are many different kinds of typewriter and as several
firms make most of them there is an enormous choice of
machines. With the widespread application of electronics and
the microchip to office machines, and in particular with the
expanding range of operations provided by the electronic typewriter, it seems inevitable that some of the special-purpose typewriters still in present use will in the course of time be phased
out.

The "Auto-typist"
This is an electric typewriter that enables an indefinite number
of "originals" to be typed from a "master" consisting of a perforated paper roll like that used to operate a pianola.

The "Copy-typist"
This is a composite piece of apparatus consisting of a master
typewriter to which one or two or more typewriters are linked in
such a way that anything typed on the master is automatically
reproduced on the linked machines.

The "Justowriter"
This is a machine that justifies (i.e. aligns) the right-hand margin
so that all lines are of precisely the same length and finish at
the same typing point. This is made possible by proportional
spacing of the characters used.

The "Flexowriter"
This is a machine which has a paper-tape punch and a paper-
tape reader attached to it and is used for storing data (i.e.

information) and documents for future use, and for preparing data for transmission by telegraph or telephone in Datel services.

In addition there are dual-feed machines, continuous stationery machines, and machines with card-holding attachments. The specialized facilities of these and other similar special-purpose typewriters can now be provided by the electric and electronic typewriters now being widely used in offices of all kinds and size.

The electric typewriter

This is now in general use. Key depression, carriage return, line-spacing, tabulator settings and other actions are all electrically controlled and make typewriting a less physically demanding activity than with a non-electric machine.

For the electric typewriter it is claimed:

(a) that fatigue is reduced and output increased (though it is doubtful whether the increase is nearly as much as is claimed, since experiments have shown that the more highly-skilled typist gets a greater relative gain in output than the less skilled);

(b) that the superior typeface used enables as many as twenty copies to be typed in one operation;

(c) that the electrically-controlled key depression makes it ideal for stencil cutting;

(d) automatic carriage return, which operates the line-spacer at the same time, saves both time and effort;

(e) underscoring is carried out automatically;

(f) a carbon copy control enables machine pressure to be adjusted according to the number of copies required.

Many electric typewriters have dispensed with type bars and instead use a small round-shaped head, commonly referred to as a "golf ball". The surface of the head carries all the characters needed to match those of the keyboard. When the keys are operated the typing head revolves to the required printing position and prints the character. It is the printer and not the carriage that moves.

The golf ball element is easily removed and can be quickly changed and replaced by a printing head with a different style of type. This makes it useful for typing documents where a variety of typestyles and sizes are required.

Electric typewriters also frequently use printers of the daisy-wheel type normally used with electronic typewriters (*see* below).

The electronic typewriter

Electronic typewriters are operated by microchips. They differ from electric typewriters in having a variety of automatic electronically-controlled features, including paper feed, margin and tabulator stops, carriage return, underscoring, double underscoring and right-hand margin justification. Like the word processor but to a more limited degree, the more expensive machines have a memory and can store information, e.g. frequently-used phrases and paragraphs, names and addresses and letter formats, for recall and use at a later time. As text is typed the characters are registered on a fluorescent panel at the top of the keyboard or with some machines on a visual display screen (*see* Fig. 41). If for any reason it is necessary to make alterations to the text or to correct mistakes this is done quite simply by backspacing and retyping over the words or characters that need to be changed.

The printing element is normally a daisy wheel with a character at the end of each spoke (*see* Fig. 42). It gives fast printing and high print quality, with a choice of type faces in 10, 12 and 15 pitch (the width of individual characters) with proportional

Courtesy: Rank Xerox (UK) Ltd.

Fig. 41. *An electronic typewriter with storage and word processing facilities and visual display screen.*

The Xerox 640 electronic typewriter illustrated combines standard correcting electronic typewriting with disk driven word processing capabilities—the ability to store up to eighty pages of typing together with a 3–4 page visual display screen.

spacing. Daisy wheels are easy to load and can be easily and quickly changed.

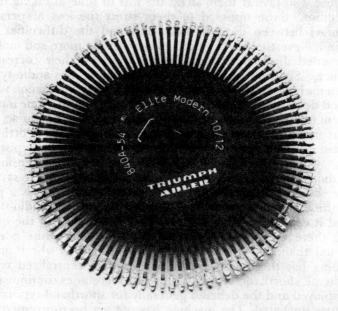

Fig. 42. *A daisy wheel.*

Other special purpose typewriters

Besides those already mentioned there are a number of typewriters and devices for special purposes to help the typist to carry out operations that would be difficult or time-consuming if performed on standard models. They include the following.

(a) Dual-feed machines which enable summaries of invoices, statements, lists of cheques, etc., to be typed as each document is completed.

(b) Continuous-stationery machines—useful when invoices and other documents are being dealt with by the same typist for much of the working day. The machine uses packs of continuous stationery that can be automatically fed with carbon paper each time a new sheet is used.

(c) Card-holding attachments, consisting of a special platen with a metal channel into which stiff cards are placed and held together firmly in position for typing.

THE DICTATION MACHINE

Opinion on the usefulness of dictation machines is divided. Those who favour them stress the loss of time in taking down dictation; those opposed to them stress the loss of personal contact between dictator and typist and the difficulties that result. Nevertheless, large offices are turning more and more to recorded dictation systems for dealing with their correspondence. Skilfully used, recorded-dictation or audio-typing systems have many advantages. But standards of dictation vary a good deal, and if these are poor much of the typist's time is often spent in unravelling what has been dictated. It is, of course, true that much of the routine work often done by the shorthand-typist can with advantage be taken over by the audio-typist and that with the raising of dictation standards an extension of audio-typing systems is to be expected. But this is not to say that the shorthand-typist is finished. Far from it. There is a place in the office for both the shorthand-typist and the audio-typist, and it cannot be claimed that either is superior to the other, for there will always be circumstances to which one is more suited than the other. Even in large concerns where audio-typing has thoroughly established itself in centralized typing systems, shorthand-typists and private secretaries continue to be employed and the demand generally for shorthand-typists continues unabated. The machine has not yet been invented that can think and reason for itself or serve as a substitute for those personal secretarial qualities which business executives continue to find indispensable. There are, moreover, many secretarial duties that defy mechanization.

Dictation machines fall into two broad classes—the magnetic and the non-magnetic. Within each class there is a variety of types. Some machines use disks, some tapes, others coated paper, and so on. Magnetic recordings may not be permanent. They are invisible and liable to inadvertent erasure by superimposed recordings. The particular medium employed can, however, be used over and over again indefinitely. Non-magnetic recordings, on the other hand, are permanent, unless deliberately erased, and have the advantage of showing the amount of dictation matter recorded.

The modern trend in large offices is to discard individual dictation machines in favour of a centralized system. Executives wishing to dictate do so from a microphone or other dictating unit in their own rooms. Centralization eliminates idle machine time, reduces the number of machines necessary, and thus cuts down installation costs. It also makes for an even distribution of work among the typists.

The case for recorded dictation

Among the advantages claimed for recorded dictation are the following.

(a) There is an estimated saving of nearly 50 per cent of the time the shorthand typist spends on correspondence. She can therefore be employed on other work while dictation is in progress.

(b) Recorded messages can be sent by post, thus eliminating both shorthand and typewriting.

(c) Dictation can take place at any time, e.g. after office hours, at home, or even during travel.

(d) Mistranscriptions of shorthand are eliminated; there can be no doubt about what was said.

(e) The dictator can listen to his recording and redictate any letter with which he is not satisfied.

(f) Dictation machines can record entire lectures or the entire proceedings of meetings.

The case against recorded dictation

The following are among the disadvantages claimed.

(a) Personal contact is lost between the executive and his typist, who is no longer available for discussion or as a source of information.

(b) Brief instructions by the executive are no longer possible; he must elaborate details on points his typist would have known or could have found out for herself.

(c) The success of the system is commensurate with the skill of the dictator, who must express himself correctly the first time, since typists find corrections confusing and sometimes hard to follow.

(d) The typist's notebook is no longer available for reference, if needed.

(e) Executives find "live" dictation quicker and less exacting to themselves.

(f) Recorded dictation is impersonal, and typists generally dislike it.

The success of any audio-typing system depends very largely on the care and skill of those who dictate. Short of first playing the dictation through, the typist has no means of knowing in advance whether the matter contains repetitions or rewordings.

The dictator's verbal corrections often prove confusing, and so it is important for those who dictate to express themselves correctly the first time. The typist must also know beforehand the length of the letters to be typed and the number of carbon copies needed, otherwise time is wasted in retyping if the paper used is too small or the number of copies taken too few. The size of paper required may, of course, be gauged from the indicated length of the recording where the dictation machine carries a recording scale or index slip. The dictaphone "Thought Master" dictation machine, for example, can be obtained with an electronic indexing facility. By pressing a button on his dictation microphone the dictator records electronic signals on the cassette tape to mark letter lengths and special instructions. These signals are recognized visually on a display panel and sub-audibly in her headset when the typist rewinds the tape on her machine, and at each point where they occur she plays the tape forward to listen to the instructions. She then resumes rewinding. She can thus begin transcribing aware of the length of each piece of dictation and of any special instructions.

A particular difficulty with audio-typing arises from homophones, the name given to different words that are pronounced alike, such as *draft* and *draught, lessen* and *lesson, principal* and *principle*. Before she can make the correct choice the typist may have to wait until she hears what follows.

Suggestions for dictators
Persons who dictate can contribute considerably to the success of audio-typing systems by observing a few simple rules.

(*a*) Make brief notes before starting to dictate. This helps to ensure straightforward dictation, free from repetitions and corrections, and greatly simplifies the typist's task.

(*b*) Speak clearly, deliberately, and at no faster than a reasonable speed, say 100–120 words a minute.

(*c*) Begin by giving the following information in the order shown:

(*i*) your name and reference;

(*ii*) size of notepaper to be used (unless you are using an individual dictation machine that carries a scale);

(*iii*) number of carbon copies to be taken;

(*iv*) correspondent's reference, if known;

(*v*) correspondent's name and address, spelling out confusing or unusual names, e.g. *Lowton, Loughton, Leominster* (pronounced *Lemster*), *Kircudbright* (pronounced *Kircoobri*), *Macleod;*

(vi) indicate salutation to be used—*Dear Sir*, or *Dear Mr ...*;

(vii) state heading, if any, to be given to body of letter.

(d) Dictate such instructions as "New paragraph" and "Bracket". It is also helpful to dictate "Full-stop", though an experienced typist may not need such help. Voice inflexion should be sufficient to indicate commas and other marks of punctuation.

(e) Spell out technical terms and unusual words and, where not obvious, indicate use of capitals.

(f) Dictate nature of subscription, e.g. whether "Yours faithfully", "Yours sincerely", etc., and also designation of the person who is to sign the letter—Managing Director, Sales Manager, etc.

(g) If enclosures are to accompany the letter, state size of envelope needed.

Where the file containing previous correspondence is passed to the typist, not all the foregoing information will need to be given.

REPRODUCTION PROCESSES

When there is a need to give the same information to a number of people we send them a circular letter. Circular letters are commonly used in sales campaigns and for announcing important developments in business, such as changes of address, extensions and reorganizations. Names and addresses of readers may be obtained from the firm's records, or from trade and other directories. Sent as they are only to selected readers, circulars should be made as personal as possible, as by addressing each letter to a particular person by name if it is known. *Dear Mr Williams* is better than *Dear Customer* or *Dear Reader,* and certainly very much better than *Dear Sir* or *Dear Madam.* Good-quality letter-headed paper should be used and the cheap-looking stencil-duplicated letter on semi-absorbent paper avoided, otherwise your letter is unlikely to capture interest and may quickly find its way into the waste-paper bin.

Where large numbers of the same letter are sent out, individual typing will not be possible. The letters must then be either printed or reproduced by one of the several office reproduction processes available. Circular letters can also be typed individually by using a word processor to merge a standard letter and a mailing list, as explained earlier (*see* p. 371). The personal touch can be maintained by printing in imitation type-writer type with the signature in facsimile.

Carbon copying

To ensure that records of all transactions conducted by correspondence are complete and available for reference, copies of outgoing letters must be taken and filed. For this, it is customary to take carbon copies. Copies may be taken either on separate sheets or on the reverse side of incoming letters to which the outgoing letters are sent in reply. The latter arrangement has the advantage of economizing filing space; it also ensures that enquiry and reply are kept together.

Carbon copying is also a convenient and inexpensive way of making copies in small numbers. By using thin carbon paper and thin typing paper as many as half a dozen clearly legible copies can be taken at a single typing, and even a dozen or more on an electric typewriter with a hard platen. The number of copies may be doubled if two-sided carbon paper is used with the kind of transparent paper known as "onion-skin", for then each carbon produces two copies—a facsimile copy on the face of one sheet and a "mirror" copy on the reverse of another, onion-skin paper being transparent enough for the mirrored impression to be read through it.

What is termed *NCR* (no carbon required) *paper* eliminates the need for carbon paper. NCR paper is specially coated with chemicals which are themselves colourless, but which produce a coloured impression when subjected to pressure by pencil, ball-point pen or typewriter keys. Because of the absence of inter-leaving carbons, copies are sharp and clear and clean to handle. NCR forms are very useful for documents where only two or three copies are needed. The method also has an important use in continuous stationery, in teleprinter rolls and computer print-outs.

Spirit duplicating

Spirit duplicating makes use of hectographic carbons similar to ordinary carbons in appearance, but coated with an aniline dye. The coated surface of the carbon is placed in contact with the glossy side of a sheet of one-sided art paper. The image to be copied is then typed, written or drawn on the front, the non-glossy, side of the art paper. The effect is to transfer a mirror impression of the typing or drawing from the "carbon" to the reverse or glossy side to provide the "master" from which copies are taken on a rotary duplicator (*see* Fig. 43).

Spirit duplicating is especially suitable for producing forms that have to be completed in ink, since the copy paper used,

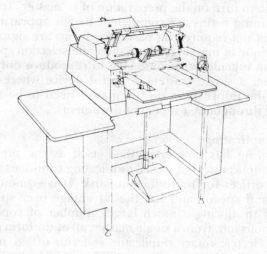

Fig. 43.   *A spirit duplicator.*

The Banda 1700 is a modern duplicator operated electrically either by switch or by foot pedal. It has a reproduction rate of seventy copies a minute.

unlike that for stencil duplicating, is non-absorbent. As hectographic carbons are supplied in a variety of colours, spirit duplicating provides an ideal medium for producing multi-coloured drawings and diagrams, but because of gradual fading as additional copies are taken the process was originally suitable for only short runs of up to about a hundred copies. This problem of fading can now be met by using a thermal copying process to prepare a new master in a few seconds (*see Photocopying* below).

This method of spirit duplicating is particularly useful in preparing series of aligned documents. In the export trade, for example, consignment details have to be entered in documents originating from many sources, each nevertheless requiring much the same information. Bills of lading from exporters, consignment notes from carriers, customs declarations and exchange-control forms from government departments, as well as forms from forwarding agents, port authorities, banks and insurance companies are among the documents regularly required. Under a system designed by the former Board of Trade an aligned series of documents is now available, i.e. a complete set of documents of standard size with the same information in the same position in each document. The benefits of the system turn on the preparation of a "master" from which the remaining forms are completed; details appearing on the master but not required on particular forms are suppressed by the technique of masking. The Banda line-selection spirit duplicator is an ingenious machine able to reproduce only selected parts from a single master—a useful device where different parts of the information on the master need to be separately recorded throughout a system of documents.

Stencil duplicating

Photocopying has now established itself as the predominant form of duplicating, but stencil duplicating continues to be used in many offices for reproduction work. It is economical, convenient and speedy and has the advantage over spirit duplicating of producing a much larger number of copies, up to several thousand, from a single master, all of uniform density. A modern electric rotary duplicator will run off as many as a hundred or more copies a minute. The process also lends itself to colour duplicating, but to a more limited extent than in spirit duplicating and with much less convenience, since a separate stencil must be cut and a fresh ink drum fitted each time a new colour is used. Correct registration of the separate printings, which must be carefully adjusted in relation to one another, may also present a problem.

Stencils covering a wide range of subjects, including photographs, pencil drawings, etc. can be prepared by photographic and electronic processes. The electronic stencil machine prepares stencils from almost any type of original in a matter of minutes, and is especially suitable for photographs and drawings.

Lithographic (offset) duplicating

The word "lithographic" means "stone writing" and offset-litho duplicating, often referred to as "offset duplicating", is so called because the inked image is "set off" or transferred from a "master" attached to the plate cylinder of a machine on to a second cylinder that does the actual printing. The master now used is no longer stone, but either a light metal plate of zinc or aluminium, or a special type of plasticized paper. The master may be prepared on a typewriter fitted with a special lithographic (oily) ribbon or by hand with special ink or a special reproducing pencil, or it may be prepared by a photocopying process.

Offset duplicating offers high quality reproduction on quite inexpensive paper. It is capable of high speeds and excellent colour work, which involves changing the ink and the cylinder, though in some machines it is necessary to replace only the cylinder containing another colour of ink. The machines used vary in size from small duplicators to large printing machines and even the small office can itself handle much of the work normally done by a printer, such as letter-headed paper and documents of various types. For producing circulars in large quantities it is excellent. Provided there is enough work to justify the cost of initial equipment, offset-litho duplicating is probably the cheapest of all reproduction processes.

Photocopying

Photocopying embraces a number of different processes in most of which the documents to be copied are placed in contact with some form of coated paper sensitive to light or heat. Dry photocopying, which dispenses with the need for dark rooms and liquid developers, is now possible with a number of processes, including the following.

(a) *The dyeline (diazo) process* is simple and clean and also very economical if only a few copies are needed. The process depends upon the action of ultra-violet light on paper coated with diazo salts. The light-rays destroy the coating on the paper, except where protected by the lines drawn on the original. When passed through a developer the paper produces a perfect copy.

(b) *The thermal process* makes use of a specially coated paper sensitive to infra-red heat rays. Thermal copiers are compact, and clean and simple to operate. They are also convenient where the number of copies needed is not large. On account of cost the process is too expensive for long runs.

(c) *Electrostatic copying* is a process that makes photographed copies direct from originals on to plain paper of almost any quality. The process can also enlarge or reduce the size of the copies taken. It is simple and speedy to operate and is especially suitable for very long runs. But the initial cost of equipment is high and is justified only where the amount of reproduction work in the office is considerable. The process currently available is called *xerography*, from the Greek *xeros* (dry) and *graphe* (writing); machines similar to the Xerox copiers, including colour copiers, marketed by Rank Xerox Ltd. are suitable (*see* Fig. 44). If a large number of copies is required, a master can be made to produce copies on an offset-litho duplicator.

Fig. 44.   *A Xerox copier.*

The Xerox 3100 is a copier for the small user, or for decentralized copying in large organizations. It has a reproduction rate of twenty copies a minute.

(d) Microfilming is a photographic process used for preserving a microscopic record of documents, which can be enlarged in projection. It is a method of commercial reproduction used in specialist libraries and by the banks for preserving copies of customers' cheques, and also by many other large organizations for copying documents of which permanent records are required. Photographing takes place at incredible speeds. As many as 1,600 documents can be photographed on to a 100 ft (some 30 metres) reel of 35 mm film, and considerably more on 16 mm film. This economical use of space is in fact the great advantage of microfilm filing, referred to in Chapter Nineteen.

(e) Colour printing. Reproduction of printing in colour is now possible. Copying is done by an electronic process, and machines are initially expensive; they also have to be maintained professionally by skilled workers.

Of these various processes only electrostatic copies and thermal copies can be made directly from an original. The other processes all involve the production of a "master". The two direct copying processes are the ones most commonly used in offices today.

One of the important advantages of office copying processes is that they are substantially cheaper than printing, except when several thousand copies of a document are required. Printer's type is expensive both to set and to store for subsequent reprintings, whereas the "masters" prepared in the office copying processes are relatively cheap, both to prepare and to store should they be needed again.

THE COLLATING MACHINE

When a number of separate sheets forming a set have been duplicated they must be collated, that is, gathered up and placed in their right order. The slow and tiresome process of doing this by hand is avoided by using a collating machine. These machines work on a variety of principles, but most of them are electrically operated and foot-controlled. Sheets for sorting are placed in individual trays or on individual shelves, from which the top sheets are ejected into the hands of the operator by means of a foot pedal. A fully automatic collator will run for several hours, collect and arrange the separate sheets and deliver them in complete sets at the rate of two dozen sets or more a minute.

In the absence of a machine a quick and easy method of sorting is to arrange the papers as in the following diagram and to use both hands, starting with sheet 10 (left hand), followed by sheet 9 (right hand), and so on alternately.

THE ADDRESSING MACHINE

Where, for example, there is a heavy mailing list, and letters, circulars, and advertising literature are sent regularly or frequently to the same persons, or wherever the same information must be repeatedly given, an addressing machine will do the work quickly, economically, and accurately, and with unfailing neatness and legibility. Machines are available which use stencils, spirit masters, metal or plastic plates, and computer and word processor disks. The principle is the same for all types—names and addresses are first placed on "masters", which are then passed through a machine, which imprints the information on to envelopes and other documents fed into the machine.

The stencil method

Where the stencil is the printing medium the process is very similar to that of the stencil duplicating machine. A stencil made of particularly durable material is first cut on the typewriter and mounted on a card frame. A pile of these frames is then placed in position on the machine, and a turn of the handle carries both stencil and envelope between a pair of rollers, the uppermost of which is inked.

The card frame may only be deep enough to take the stencil, or it may have a space at the top for a label on which is recorded the information on the stencil, or some other data. Labelled in this way the stencil can serve as a useful card index which, with the use of guide cards, may be classified in a variety of ways (*see* Fig. 45).

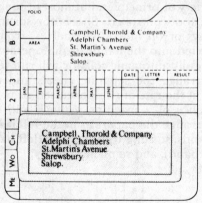

Fig. 45.   *Address stencil with record card.*

The identifying label of this stencil provides not only for the name and address, which is printed from the stencil itself, but also for additional data.

The embossed-plate method

In this method the stencil is replaced by an embossed zinc plate, prepared on an embossing machine. The plates are then put into a compartment from which they are fed into the machine under an inked ribbon. Envelopes lie face downwards on top of the ribbon and are pressed by a movable arm against the face of the plate underneath to give a facsimile. Embossing machines are available for firms who prefer to make their own plates.

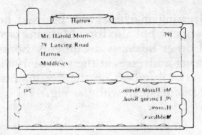

Fig. 46. *Embossed address plate with index.*

The plate provides for a slide-in index card printed from the plate itself. Coloured tabs, similar to the one on the top left-hand of the plate, may be used for signalling and classification, and also for selection of plates during printing.

The embossed plate, like the stencil card frame, may be fitted with a visible index card (*see* Fig. 46) which is printed from and is identical with the plate. The use of metal signal tabs (plain, coloured, numerical, alphabetical, geographical, etc.) provides facilities for many different systems of classification, and also enables particular plates to be automatically selected for printing without disturbing the filing sequence.

The hectographic method

For the preparation of the necessary "masters" this method uses hectographic carbon paper on the spirit duplicator principle. Carbons are placed coated side upwards in contact with the glossy surface of the master sheet. Names and addresses are then typed in the usual way, leaving a "mirror" impression on the reverse (the glossy) side of the master sheet. Master sheets may be obtained perforated to give the size of original required for fitting into special frames. On being passed through the addressing machine each frame is brought in contact with an envelope on which it leaves a facsimile of its details. One of the drawbacks of spirit duplicated masters is that impressions become progressively fainter with each copy taken, the maximum number of satisfactory copies from any one master being not more than about two hundred.

The electronic method

By this method records of names and addresses are held on mini-diskettes (floppy disks). Additions and alterations are typed on the keyboard of a visual display unit. Using this system labels can be addressed automatically at the rate of 100 a minute. There is also provision for alphabetical sorting by name or by post town.

Modern addressing machines can be used not only for envelopes and wrappers, but also for addressing circulars, invoices, statements and other business documents. Some machines are capable of printing addresses at the rate of 100 a minute. They can also print serial numbers on the documents and count the number of documents dealt with (*see* Fig. 47).

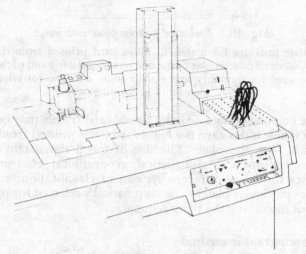

Courtesy: Addressograph-Multigraph Ltd.

Fig. 47.   *Model 1950 Addressograph.*

This electrically operated machine is capable of imprinting and listing information on all types of business forms at speeds thirty to fifty times faster than handwriting or typewriting.

SOME FURTHER OFFICE MACHINES

Adding and add-listing machines

Machines for adding and listing form part of the equipment of most offices. In its simplest form the adding machine is a small model with only one key for each of the digits 0 to 9. Add-listing machines are equipped with a carriage to hold either a paper tally-roll or a loose sheet. They are used for totalling cash sales, wages sheets, ledger accounts, etc.

Calculators

Unlike the adding and listing machines from which they have developed calculators have full facilities for all four arithmetical processes: they can add, subtract, multiply and divide at speed. They range in size from the pocket calculator to full desk-size models with display units. In addition to their display dials printing calculators, like add-listing machines, record the figures at each stage in a calculation and the result on a tally-roll. The roll is useful for providing proof that the calculation is accurate, and also for attaching to a document for future reference. There are also calculators that can read instructions from punched cards or punched paper and, like computers, store and recall information. Some desk calculators can also be programmed, for example to calculate discounts on the basis of pre-set percentages.

In the hands of an expert operator the electronic calculator can perform in seconds, and with strict accuracy, calculations which, if performed non-mechanically, would take as many minutes.

Cheque-writing and signing machines

Cheque-writing machines can be used for preparing cheques. They will enter the date, the payee's name and the sum of money, cross and sign the cheque and meter the number of cheques used. These machines are more comprehensive than cheque-signing machines, which are useful where large numbers of documents such as share certificates, dividend warrants and letters have to be signed.

Apart from speed cheque-writing machines provide protection against fraud because cheques prepared and signed in this way cannot be altered without detection.

Stamping and franking machines

For use in the smaller office there are machines for affixing postage stamps. For these machines stamps of various denominations are supplied by the Post Office in rolls. Some machines take only one denomination at a time; others take several. The rolls are locked in the machine, and as stamps are used the total is recorded on an automatic counter.

As a safeguard against improper use stamps may be perforated with initials. Perforation is not undertaken by the Post Office, but no objection to it is raised, provided the perforating holes are no larger than those dividing one stamp from another.

Firms with a large amount of correspondence prefer to use franking rather than stamping machines. These machines enable printed impressions of stamps to be made on all types of mail, including letters, parcels and telemessages. If desired, the name of, or an advertisement for, the user may be incorporated in the stamp.

Franking machines may be hired or purchased from one of the supplying companies licensed by the Post Office. Their names and addresses are given in the *Post Office Guide*. Users must conform to the following conditions.

(*a*) They must hold a Post Office licence.

(*b*) An account must be opened at the Post Office and an agreed amount prepaid. Depending on the amount prepaid, the machine is set and locked by Post Office officials. When the amount prepaid is exhausted the machine ceases to function until reset by the Post Office.

(*c*) Franked correspondence must be arranged with names and addresses facing in the same direction, tied in bundles, and handed in at a specified Post Office, and not posted in a pillar box, except after closing time and under certain conditions.

(*d*) A docket must be tendered at the end of every week showing the readings of the meter at the end of each weekday, whether or not the machine has been used.

(*e*) The machine must be inspected by the manufacturers not less frequently than twice in every period of six months.

The great advantage of the franking machine is the speed at which it works. The most up to date models can frank at the rate of 100 letters a minute.

Envelope machines
An envelope-opening machine shaves a minute portion from one edge of sealed envelopes and enables the contents to be quickly and easily removed. Electronically operated machines are capable of dealing with 600 envelopes a minute.

The envelope sealer moistens and presses the flaps of envelopes for post. Electronically operated letter-sealing machines can deal with letters of different shapes and sizes at the rate of 300 a minute.

There are also machines that fold and insert papers into envelopes, seal the flaps and stack the envelopes at speeds of up to 60 a minute.

Besides the machines mentioned there are many others concerned with the accountancy side of business, such as the machines for billing and ledger posting, but consideration of these is outside the scope of this book.

EXERCISES
1. Suppose you had, say, 4,000 circular letters to send by post, explain how you would avoid the labour of stamping them, and the rules it would be necessary to observe.

2. The head of your department suggests using a dictation machine. How would you advise him?   (RSA)

3. You are allowed to choose a dictating machine for your office. State the type of machine you would prefer, giving reasons for your choice.   (RSA)

4. Your employer suggests buying an electric typewriter to replace your office standard model. Reply, in the form of a memorandum, to this suggestion, giving your reasons for agreement or disagreement with the suggestion.   (RSA)

5. (a) What is the difference between magnetic and non-magnetic types of dictating machines?

(b) When would you consider it useful to use a photocopying machine?

(c) For what purpose is a guillotine used in an office?   (RSA)

6. Some of the executives in your office use a dictating machine, and cause you extra work by failing to give clear instructions. For example, one of them always forgets, until the end of the letter, to mention how many carbon copies are required.

Draw up a list of suggestions which will remind each dictator to give you at the appropriate time all the instructions you need.   (RSA)

7. In your office there are a spirit duplicator and an ink duplicator, but no addressing machine. Each month you send to the same fifty addresses a small booklet. To avoid typing individual envelopes, how can you use the machinery at your disposal?   (RSA)

8. At the time when he is considering purchasing a dictation machine, your employer receives literature advertising a new model of a well-known machine. This causes him to compare details of other machines, and he sends for you to discuss the matters with him. Explain to him the following:

(a) the advantages and disadvantages of a very small portable machine;
(b) the difference in use between magnetic and non-magnetic recording;
(c) the use of a foot or hand control for transcription.   (RSA)

9. A stencil is the "master-sheet" from which copies are made on an ink duplicator. How do you prepare the "master"for:

(a) a spirit duplicator;
(b) an offset litho machine;
(c) an addressing machine?   (RSA)

10. What are the advantages of using a franking machine in your out-going post room? Give any other uses to which a postal franking-machine can be put.   (RSA)

11. Your employer wishes to send out 2,000 circular letters on your normal business notepaper. What alternative methods of printing or duplication would you suggest to him? Give your reasons.   (RSA)

12. Describe with as much detail as you can, a remote control audio dictating installation. Include in your answer the advantages and disadvantages of such an installation compared with the use of shorthand-typists.

13. Choose one method of duplicating and explain:

(a) how to prepare a master;
(b) the method by which corrections can be made;
(c) the minimum and maximum number of copies you would expect to produce;
(d) an alternative method of producing a master.

(*LCCI Priv. Sec. Cert.*)

14. Within your organization it is necessary to have reproduced certain forms and documents for distribution internally and externally. State the methods of reproducing such forms and documents you would propose for up to 10 copies, 50 copies and 150 copies.

(*ICSA Pt. 2*)

CHAPTER TWENTY-TWO

For the Typist

To act with common sense, according to the moment, is the best wisdom I know.

Horace Walpole

This chapter is specially for you.

To have read through the previous chapters and worked some of the exercises should help you with your correspondence. Remember, above all, that it is your job and not that of the dictator to see that letters sent out are grammar perfect and free from misspellings and faulty punctuation. To quote Lord Luke, the secretary "should have enough knowledge of English to correct ungrammatical sentences and wrongly spelt words. She must see, too that the letters make sense." The typist who produced, "This kind of cigars" for "With kindest regards" (and it did in fact happen) may be lacking in common sense, but she is a perfect specimen of the type for whom thinking is an arduous and disagreeable exercise.

In return for your monthly cheque your employer will look not only for competence in shorthand and typewriting, and a good working knowledge of English, but also for certain personal qualities, some of which—like interest in work, tact, good manners, tidiness, and punctuality—can be taught. Others, like intelligence, initiative, and what is commonly called *savez*, have their roots in personality. They cannot be taught, but may be developed.

Some time ago the writer was approached by a business friend who wanted help in finding a new secretary. He was getting rid of the one he had "because", he said, "as a shorthand-typist she would get by, but she has no initiative, is lacking in common sense, and can't even spell." "My job", he went on, "takes me from my desk a good deal, but I daren't remain away for more than three or four days at a time, because I never know when the girl is going to drop a brick or what she is going to shelve. Above

anything else I want a girl with *nous*, and mine just hasn't got it."
Is not this the heartfelt cry of many an employer? "I don't mind
so much about the shorthand speed," he says, "provided she can
type decently and use her wits."

Yes, you must certainly type decently, because the letters you
type will convey the tone of your office to the outside world, and
your own character will be revealed in the quality of your workmanship. Poor display and messy erasures will reveal you for
what you are—slapdash and careless and, if your English is
shaky, only half qualified for your job into the bargain. If, on the
other hand, your letters are miniature works of art, as all letters
should be—neatly typed, free from erasures, nicely displayed,
correctly spelt, and intelligently punctuated—your correspondent will appreciate the care you have taken and look upon it as
a mark of considerateness, even of courtesy, as in fact it is. Good
taste in letters is as important as good taste in dress; it is one
aspect of good manners.

PREPARING FOR DICTATION

The time will come when you must take down your first real
letter, if you have not already done so. No doubt you will be
nervous, wondering whether you can cope. You might even
wonder whether you will be able to read your notes back. If you
are slow in your first attempts do not worry; you will improve
quickly, and when your shorthand speed is high enough to give
you a margin you will no longer feel anxious about these "interviews"; you will even look forward to them.

Be careful to create a good first impression. Show that you are
alert and interested, and avoid any suggestion of slackness.
During the dictation you will be immediately under the eye of
your employer. Let him see that you went to him well prepared.
See to it that your notebook is *at the ready*—date written in, left-
hand margin ruled, and a rubber band round the pages already
used so that you may start taking down without licking your
finger and fumbling the pages while he looks on, and waits. If
you take down with pencil make sure that you have by you a
"spare" in case the point breaks. If you use a pen, as most high-
speed writers do, make sure that it is filled at the beginning of
each day—it would be a humiliating experience if it ran dry in
the middle of a dictation. And just in case of accident always
keep a pencil in reserve.

TAKING DOWN

You will probably be asked to sit down, though you may occasionally be expected to take short notes standing up. If the dictation does not begin at once don't fidget, but wait quietly until your employer has arranged his papers, finished his phone talk, or filled his pipe. While waiting don't day-dream and jump like a startled rabbit when suddenly he begins to dictate. Be quite ready for him.

To save their typists' time many employers prepare their dictation beforehand. They arrange their papers and make brief notes of the replies they propose to dictate. This helps to make for a continuous dictation, and the morning's letters are cleared quickly and without fuss. To take down letters in such conditions is a real pleasure—and excellent practice for your shorthand. But not all employers are as considerate as this. Some will suck their pipes and talk through their teeth; others, with hands clasped behind them will walk distractingly up and down, and, believe it or not, some will even seem to ignore you, turn their backs on you and dictate to the sparrows on the roof opposite.

Try to follow the *sense* of what is dictated, and in your notes insert full-stops at the end of sentences or at points where you think they should be. These two things will help you greatly when you come to type back your notes, and will insure you against mistranscriptions like the following:

We are not in any way connected with the local office for administrative purposes. Our office comes directly under the central board.

instead of:

We are not in any way connected with the local office. For administrative purposes our office comes directly under the central board.

Never interrupt in the course of a dictation, not even when the dictator pauses to think out his next point; you may ruin his train of thought. If there is a word you have not heard, or a name or figure you wish to confirm, wait until dictation of the letter is finished, or at least until there is a convenient break in the dictation, and then politely put your question, "I am sorry, but would you mind repeating ...?" If the letter dictated contains any inconsistencies, as where two different times are mentioned for the same appointment, draw attention to them tactfully— once again when the dictation is finished, and not before.

During pauses in the dictation (and there are bound to be some), don't stare at the dictator, as much as to say, "Come along, I'm waiting", and don't stare round at the furniture, or out of the window. Keep your interest fastened on your note-book, and take advantage of these lulls in the dictation to glance through the notes you have just written. You may even have time to touch them up by inserting the punctuation marks you propose to use; it will save you time when you come to type back, and at the worst, find you something to do during pauses that might otherwise prove embarrassing.

Keep an orderly notebook—one to which you can refer back easily at any time. Using your margin, number each separate letter and head it with the name of your correspondent *in longhand*, not in shorthand. You can then note alternative or unfamiliar spellings—*Green* or *Greene*, *Pullen* or *Pullin*, Mrs *Duchenne*, etc.—and refer back to particular letters easily. In addition, leave one spare line after each letter so that each separate letter stands clearly by itself.

For efficient work your left-hand margin is indispensable; certainly it is one of your best friends. Use it for numbering the letters you take down, and for noting points to be clarified. For the latter a small cross is all you need. Use it also for personal reminders about phone calls to be made, messages to be de-livered, extra copies required, and so on. For noting urgent letters requiring priority, a bold asterisk is recommended.

Your dictator will occasionally wish to change the text of his dictation and ask you to refer back to a previous note. Any attempt to insert additional matter between two existing lines of shorthand can only end in confusion. You must therefore make such changes methodically. They will be of three different kinds: *(a)* to delete; *(b)* to delete and substitute; and *(c)* to add or intersperse.

The pure deletion is simple; use a squiggly line. If something is to be substituted, delete what is no longer needed and add a circle, and inside put ⓐ, ⓑ etc., making a corresponding foot-note at the bottom of the page, as in Fig. 48.

Treat interspersions in the same way.

You may or may not be given the previous correspondence dealing with the subject-matter of the dictation. If not, be care-ful to get your correspondent's correct name and address, or at least the correct name; you can look up his address later. If, on the other hand, the previous correspondence is given you, then all the details can be found from it and you will not, of course, ask unnecessary questions about name spellings, reference numbers, etc., all of which you will find in the correspondence itself

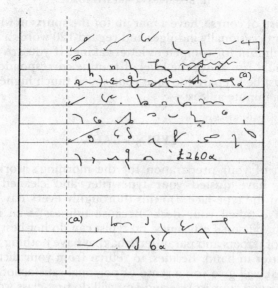

Fig. 48. *Deleting a shorthand note.*

The footnote at (a) replaces the note deleted from lines 2–3.

If your dictator is considerate he will put the previous papers together for you, turning each one face downwards as he completes his dictation. The order will then correspond to that of the letters in your notebook. Not all dictators may be as considerate as this, but few will be as inconsiderate as the one who, having dictated a letter, had an objectionable habit of throwing the papers on the floor, leaving his secretary to pick them up.

If the salutation is not dictated you may have to ask whether it is to be *Dear Sir,* or *Dear Mr . . .*; similarly with the complimentary close, *Yours faithfully, Yours truly,* or *Yours sincerely.* But avoid asking this if you are able to find it out from previous correspondence or from other members of the office staff. You must always aim at being as independent and resourceful as possible. Your employer is not there to help you to do *your* job; it is your job to help him to do *his,* and to worry him as little as possible.

If your shorthand speed is adequate you will find this part of your work both interesting and enjoyable. If your shorthand speed is not adequate your work will be difficult and trying, but it is not out of your power to raise your speed to a level at which you can hold the job down; there are plenty of facilities for this. Not many dictators average more than 100 words a minute, but you must, of course, have a margin for the spurts in which every dictator occasionally indulges and regard 120 words a minute as the minimum for competent letter-taking. If you are ambitious and would rise above the level of routine correspondence, then you must be prepared to take your speed much higher—to 140 words a minute at least.

TYPING BACK

As part of your preparation for the morning's work you will already have dusted your typewriter and cleaned out and brushed the type-face. Do this thoroughly every day. You will, too, have tidied your desk. Because tidiness is an important factor in personal efficiency, no typist can do her best work in a welter of papers and paraphernalia that have nothing to do with the matter in hand. Besides, to return from your dictation to a tidy desk will give you a sense of personal satisfaction and help you to enjoy your work—and you will do first-class work only if you enjoy doing your job.

The following hints on the typing of letters from shorthand notes are based on the experience of a very competent secretary. There is a saying that wise men learn from the experience of others, while fools learn from their own. It will pay you to study these hints carefully.

Stationery requirements
You will need three kinds of paper: headed paper, carbon paper, and paper for the file copies. Carbon paper is expensive. Keep it in a folder in your drawer, taking care not to crease or dog-ear it. Keep the headed paper and the paper for copies in a rack on your desk and withdraw it sheet by sheet as you need it. You may also need plain, unheaded paper for long letters with continuation sheets. This should be of the same texture and quality as the headed paper.

Selection of paper
Select the size of paper, quarto or octavo (or, if using international-size paper, A4 or A5, appropriate to the length of letter you have to type. To select octavo or A5 and then find yourself short of room so that you must continue or another sheet is evidence of bad judgment. If this happens the only decent thing to do is to retype your letter on quarto or A4, even if it does mean wasting time and paper.

Continuation sheets

If a letter extends beyond a single sheet never suggest to your correspondent that he is not worth a second sheet by typing on the reverse side of the first; continue on a separate sheet. Plain paper of the same quality as the letter-head must be used and typed with a heading to show:

(*a*) the number of the sheet (in the centre of the page);
(*b*) the name of your correspondent (on the left-hand side);
(*c*) the date of the letter (on the right-hand side).

This provides an adequate safeguard should sheets become separated.

```
L A Brazier & Co Ltd           2            15 March 19..
```

To type only one or two lines of a new paragraph at the bottom of a sheet looks bad, and unless there is room for at least three lines of type the new paragraph should be started at the top of the continuation sheet.

A catchword is sometimes used to carry a passage from one sheet to another; the last word on the first sheet is typed in the bottom right-hand corner below the last line of type, thus:

```
Sorry to complain that the goods were not in accordance
                                              with /
```

The word *with* is then repeated as the first word on the next sheet. The use of continuation sheets connected as shown above makes the use of catchwords an unnecessary elaboration.

Paper economy

Letter-head paper is expensive; don't waste it. First read your shorthand note through, marking with a double oblique the points at which new paragraphs are to begin, inserting at the same time the punctuation you propose to use. Typing back will then resolve itself into a piece of straightforward transcription, and second attempts at the same letter will be much less likely.

Importance of layout

In many offices it is a practice to identify letters by including the initials of both dictator and typist. In some cases the serial number of the letter is also added, thus:

This is best done at the head of the letter on the same line as the date, except when using the blocked style, when the reference is placed *above* the date. Placing references in the top left-hand part of the paper has the advantage of leaving the bottom left-hand corner of the letter free for noting enclosures.

Always type the date in full, thus:

3 September 19..

As with the date always type in full words such as *Road, Street,* and *Avenue*. Use capitals for the name of the town; by relieving the monotony of all-lower-case characters it adds to the artistic appearance of the letter. To reduce the number of lines occupied by a lengthy inside name and address, type the county name on the same line as the post town, reserving the final line for the postcode. If the county name is given a separate line the postcode may share the same line provided adequate space is left between county name and postcode.

Whether you use the blocked or the indented form of address will depend on the practice in your particular firm. Because it provides a better display, the former is to be preferred and is now usual. Make sure to use courtesy titles correctly. For the use of *Mssrs* follow the practice recommended on pp. 278–80.

You will find some specimen layouts in the next chapter.

Display and neatness

See that your typing is accurate and the display artistic. Aim at an attractive and pleasing appearance for your letters. Margins especially are important, since they serve to "frame" your letter.

For very short letters you may adopt double line-spacing except for your correspondent's name and address for which single line-spacing should always be used.

Perusal of shorthand note

Before beginning to type examine your notebook for special instructions, such as extra carbon copies, otherwise you may make unnecessary work for yourself. Look out, too, for badly formed sentences, unnecessary repetitions, incorrect verb forms, and so on. Remember that *shall* always pairs with *will*,and *should* with *would*. These sequences cause trouble because dictators often say what sounds very much like *I'sh be glad if you will* or *I'sh be glad if you would*. It is left to you to supply the verb *shall* or *should* to give the correct sequence.

Note similarly:

$$\text{I } shall \text{ be glad if } \begin{cases} \text{you } can \\ \text{I } may, \\ \text{they } do \end{cases} \quad \text{BUT} \quad \text{I } should \text{ be glad if } \begin{cases} \text{you } could \\ \text{I } might \\ \text{they } did \end{cases}$$

When making an alteration to the text of a dictated letter make sure your alteration is for the better and that you can justify it if asked to do so. A knowledge of sentence structure as outlined in Chapter Three will enable you to make many minor improvements in the letters you type.

The following are extracts from actual letters that might easily have been improved by the typist:

(a) There is a strong tendency for grammar-school pupils to stay on for sixth-form courses and, of course, we depend mainly on the grammar schools for our junior staff. (For *of course* substitute *as you know*, or some similar phrase.)

(b) If she is to begin the course it is important that she should begin without delay. (Substitute *do so* for the second *begin*.)

(c) There has been some difficulty in tracing your record of work, and I am afraid it is difficult to give you the certificate for which you ask. (Reconstruct the sentence so as to avoid using *difficulty* and *difficult* so close together. E.g. *It has not been possible to trace your record ...*, or *I am sorry I am unable to give you the certificate ... because ...*)

Verifying references

"Never trust your boss" is a sound maximum when applied to references, dates, etc., quoted in correspondence. Your employer is a busy man concerned with the broader issues that arise in the course of his work. He has little time for details of the kind you yourself are quite capable of looking after. If he replies to "your letter of 17th August" make sure that the letter is in fact dated the 17th, and not the 19th, or some other date. And if he makes an appointment for "Tuesday, the 5th" make sure that the 5th is a Tuesday, and not some other day. To allow slips of this kind to pass may cause much inconvenience. It is *your* business to verify reference numbers, invoice numbers, amounts of cheques, and so on, dictated to you. Your employer may easily make a mistake, and in any case it is always possible that you may have misheard.

Erasures

Nothing will brand you more certainly as an incompetent, slovenly typist than obvious erasures. Strictly, there should be no erasures at all in any letter, but if you *do* make an occasional one see that it is made so carefully as not to be apparent upon a normal scrutiny of your letter. If you use one of the so-called "mechanical erasers", consisting of strips of coated paper that blot out wrongly-typed characters retyped through the tape, or the kind of eraser that "paints out" mistakes, make sure that the substance you use matches exactly the shade of the typing paper, otherwise your correction will be apparent. And treat your carbon copies with much the same care. A smudged carbon is a sign of laziness, besides being offensive to those who have to refer to the office file later on. You can avoid a smudge by putting a slip of paper between the carbon and copy, and by first using a soft and then a hard eraser.

Never remove a letter from your machine until you have read it through carefully. Retyped characters will then fall precisely into their right places.

Checking your typing

The most frequently voiced criticism of the modern typist is that "She can't spell"; the next, that "She can't see a mistake". Over and over again employers are asked to sign letters that should never have been passed to them in the first place, with letters transposed, words carelessly omitted, obvious wrong spellings, and so on. Avoid stupidities such as the following:

(a) I shall also *meed* fifteen more forms.
(b) I am sorry to *lear* from your letter that ...
(c) I *understnad* that he was unable to come.
(d) We can provide a class that is less *advances* than the one you are taking.

These are samples from letters actually passed in for signature. To hand in for signature a letter that contains any mistakes of this sort is unpardonable; not only does it destroy your employer's confidence in you but you also betray a trust. The mistakes also suggest that the firm itself is as negligent and inefficient as its typist.

Cancelling shorthand notes

As you type each letter cancel the shorthand note by drawing a *vertical* line through its full length. When you have cancelled all the notes on a page in this way the vertical lines will join up to form a continuous line running the full length of the page, and provide you with a clear indication that no letters have been skipped.

This method of cancelling is recommended, because your

letters may not always be typed in order of dictation, and any break in the vertical line will show at once that work on the page is incomplete. The use of oblique rather than vertical lines is open to the objection that a letter, especially if very short, is liable to be overlooked—and the letter overlooked may well be an important one.

ENVELOPES AND CARBON COPIES

Type your envelopes as you go along, letter by letter. Don't hand them in with your letters; the person who has to sign the letters has no need for them, and does not want them.

Attach carbon copies to the top of the papers handed to you at the time of dictation. Don't leave this fiddling little job to your employer. Then hand in your letters for signature—the original with attached enclosures first, then the remaining papers with carbon copies on top. Your service in arranging and submitting your work methodically in this way will be appreciated. Your employer may not express his appreciation; he is, after all, entitled to take such elementary service for granted.

EXERCISES

1. You are acting as receptionist/switchboard operator relief in the lunch-hour. Everyone else, except some of the juniors, is out. What would you do in each of the following circumstances?

(a) A van-driver delivers four boxes of envelopes and hands you the advice note for signature.

(b) A policeman calls to say that the firm's van is obstructing the traffic. (RSA)

2. A junior from another department comes to you in an unhappy frame of mind. She says that she "can do nothing right" in the eyes of the head of her department. The head of that department is a woman senior to you. What could you do? (RSA)

3. Where would you find the following information:

(a) how to address an ambassador;
(b) the name of the head of a government department;
(c) official reports of proceedings in parliament?

4. What would you suggest to your telephone operator that she should say instead of the following expressions, which she uses consistently?

(a) (on lifting the receiver) "Hullo",

(b) "Okeydoke" or "OK",

(c) (if she cannot hear) "Mr Who?",

(d) "Hold on, will you?"

(e) "The gentleman you want is out," or, "the gentleman you want is busy",

(f) "Just a minute, dear."   *(RSA)*

5. In what order of importance do you place those skills and attributes necessary for a private secretary?   *(RSA)*

6. Your employer wishes you to increase your shorthand speed so that you can go with him to the meetings of departmental heads and take notes. He has offered either to pay your evening-class fees or to release you for one day each week to attend special day classes. Which would you choose, and why?   *(RSA)*

7. The stationery cupboard for your department is kept locked, but everyone knows where the key is kept, and staff help themselves. The result is that stationery gets muddled up and supplies of items often run out without being re-ordered.

You are asked to take charge. What would you do?

8. How would you, as secretary, deal with the following situation? An executive, based on London, has an important appointment in Edinburgh on the following morning. It has been arranged that he shall fly from London airport to Edinburgh in the late afternoon, and a reservation for the night has been made for him in an Edinburgh hotel. Owing to fog, the flight is cancelled.   *(RSA)*

9. Your employer has been away for a few days visiting customers. He is due back at his home on Wednesday evening, and appointments in the office have been made for him for the following day. On Wednesday afternoon you receive a telephone message to say that he has had a slight accident in the car and will not be fit to travel until Thursday.

What action would you take?   *(RSA)*

10. Much stationery has been wasted owing to departments ordering too much at one time. It has been decided to have a weekly issue, and each department has been instructed to complete a requisition form showing the estimated needs for the coming week.

A simple, standard form must be drawn up and duplicated. Design a form to include ten items of stationery.   *(RSA)*

11. State briefly how you would deal with the following situation: Mr X, an important client, telephones you at lunch time to say that he has been waiting for over half an hour in a restaurant for your employer to join him. He wants to know what has happened. You know that your employer is at a meeting in another part of the city. He has not told you of his appointment with Mr X, which he seems to have forgotten.

                                                                     (RSA)

12. You work for a small charity. A number of people call or write for information, and the literature which they receive includes a form on which interested persons may apply for membership. Many enquirers do not return these forms. Write a suitable follow-up letter to such enquirers.   *(RSA)*

13. The room in which you house your addressing machine and electric duplicator is uncarpeted. The room underneath is occupied by the editor of a small magazine. During your employer's absence you receive an angry letter from the editor saying that, because of the noise overhead, he cannot concentrate, and asking you to take immediate steps to stop the noise. Reply by letter. *(RSA)*

14. You are employed as secretary to the principal of a small secretarial college which holds evening classes in typewriting. You send a prospectus to each enquirer. Too many enquiries are received to allow a typed letter to be sent to each, but a duplicated letter, giving dates and vacancies, is sent with the prospectus. Draft a letter, to be used throughout the year, leaving spaces in which future dates can be inserted.

(RSA)

15. Your employer has left the instructions shown below. Carry out his requests. *(RSA)*

Miss A.   So sorry I forgot to give you this last night.

I want to sign ~~this~~ a letter when I come in in the morning. ‡

Have it ready ~~in duplicate~~ with ~~one copy~~ two copies. The letter is to

X Fred Smith - you've got his address - begin the letter

Dear Fred and tell him that I should be glad to see him

about the renewal of the Insurance policy in this office on Monday next

stet at ~~11 o'clock~~ 3 o'Clock. Ask him to ~~at~~ telephone me at home

to let me know if its convenient. No, on second

thoughts ask him to telephone me at the office.

My typing isn't as good as yours, is it?

I've looked up the policy no. it is 51870, and his

X address I remember is 67 West minster Road, W.1.

‡ I must be away again by 12 o'clock.

CHAPTER TWENTY-THREE

Letter Styles

Men trust rather to their eyes than to their ears; the effect
of precepts is therefore slow and tedious, whilst that of
examples is summary and effectual.

Seneca

The conventional layout adopted for letters in this country is
illustrated by the example given on p. 224. But as already mentioned, choice of layout is a matter of personal taste, and in
recent years there has been a general movement to depart from
what is still regarded by many as the most attractive form of
display.

Many firms adopt a particular letter style and standardize its
use throughout the entire organization. Clear instructions are
given, often in an office manual, to all typists, who must then
follow the prescribed practice in dealing with such details as
arrangement and placement of dates, reference numbers, complimentary closures, and in matters of margins, spacings, and
paragraph arrangement. The letter style, like the letter-head,
thus becomes an expression of the firm's personality. Some
firms, on the other hand, allow each department to adopt its
own style, while others leave the arrangement to the personal
preferences of their typists. Many firms have adopted the style
of layout prescribed for use in government departments and
given in the *Manual for Civil Service Typists* (HMSO, 1974).

The six examples that follow, reproduced half actual size,
illustrate the various letter styles sometimes adopted. The styles
fall into two main classes—the indented and the blocked—
though within each class there are variations. Notes explaining
the special features of each style illustrated are included in the
body of the letters. Brief comments on the style used are given
after each letter.

Telephone: 0772 51662

THE CAXTON FIRE APPLIANCE CO., LTD.
FIRE PROTECTION ENGINEERS

Directors:
J. Beaumont, A.C.A.
H. J. Willis, F.I.A.

53–55 Berwick Street
PRESTON
PR1 5QS

13th February 19..

Miss Elizabeth Groves
11 Osborne Road
WATFORD Herts
WD2 4TJ

Dear Miss Groves

Fully-blocked Letter Style

This letter style is up to date and is in general use in this country.
Its outstanding feature is the commencement of all typing lines,
including those for the date, the inside name and address, the subject
heading and the complimentary close, at the left-hand margin.

For this letter the open pattern of punctuation has been adopted; that
is to say, none except essential punctuation marks are used outside the
body of the letter. You will notice, for example, a complete absence
of punctuation marks from the date, the salutation, the complimentary
close, and from the ends of the lines forming the inside name and
address.

Some people who use this style prefer to place the date in its usual
position on the right, because it helps to give the letter a more
balanced appearance. It also facilitates reference to the files.

Yours sincerely
for THE CAXTON FIRE APPLIANCE CO LTD.

J Beaumont

J Beaumont
Director

Example 1: Fully blocked style letter

This style has a business-like appearance, and is the most effective since
the absence of indentations reduces typing time. Those who dislike it
say it is side-heavy and unbalanced. The loss of clarity occasioned by the
absence of indentations can be made good by increasing the number of
separate line-spacings between paragraphs from two to three.

The open pattern of punctuation used is in keeping with the modern
letter style, but is not essential to it. If closed punctuation is preferred it
could be used.

This is the letterstyle recommended for Civil Service Departments
(*see* p. 223) and is now in general business use.

Excelsior Furniture

the excelsior furniture company limited
excel house piccadilly london WIV 9QS
tel: 01-196 0123   telegrams: excel london

WRH/JFD   3rd October 19..

Miss W Livingstone
5 Lyndhurst Road
OXFORD
OX3 4NG

Dear Miss Livingstone

                        Modified Block Letter Style

This style is similar to the fully-blocked style used in the preceding
example, differing from it only in the positioning of the date, the subject heading, and the closing lines.

The date is given its normal position on the right-hand side and the
subject heading is centred over the body of the letter. For the complimentary close and signature data either the centred or the indented
method illustrated in Fig. 5 may be used. The centred closure is more
in keeping with the general style of the letter and is the one used in
this example. The open pattern of punctuation has been adopted.

This letter style is popular in the United States and is now being used
by a growing number of business houses in this country.

                        Yours sincerely
                  for THE EXCELSIOR FURNITURE CO LTD

                        W. R. Harrison

                        W R Harrison
                        Sales Manager

Example 2: Modified block letter-style

Those who favour this style claim that the unbroken left-hand margin
gives the letter an attractive appearance, and that it is easier and quicker
to type than the indented styles. There are, on the other hand, many
who do not like it because of its strong departure from the conventional indented styles to which they have become accustomed.

If desired treble-line spacing can be adopted to compensate for the
loss of clarity occasioned by the loss of indentation.

Macdonald & Evans

Estover, Plymouth PL6 7PZ
Telephone: Plymouth (0752) 705251
Telegraphic address: MACEVANS Plymouth
Telex: 45635

GBD/FM

17 May 19..

Miss J. W. Preston,
    4 Glen Eldon Road,
        SOUTHPORT, Lancs.
           PR8 9UL

Dear Miss Preston,

<u>Fully-indented Letter Style</u>

     This letter is typed in the fully-indented style, with closed
punctuation. The inside name and address, and the paragraphs forming
the body of the letter are all indented five spaces. Some typists prefer
a deeper indentation and may use as many as ten spaces, though five are
quite enough to show the separation of paragraphs clearly.

     Left-hand and right-hand margins of 3cm have been adopted, and the
date is so placed that the terminal figure serves as a guide for the
right-hand margin.

     The letter is of course typed in single line-spacing. The subject
heading is centred two line-spacings below the salutation, which in turn
begins three line-spacings below the inside name and address. The paragraphs are separated by double line-spacing.

     The complimentary close begins at the centre of the typing line, and
the designation, following the general plan for indentation, is typed
five spaces to the right of this. The effect is to offset the inside
name and address and to give the letter an appearance of balance.

               Yours sincerely,
         for MACDONALD & EVANS (Publications) LTD.

                 G. B. DAVIS
               Managing Director

Macdonald & Evans Ltd. Directors: R B North M A (Oxon) M W Beevers FCA W D J Argent A L Rowins FCA (non-executive) Registered in England Number 488368
Macdonald & Evans (Publications) Ltd. Directors R B North M A (Oxon) M W Beevers FCA W D J Argent W D Antrobus A L Rowins FCA (non-executive) Registered in England Number 590428
Macdonald & Evans Distribution Services Ltd. Directors R B North M A (Oxon) M W Beevers FCA W D J Argent A L Rowins FCA (non-executive) Registered in England Number 1253536

Example 3: Fully indented letter style

Until comparatively recently this letter style was the style in general use.
It was liked because it has balance and the suggestion of a light touch;
each paragraph is prominently displayed. There are many who do not
like this style; they claim that the numerous indentations are time-
wasting and that the style has been in use for so long that it has become
old-fashioned. Mainly because it is time-saving most business houses
have now adopted the blocked style shown in Example 1.

TELEPHONE: HARTLEY 396   LEATHER MERCHANTS

HARCOURT, GROVES & CO. LTD.
24-30 Queen Victoria Street, Hartley HA8 6UF

DIRECTORS:
R. WILLIAMSON
W. F. GROVES
C. J. GROVES   WPG/LC   24 September, 19..

Mrs. Frank Fairclough,
31 Dunster Road,
GUILDFORD, Surrey
GU5 6EW

Dear Mrs. Fairclough,

<u>Semi-indented Letter Style</u>

     This style is a modified version of the fully-indented style. The main differences lie in the inside name and address, which is typed in block form, and in the complimentary close, which is typed to fall evenly across the centre of the typing line, with the designation similarly centred. Some typists using this style prefer to place the closing lines to the right, as in the preceding example.

     The closed pattern of punctuation has been adopted. This makes free use of commas, for example in the date after the name of the month, at the end of each line of the inside address except the last, and after both the salutation and complimentary close.

     Another point to note about the pattern of punctuation is the absence of full-stops after the date, and also at the end of the inside address unless the name of the county is abbreviated, when the normal abbreviation full-stop is used.

     The pattern of end-punctuation used does not of course affect the punctuation used in the body of the letter, to which the normal rules of punctuation apply. All abbreviations are marked with a full-stop.

                   Yours sincerely,
             for HARCOURT, GROVES & CO. LTD.

                      W. F. Groves
                      Director

Example 4: Semi-indented letter style

Many people still regard this as an attractive letter style. The blocked inside name and address is liked because of its compactness and the added tidiness it gives to the left-hand margin. The placement of the complimentary close and signature data over the centre of the typing line provides a fitting counterpart to the inside name and address.

This style appeals to the more conservative reader, who likes the indented paragraphing which reading of printed matter has made so familiar.

PHOENIX INSURANCE CO., LTD.

Phoenix Buildings   Bulawayo

Manager
J.R.Clements   3rd October 19..   *Telephone:*
                                                                    BULawayo 3546

RLS/ALH

Miss M Llewelyn
18 Deneway Avenue
BATH Somerset
BA2 3ER

Dear Miss Llewelyn

                    The Hanging-paragraph Letter Style

This letter style is a most unusual one. It makes use of the hanging
    paragraph described in Chapter 4. The effect is to throw the first
    few words of each paragraph into prominence. It is therefore used
    for letters that deal with a variety of topics.

The first word of each paragraph begins at the left-hand margin, the
    remaining lines being indented, usually three to five spaces. The
    date is given its normal position on the right, though it is centred
    in this example to fill the open space provided for it in the
    letter head.

As this style is a reversal of the indented styles, the indented form of
    inside address would not be appropriate; the blocked form is there-
    fore used. Complimentary close and signature data are centred.

The placing of the date within the letter-head allows more room for the
    letter itself, and because of this the margins have been widened
    to 3½cm.

                        Yours sincerely

                        R. L. Stevens

                        Mrs R L Stevens
                        Typing Pool Supervisor

Example 5: Hanging paragraph letter style

This style is well adapted to letters that deal with a number of separate
topics. On the other hand, the use of the tabular stop at the commencement of each line except the first in the paragraphs slows down the
typing. Critics of the style also claim that it has a distracting effect, since
it tends to focus attention on the form rather than the substance of the
letter. In this example open punctuation has been used.

Tel. 01-405 3546

BLOOMSBURY
SECRETARIAL
COLLEGE

ARCADIA HOUSE , BLOOMSBURY SQUARE , LONDON, WC1A 2AL
Principal: J.Harris, M.A., B.Com.

11 April 19..

Advanced Letter Styles Ltd
Standard Buildings
UTOPIA

THE NOMA SIMPLIFIED LETTER STYLE

This style is the one recommended by the National Office Management
Association of America for business letters. In a modified form it has
been adopted in the United Kingdom by the Institute of Office Management
and some business houses.

In most respects it follows the fully-blocked style illustrated in
Example 1. Open punctuation, for example, is used, and all typing lines,
including those for the date and subject heading, begin at the left-hand
margin.

The style has the following special features:

1   The formal salutation and complimentary close are omitted

2   The subject heading is given in capitals at least three spaces below
     the inside address

3   The writer's name and designation are also typed in capitals - both
     on the same line

4   Enumerations like the ones here listed begin at the left-hand margin,
     but if not preceded by a number or letter may be indented five spaces.
     Full-stops are not used

5   The typist's initials are placed in the bottom left-hand corner

Trevor B. Hanson
TREVOR B HANSON - REGISTRAR

ogs

Example 6: Noma simplified letter style

Those who like this style claim that the omission of meaningless salutations and closures is sensible, and that the style is business-like and time-saving.

Those who dislike it condemn it as blunt, impersonal, lacking in feeling, and too far removed from the forms to which we are accustomed and which most readers like.

APPENDIX A

Numerals in Correspondence

Conventionally, numerals in correspondence are represented in the following ways.

Numbers up to one hundred

Use words for all numbers up to and including one hundred, and for all round numbers over one hundred:

> *twenty-six* days from now
> a membership of *one hundred*
> *six thousand* letters

Exceptions

> *Dates*: 10 February 19..
> *Addresses*: 25 Folkestone Road, London E4 6AT
> *Ages*: 18 years old
> *Quantities and measurements*: 500 kilos, 1,000 metres
> *Percentages*: 12 per cent

At the beginning of sentences

Use words for all numbers that begin sentences:

> *One hundred and twenty years* ago

Time of day

Use words before *o'clock* and figures before *a.m* and *p.m.*:

> *six* o'clock but *6.0* a.m.

When expressing time in the 24-hour system always use four figures, with no spaces and no punctuation:

0025	i.e.	0.25 a.m.
1140	i.e.	11.40 a.m.
0716	i.e.	7.16 a.m.
1320	i.e.	1.20 p.m.
2114	i.e.	9.14 p.m.

In this system the abbreviations *a.m.* and *p.m.* are unnecessary and are not used.

Money in correspondence
Sums of money occurring in sentences are typed as follows:

£10 (or £10·00); £64·06; 76dp (or (£0·76d)

(a) Neither the £ sign nor the *p* sign takes a full-stop, except at the end of a sentence.

(b) The *p* sign is not used in amounts expressed in £s:

£84·18 (not £84·18p)

(c) The decimal point may be replaced in typewriting by a full-stop.

(d) There are two ways of expressing amounts below £1 (100p):

29p (or £0·29); 82dp (or £0·82d)

Note carefully that in the decimal form the £ sign is followed by a nought (to prevent confusion with £29 and £82d).

Quotations and estimates .
As a precaution against mis-typings, amounts in figures are often repeated in words with brackets:

£16·00   (Sixteen pounds)
£67·06d   (Sixty-seven pounds 06d)
£0·54d   (Fifty-four-and-a-half pence)

Money in accounts
All amounts are expressed in decimal form:

£0·46 (not 46p); £0·05 (not 5p)

Note that for amounts below 10p the amount in pence is preceded by a nought.

Money in columns
Amounts are typed as follows:

Method 1	Method 2
£	£
110.51½	110.515
0.67	0.67
12.24½	12.245
£123.43	£123.43

(a) Method 1 is used for statements to the public. For internal accounting, Method 2 may be preferred.

(b) The £ symbol is centred over the longest entry, though it is now becoming common commercial practice to place it over the unit pounds position.

(c) The nought in the £ column may be omitted from amounts below £1 (e.g. from 0.67), but must be retained in amounts appearing singly.

(d) Totals are preceded by the £ symbol and underscored as shown above.

Money in cheques

Amounts are expressed in both words and figures.

(a) Where the amount is typed, the decimal point in the figures may be replaced by a full stop (*see Money in correspondence, (c)*, above).

(b) Where the amount is handwritten, the decimal point is replaced by a hyphen to lessen the risk of misreading or fraudulent alteration.

Figures	Words
£20-00	Twenty pounds only
£19-55	Nineteen pounds 55
£0-74	Seventy-four pence

(a) Half-pence are not used on cheques; if included, the banks will ignore them.

(b) The term *guineas* is no longer accepted; the amount should be expressed thus:

Figures	Words
£1·05 (if typed)	
£1·05 (if handwritten)	One pound 05

Measurements and quantities

When figures are used, the appropriate following words are sometimes typed in full, but are more commonly abbreviated, thus (using open punctuation):

5ft 3 in   8lb 3 oz

The Metrication Board treat shortened forms for metric units as symbols and not as abbreviations and accordingly full stops should always be omitted, e.g.

3.5 m   16 cm   13·5 kg (or kilo)

The figures are followed by a space, but it is usual to omit the letter "s" for plurals. The extremely abbreviated form $5'\ 3''$ is seldom used in running text, but is often found in invoices, price-list, etc.

Fractions

When it is necessary to type a fraction not included in the key board, either of the following methods is adopted:

$$3/5 \qquad\qquad 7/16$$

$$\frac{3}{5} \qquad\qquad \frac{7}{16}$$

Decimals

Except in mathematical work, it is unnecessary to raise the full stop for the decimal point, but it is necessary to include the zero sign in the units position to avoid misreading when the amount is less than unity. For example, .73 may easily be misread as 73, but 0.73 is unmistakable.

The pence column must always contain two digits, i.e. £0·07 and not £0·7, which would be misread as £0·70.

The £ symbol should always be shown when the decimal point is used and, if there are no pounds, should be followed by a nought: £0.75 and not £·75, which would easily be read as seventy-five pounds.

Legal documents

Use words for numerals, including those for dates and sums of money, but not for those in addresses:

THIS ASSIGNMENT *is made the ninth day of January one thousand nine hundred and eighty-five* in consideration of the sum of *three thousand and six hundred and seventy-five pounds* between James Brown of 110 Normanshire Drive, Chingford and ...

Ordinal numbers

Use words for ordinal numbers, except in dates:

the *twentieth* century; the *thirty-first* annual general meeting

Use of commas in figures

In all numbers consisting of more than three figures insert

commas before the third and the sixth figure, except in dates, telephone numbers, or in figures denoting page numbers:

3,476,312;   £4,583

but

the 1914–18 war;   01-242-2177;   Page 1152

On the continent the comma is used as the decimal point, and because of this it is recommended that in scientific notation the comma should be omitted and replaced by a space.

Singulars used as plurals
The singular forms of certain nouns signifying number, weight and measure are sometimes used to express the plural:

two *ton* of coal; five *pound* of sugar; six *foot* square

Follow the modern tendency, however, and use the plural forms, except when the numeral and its noun make a compound adjective:

five *tons* of coal, but a five-*ton lorry;*
two *gallons* of petrol, but a two-*gallon* can;
three *years* old, but a three-*year* plan.

APPENDIX B

CEREMONIOUS FORMS OF ADDRESS

Rank or title	Form of address	Salutation, and style of address	Complimentary close
The Queen	The Queen's Most Excellent Majesty OR Her Majesty Queen Elizabeth II	Madam OR May it please your Majesty (Your Majesty)	I have the honour to remain Your Majesty's faithful subject
Royal Prince	His Royal Highness Prince (Christian name) OR if a duke His Royal Highness the Duke of …	Sir (Your Royal Highness)	I have the honour to remain Your Royal Highness's most dutiful subject
Royal Princess	Her Royal Highness the Princess (Christian name) OR if a Duchess Her Royal Highness the Duchess of …	Madam (Your Royal Highness)	I have the honour to remain Your Royal Highness's dutiful and obedient servant
Ambassador (British)	His Excellency (followed by rank), HBM's Ambassador and Plenipotentiary,	Sir, My Lord, etc. (according to rank) (Your Excellency)	I am, etc. (according to rank) Your obedient servant

Rank	On the envelope	Salutation	Complimentary close
Archbishop	His Grace the Lord Archbishop of ...	My Lord Archbishop (Your Grace)	I have the honour to be Your Grace's obedient servant
Archdeacon	The Venerable the Archdeacon of ...	Venerable Sir	I have the honour to be Your obedient servant
Baron	The Rt Hon the Lord .... OR The Lord	My Lord (Your Lordship)	I have the honour to be Your Lordship's obedient servant
Baroness	The Rt Hon Lady	Madam (Your Ladyship) / Sir	I have the honour to be Your Ladyship's obedient servant / I am, Sir Your obedient servant
Baronet	Sir Thomas Marsden Bt	Sir	I am, Sir Your obedient servant
Baronet's Wife	Lady Marsden	Madam	I am, Madam, Your obedient servant
Bishop	The Right Rev the Lord Bishop of ... OR The Lord bishop of ...	My Lord Bishop OR My Lord (Your Lordship)	I have the honour to be, Your Lordship's obedient servant,
Bishop (Suffragan)	The Right Rev. the Bishop Suffragan of ...	Sir OR Right Reverend Sir	I am, Sir, Your obedient servant
Bishop (Roman Catholic)	the Right Rev the Bishop of ...	As above	As above
Cardinal	His Eminence Cardinal ...	My Lord Cardinal OR My Lord (Your Eminence)	I have the honour to be Your Eminence's obedient servant

Rank or title	Form of address	Salutation, and style of address	Complimentary close
Clergy	The Rev . . .(Christian name and surname)	Dear Rev Father, for a Roman Catholic priest; Dear Sir (formerly Reverend Sir), for other denominations	I am, dear Sir, Your obedient servant
Consul (British)	. . . Esq., HBM's Consul-General (or Consul, Vice-Consul, as may be)	Sir	I am, Sir, Your obedient servant
Countess (Wife of Earl	The Rt Hon the Countess of . . .	Madam (Your Ladyship)	I have the honour to be Your Ladyship's obedient servant
Dame (Order of the British Empire)	Dame Irene Whitehead	Dear Madam	No set form
Doctor	Mr H Loveridge DSc OR Dr H Loveridge	No set form	No set form
Dowager (Widows of Peers or Baronets)	The Rt Hon the Dowager Duchess (Countess, etc.) of . . . OR more usual nowadays The Rt Hon Alice, Countess of . . .	As for Duchess, Countess, etc.	As for Duchess, Countess, etc.
Duchess (not Royal)	Her Grace the Duchess of . . .	Madam (Your Grace)	I have the honour to be Your Grace's most obedient servant

Title	Address	Salutation	Closing
Duke (not Royal)	His Grace the Duke of ...	My Lord Duke (Your Grace)	I have the honour to be Your Grace's most obedient servant
Earl	The Rt Hon the Earl of ... OR The Earl of ...	My Lord (Your Lordship)	I have the honour to be Your Lordship's most obedient servant
Judge (High Court)	The Hon Sir Thomas Clay, if not a Knight OR The Hon Mr Justice Clay	Sir	I have the honour to be, Sir, Your obedient servant
Judge (County Court)	His Honour Judge Clay	Sir	I have the honour to be, Sir, Your obedient servant
Knight	Sir James Pitt KCB, etc.	Sir	I am, Sir, Your obedient servant
Knight's Wife	Lady Pitt	Madam (Your Ladyship)	I am, Madam, Your obedient servant
Lord Mayor	(*For London, York, Belfast*) The Rt Hon the Lord Mayor of ... OR The Rt Hon ... Lord Mayor of ... (*For others*) The Right Worshipful the Lord Mayor of ...	My Lord (Your Lordship)	I am, my Lord Mayor, Your obedient servant
Lord Mayor's Wife	The Rt Hon (or *Hon* according to husband's title) the Lady Mayoress of ...	My Lady Mayoress OR Madam (Your Ladyship)	I am, my Lady Mayoress, Your obedient servant

APPENDIX B—*continued*

Rank or title	Form of address	Salutation, and style of address	Complimentary close
Marchioness	The Most Hon the Marchioness of …	Madam (Your Ladyship)	I have the honour to be Your Ladyship's obedient servant
Marquess (or Marquis)	The Most Hon the Marquess of …	My Lord Marquess (Your Lordship)	I have the honour to be My Lord Marquess, Your obedient servant
Mayor	*(For certain cities)* The Right Worshipful the Mayor of … *(For others, and towns)* The Worshipful the Mayor of …	Sir (or Madam)	I am, Sir (or Madam), Your obedient servant
Mayor's Wife	The Mayoress of …	Madam	I am, Madam Your obedient servant
Member of Parliament	According to title, with the addition of *MP*	Sir	I am, Sir, Your obedient servant
Privy Councillor	The Rt Hon … (Christian name and surname)	According to rank	According to rank
Secretary of State	HM Principal Secretary of State for the … Department	Sir	I am, Sir, Your obedient servant
Viscount	The Rt Hon the Viscount …	My Lord (Your Lordship)	I have the honour to be Your Lordship's obedient servant
Viscountess	The Rt Hon the Viscountess …	Madam (Your Ladyship)	I have the honour to be Your Ladyship's obedient servant

Glossary of Business Terms

(For terms printed in capitals see separate items)

ACCEPTANCE. The assent given by a person to the terms of a bill of exchange drawn on him when he signs his name across the face of the bill. Usually it takes the form of the word *Accepted*, followed by the drawee's signature, the date and place of payment, though mere signature is alone sufficient. The acceptance may be qualified in a number of ways.

ACCEPTING HOUSES. Wealthy merchant bankers such as Rothschilds whose primary business is to help in financing international trade by accepting bills drawn on them by trustworthy clients. They also raise loans especially for foreign governments and thus perform the functions of ISSUING HOUSES as well. The post-war decline in both accepting and issuing business has led them to develop new types of business, and they now deal extensively in foreign exchange.

ACCOMMODATION BILL. A bill drawn by one person and accepted or endorsed by another without CONSIDERATION, merely to enable the drawer or some other person to raise money on the bill by discounting it. Such bills are sometimes called *fictitious bills, kites,* and *windmills.*

ACCOMMODATION PARTY. The drawer, acceptor or endorser of an ACCOMMODATION BILL.

ACCOUNT CURRENT. A statement made out in debit and credit form summarizing business transactions between two parties over a given period. Interest is generally charged on each item debited and allowed on each item credited, from the date of the item to the date on which the account is made up. It is used by merchants who have extensive dealings with overseas traders.

ACCOUNT DAYS. The days on which bargains entered into by

members of the STOCK EXCHANGE are settled. There are usually two such days each month. Sometimes called *settlement days*.

ACCOUNT SALES. An account of goods sold rendered by an agent to the owner or consigner. The credit side shows the gross proceeds of the sale and the debit side the charges paid for freight, dock charges, etc., the agent's commission, and the balance due to the consignor. It is usually accompanied by a CHEQUE or DRAFT in settlement.

ACT OF GOD. A term used in insurance policies and other documents to denote risks and dangers that are beyond human control, i.e. which could not be foreseen, or if foreseen could not be guarded against, e.g. a thunderbolt.

ACTUARY. One who makes the calculations that regulate the premiums payable for various classes of insurance.

AD REFERENDUM CONTRACT. A contract for the sale of goods, containing a proviso that certain minor points are left *for further consideration*.

AD VALOREM DUTY. *See* DUTIES.

ADJUDICATION ORDER. An official declaration by the court that a debtor is bankrupt. It vests his property in a TRUSTEE for distribution to the creditors.

ADMINISTRATION ORDER. An order by the court for the administration of the estate of a deceased debtor, made upon the petition of a creditor. It vests the debtor's property in the OFFICIAL RECEIVER, as trustee, for realization and distribution to the creditors.

ADMINISTRATOR. *See* EXECUTOR.

ADVANCE NOTE. A draft, payable as a rule three days after a ship has sailed, issued when a seaman signs on for a voyage. It enables him to make provision for his dependants while he is absent.

ADVICE NOTE. A document informing a customer that his goods are on the way. It usually gives the date of despatch and the method of transport, and gives details of the goods, but not their price. An INVOICE sent in advance of the goods serves the same purpose.

AFFIDAVIT. A statement made in writing and on oath, and sworn before a judge or other authorized person, usually a COMMISSIONER FOR OATHS, for use as evidence in court.

AFFREIGHTMENT. The freight of a ship. The contract of affreightment may be either a CHARTER PARTY or a BILL OF LADING.

AGENDA. A programme of the items of business to be transacted at a meeting.

AGENT. A person authorized expressly or impliedly to transact business for another, called the PRINCIPAL. His reward usually takes the form of a COMMISSION. The agent may be either *general*, with general authority in all matters of a particular trade or business (e.g. a company secretary), or *special*, employed to act only in a particular transaction (e.g. an estate agent employed to sell a house), or *universal* (rare in business). Agents with power to make contracts by deed must themselves be appointed by deed, i.e. by POWER OF ATTORNEY.

AGIO. The difference between the real and the nominal value or MONEY, e.g. the amount by which a currency deviates from the fixed par of exchange; also the charge made for exchanging one kind of money for another.

ALLONGE. A slip of paper pasted on the back of a BILL OF EXCHANGE to accommodate endorsements for which there is no room on the bill itself. The first ENDORSEMENT should appear partly on the allonge and partly on the bill.

ALLOTMENT. The number of SHARES granted to a person who has applied for shares in a public company and paid the required deposit per share. The applicant is notified by *letter of allotment*.

AMALGAMATION. The amalgamation of companies is primarily designed to effect economies by eliminating duplication of effort arising from competition. It may be effected in a variety of ways: *(a)* by one company acquiring a controlling interest in another; *(b)* by one company purchasing the entire assets of another; *(c)* by the formation of a new company to take over two or more others; *(d)* by the formation of a HOLDING COMPANY.

AMORTIZATION. The extinction of a LIABILITY over a period, especially by means of a SINKING FUND. Loosely, the DEPRECIATION of such wasting assets as LEASES and ROYALTIES.

ANNUAL RETURN. A statutory return submitted to the Registrar of Companies within forty-two days of the annual general meeting of a registered company. The returns, submitted by both public and private companies, must be accompanied by a certified copy of the BALANCE SHEET and auditor's report.

ANNUITY. A stated yearly sum payable for the whole or a portion of a person's life. The annuity may arise from the investment of a capital sum, or under the terms of a will, etc.

ANTE-DATE. To affix to a document a date earlier than that of its signature or execution.

ARBITRAGE. Dealings in securities which aim at profiting from the different prices prevailing in different financial centres at a given moment.

ARBITRATED EXCHANGE. A RATE OF EXCHANGE resulting from the intermediate purchase and sale of a third currency, e.g. the purchase of French francs by first purchasing Dutch guilders, which in turn purchase the francs, gives an arbitrated rate between sterling and francs.

ARBITRATION. The method by which matters in dispute between two parties are submitted to a third independent party, by whose decision the contending parties agree to be bound. The third party is termed an *arbitrator*.

ARTICLES OF ASSOCIATION. The regulations governing the constitution and internal management of a registered company and the relations of its members to one another. The almost invariable practice is for companies to adopt, with modifications to suit their special circumstances, the model Articles known as Table "A" as amended by the Companies Act 1985.

ARTICLES OF PARTNERSHIP. *See* PARTNERSHIP.

ASSETS. The entire property of all kinds possessed by or owing to a person or organization.

   (*a*) *Current or circulating assets*. Assets, such as stock and book debts, whose value is constantly changing as trade proceeds.

   (*b*) *Fixed assets*. Assets, such as land and machinery, acquired for use and not for resale.

   (*c*) *Fictitious assets*. Assets, such as PRELIMINARY EXPENSES, of no real value, but included in the BALANCE SHEET for technical or legal reasons.

   (*d*) *Intangible assets*. Assets, such as GOODWILL, that cannot normally be sold on the market.

   (*e*) *Liquid assets*. Assets that can readily be turned into cash.

   (*f*) *Wasting assets*. Those fixed assets which gradually depreciate, e.g. LEASES, machinery.

ASSIGNMENT. A transfer of title or of an interest in any property. Assignment may be automatic by operation of the law (e.g. upon death or BANKRUPTCY), or by arrangement between the parties themselves. An assignment of the latter kind may take the form of a MORTGAGE (in the case of real property), a BILL OF SALE (in the case of goods), or an assignment of rights and duties under a contract.

ASSURANCE. The form of insurance that relates to events which must necessarily happen sooner or later, e.g. death; hence the term *life assurance*. The term INSURANCE, on the other hand, is identified with contingencies, e.g. fire insurance.

ATTORNEY. A person legally authorized to act as agent for another, especially a solicitor.

AUCTIONS. Public sales in which the bidder offers an increase on the price offered by another, the article going to the highest bidder. A sale is completed by the fall of the hammer; until then, any bidder may retract his bid.

The auctioneer is a person authorized by LICENCE to sell goods on COMMISSION at a public auction. He must obtain the best price possible, and has a LIEN for his charges on the goods he sells.

AUDIT, INTERNAL. An examination of the accounts of an organization carried out by members of its own staff. Many large concerns have internal audit departments, whose members visit branches to audit the accounts kept there.

AUDITOR. A person appointed to examine accounts and to report on them. Every registered company is required to appoint an auditor, who must be a member of a professional body recognized by the Department of Trade and Industry, and be appointed at each annual general meeting.

AVERAGE. A term denoting the apportionment of loss or damage to a ship or cargo.

(a) General average. Where a *deliberate sacrifice* is made (e.g. the flooding of a hold to extinguish a fire, or the JETTISON of cargo to lighten the ship in a storm) for the benefit of all persons interested in the voyage, the loss is borne by them in proportion to their financial interest in the venture. The adjustment of their respective contributions is the work of a special class of persons called *average adjusters*.

(b) Particular average. Where the loss or damage is *accidental* it must be borne wholly by the particular party interested, e.g. damage to goods by sea-water, or the loss of an anchor.

AVERAGE BOND. A signed undertaking by a contributor to pay his share of a general AVERAGE loss as soon as the amount is known.

BACKWARDATION. A premium payable by a "BEAR" operator on the STOCK EXCHANGE when he wishes to defer delivery of shares he has sold.

BAILIFF. *See* SHERIFF.

BAILMENT. The delivery of goods by one person (*the bailor*) to another (*the bailee*) either to be handed over to a third person, or to be returned to the bailor in a certain event (e.g. a borrowed lawn-mower when finished with).

BALANCE OF PAYMENTS. The BALANCE OF TRADE includes only tangible commodities or "visible" items, whereas a country's Balance of Payments includes also "invisible" items such as payments for shipping and financial services, income from investments and property held abroad, tourism, and government income and expenditure, including loans.

ֵALANCE OF TRADE. The difference between a country's recorded imports and exports of goods. The Balance of Trade is said to be favourable when exports exceed imports, and unfavourable when imports exceed exports.

BALANCE SHEET. A statement prepared at the end of each trading period to show the financial position of an undertaking at a particular date. It is customary, though not obligatory, to set out the ASSETS on the right-hand side and the LIABILITIES on the left-hand side.

Registered companies must prepare a balance sheet once a year, and JOINT-STOCK BANKS every six months. To ensure the disclosure of adequate information, the 8th Schedule of the Companies Act 1985 imposes on the directors an obligation to present certain items of information under prescribed headings. A copy of the auditor's report must be attached to all balance sheets issued to SHAREHOLDERS.

BALLAST. Heavy material put into the hold to steady a ship that sails with less than a full cargo.

BANK LOAN. *See* OVERDRAFT.

BANKNOTE. A currency note issued by a bank. Only the Bank of England is now allowed to issue notes in England and Wales, the right of other banks to do so having gradually lapsed under the Bank Charter Act 1844. By an Act of 1954 the Bank may issue notes for *any* denomination approved by the Treasury, but at present does so for only £50, £20, £10, £5 and £1. (£1 notes will cease to be issued after 1985 and will be replaced by the £1 coin.) In 1931 Bank of England notes ceased to be redeemable in gold, and the *Promise to pay the Bearer on Demand*, which appears on the face oof every note, is virtually meaningless, since payment would no longer be made in gold, but only in notes of the same kind. Several banks in Scotland and Northern Ireland have their own note issues, but these are not LEGAL TENDER.

BANK OF ENGLAND. Founded in 1694 by royal charter granted by William III in exchange for a loan of £1,200,000 to enable him to prosecute the war with France.

The Bank was reorganized in 1844 under the Bank Charter Act which established two separate departments—the Issue Department and the Banking Department, the former to be responsible for providing and issuing notes and the latter for conducting ordinary banking business for the Government and the public. Every Thursday it publishes a *Weekly Return* showing the ASSETS and LIABILITIES of the two departments. In 1946 the Bank was nationalized and became a State bank, but continued to be administered by the Governor and Court of Governors. It now has branches only in Birmingham, Bristol, Leeds, Liverpool, Manchester, Newcastle, Southampton, and at the Law Courts in London.

BANK RECONCILIATION STATEMENT. A statement prepared by a customer to check his BANK STATEMENT with his cash book, the balances of which often differ by reason of the inclusion in the BANK STATEMENT of bank charges and of the omission from it of CHEQUES drawn by the customer and not presented to the bank for payment.

BANK STATEMENT. A statement in loose-leaf form that has now replaced the bank pass book. It is recorded mechanically to show, in columnar form, all transactions affectiung a customer's CURRENT ACCOUNT, with dates, cheque serial numbers instead of names, amounts paid in and withdrawn, and the balance on the account.

BANKERS' CLEARING HOUSE. *See* CLEARING HOUSE.

BANKER'S DRAFT. A document that may be bought by a customer from the bank ordering one of its branches or agents to pay on demand a certain sum of money to a specified person.

BANKER'S ORDER. *See* STANDING ORDER.

BANKRUPTCY. A person who has not enough funds to meet his LIABILITIES is said to be *insolvent,* but before he can be made bankrupt by the proceedings of the court he must commit some act which shows that in all probability he cannot pay his debts. The effect of bankruptcy is to vest the debtor's property in a TRUSTEE, to be divided *pro rata* among his creditors.

BARRATRY. Any unlawful act wilfully committed by a ship's master or crew to the prejudice of the owner or charterer. Examples are smuggling, mutiny and attempts to scuttle the ship.

BARTER. The direct exchange of goods for goods, that is without the use of MONEY.

BEAR. A dealer on the STOCK EXCHANGE who sells for future

delivery securities he does not possess, hoping that their prices will fall and so enable him to acquire the securities at a reduced price in time for delivery.

BEARER SECURITIES. Securities that can be transferred by mere delivery (e.g. bearer bonds, bearer stock, TREASURY BILLS). They are not registered by the issuing body and do not require completion of a transfer form.

BEDAUX SYSTEM. A scheme for encouraging higher output by the grant of a bonus on wages.

BILL OF EXCHANGE. A document now used less extensively than formerly in settlement of international indebtedness, and one that has now virtually disappeared from the home trade. It is an order requiring the person to whom it is addressed to pay on demand or at some future date a stated sum of money to, or to the order of, a specified person, or to bearer. It requires ACCEPTANCE by the drawee.

BILL OF HEALTH. A certificate granted by a CONSUL or other authority to the master of a ship sailing from a port suspected of infectious disease, stating the conditions in the port at the time.

BILL OF LADING. A document in the form of an acknowledgment given by a shipowner or shipping agent as a receipt for goods taken on board ship, and setting out the terms on which the goods are to be carried.

BILL OF SALE. A document transferring the ownership of goods from one person to another, possession of the goods remaining with the former. A *conditional bill of sale* mortgages the goods as security for a loan. An *absolute bill of sale* is one given otherwise than by way of mortgage. Both classes must be registered.

BILL OF SIGHT. A customs document that allows an importer who has insufficient knowledge of the goods to inspect them before he can complete the necessary customs entry.

BINARY NOTATION. A number system having only two digits, 0 and 1. Any number can be expressed using combinations of these digits. The system is used in computers, as the digits 0 and 1 can be represented by an electrical system in the "off" and "on" states.

BLUE CHIPS. Ordinary shares which, though not GILT-EDGED, are of the highest standing in well-established and flourishing companies, considered to be so safe that there is little risk of losing either CAPITAL or income.

BOND. A written undertaking, given under seal, to do or to refrain from doing the things specified. Bonds are frequently issued by governments, nationalized corporations and companies as security for loans. They carry a fixed rate of interest. *See* DEBENTURE.

BOND NOTE. A note given by the Customs authorities in exchange for a BOND executed by an exporter of BONDED GOODS. On the back is the WAREHOUSEKEEPER'S ORDER authorizing release of the goods.

BONDED GOODS. Goods liable to CUSTOMS DUTY or EXCISE DUTY and stored in a BONDED WAREHOUSE pending either export or payment of duty.

BONDED STORES. Dutiable goods removed free of duty from a bonded warehouse for consumption on board ship.

BONDED WAREHOUSE. *See* WAREHOUSE.

BONUS SHARES. *See* SHARE.

BOTTOMRY BOND. A MORTGAGE of a ship as security for a loan required for immediate repairs. Repayment of the loan is enforceable only if the ship reaches port safely. Modern telegraphic facilities have now virtually abolished such transactions.

BOUGHT NOTE. A formal document, giving particulars of the transaction, sent by a BROKER to the buyer. The corresponding document he sends to the seller is called a SOLD NOTE.

BRASSAGE. *See* SEIGNIORAGE.

BROKER. An agent who buys and sells for a PRINCIPAL on commission. He does not have possession of the goods, shares, or policies in which he deals. His commission is sometimes called *brokerage*.

BUCKET SHOP. The office of a stockbroker who is not a member of the STOCK EXCHANGE, and who deals in highly speculative securities.

BUDGET. A plan of expenditure based on estimated income; especially the financial statement of national revenue and expenditure annually presented to Parliament by the Chancellor of the Exchequer. It consists of a statement of actual revenue and expenditure for the past year, an estimate of that for the year to come, and a statement of proposed changes in taxation.

BULL. A dealer on the STOCK EXCHANGE who buys securities with no intention of taking them up, hoping to sell them at a higher price before pay day.

BULLION. Gold or silver in mass or in bars, as distinct from coined metal.

BUREAU DE CHANGE. A bank or other place where foreign currency can be exchanged or dealt in.

CALL. A demand for payment of an instalment due on a share in a public company.

CALLED-UP CAPITAL. *See* CAPITAL.

CAMBIST. A dealer or speculator in foreign currencies or BILLS OF EXCHANGE.

CAPITAL. The term has many different uses. To the ordinary person it means money invested; to the businessman, the excess of assets over liabilities, or his available resources for carrying on the business; to the economist, capital goods such as buildings and machinery; while the capital of a company is qualified to mean different things, as follows:

(*a*) *Authorized (nominal, or registered) capital.* The maximum amount a company is empowered by its MEMORANDUM to raise.

(*b*) *Issued (or subscribed) capital.* The amount offered for subscription, and allotted to SHAREHOLDERS.

(*c*) *Called-up capital.* That portion of the *issued capital* for which payment has actually been demanded from the SHAREHOLDERS.

(*d*) *Paid-up capital.* That portion of the *called-up capital* actually received from the shareholders.

(*e*) *Loan capital.* Capital borrowed, e.g. by the issue of DEBENTURES.

(*f*) *Fixed capital.* Capital invested in fixed ASSETS, or the fixed assets themselves.

(*g*) *Circulating (or floating) capital.* Capital in the form of circulating ASSETS.

(*h*) *Liquid capital.* Capital in a form available immediately or at short notice for the payment of debts, e.g. cash in hand and in bank, and assets that are readily saleable, e.g. BILLS OF EXCHANGE available for discounting.

(*i*) *Working capital.* (i) *of a new enterprise*, the amount of invested capital remaining after the fixed ASSETS have been bought; (ii) *of a going concern*, the excess of current assets over current LIABILITIES.

(*j*) *Watered capital.* Capital for which no assets exist, as where an excessive price is paid for GOODWILL. Another example is the issue of bonus shares the effect of which is to reduce the average rate of DIVIDEND.

(*k*) *High-geared capital.* Capital in which the proportion of preference (or fixed-interest) SHARES to ordinary shares is high. Capital is *low-geared* when the reverse situation prevails.

CAPITAL EXPENDITURE. Expenditure devoted to the acquisition or improvement of fixed assets, and not chargeable against profits.

CAPITAL GAINS TAX. A comprehensive tax levied on gains from the disposal of ASSETS of whatever kind, including movable property, securities and land, but not on owner-occupied residences, British Government SECURITIES held for more than a year, life assurance POLICIES, privately-owned motor cars and household goods worth less than £3,000.

CAPITAL RESERVE. A reserve resulting from a capital profit, e.g. from writing up the value of fixed assets.

CAPITAL TRANSFER TAX. This tax applies broadly to all transfers of personal wealth exceeding in aggregate a figure that varies with each Finance Act (£64,000 in 1985). Exemptions include transfers between husband and wife and the first £3,000 of gifts made in any one year, and all gifts of up to £100 per recipient and some wedding gifts.

CARAT. A twenty-fourth part of a unit of pure gold. Eighteen carats, for example, means that the gold of which the article is made consists of eighteen parts pure gold and six parts alloy.

CARRYING OVER. A STOCK EXCHANGE term signifying that settlement of a transaction is deferred to the next settling day. Payments in the form of CONTANGO or BACKWARDATION are made for the accommodation.

CARTEL. A voluntary association of firms that concentrate on production, leaving the marketing function to a central organization on which they are represented.

CASE LAW. That part of established law, sometimes called judge-made law, which is to be gathered from decisions made in the Higher Courts in what are known as "leading cases", i.e. cases which lay down legal principles that must be followed in similar subsequent cases. Examples are to be found in both COMMON LAW and EQUITY.

CASE OF NEED. A person known as the REFEREE IN CASE OF NEED to whom the holder of a BILL OF EXCHANGE may resort should the bill be dishonoured by non-acceptance or non-payment, his name and address being placed upon the bill.

CASH DISCOUNT. *See* DISCOUNT.

CATALOGUE. A list containing a description of goods, their purpose, and their prices, published to help customers who wish to place orders. As catalogues issued by wholesalers are often expensively produced, variations in the prices charged to retailers are made by adjustments in the percentage of trade discount allowed.

CAVEAT EMPTOR. *Let the buyer beware*, the doctrine that a buyer must bear any loss resulting from any failure to satisfy himself as to the nature and quality of the goods he buys.

CERTIFICATE OF INCORPORATION. A document issued by the Registrar of Companies, from the date of which a company comes into legal existence.

CERTIFICATE OF ORIGIN. A document signed by an exporter declaring the place of origin of the goods, and used to secure preferential customs DUTIES in the importing country. These documents are also issued by certain CHAMBERS OF COMMERCE.

CERTIFICATE OF REGISTRATION. A certificate issued upon the registration of a ship, stating her name, tonnage and other particulars.

CHAIN STORE. *See* MULTIPLE STORE.

CHAMBER OF COMMERCE. A voluntary association of businessmen formed for the protection and furtherance of their trading interests. Almost every town has its chamber of commerce, many of them with strong industrial sections. The chambers of commerce act as clearing houses of information for their members, discuss matters of interest to them, and arbitrate in mercantile disputes. Those established in the ports also issue CERTIFICATES OF ORIGIN and keep members informed concerning import, export and shipping matters. The *London Chamber of Commerce and Industry* is by far the largest and has performed a valuable national service in organizing schemes of commercial education and holding examinations. The *Association of British Chambers of Commerce* works in close co-operation with government departments concerned with overseas trade.

CHAMPERTY. Maintenance of a person in a legal action in return for a share in any proceeds that might result. Such an arrangement is illegal at COMMON LAW.

CHARTER PARTY. A contract for the hire of a ship, or part of a ship, made between owner and charterer. The charterer may use the ship either for carrying his own goods only, or for completing his cargo by accepting the goods of others.

(a) *Time charter*. One by which the ship is placed at the charterer's disposal for a specified period of time.

(b) *Voyage charter*. One by which the ship is engaged to sail on a specified voyage or series of voyages. The time taken for loading and unloading can appreciably affect the time the ship is with the charterer. To control this a certain number of LAY DAYS are specified in the charter.

CHATTELS PERSONAL AND REAL. *See* PERSONALTY.

CHEQUE. A bill of exchange drawn on a banker and payable on demand.

(a) *Blank cheque*. One in which particulars as to amount, payee, etc. are not inserted.

(b) *Crossed cheque*. One with two transverse parallel lines (*general crossing*), or the name of a bank (*special crossing*) written across the face. Such cheques must be paid into a bank account, the former at any bank; the latter at the bank named.

(c) *Open cheque*. One not crossed, and payable at the bank's counter.

(d) *Order cheque*. One payable to a named person *or Order*. Such cheques require ENDORSEMENT, except when paid into payee's account.

(e) *Bearer cheque*. One payable to bearer. No endorsement is required.

CHOSES IN ACTION, AND POSSESSION. *See* PERSONALTY.

CIRCULAR NOTE. Serves much the same purpose as a circular LETTER OF CREDIT. It is an instruction from a bank to its correspondent abroad to pay the person named the equivalent of the sterling amount mentioned. Circular notes were formerly issued by the banks in return for money deposited with them, but as more convenient methods of payment are now available, they have fallen into disuse.

CIRCULATING ASSETS. *See* ASSETS.

CIRCULATING CAPITAL. *See* CAPITAL.

CIVIL WRONG. *See* OFFENCES.

CLEARING HOUSE. Situated in the City of London, the Bankers' Clearing House is the centre through which the member banks and the Bank of England exchange and settle CHEQUES drawn on one another. At the Clearing House each bank receives from the other banks cheques drawn on itself and its branches, and in exchange delivers cheques drawn on the other banks and paid into its branches by customers. The cheques it receives from other banks are termed its *in-clearings*, while those given out are its *out-clearings*. Differences between the totals of a bank's in-clearings and out-clearings are settled by means of balance or transfer tickets to and from their accounts at the Bank of England.

Two clearings operate daily:

(a) *Town Clearing*—dealing with cheques drawn on, and paid into, branches of the clearing banks and the Bank of

England in the Town Area, which is roughly that of the City of London.

(b) General Clearing—dealing with all other cheques, drawn on branches of the clearing banks and the Bank of England, that may not be passed through the Town Clearing.

A *Credit Clearing* is also operated on similar lines. It serves the whole credit transfer or Bank Giro system, including standing orders.

Cheques drawn on a branch and paid in at other branches of the same bank do not pass through the Clearing House, but are cleared internally, usually through a central clearing department at the bank's head office.

CODICIL. A supplementary clause attached or referring to a will, adding to, altering, or cancelling some of its provisions.

COLLATERAL SECURITY. Security additional to that already given. The name is usually applied to documents representing a right to the ownership of property of any kind.

COMMERCE. The wide and complex field of economic activity concerned with the buying and selling of goods and their movement from producer to consumer. It includes *trade*, i.e. the activities directly concerned with transferring the ownership of goods, and a number of specialized activities *auxiliary to trade*, as shown in the following diagram:

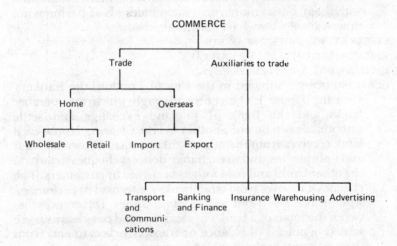

COMMERCIAL TRAVELLER. A person appointed to represent his firm by visiting likely customers. He is frequently paid a basic salary and, in addition, a COMMISSION on the orders he takes.

COMMISSION. The reward paid to an agent for his services, consisting usually of a percentage of the value of the transactions carried out for his principal.

COMMISSION AGENT. One employed to buy or sell goods for his principal. He does not establish privity of contract between principal and third party, but buys and sells in his own name, receiving a commission for his services. Such agents are common in overseas trade. When he guarantees payment for the goods supplied he is known as a DEL CREDERE AGENT.

COMMISSIONER FOR OATHS. A solicitor of not less than six years' standing appointed by the Lord Chancellor and authorized to take and authenticate STATUTORY DECLARATIONS and other AFFIDAVITS.

COMMON CARRIER. A carrier who exercises the business of carrying as a public employment, and undertakes to carry goods for anyone who cares to engage him. With certain exceptions, e.g. ACTS OF GOD, he is liable to compensate the owner for loss of or damage to the goods he carries.

COMMON LAW. The ancient customary law of the land, consisting of customs and usages handed down orally from generation to generation, and subsequently recognized and administered by the courts of law. It includes what is known as CASE LAW.

COMPANY. A body of persons incorporated as an association for trade or business. Companies are formed: *(a)* by charter; *(b)* by Act of Parliament; *(c)* by registration under the Companies Acts. *Registered companies* are either public or private. A *public company* (minimum capital £50,000) may offer its shares to the public. It may have as many members as there are shares, with a *minimum of two*. A *private company* restricts the transfer of its shares, and prohibits any invitation to the public to subscribe to its capital. Both public and private companies are usually formed with LIMITED LIABILITY.

COMPOSITION. A payment, as by an insolvent or bankrupt person, of so much in the £ in settlement of the full amount owing.

CONDITION. An obligation that forms a vital element in a contract, and breach of which entitles the injured party to rescind the contract.

CONFIRMING HOUSE. A concern that places and confirms orders with suppliers on behalf of overseas buyers and, as a rule, takes charge of the appropriate details, such as export documentation and shipping arrangements. It undertakes that its buyers will not default on their contracts, and in placing orders normally acts as principal, thereby becoming primarily liable for payment.

CONSIDERATION. Something given by each party to a contract in return for the promise of the other. It must support every contract not under seal, and all contracts in restraint of trade (even if under seal).

CONSIGNMENT. A transfer of goods to an agent for sale at the best price possible. The agent receives a PRO FORMA INVOICE to enable him to fix a suitable selling price, and notifies the proceeds of the sale to the consignor in an ACCOUNT SALES.

CONSIGNMENT NOTE. A document completed by the consignor of goods sent by rail, or other form of transport. It contains particulars of the quantity, weight, nature and destination of the goods, includes printed details of the terms on which they are carried, and is the contract between the carrier and the consignor.

CONSOLS. A term first used in 1751 to refer to the *consolidated annuities* which form part of the NATIONAL DEBT, and since applied to other Government borrowings. Consols carry interest at $2\frac{1}{2}$% and 4%. They have no redemption date and are transferred by entry in the register kept by the BANK OF ENGLAND. *See* INSCRIBED STOCKS.

CONSUL. A person appointed by a government to reside in some foreign country to watch over the commercial interests of the state he represents and to assist those of its subjects who are in his district.

CONSULAR INVOICE. A detailed invoice authenticated by the consul of the country to which the goods are being exported. Its purpose is to give the customs authorities of the importing country reliable information on which they can assess duty without examining the contents of cases in detail.

CONTANGO. Payment made to a JOBBER by a "BULL" operator on the STOCK EXCHANGE for being allowed to carry over his transaction to the next Settlement.

CONTINGENT LIABILITY. A liability to pay a sum of money only upon the occurrence of a specified event that may or may not occur, e.g. subsequent dishonour of a discounted BILL OF EXCHANGE, or a guarantor's secondary liability for a debtor's default.

CONTRACT. An agreement made with the intention to create a legal obligation enforceable at law. Ordinary domestic and social arrangements do not contemplate such obligations and, while they are agreements, they are not contracts and cannot be enforced at law.

All contracts not under seal must be based on CONSIDERATION. *See* OFFENCES, *(c) Contractual.*

CONTRACT NOTE. A document issued by a BROKER giving details of a transaction, e.g. the purchase or sale of shares on the STOCK EXCHANGE, or of goods on the commodity exchanges.

CO-OPERATIVE SOCIETY. A type of trading association originating in Rochdale in 1844. The share capital is provided by the customers, the maximum holding being restricted by legislation to £5,000. Members receive a fixed rate of interest on their share capital and, in addition, share in the profits on the basis of their purchases. Almost every large town has its own retail co-operative society, with localized branches. According to the 1971 Census of Distribution the societies accounted for 7% of the country's retail trade. The retail societies contribute to the capital of the CWS (Co-operative Wholesale Society), which engages in manufacture as well as in selling. Like their own customers, the retail societies receive a dividend on their purchases from the Wholesale Society.

CO-PARTNERSHIP. An arrangement whereby labour is given not only a share of the profits of a concern but also a share in its control, the degree of which varies considerably between different concerns.

COPYRIGHT. The sole right to produce or reproduce literary, dramatic, musical, or artistic work, or to perform or display it in public. The right continues for fifty years after the calendar year in which the author dies.

CORONER. An officer of the Crown, being a barrister, solicitor or legally qualified medical practitioner. He is appointed by the district council or county council to hold inquests in cases of violent, unnatural and sudden death, and in cases of treasure trove. Since 1927 he may sit without a jury, except in certain cases.

CORPORATION TAX. A straight levy on the profits and other income of both incorporated and unincorporated associations, but not PARTNERSHIPS, whose members are taxed individually. It was introduced in 1965 and is fixed each year in the Finance Act.

COST ACCOUNTING. The branch of accountancy concerned with establishing procedures for the systematic recording, analysis and presentation of information relating to production costs.

COST, INSURANCE AND FREIGHT. A price quoted *c.i.f.* includes, in addition to the cost of the goods, the cost of the freight and insurance to the port or place of destination.

COST OF LIVING. *See* INDEX NUMBERS.

COUPON. An interest certificate. BONDS issued for a term of years bear a number of these certificates, which are detached as they fall due and paid into the bank for collection. *See* TALON.

COVERING NOTE. A note issued by an insurance company to cover the insured until a formal policy is prepared and issued to him.

CREDIT. A word meaning "belief" or "trust". To give credit is to deliver goods or perform work under an arrangement for payment to be made at a later date, which may or may not be specified. If no date is specified, payment must be within a reasonable time.

CREDIT NOTE. A document sent by a seller to a buyer to rectify an over-charge in the original invoice, or to acknowledge and allow credit for goods, cases, etc., returned by the buyer. It is usual to print credit notes in red.

CREDIT SALE. *See* HIRE PURCHASE.

CREDIT TRANSFER. (Bank Giro) A slip used for the transfer of money from the bank account of the payer to that of the payee. A slip is completed for each separate transfer and entered on a list, which the payer passes, together with the slips and a cheque to cover the total amount, to his banker, who then distributes the slips to the banks of the payees.

CRIME. *See* OFFENCES.

CROSSED CHEQUE. *See* CHEQUE.

CUM DIVIDEND. (Literally, *"with dividend"*.) When securities are sold *cum div.* the buyer is entitled to dividends declared but not yet paid, or about to be declared.

CURRENCY. That which circulates in a country as money. *See* MONEY.

CURRENT ACCOUNT. A bank account from which withdrawals may be made by cheque at any time without notice. The bank does not usually pay interest on such accounts, but, if the balance is small, makes a charge for its services.

CURRENT ASSETS. *See* ASSETS.

CURRENT LIABILITIES. *See* LIABILITIES.

CUSTOMS DUTIES. *See* DUTIES.

CUSTOMS WARRANT. A document issued by the Customs authorities consisting of a receipt for duty paid on BONDED GOODS and containing a WAREHOUSEKEEPER'S ORDER authorizing their release from WAREHOUSE.

DAISY WHEEL. A printing device, used especially in the printing machines attached to computers and word processors, consisting of printing characters fixed at the end of spokes on a wheel, which rotates until the right character is in position for striking the paper.

DAMAGES. Monetary compensation awarded by the court in a civil action for wrong suffered by the plaintiff, e.g. for a breach of contract.

DATAPOST. A highly reliable door-to-door overnight delivery service operated by the Post Office, which collects from customers and delivers next day. An international Datapost service is also in operation.

DEBENTURE. There are two types of debenture.

(a) *Customs.* A customs certificate entitling an importer to repayment of duty, called DRAWBACK, in respect of goods re-exported.

(b) *Loan.* A fixed interest-bearing BOND issued as an acknowledgment of and security for a debt.

Debentures are usually issued by JOINT STOCK COMPANIES for the purpose of raising loan capital. If the loan is secured by a charge upon the company's property the bond is termed a *mortgage debenture*. Debentures may be *redeemable*, i.e. repayable at or after a certain date, or *irredeemable*, i.e. not repayable except on default of interest or on liquidation of the company.

DEBIT NOTE. A document similar to an invoice. It is sent by a seller to a buyer to rectify an undercharge in the original invoice, and sometimes to the seller by a buyer who has returned goods or been overcharged, though it is more usual for him to write a letter requesting a credit note.

DEED. A written instrument signed, sealed, and delivered. The right to sue on a contract made by deed is extinguished after twelve years.

DEED OF ARRANGEMENT. Any instrument, whether under seal or not, whereby an insolvent debtor, without being bankrupt, arranges: (a) to assign his property to a trustee for the benefit of the creditors, OR (b) to compound with his creditors for payment of a proportion only of their claims.

DEFERRED SHARES. *See* SHARE.

DEL CREDERE AGENT. An agent who, in return for an extra commission, guarantees payment for the goods he sells for his principal.

DELIVERY NOTE. A document prepared for signature by the buyer when the goods are delivered to him. A *delivery book* is sometimes used for the purpose.

DELIVERY ORDER. A DOCUMENT OF TITLE addressed by the owner of goods to a warehouse-keeper or other bailee instructing him to deliver specified goods to the person named in the document.

DEMURRAGE. The daily charge made for detention of a ship beyond the agreed number of LAY DAYS. The term is also used for the daily charge made for detention of railway rolling stock.

DEPARTMENT STORE. A large retail store divided into separate departments, each specializing in a particular line of business. Each department is managed by a *buyer*, and is in reality a separate shop that is expected to make a profit. Such stores are organized as JOINT-STOCK COMPANIES and are characterized by their central position, fine buildings, luxurious appointments, attractive window displays, and the special amenities they provide for their customers.

DEPOSIT ACCOUNT. An account, bearing interest, in which money is deposited with a bank subject to notice of withdrawal.

DEPRECIATION. The fall in value of a fixed asset due to wear and tear or lapse of time. One method of dealing with depreciation in accounts is to "write off" such an amount each year as will reduce the book value of the asset to that of its residual value when it comes to be discarded and has to be replaced. Another method is to provide for replacement of the asset by means of a SINKING FUND.

DEVISES. Gifts of real property made by will.

DIRECTORS. Persons elected by the SHAREHOLDERS of a JOINT-STOCK COMPANY to conduct the affairs of the company in accordance with the powers conferred by the ARTICLES OF ASSOCIATION. Every public company must have at least two directors, and every private company at least one.

DISCOUNT. There are two types of discount.

(a) *Cash discount.* An allowance made to encourage prompt payment of an account or payment before the expiration of the period allowed for credit, thus enabling the creditor either to earn interest on the money or to use it in promoting further business.

(b) *Trade discount.* A deduction from the gross or catalogue price allowed to traders who buy to sell again. It constitutes the trader's profit, or part of it, and enables the supplier to meet price fluctuations by adjusting the rate of discount instead of altering the prices in the catalogue.

DISCOUNT HOUSES. Institutions that formerly specialized in discounting BILLS OF EXCHANGE offered to them, borrowing from the joint-stock banks for the purpose. Owing to the decline of the BILL OF EXCHANGE during the inter-war years their main activities are now devoted to dealings in TREASURY BILLS.

DISCOUNTED BILL. A bill of exchange encashed before its due date, a charge in the nature of INTEREST, but called DISCOUNT, being made for the money advanced.

DISHONOURED BILL. A bill of exchange is dishonoured when either acceptance or payment is refused by the drawee. In either case the holder has an immediate right against the drawer and endorsers, provided he gives them prompt notice of dishonour. A dishonoured foreign bill must be *protested*; an inland bill is only *noted*. *See* NOTING AND PROTEST.

DISTRAINT. A seizure of goods in payment of a debt that is overdue.

DISTRESS WARRANT. A warrant empowering a creditor to distrain on the goods of the debtor. Among the most common occasions of distress are distress for unpaid rent, rates, and taxes.

DIVIDEND. A variable return upon an investment, as distinct from a fixed return, which is termed INTEREST.

  (a) Dividend on shares. A share in the profits of a company calculated as a percentage on the capital invested. Dividends are proposed by the directors and declared by resolution passed in general meeting. An *interim dividend* is one declared prior to the making up of the balance sheet, and may be paid on the authority of the directors.

  (b) Dividends in bankruptcy. A *pro rata* sum distributed by a bankrupt or insolvent person among his creditors, e.g. 37dp, or £0·37d in the £.

DIVIDEND WARRANT. A certificate entitling the holder to payment of dividend. It is *negotiable*, and may also be crossed like a cheque.

DOCK (OR WAREHOUSE) WARRANT. A DOCUMENT OF TITLE issued to the owner of goods imported and deposited with a dock company or warehouse-keeper. The title passes by ENDORSEMENT.

DOCUMENT OF TITLE. A document which upon transfer gives to the transferee a more or less good title to the goods to which it refers. Such documents include BILLS OF LADING, MATES' RECEIPTS, DOCK (OR WAREHOUSE) WARRANTS, and DELIVERY ORDERS. Although they have some of the characteristics of negotiability, they are not negotiable. *See* NEGOTIABLE INSTRUMENT.

DOCUMENTARY BILL. A BILL OF EXCHANGE to which are attached the BILL OF LADING, certificate or policy of insurance, and INVOICE for goods exported. The bill and documents are handed to a bank, whose agent abroad will pass the documents to the consignee only when he has accepted or paid the bill of exchange. Meanwhile, the bank usually makes an advance to the exporter against the security of the goods.

DOCUMENTARY CREDIT. A method frequently adopted to finance exports. The credit is issued to the exporter by the importer's bank through its branch or agent bank in the exporter's country. Upon shipment of the goods the exporter hands the shipping documents, together with a BILL OF EXCHANGE drawn on the importer, to the agent bank, which buys them for cash and sends them by air mail to the importer's bank, which in turn hands the documents to the importer either against payment, where the bill is payable on demand, or against acceptance, where the bill is payable at USANCE.

DORMANT PARTNER. *See* PARTNERSHIP.

DRAFT. An order for the payment of money; a BILL OF EXCHANGE before acceptance.

DRAWBACK. A refund of customs or excise duty in respect of goods exported.

DUNNAGE. Packing materials used to protect the cargo of a ship from damage.

DURESS. In law, coercion consisting of actual or threatened violence to, or confinement or imprisonment of, a person or his near relative. A threat to destroy property is not duress. A contract induced by duress is voidable at the option of the person coerced.

DUTIES. There are two kinds.

(a) *Customs*. A form of indirect taxation, imposed on certain classes of imported goods. The duties are either *specific* (levied on goods according to quantity) or *ad valorem* (levied on goods according to value). They may be used solely to raise revenue, or to afford protection to home industries.

(b) *Excise*. Taxes levied on dutiable goods produced at home, e.g. beer, whisky. Licences for the sale of beer, spirits, tobacco, etc., also come under the heading of excise duties.

EARNEST. An amount of money or other thing given by a buyer to a seller to bind a bargain made orally.

ECONOMICS. Has been given many definitions in course of time. It is a practical science, concerned with the material satisfaction of human wants. It studies human behaviour in reference to the production and distribution of the limited resources available, and the price mechanism by which their exchange is regulated.

EMBARGO. A temporary government order to prevent the arrival or departure of ships, especially in times of war; also a temporary prohibition of trade by authority.

ENDORSEMENT. A writing on the back of a document. BILLS OF EXCHANGE (including cheques) drawn payable to order (but not if drawn payable to bearer) must be endorsed by the payee before they can be negotiated. Endorsement may be either: *(a)* in blank; *(b)* special; or *(c)* restrictive.

(a) Endorsement in blank, i.e. a mere signature, whereupon the bill becomes payable to bearer.

(b) Special endorsement. One directing payment to a specified person, or to his order, e.g. *Pay R. Simpson, or Order.*

(c) Restrictive endorsement. One that prohibits further negotiation of the bill, e.g. *Pay R. Simpson only.*

ENDOWMENT POLICY. *See* POLICY.

ENTREPÔT TRADE. Trade in merchandise imported merely to be re-exported elsewhere. The goods are placed in a warehouse pending transhipment.

EQUITIES. The ordinary shares or stock of a company, i.e. shares that carry the risk of enterprise.

EQUITY. A body of legal principles, essentially different from those of the COMMON LAW, built up from the precedents of the old Court of Chancery, which aimed at natural justice. Since 1873 both types of law have been administered in the same courts.

ESCROW. A deed delivered to a person who is not a party thereto, to be held by him until some condition is fulfilled by the party for whom the deed is intended.

ESTIMATE. A written offer *to do certain work* for a specified price. The term is also sometimes used for the supply of goods. It is usually no more than an approximation of the actual cost and may be subject to variation, thus differing from a TENDER or QUOTATION, which states the exact price payable. *See* QUOTATION.

EX DIVIDEND. A QUOTATION *ex div.* means that the price quoted does not include the DIVIDEND declared or about to be declared. Three weeks before dividend date share transfers cease for dividend purposes to enable DIVIDEND WARRANTS to be prepared. On SHARES transferred during this period the dividends declared are payable to the sellers.

EX QUAY. A price quoted *ex quay* means that the buyer must take delivery of the goods, and pay all expenses, *after* the goods are landed on the quay.

EX SHIP. A price quoted *ex ship* includes delivery over the side of the ship into lighters, the buyer being responsible for payment of the lighterage.

EX WAREHOUSE. A price quoted *ex warehouse* is for delivery at the seller's warehouse, the buyer bearing the cost of the subsequent transport.

EXCHANGE CONTROL. A system of controlling foreign-exchange rates under which all useful foreign currencies are surrendered to the authorities in return for national currency at officially fixed rates.

EXCHANGE EQUALIZATION ACCOUNT. The method adopted in the United Kingdom to counter short-term fluctuations in rates of exchange between 1947–79. The Account operated as a department of the Bank of England.

EXCHEQUER BILL. An interest-bearing bond, payable to bearer, formerly issued by HM Treasury, and repayable usually after three or five years.

EXCISE DUTIES. *See* DUTIES.

EXECUTOR (MALE), EXECUTRIX (FEMALE). The person named in the will of the deceased testator to administer its provisions. The personal representative of an intestate (a person who dies without making a valid will) is called an *administrator*. An administrator may also be appointed if no executor is named in the will, or if the executor is unwilling or unable to perform the necessary duties. *See* LETTERS OF ADMINISTRATION.

EXPORT CREDITS GUARANTEE. A form of insurance that covers the risk of non-payment for goods exported. It is undertaken mainly by a government scheme managed by the *Export Credits Guarantee Department*, which deals with exporters either direct or through insurance brokers. It does not work for profit, but aims at covering its costs.

FACTOR. A mercantile agent dealing in his own name, entrusted with the custody and disposal of the goods of his principal on terms which he himself considers favourable.

FELONY. *See* OFFENCES.

FICTITIOUS ASSETS. *See* ASSETS.

FICTITIOUS BILLS. *See* ACCOMMODATION BILL.

FIDELITY GUARANTEE. An insurance policy taken out to cover the risk of fraud by an employee. These policies sometimes cover only the individual named, but may cover the whole of the employer's staff.

FIDUCIARY ISSUE. That portion of the banknote issue which is backed by first-class securities and not by gold. Since 1970 the Bank of England note issue has been entirely fiduciary.

FIDUCIARY LOAN. One granted in reliance upon the borrower's trustworthiness without security of any kind.

FINANCIAL ACCOUNTING. The branch of accounting concerned with the ascertainment of profit and loss, and the effect of operations upon the financial structure and stability of an undertaking.

FIRM. The collective name applied to partners in business, though the term is applied loosely to most types of business undertaking. See PARTNERSHIP.

FIRM OFFER. A promise to sell certain goods at a certain price subject to acceptance within a specified time. Like any other offer it is not legally binding unless made under seal or in return for a valuable consideration and may therefore be withdrawn at any time before acceptance.

FIXED ASSETS. See ASSETS.

FIXED CAPITAL. See CAPITAL.

FIXED TRUST. See UNIT TRUST.

FLOATING CAPITAL. See CAPITAL.

FLOATING POLICY. See POLICY.

FLOTSAM. Goods lost by shipwreck and found floating on the sea. They belong to the Crown unless claimed by the owner within a year and a day.

FORECLOSURE. The legal process by which a defaulting mortgagor forfeits, by order of the court, his right to redeem his property, which thereupon passes to the mortgagee.

FOREIGN EXCHANGES. A term restricted by custom to the mechanism whereby debts between persons in different countries are settled by means of TELEGRAPHIC TRANSFERS, BILLS OF EXCHANGE, etc., without the actual transmission of money. The JOINT-STOCK BANKS and the MERCHANT BANKS are the main dealers in foreign exchange, which can no longer be bought and sold in the free market. See EXCHANGE CONTROL.

FORFEITED SHARES. See SHARE.

FORWARD DELIVERY. A term signifying that goods are sold for delivery within a specified future time, either by instalments or in one lot.

FOUNDERS' SHARES. See SHARE.

FREE ALONGSIDE SHIP. A price quoted *f.a.s.* includes lighters to bring the goods to the ship, the cost of actual loading to be borne by the buyer.

FREE ON BOARD. A price quoted *f.o.b.* means that the goods will be put on board ship at the seller's expense, freight being payable by the buyer.

FREE PORT. A port where goods can be transhipped without payment of CUSTOMS DUTY. Most free ports have now been replaced by the BONDED WAREHOUSE system, but Singapore, Hong Kong, Hamburg and Rotterdam are important surviving examples. In 1984 the Government announced that, as an experimental measure for a period of five years, free ports would be established at Belfast, Birmingham, Cardiff, Liverpool, Prestwich and Southampton.

FREE TRADE. The policy of allowing the free interchange of commodities between countries by the non-imposition or abolition of protective duties. *See* PROTECTION.

FREIGHT. The consideration paid to a shipowner for the carriage of goods or the chartering of a ship. In the absence of agreement to the contrary freight is not payable until the voyage is completed and the goods have been delivered. The term is also used to denote the cargo itself.

    (a) Back freight. The amount payable by the owner of a cargo when a ship is unable to deliver at the port named and has to return to the port of loading.

    (b) Dead freight. Freight payable for cargo which a charterer has failed to provide.

FREIGHT NOTE. An account giving details of freight payable.

FUNDED DEBT. The *permanent* debt of the British Government for which there is no fixed date for redemption. Repayment takes place at current market prices as the revenues of the country permit, a SINKING FUND having been created for this purpose. The *unfunded* debt consists of all debt which the Government has an obligation to repay either at some fixed future date or on demand of the holder, and consisting in the main of TREASURY BILLS and dated GILT-EDGED SECURITIES.

FUTURES. The purchase of goods for delivery at some specified future time, providing the buyer with a form of insurance against a possible rise in the price of his raw material.

GARNISHEE ORDER. An order of the court instructing a person who owes money to a judgment debtor to hold the judgment debtor's funds, or goods, for the benefit of the judgment creditor in whose favour the order is granted.

GENERAL AVERAGE. *See* AVERAGE.

GILT-EDGED SECURITIES. Those offering the highest degree of safety, and consisting chiefly of trustee stocks, i.e. securities in which trustees are authorized to invest. They include securities of the British and Commonwealth Governments, the nationalized corporations and certain municipal stocks.

GOLD STANDARD. A monetary system under which a country's paper currency is freely convertible into gold. The gold standard in this country ceased to exist in practice (but not in theory) with the outbreak of war in 1914, by reason of restrictions on gold exports. It was restored in modified form by the Gold Standard Act 1925 but taken away by the Gold Standard Amendment Act 1931 and has not since been restored.

GOODWILL. The value of a business over and above that attached to its net worth, arising from its reputation and connections. There is little justification for the commonly held view that the goodwill of a business is worth three years' purchase, i.e. the profits of the three previous years, which may have been abnormally good or bad. It is worth what it will fetch—no more, and no less. Goodwill is an ASSET, but appears in the BALANCE SHEET only when it has been bought and paid for. Being intangible, it is not normally available as security, and most traders prefer to write it off, usually by instalments.

GREAT HUNDRED. The equivalent of 120 articles.

GRESHAM'S LAW. The principle that inferior currency will drive out superior currency from circulation, e.g. where a coinage has been debased, as by wear and tear or clipping, there is a tendency for the debased coins to remain in circulation and for the new coins to be hoarded.

GROSS PROFIT. The difference between the selling price and the cost price of goods when the former is greater than the latter, and before the deduction of any expenses incurred in selling the goods.

GROSS WEIGHT. *See* TARE.

GUARANTEE. An undertaking by a person to be answerable for the conduct of another. The liability of the guarantor, or SURETY as he is called, is secondary only, i.e. it arises only if the person whose conduct is guaranteed defaults.

A guarantee must be distinguished from an *indemnity*, which does not imply default. The indemnifier's liability is primary and does not depend upon the conduct of the person indemnified. The distinction is important in law, since a guarantee must be evidenced in writing and an indemnity need not be.

HAGUE RULES. A code of rules drawn up at The Hague in 1921 setting out the rights and liabilities of shipowners. In 1968 the Rules were modified and in their extended form (known as the *Hague–Visby Rules*) are embodied in the Carriage of Goods by Sea Act 1971.

HALL-MARK. Official marks stamped on gold and silver articles at the Goldsmiths' Hall in London and at other Assay Offices in the provinces, indicating date, maker, fineness of metal, etc. Each Assay Office has its own particular device, e.g. in London, a leopard's head; in Birmingham, an anchor; in Edinburgh, a castle, and so on.

HAMMERED. A STOCK-EXCHANGE term signifying expulsion of a member through inability to fulfil his obligations either to take up securities he has bought or to deliver those he has sold. A brief announcement is made in the "House" after three blows with a mallet have been struck on the rostrum.

HARDWARE. The equipment directly involved in the performance of data processing, e.g. the computer itself and any of the associated equipment.

HIGH SEAS. All seas outside territorial waters (usually three miles from shore) and free to all nations.

HIRE PURCHASE. An agreement to *hire* goods with an option to purchase after payment of the agreed hire instalments. Ownership of the goods remains with the vendor until the option to purchase is exercised. A hire-purchase must be distinguished from a *credit-sale agreement*, which is an agreement to *buy* goods when the purchase price is payable in five or more instalments, and under which ownership of the goods passes to the buyer at once.

HOLDER IN DUE COURSE. A person who has taken a BILL OF EXCHANGE or PROMISSORY NOTE in good faith and before it was overdue. His title to the document is good, but is defeated if the document contains a forged signature, since no title can be obtained by, through, or under a forgery.

HOLDING COMPANY. A company formed to purchase and hold a majority, and sometimes all, of the shares of other companies in order to bring them under unified control. The subsidiary companies preserve their legal identities and continue to function as separate concerns.

HYPERMARKET. A form of mammoth supermarket, defined in *The Architect* as an out-of-town store with a floor area of between 60,000 and 100,000 sq. ft. (compared with the average of about 10,000 sq. ft. for the larger supermarket), and accompanied by parking facilities for several hundred cars.

HYPOTHECATION. The act of pledging or mortgaging property. *See* LETTER OF HYPOTHECATION.

I.O.U. An acknowledgment of a debt containing no specified date for repayment, usually given as a voucher for, or as evidence of, a temporary loan for a small sum. It does not require stamping, but the addition of a specified date of repayment would convert it into a PROMISSORY NOTE.

IMPREST SYSTEM. The periodical reimbursement of expenditure so as to bring the allocation or "float" at the commencement of each new period up to the original or imprest amount. The system is commonly used for PETTY CASH.

INCOME AND EXPENDITURE ACCOUNT. An account prepared to show the financial results of non-trading concerns, such as hospitals, clubs, and voluntary societies. It differs from a *Receipts and Payments Account* mainly by including income accrued but not received and expenditure due but not paid, and aims at showing the profit or loss for the period. The *Receipts and Payments Account*, on the other hand, is a summary of the cash book, and records only actual receipts and payments of cash, the balance representing cash in hand.

INCOME TAX. A direct tax imposed by the Government upon a person's total income, whether earned or not. It is graduated to fall heaviest on those with the highest incomes, and exempts completely many in the lower income groups. A new unified system came into operation in 1973 and greatly simplified the former structure of the tax.

(a) It replaced the dual system of income tax and surtax by a single graduated tax.

(b) It abolished the distinction between earned and unearned income and now charges tax at the same rate on both.

(c) For the former standard rate, with its associated reduced rates and complicated system of allowances, it substitutes a new basic rate.

Starting from a specified basic rate (30% in 1985) the rate is highest on incomes above £40,200 (60% in 1985). These rates and the various allowances are determined each year by Parliament in the annual Finance Act, commonly known as the BUDGET.

For 160 years income tax has been charged on the basis of five schedules, each dealing with a different class of income:

Schedule A—Income from rent or other receipts from the ownership of land and buildings.

Schedule B—Income from the occupation, as distinct from the ownership, of land.

Schedule C—Income from interest and annuities payable out of public revenue in the United Kingdom.

Schedule D—Income from trades, professions, bank interest, overseas securities and possessions, short-term capital gains, and from any other source not included in any other schedule.

Schedule E—Income from wages, salaries, and pensions derived from offices and employments. *See also* SURTAX.

INCORPORATION. The act of bringing an association into legal existence. It may take place by royal charter, by special Act of Parliament, and by registration under the Companies Acts. Joint stock companies registered with limited liability are by far the commonest type of incorporated body in the UK.

INDEMNITY. *See* GUARANTEE.

INDENT. An order sent to an agent to buy goods. A foreign indent will usually include instructions as to marks and numbers, method of packing, means of forwarding, insurance, and the method of reimbursement to be employed. The indent may be either *specific*, stating precisely the brand of goods required, or *open*, not specifying the source from which the goods are to be obtained, in which case the agent will obtain quotations from several suppliers.

INDENTURE. A deed made between two or more parties, as distinct from a deed made by one party, and so called because there may be as many copies as there are parties. Formerly, two or more copies were made on parchment, the separate copies then being cut with a waved or indented edge to guard against forged substitutes.

INDEX NUMBERS. The mechanism adopted for measuring changes in the cost of living, commodity prices, and the value of money generally. A group of commodities is taken, their combined prices for a particular year (known as the *base year*) being noted and given the number 100. A subsequent increase of, say, 2% in the combined prices would then be represented by the index number 102.

Several index numbers are in use, the best known being

the Department of Employment's Index of Retail Prices, which measures changes in the cost of living. The base year, originally 1914, has frequently been changed to reflect changes in spending habits.

INFANT. Formerly a person under twenty-one years of age, but under the Family Law Reform Act 1969 persons not of full age (now eighteen instead of twenty-one) are to be known as *minors. See* MINOR.

INFLATION. An increase in available currency that has the effect of raising general prices.

INJUNCTION. An injunction (*interdict* in Scotland) is a court order requiring a person to perform (a mandatory injunction) or to refrain from performing (a prohibitory injunction) some specified action. Injunctions are frequently granted to prevent someone from acting in a manner harmful to someone else.

INQUEST. An inquiry held by a CORONER into the manner of the death of a person who has been killed, or died suddenly or in prison. It is not a trial, though it may terminate in the committal of a person for trial. *See* CORONER.

INSCRIBED STOCKS. Stocks for which no DOCUMENT OF TITLE is given, but ownership of which is inscribed in the books of the bank that has charge of the issue. They include CONSOLS of the British Government and many Commonwealth government securities inscribed with the BANK OF ENGLAND.

INSOLVENCY. The condition in which LIABILITIES exceed ASSETS or, within the meaning of the Sale of Goods Act 1979, inability to pay one's debts as they become due, notwithstanding that the assets may exceed liabilities. Insolvency differs from bankruptcy, which results from a judicial act by the COURT. *See* BANKRUPTCY.

INSTRUMENT. A deed, will, certificate, or other formal legal document.

INSURABLE INTEREST. A term used in insurance to denote some pecuniary interest in the risk against which it is desired to provide. Such an interest must exist in all contracts of insurance, without it the contract will be void.

INSURANCE. The system whereby all who have interests at risk contribute premiums (the amount of which varies with the nature and extent of the risk) to a general fund, from which losses sustained from the risk insured against are made good. The person paying the premium is the *insured*; the one who receives it and bears the risk is the *insurer* or UNDERWRITER.

Fire and marine insurance contracts are contracts of indemnity, that is the insured is given compensation, and no more, for the loss he sustains. Life assurance policies, on the other hand, are not contracts of indemnity but undertakings to pay a fixed sum of money upon death or at some stated time. (*See* POLICY, *(a) Endowment policy*.) Personal accident insurances are not strictly contracts of indemnity, except in theory, since exact calculation of loss occasioned by death or disablement is clearly impossible.

INTANGIBLE ASSETS. *See* ASSETS.

INTERDICT. *See* INJUNCTION.

INTEREST. A payment made for the use of borrowed capital, and as an inducement to people to save. It is usually calculated at a fixed percentage per annum.

INTERIM DIVIDEND. *See* DIVIDEND.

INTERNAL AUDIT. *See* AUDIT.

INTESTATE. Not having left a valid will.

INVENTORY. A list or schedule of furniture or other items.

INVESTMENT TRUST. A company formed for the purpose of investing the capital of its shareholders in a wide range of securities in such a way as to minimize risk. By so doing it applies the principle of insurance to the work of investment. The investment trust has a special value to the small investor who seeks a better return on his capital than GILT-EDGED SECURITIES provide but does not want to risk his capital. Unlike the UNIT TRUST, the investment trust has no trustees—the safety of the capital lies, as with any other business, in the hands of the managers.

INVISIBLE IMPORTS AND EXPORTS. *See* BALANCE OF PAYMENTS.

INVOICE. An account sent by a seller of goods to the buyer, stating details of the quantity, description, and price of the goods and showing the total amount due. It may also include the buyer's order number, the mode of dispatch, and the terms of payment. It serves to inform the buyer of the amount due, and provides him with a basis for checking the goods when they arrive and for the entry in his books of account. It communicates a charge, but is *not* a demand for payment. *See* PRO FORMA INVOICE and STATEMENT.

ISSUED CAPITAL. *See* CAPITAL.

ISSUING HOUSE. An institution that specializes in marketing new issues of SHARES or DEBENTURES. It carefully examines projects submitted to it and gives advice to those who sponsor them. It also undertakes the routine work connected with the issue, such as the preparation and distribution of the

PROSPECTUS. Issuing houses are particularly active in the field of overseas investment. *See* ACCEPTING HOUSES.

JERQUER. A customs official appointed to examine a ship's cargo for concealed or prohibited goods. *See* RUMMAGING.

JETSAM. *See* JETTISON.

JETTISON. To throw goods or tackle overboard to lighten a ship in distress. Goods jettisoned and *washed ashore* (or, according to some, which *sink*) are called JETSAM; those which remain afloat are called FLOTSAM.

JOBBER. A member of the STOCK EXCHANGE who, through the medium of BROKERS, buys and sells STOCKS and SHARES on his own account. A jobber specializes in a particular class of securities, and often in a limited number of securities in that class.

JOINT AND SEVERAL LIABILITY. *See* PARTNERSHIP.

JOINT STOCK BANK. Includes banks formed under royal charter, e.g. the BANK OF ENGLAND, and those registered under the Companies Acts as LIMITED LIABILITY companies. In addition to the statutory obligations applicable to all registered companies, the latter type are required to publish a BALANCE SHEET twice yearly. The largest joint stock banks are known as the "Big Four"—Barclays, Lloyds, Midland and National Westminster.

JOINT STOCK COMPANY. A body of persons who unite to subscribe the necessary CAPITAL to carry on some trade or business, the subscribers being known as SHAREHOLDERS. A few privileged companies are incorporated by royal charter, public utility companies by special Act of Parliament, and trading companies by registration under the Companies Acts. *See* COMPANY.

Three types of registered company may be distinguished: *(a)* companies with members whose liability is unlimited (few in number); *(b)* companies limited by guarantee (professional bodies, trade associations, clubs, etc.); *(c)* companies limited by shares (business concerns). The contractual powers of a company are prescribed by its instrument of INCORPORATION, in the case of a registered company by its MEMORANDUM OF ASSOCIATION.

JUDGMENT. The decision of a court of law in either a civil or a criminal proceeding.

JUDGMENT DEBTOR. A person against whom a judgment has been given ordering him to pay a sum of money to the *judgment creditor*. Until the JUDGMENT is satisfied the debtor is liable to have his property taken in execution.

JURY. A body of persons appointed to hear evidence at a criminal trial in a County, Crown or High Court, and to give their verdict upon it. Jurors are drawn from the lists of the rating authorities and must be between twenty-one and sixty years of age. Many persons, including Members of Parliament, clergymen, lawyers, and civil servants, are exempt from jury service.

Juries in civil cases are now rare, but a jury of not fewer than seven nor more than eleven members is sometimes appointed to assist a CORONER.

KAFFIRS. A STOCK EXCHANGE term for South African gold mining shares.

KANGAROOS. A STOCK EXCHANGE term for Australian land, tobacco and mining shares.

KEELAGE. Dues payable by a ship in certain ports.

KITE. *See* ACCOMMODATION BILL.

LANDING ACCOUNT. A document prepared and sent by a port authority to an importer informing him of the landing of goods from the ship and giving him details. The account states when warehousing commences, and includes particulars of any damage to the goods discovered.

LANDING ORDER. A customs document authorizing the ship's captain to deliver overside the goods of an importer who has completed the necessary formalities and paid any duty due.

LAY DAYS. The number of days allowed in a CHARTER PARTY for the loading or discharge of a cargo. Should the number of lay days be exceeded the charterer must pay DEMURRAGE; should the work be completed in less than the number of days allowed he receives *dispatch money*.

LEASE. A grant of property for a term of years, for life, or at will, by one person (the *lessor*) to another (the *lessee*), usually in return for a rent. Leases of three years and over must be made by deed; those for a shorter period may be made in writing, or even orally. A long lease applies to a term exceeding 50 years; a short lease to a term of 50 years or less.

LEGAL TENDER. That form of money which may be legally offered in settlement of a debt, or in payment for goods supplied or services rendered. To be legal the tender must be for the exact amount due. The following are legal tender:

Bank of England notes: £50, £20, £10, £5, £1—for any amount (Currency and Bank Notes Act 1928).

Gold coins of the realm (dated 1838) onwards: any amount (Coinage Act 1970).

Nickel-brass £1 coin: any amount.

Cupro-nickel ("silver") coins:

50p pieces } amounts up to £10.
20p pieces

10p pieces } in any combination—amounts up to £5.
5p pieces

(Decimal Currency Act 1969)

Bronze ("copper") coins:

2p pieces
1p pieces } in any combination—amounts up to 20p.
d p pieces

(Decimal Currency Act 1969)

At the end of 1985 the dp coin is due to be demonetized, and the £1 note replaced by the £1 coin, although existing notes will remain legal tender for at least another year.

Notes for £1, but not for other amounts, are legal tender in Scotland and Northern Ireland. Notes of the Scottish banks of issue, however, are not legal tender even in Scotland, but are accepted by the English clearing banks and the Post Office. In Scotland itself they customarily enjoy a status equal to that of the Bank of England note.

LEGISLATURE. The Queen and Parliament, i.e. that part of the Government concerned with the making of laws, as opposed to the *Executive*, which is concerned with carrying them out.

LETTER OF ALLOTMENT. *See* ALLOTMENT.

LETTER OF CREDIT. A letter addressed by a banker or other person to a correspondent abroad requesting him to advance money to the beneficiary against the credit of the bank or other person issuing the letter. *Circular Letters of Credit* are those addressed to several correspondents in different places, and are frequently issued by banks to persons travelling abroad. They are accompanied by a *Letter of Indication* containing the bearer's signature and the names of the banks to which they may be presented. As payments are made they are recorded in the space provided on the back of the letter of credit. Inasmuch as banking facilities are now extensive in almost every country, letters of credit, with the exception of those issued by the banks, have more or less fallen into disuse.

LETTER OF HYPOTHECATION. A letter empowering a bank that has advanced money on a DOCUMENTARY BILL to sell the goods should the bill be dishonoured. An exporter who regularly obtains advances often signs a *general letter of hypothecation*, which covers all future transactions.

LETTERS OF ADMINISTRATION. The form in which official sanction is given by the Probate Division of the High Court to an administrator to act in reference to the property of the deceased. The administrator, whose appointment is within the discretion of the Court, is first required to give a BOND, with SURETIES, that he will faithfully administer the estate. *See* EXECUTOR.

LETTERS PATENT. Letters under the Great Seal of England, usually granting a special privilege, e.g. a patent right, to some person or company, so called because they are addressed, not to any particular person, but to all.

LIABILITIES. Debts or other obligation for which a person or body of persons is responsible.

(*a*) *Fixed liabilities.* Liabilities which, like proprietor's capital, will not be payable until the business is wound up; also loans repayable in the distant future.

(*b*) *Current liabilities.* Liabilities, such as trade creditors, bills payable, and bank OVERDRAFTS, which must be met in the near future.

(*c*) *Contingent liabilities.* Liabilities that may or may not have to be met; DISCOUNTED BILLS not yet matured are the most common example.

LIBEL. Defamatory matter published in permanent form, as in a written or printed statement, a picture, or a gramophone record. DAMAGES for libel are recoverable even though no special damage is suffered. Libel differs from slander in that *slander consists of oral defamation only* and, with certain exceptions, damages are not recoverable unless damage can be shown to have been suffered.

LICENCE. An authorization from competent authority to do something that would otherwise be unlawful.

LIEN. The right to retain another's property until some debt or claim is settled, e.g. a watchmaker, the watch he has repaired.

(*a*) *General lien.* The right of a creditor to retain *any property* of the debtor's that he has, or will have later, in his possession. It exists by custom with solicitors, bankers, FACTORS, and stockbrokers.

(*b*) *Particular lien.* The right to retain only the *particular property* connected with the claim.

LIGHTER. A barge used in loading and unloading ships; the payment for use is termed *lighterage*.

LIMITED LIABILITY. The liability of a member of a company registered under the Companies Acts may be limited either by the number of shares he has taken or by guarantee, so that he cannot be called upon to contribute beyond the amount of his shares or guarantee.

(a) Limitation by shares. Until shares are fully paid the holder is· liable for the difference between their nominal value and the amount paid on them either by himself or by previous holders. Once the shares are fully paid he cannot be called upon to pay more.

A holder who transfers his shares has no further liability on them, unless within one year of the transfer the company is wound up, when he becomes liable for any uncalled balance his transferee is unable to pay.

(b) Limitation by guarantee. Many professional societies and associations formed for the promotion of science, art, religion, charity, etc., are registered under the Companies Act as companies *limited by guarantee*. Each member undertakes to contribute a specified sum should the company be wound up during his membership or within one year afterwards, and is liable for no greater amount. Such companies may or may not also have a capital divided into shares.

A company limited by shares must use the word *Limited* (*PLC* or *plc* if a public limited company), or some abbreviation of it, as part of its title, but non-profit-making companies limited by guarantee, and which do not propose to pay dividends, may be empowered by the Department of Trade and Industry to dispense with the word *Limited*.

LIMITED PARTNERSHIP. *See* PARTNERSHIP.

LINERS. Ocean-going vessels that sail on specified routes and to schedule, whether they have a complete load or not, as distinct from *tramps*, i.e. vessels sailing to no fixed route, but picking up cargoes, usually in bulk, wherever they are offered.

LIQUID ASSETS. *See* ASSETS.

LIQUID CAPITAL. *See* CAPITAL.

LIQUIDATOR. An official appointed to conduct the WINDING-UP proceedings of a company. He may be appointed either by resolution of the SHAREHOLDERS in a voluntary winding-up or by the court in a compulsory winding-up.

LLOYD'S. An incorporated association of marine insurance UNDER-WRITERS with more than 14,000 underwriting members. Insurance business is done, not by the Association, but by the individual members, who usually work in SYNDICATES. Their activities are not confined to the insurance of marine risks.

(a) *Lloyd's List*. Lloyd's is also the world's main centre for compiling shipping intelligence. It maintains signal stations and agencies all over the world and publishes daily *Lloyd's List and Shipping Gazette*, which gives detailed information about the movements of ships, their cargoes, etc.

(b) *Lloyd's Register*. A register, published annually by a committee distinct from the incorporated association, giving the tonnage, age, building, ownership, and nationality of almost every ocean-going ship in the world. Initially, ships were graded according to their seaworthiness as A1, 90–A1 or 80–A1, but only one standard is now recognized (100–A1), to which all classed ocean-going ships of over 100 tonnes are required to conform.

LOAN CAPITAL. *See* CAPITAL.

LONG DOZEN. A term used in certain trades to indicate *thirteen*.

LOSS LEADER. A resale of goods effected by a dealer, not for the purpose of making a profit, but for the purpose of attracting customers who are likely to purchase other goods. The term does not apply to goods sold at a genuine seasonal or clearance sale.

MAINTENANCE. Assistance, financial or otherwise, given to a litigant by a person who has no legal interest in the case. Like CHAMPERTY, such an arrangement is illegal at COMMON LAW, but no legal offence is committed where the assistance arises from an interest in the action, a mere motive of charity being sufficient to establish this.

MANAGEMENT ACCOUNTING. "The presentation of accounting information in such a way as to assist management in the creation of policy and in the day-to-day operation of an undertaking" (*Report of the Anglo-American Council on Productivity*).

MANIFEST. A customs declaration by the master of a ship about to leave port, giving particulars of the cargo, the number of passengers and crew, port of destination, etc.

MARKET. A place where goods are bought and sold or other buying and selling transactions are arranged. The term is also applied to the collective operations of buyers and sellers (e.g. of FOREIGN EXCHANGE, for which there is no recognized meeting place).

MARKET OVERT. An expression applied to the sale of goods in *open market*, which includes every shop in the City of

London, except on Sundays, but elsewhere only in the market-places and on the special days prescribed for particular towns. The effect of a sale in market overt is to give the buyer a good title to the goods he buys, notwithstanding defects in the vendor's title, though the rule does not extend to Crown property.

MATE. The deputy of the master of a merchant ship. There are sometimes more than one.

MATE'S RECEIPT. A receipt given by the mate of a general cargo ship for goods received on board direct from a barge or lighter instead of from the quay. A note of any damage to the packages, or of any discrepancy in their number, is made on the receipt, which is subsequently exchanged for a BILL OF LOADING.

MEMORANDUM OF ASSOCIATION. The principal document filed with the Registrar of Companies upon the incorporation of a company under the Companies Acts. It sets forth the company's relations with the outside world. It must be subscribed by two or more persons and state: *(a)* the proposed name of the company; *(b)* the domicile of the registered office; *(c)* the objects of the company; *(d)* a statement that the liability of the members is limited (if such is the case); and *(e)* the amount of capital and the manner of its subdivision into shares. A company cannot exceed the powers circumscribed by its memorandum. For this reason the objects are drawn as widely as possible to permit of an extension of operations if necessary.

MERCANTILE AGENT. Defined in s. 1 of the Factors Act 1889 as an agent to whom authority is given to sell, consign, or buy goods, or to raise money on the security of the goods. *See* FACTOR.

MERCHANT BANK. *See* ACCEPTING HOUSES.

MERGER. A permanent amalgamation of business units for centralizing control. The participating concerns lose their independence, but for purposes of GOODWILL often retain their original names. The Imperial Tobacco Company is an example of such an amalgamation. The amalgamation may be either *horizontal*, i.e. a combination of undertakings engaged in the same stage of production, or *vertical*, i.e. engaged in different stages of production.

Another name for a merger is a *trust*.

METRIC SYSTEM. A logical system of weights and measures based on decimal notation. It takes its name from the *metre* as the unit of length. There are three other units—the *gram* for weight, the *litre* for capacity, and the *are* for area. The great advantage of the system lies in the speed with which calculations in metric can be made since all weights and measures are either multiples or sub-multiples of 10, formed by using the appropriate prefix.

	Prefix	Symbol	Meaning
Multiples	mega	M	million
	kilo	k	thousand
	hecta	h	hundred
	decca	da	ten
	(Basic unit)		
Sub-multiples	deci	d	one-tenth
	centi	c	one-hundredth
	milli	m	one-thousandth
	micro	μ	one-millionth

These prefixes are the same for all four units, e.g.

1 *kilo*metre (km) = 1,000 metres
1 *kilo*gram (kg) = 1,000 grams

Conversion Equivalents

A metre (m)   = 1·0936 yds. (approx. 3 ft. 3 in.)
A square metre (m^2) = 1·1960 sq. yds. (approx. 1⅖ sq. yds.)
A kilogram (kg)   = 2·2046 lbs. (approx. 2⅕ lbs.)
A litre (l)   = 0·2200 gals. (approx. 1f pints)

The metric system is now used by nearly all countries. In 1965 Britain decided to adopt the system and in 1969 set up a Metrication Board to implement its gradual adoption throughout the United Kingdom.

MICROFICHE. A sheet of microfilm usually measuring 10 by 15 centimetres (4 by 6 inches) capable of accommodating and preserving the equivalent of a considerable number of book pages in reduced form. Also called *fiche*.

MICROFILM. A photographic film for preserving a microscopic record of a document, which can be enlarged in projection. The practice of microfilming is justified only for records that must be kept for long periods, and where normal filing or storage accommodation is not available.

MIDDLEMAN. An intermediary, especially a wholesaler. His elimination does not necessarily lower prices, since the functions he carries out still remain to be performed, possibly with less efficiency, either by the manufacturer or by the retailer.

MINIMUM LENDING RATE. Like the *Bank Rate* which it replaced in 1972 the MLR was a device to control the general monetary situation. The rate is no longer published. Instead, the Bank now publishes each day its estimate of the cash position of the MONEY MARKET and details of its own operations, an arrangement that permits market forces to influence the structure of short-term interest rates to a greater extent than before.

MINIMUM SUBSCRIPTION. The minimum amount, details of which must be stated in the PROSPECTUS of a company, estimated by the directors to be necessary to enable the company to function. It must be sufficient to cover the purchase price of any property to be acquired, PRELIMINARY EXPENSES, and WORKING CAPITAL. If the minimum stated is not reached the directors cannot proceed with the ALLOTMENT of shares, and within forty days of the first issue of the prospectus must return the moneys received to the applicants.

MINOR. In law, a person under eighteen years of age. Because of their youth and inexperience minors are given only a limited capacity to make legally binding agreements.

MINUTES. A summarized record in the third person of the proceedings at a meeting, stating the date and place of meeting, the names of those present, the matters discussed, and the decisions reached. They are prepared by the secretary and signed by the chairman at the next meeting as being a correct record.

MISDEMEANOUR. *See* OFFENCES.

MIXED POLICY. *See* POLICY.

MONEY.

(a) *Definition*. Broadly, that which is given in exchange for commodities or services and is generally acceptable to the community at large. More specifically, it consists of the currency of the realm in the form of coins and banknotes, but is sometimes regarded as including cheques and postal orders, though less correctly since these documents enjoy only a limited acceptability.

(b) *Functions*. Money serves as : (*i*) a medium of exchange, and disposes of the difficulties associated with barter; (*ii*) a measure of value, enabling commodities and services to be valued in terms of one another; (*iii*) a means of saving.

With the development of clearing systems and the principle of set-off, money has come to be regarded by businessmen mainly as a unit of account, in terms of which they settle their indebtedness to one another.

(c) Token money. Token coins are those whose nominal or face value is greater than the value of the metal contained in them. All nickel-brass cupro-nickel and bronze coins circulating in the United Kingdom are of this kind—they represent certain amounts of standard money without being worth it as metal. Bank of England notes, no longer convertible into gold since 1931 notwithstanding the "Promise to pay" which they represent, are now also token money.

MONEY MARKET. The name given to the financial institutions, banks, bill brokers, DISCOUNT HOUSES and ACCEPTING HOUSES concentrated in the neighbourhood of the BANK OF ENGLAND, and who are engaged in borrowing and lending money (generally known as the *Short Loan Fund*) for periods not exceeding seven days. The main lenders are the JOINT-STOCK BANKS, and the bill brokers are the main borrowers.

MONEY ORDER. The inland money order services by which amounts of up to £50 could be sent by post have been withdrawn. Remittances by post can still be made in cash by registered post, and also by National Giro to persons or organizations who have a Girobank Account or Freepay number.

MONOPOLY. An exclusive right, privilege, or power, either granted by prescription or acquired by obtaining and exercising control over the manufacturing or marketing of a commodity or service with a view to regulating its price. Public monopolies such as the Post Office, Telecom, the railways, the National Coal Board, and the Central Electricity Board are exercised for the public benefit, but others are often injurious to the public interest. *See* PRICE MAINTENANCE.

MORATORIUM. An extension of time allowed by the government of a country in times of national crisis for the payment of debts.

MORTGAGE. A means whereby the owner of land or other REAL PROPERTY may borrow money on the security of that property. The borrower (the *mortgagor*) may either execute a deed charging his estate or may grant to the lender (the *mortgagee*) a LEASE, with a provision that it shall terminate on repayment of the loan with interest. If the mortgagor defaults in payment the mortgagee at COMMON LAW can take over the property, but it is the practice of EQUITY to allow the mortgagor to redeem his property by payment of principal, interest, and costs.

MORTGAGE DEBENTURE. *See* DEBENTURE.

MULTIPLE STORE. A retail selling organization with a number of branches (ten in the Census of Distribution). Each branch is in the charge of a manager, who receives his instructions from headquarters and obtains his stocks from a central depot. Such shops may be either: *(a)* variety stores (e.g. Woolworths), or *(b)* specialist shops (e.g. in furniture, footwear, and groceries). The specialist shops are usually owned by manufacturers who seek the security of their own outlets for their goods. It is estimated that multiple shops with ten or more branches account for about 40 per cent of the country's retail trade.

NATIONAL DEBT. Money borrowed at various times by the government for national purposes. It is in part funded (i.e. permanent) and in part unfunded (i.e. temporary), and is managed by commissioners. *See* FUNDED DEBT.

NECESSARIES.

(a) Infants (or minors). Necessaries include food, clothing and instruction, and are defined by s. 2 of the Sale of Goods Act 1979 as "goods suitable to the condition in life of such infant or minor or other person, and to his actual requirements at time of sale and delivery". *See* INFANT.

(b) Married women. Similarly, as for infants, things suitable to her station in life, and for the supply of which her husband is normally responsible.

NEGOTIABLE INSTRUMENT. An INSTRUMENT representing title to money in which the property (i.e. ownership) passes to a transferee who takes it in good faith, notwithstanding that the title of the transferor may be defective. Negotiable instruments provide an important exception to the general rule that a person cannot transfer to another a better title to a thing than he himself has. If the instrument is payable *to bearer* it may be negotiated without ENDORSEMENT, but if *to order* it must first be endorsed. Negotiable instruments include BANKNOTES, BILLS OF EXCHANGE (with CHEQUES), PROMISSORY NOTES, TREASURY BILLS, bankers' CIRCULAR NOTES, DIVIDEND WARRANTS and SHARE WARRANTS (but not SHARE CERTIFICATES or SHARE TRANSFERS), bearer bonds, and bearer debentures. Although DOCUMENTS OF TITLE have some of the characteristics of negotiable instruments, they are not negotiable. The tendency is for the list of negotiable instruments to increase as they come to be regarded by custom as negotiable.

NET PROFIT. The profit remaining after all expenses have been deducted from the gross profit. It represents the real gain of a business, available in the case of a company for distribution as DIVIDEND, and in the case of a sole trader or partnership as the reward of enterprise. Whether a given return by way of net profit is regarded as satisfactory or not depends upon a consideration of the following: *(a)* the value of the personal services given; *(b)* the interest the capital employed would have earned from investment; *(c)* the degree of risk undertaken.

NET WEIGHT. *See* TARE.

NOMINAL CAPITAL. *See* CAPITAL.

NOTARY PUBLIC. A person who attests or certifies documents, mainly relating to DISHONOURED BILLS OF EXCHANGE. In Great Britain notaries are appointed by the Lord Chancellor from solicitors (in England) or from law agents (in Scotland). There is a society of public notaries.

NOTING AND PROTEST.

(a) *Noting.* A minute made on or attached to a DISHONOURED BILL OF EXCHANGE by a NOTARY PUBLIC who has re-presented it to the drawee. The minute notes the reply received and provides formal proof of dishonour.

(b) *Protest.* A formal declaration by a NOTARY PUBLIC attesting the dishonour of a bill and containing a copy of it. It is usually preceded by noting. Foreign bills must be protested in order to preserve the rights of the holder against other parties to the bill. Neither noting nor protest is necessary for inland bills, though noting is usual as a precaution.

NOVATION. The substitution, with the consent of all parties concerned, of a new obligation for an old one, or of a new debtor for an old one.

OFFENCES. The Criminal Law Act 1967 abolished the former distinction between *felonies* (grave crimes) and *misdemeanours* (lesser crimes), and all non-civil offences are now classified as misdemeanours divided as shown.

(a) *Arrestable offences*—crimes for which a person may be summarily arrested, e.g. treason, murder, piracy, arson on HM ships, and certain common law offences, including breach of the peace.

(b) *Non-arrestable offences*—crimes for which arrest can be made only on a warrant or court summons, e.g. common assault, careless driving, no TV licence, fare evasion.

(c) *Contractual*—breach of contract, for which the usual remedy lies in damages.

(d) *Torts*—wrongful acts other than crimes or breach of

contract, e.g. trespass, slander, fraud, negligence. The remedy lies in damages.

OFFER FOR SALE. An offer by an ISSUING HOUSE to sell SHARES it has bought outright, usually where a business is too small for a quotation on the STOCK EXCHANGE.

OFFICIAL RECEIVER. An official appointed by the Department of Trade and Industry to act as interim receiver and manager of a bankrupt's estate pending the appointment of a TRUSTEE.

OFFSET LITHO. Offset lithography—a printing or copying process that makes use of a metal or paper "master" typed with a special typewriter ribbon or prepared with special inks, from which upwards of 40,000 copies can be taken.

ONCOST. Indirect expenses or OVERHEADS; more precisely, the estimated amount of such expenses chargeable to the cost account of the current period. *See* OVERHEADS.

ONE-MAN COMPANY. A private company the capital of which is held almost entirely by one person.

OPEN CHEQUE. *See* CHEQUE.

OPEN POLICY. *See* POLICY.

OPTION. There are two types of option.

(a) General. A contract whereby one party has the right within a specified time to require the other to perform some nominated act. It must be supported by CONSIDERATION.

(b) Stock Exchange. The purchase of a right to buy or sell specified securities at a fixed price at or within an agreed future time: *(i)* a *put option* is an option to sell; *(ii)* a *call option* is an option to buy; *(iii)* a *put and call, or double, option* is an option to buy or sell; the PREMIUM paid for an option is so much per share or per cent, the premium for a double option being twice that for a single option. The maximum period for a STOCK EXCHANGE option is three months.

ORDER CHEQUE. *See* CHEQUE.

ORDINARY SHARES. *See* SHARE.

OVERDRAFT. An amount withdrawn from a bank CURRENT ACCOUNT in excess of the balance available. INTEREST is charged on the fluctuating amount overdrawn. An overdraft must be distinguished from a *loan*, which is a fixed sum credited to the customer's current account, and on which interest is charged for the full amount. Overdrafts and loans are both made against security, the banker having a general LIEN on securities in his possession.

OVER-ENTRY CERTIFICATE. A customs document entitling an importer to a refund of excess duty paid on a PRIME ENTRY.

OVERHEADS. The indirect expenses of production, such as rent, lighting and heating, administration and advertising, which cannot be allocated with precision to any particular cost unit, but which are incurred for the general benefit of production. They represent the difference between the prime cost and the total cost of a product. *See* PRIME COSTS and ONCOST.

OVERTRADING. Trading beyond one's means, as when the amount due to creditors exceeds the amount of liquid ASSETS. In such circumstances a concern may be solvent, but would face a crisis if creditors pressed for payment.

PAYE. *Pay as you earn.* The method used for the recovery, by deductions from wages and salaries, of INCOME TAX due under Schedule "E". Deductions are made by the employer on the basis of the employee's *code number*, a number determined by the allowances to which the employee is entitled.

PAID-UP CAPITAL. *See* CAPITAL.

PAR. STOCKS, SHARES, and other securities are said to be *at par* when their actual value is equal to their nominal value. If the actual value is less, then they are said to be *at a discount*; if more, then *at a premium*.

PAR OF EXCHANGE. The basic value of one currency expressed in terms of another.

(a) Mint par. When two countries are on a GOLD STANDARD the par of exchange is determined by the relative quantities of pure gold in the standard coins of the countries. For example, if a sovereign contained just as much pure gold as 4.86⅔ American dollars, then the mint par of exchange with the United States would be expressed as £1 : $4.86⅔.

(b) Purchasing power par. Between two countries not on a gold standard, par of exchange is determined by the respective purchasing powers of the currencies. If, for example, $2.00 will buy just as much in the United States as £1 will buy in the United Kingdom, par would be expressed as £1 : $2.00.

PARKINSON'S LAW. The natural tendency for the number of officials to multiply and *to make work*. The law, based on statistical proof, strikes at the assumption that an increase in the number of staff reflects an increase in the amount of work to be done.

PARTICULAR AVERAGE. *See* AVERAGE.

PARTNERSHIP. Defined by s. 1 of the Partnership Act 1890 as "the relation which subsists between persons carrying on a business in common with a view to profit". A partnership is collectively known as a FIRM, but does not include bodies formed by INCORPORATION. Unlike an incorporated body, a partnership has no existence independent of that of its members. Partnerships are common among the professions, e.g. solicitors (but not barristers), doctors, accountants, etc., and in retail and wholesale trade.

A partnership may consist of two or more members, restricted by the Companies Act 1985 to twenty (ten for banking). But by the Companies Act 1967 this restriction no longer applies to partnerships of solicitors, accountants or members of a recognized STOCK EXCHANGE. The partnership is often constituted by a deed or other written instrument known as the *Articles of Partnership*, in which are set out the respective rights and responsibilities of the partners, who provide the firm's capital and run the business. A new partner cannot be admitted without the consent of all.

(a) Types of partner. There are three types: *(i)* an *active partner* is one who takes an active part in the conduct of the business; *(ii)* a *dormant* or *sleeping partner* provides capital and shares in the profits, but neither takes part in the conduct of the business nor lends his name to it; *(iii)* a *nominal* or *ostensible partner* lends his name to the business, but takes no part in its conduct and may not even share in the profits, and yet he is liable as other pertners.

(b) General partnerships. The essence of partnership is *equality*, and *in the absence of agreement to the contrary* the following rules apply; *(i)* all partners are entitled to share equally in the capital and profits, and must contribute equally towards all losses; *(ii)* a partner is entitled to interest at 5 per cent per annum on payments advanced in excess of his agreed capital; *(iii)* a partner is not entitled, before profits are ascertained, to interest on capital; *(iv)* a partner is not entitled to remuneration for his services; *(v)* every partner may share in the conduct of the business and have equal access to the books.

Every partner is an AGENT of his FIRM and of his co-partners for the purpose of the firm's business. He is *liable jointly* (but not severally, except in Scotland) for all *debts and obligations* of the firm incurred while he is a partner. This means that a judgment obtained against some but not all of the partners frees the others from liability, so that a creditor cannot afterwards obtain judgment against these others if the judgment fails. A partner's liability for the *torts* of a co-partner committed in the course of the firm's business is, however, *joint and several*, so that a judgment against one is not a bar to a subsequent action against the others.

(c) Limited partnerships. Partnerships formed under the Limited Partnerships Act 1907, with one or more general partners liable for all the firm's debts and obligations, and one or more partners whose liability is limited to the amount of capital contributed. A limited partner shares in the profits, but may not take part in the management of the business and has no power to bind the firm. Limited partnerships must be registered, otherwise every limited partner will be liable as a general partner.

A partnership is dissolved by the retirement, death, or bankruptcy of a partner, but not by the death or bankruptcy of a limited partner.

PASS BOOK. A small book showing payments into and withdrawals from a customer's CURRENT ACCOUNT, prepared periodically by a banker and *passed* by him to the customer, thus enabling the latter to check the state of his account and the accuracy of the entries in it. With the growth of computerization the pass book now takes the form of a machine-recorded statement in loose-leaf form. *See* BANK STATEMENT.

PASSPORT. A document of identification granted by the government of a country to ensure protection and safe conduct to those of its subjects who travel abroad. In the United Kingdom passports are issued to British subjects by the Foreign Office through its six regional passport offices, on the recommendation of a banker, magistrate, or other person of standing, and since 1970 are valid for ten years, subject to renewal. To forge a passport or to make a false statement to obtain one is a MISDEMEANOUR punishable by fine, or imprisonment, or both.

PATENT. A patent right or privilege, granted by LETTERS PATENT, to an inventor, called the *patentee*, enabling him alone to benefit from the proceeds of his invention for a period of fourteen years from the original date of his application. The grant of a patent is not a legal right but an act of royal favour, though in fit cases it is never refused.

PAYEE. One to whom money is payable, or in whose favour a BILL OF EXCHANGE, PROMISSORY NOTE, or CHEQUE is drawn. If the instrument is drawn payable *to order* it can be negotiated only after ENDORSEMENT by the payee, though such an instrument made payable to a fictitious or non-existing person, e.g. *Pay Wages*, may be treated as payable to bearer and does not require endorsement.

PAYING-IN SLIP. A form provided by the bank for the enumeration of items of money paid into a CURRENT ACCOUNT. A duplicate (or counterfoil) initialled and stamped by the bank cashier serves as an acknowledgment. For the convenience of the customer paying-in slips are frequently bound together to form a *paying-in book*.

PER PROCURATIONEM. A Latin phrase, usually abbreviated *per pro*. or *p.p.*, signifying that the person so signing is acting as an agent with special authority. The authority is granted by a deed called a POWER OF ATTORNEY, though it may also arise from custom. Unless a person has been appointed to sign *by procuration* he is correctly entitled to use only the word *per* for *for*, and not *per pro*. The phrase is especially applied to the signing of BILLS OF EXCHANGE, where it serves as an express intimation that the AGENT signing possesses no more than a special and limited authority, so that his PRINCIPAL is not bound if the agent exceeds the limits of the *actual* authority given to him.

PERSONAL REPRESENTATIVE. An EXECUTOR or administrator. His duties are: *(a)* to bury the deceased; *(b)* to make an INVENTORY of the deceased's estate; *(c)* to obtain PROBATE or LETTERS OF ADMINISTRATION as the case may be; *(d)* to collect the estate and pay the debts; and *(e)* to pay the legacies and distribute the residue.

PERSONALTY. Personal property or personal estate. It consists of two main categories—chattels real and chattels personal.

(a) Chattels real. Interests in land less than freehold (e.g. leaseholds) as opposed to freeholds, which are real and not personal property.

(b) Chattels personal. Further subdivided into: *(i) choses in possession* (or corporeal chattels), i.e. tangible movables, which can actually be possessed; *(ii) choses in action* (or incorporated chattels), i.e. intangible property such as debts, shares in a company, rights under contract, PATENTS, TRADE MARKS, etc., rights to which cannot be asserted by taking possession but only by means of a legal action.

PETTY CASH. A ready sum of money kept for the special purpose of meeting miscellaneous expenses of small amount (from the French word *petit*, meaning small). *See* IMPREST SYSTEM.

PIECE-WORK. Work for which payment is made according to the amount done and not the time taken in doing it.

PLACING. An arrangement by an ISSUING HOUSE to "place" or sell new issues of SHARES privately to a selected number of investors.

PLIMSOLL LINE (OR MARK). The mark or marks on a ship indicating the load-line, or set of load-lines for different waters and different conditions, required by the Merchant Shipping Act 1870.

POLICY. The document issued by an insurance company setting out the terms of a contract of INSURANCE or ASSURANCE, such as the risks covered, the sum insured, the amount of premium, and the renewal date. It is a document capable of ASSIGNMENT and is in fact often assigned as security.

(a) *Endowment policy.* Provides for payment of a stated sum on the attainment of a specified age, or at death if earlier.

Marine insurance policies are of several kinds.

(b) *Open (or unvalued) policy.* One in which the value of the subject-matter is not stated, but is left to be assessed when a claim is made.

(c) *Valued policy.* One in which the value of the subject-matter is expressly stated.

(d) *Voyage policy.* One covering a specified voyage.

(e) *Time policy.* One effected, not for a voyage, but for a specified *period*—usually for the insurance of the ship itself.

(f) *Floating policy.* A policy attached to any ship or ships that may be assigned for a specified voyage. As each shipment is made its value is written off the policy, a new policy being taken out when the total value of the shipments equals the face value of the original policy.

(g) *Mixed policy.* One that covers a ship on a specified route for a specified period, thus combining the elements of the voyage and the time policy.

PORTFOLIO. The list of SECURITIES owned by a person or financial institution. In a more general sense, a portable case for holding papers, drawings, etc.

POST ENTRY. A supplementary customs entry lodged by an importer when the amount of duty paid on the PRIME ENTRY was less than that subsequently found to be due.

POSTAL ORDER. Orders with counterfoils attached issued by the Post Office for sums ranging from 25p. to £10, in which the names of payee and post office are left to be inserted by the remitter. They are *not negotiable.*

POST-DATE. To affix to a document a date later than that of its signature or execution.

POSTE RESTANTE. A French term denoting a department of the

Post Office where correspondence may be left "to be called for" by the addressee. The service is designed solely for the convenience of travellers, and may not be used in the same town for more than three months. Any letter not called for within two weeks is treated as undeliverable and returned to the sender. To facilitate this it is helpful if the sender's name and address is placed on the back of the envelope.

POWER OF ATTORNEY. A deed executed by one person authorizing another to act on his behalf, e.g. to receive debts and sign documents. The party so authorized is called the ATTORNEY or AGENT of the one giving authority.

PREFERENCE SHARES. *See* SHARE.

PRELIMINARY EXPENSES. Expenses incidental to the formation and incorporation of a company, incurred for such items as legal charges, stamp duties, and printing costs of memorandum and articles.

PREMIUM. *See* INSURANCE AND PAR.

PRICE-LIST. A list of prices intended to remain in force for a period of time, representing the *actual prices*, usually of manufactured goods, at which the supplier is prepared to sell. *See* PRICES CURRENT.

PRICE MAINTENANCE. It is illegal for any supplier, at any level of trade, to impose minimum (but not maximum) prices for goods, or to withhold supplies from dealers merely because they have cut prices, except where they are using his goods as LOSS LEADERS. This does not preclude suppliers from *recommending*, as distinct from *fixing* resale prices.

PRICES CURRENT. A periodical price list of commodities subject to frequent price fluctuations, sent by a merchant to customers showing prices prevailing on date of issue, these being the *approximate prices* at which he is prepared to sell. *See* PRICE-LIST.

PRIMAGE. A percentage formerly paid to the master of a ship to ensure care in loading and unloading cargo, but now paid to the ship's owners as an integral part of the freight, the rate usually being 10 per cent of the charge for freight proper.

PRIME COSTS. Those costs which vary directly with the quantity produced, comprising expenses such as wages and materials that can be identified with the actual product. *See* OVERHEADS.

PRIME ENTRY. A customs entry completed by an importer of dutiable goods when he means to remove the goods at once and pay the required duty. Different forms of entry are used for *ad valorem* and *specific* duties. *See* DUTIES.

PRINCIPAL. This term has two meanings:

(a) *Finance*. The capital sum of money on which interest is paid.

(b) *Agency*. The person for whom an agent acts. Except where expressly required by statute, the agent's appointment need not be in writing, and an agent appointed verbally may make contracts required by law to be in writing. But an agent cannot contract for his principal under seal unless he himself has been appointed under seal, the deed of appointment being termed a POWER OF ATTORNEY. *See* AGENT.

PRIVATE COMPANY. *See* COMPANY.

PROBATE. Official acceptance of the authenticity of a will and official sanction of the executor's right to act.

PRO FORMA INVOICE. An invoice sent *for form's sake*. It differs from an ordinary invoice only in being marked *Pro Forma*. It is not entered in the books of account and does not debit the receiver with the amount. It is used: (a) to cover goods sent on approval, or on consignment; (b) to serve as a quotation; (c) to serve as a request for payment in advance if the goods are required.

PROMISSORY NOTE. A signed promise to pay a specified sum of money at a certain date. It is subject to the rules that apply to BILLS OF EXCHANGE, but, unlike a bill, does not require ACCEPTANCE. It is not commonly used in business, but as a *note of hand* is frequently given to a money-lender as security for a loan.

PROMOTER. One who specializes in promoting companies either from existing businesses or from new resources. He negotiates for the purchase of property, prepares the PROSPECTUS, finds persons willing to act as directors, and arranges with UNDERWRITERS to guarantee the proposed issue of shares. He does not usually retain a permanent interest in the companies he promotes. The ISSUING HOUSE has now largely replaced the older type of promoter.

PROPOSAL FORM. A form completed by a person seeking insurance cover containing details of the risk. The proposer must make a full disclosure of all material facts bearing on the contract, whether or not the form includes questions about them, otherwise the contract is voidable at the option of the insurer. (*See* UBERRIMAE FIDEI.) In most proposals the proposer is required to sign a declaration warranting the truth of the statements made, in which case it is of no importance whether the fact enquired into is or is not material to the risk.

PROSPECTUS. Any document inviting the public to subscribe to the capital of a company. Before it can be issued a copy, signed by the directors, must be filed with the Registrar of Companies. It must state the contents of the MEMORANDUM OF ASSOCIATION and include other statutory information to enable the public to form a fair judgment of the company's prospects. False statements in a prospectus, even though made innocently, will be construed as fraud and entitle a subscriber misled by the information to claim DAMAGES against those responsible for the issue of the prospectus. It is then upon the defendants to show not only that they believed the statements to be true but also that they had reasonable grounds for so believing.

PROTECTION. The policy of fostering home industries. This may be done in various ways: (a) by prohibiting imports of competing goods; (b) by imposing protective taxes on imports; (c) by subsidizing home production.

PROTEST. *See* NOTING AND PROTEST.

PROXY. One appointed to act or vote for another, and also the document of authorization. Proxies are commonly used for company meetings; a shareholder's proxy may vote but may not address the meeting.

PUBLIC COMPANY. *See* COMPANY.

PUBLIC UTILITY COMPANY. A public corporation concerned with the supply of essential services, e.g. gas, water, electricity. Because of their monopoly of vital public services, gas, electricity and coal undertakings, and rail and canal transport, now operate as nationalized industries under non-profit-making public corporations which, while working within the framework of government policy, enjoy a substantial measure of autonomy.

PYX. A box at the Mint in which sample coins are preserved for testing. The test is carried out annually before a jury of the Goldsmiths' Company summoned by the Lord Chancellor to what is called *The Trial of the Pyx*, to ensure that the legal weight and fineness of the coins are maintained.

QUANTUM MERUIT. A legal term meaning *as much as he deserves*. Under the doctrine a person is entitled in two cases to recover reasonable payment for the actual work done: (a) where he has not completed the whole of the work undertaken, and where non-completion is due to the fault of the other party, but not otherwise; (b) where a contract makes no mention of specific remuneration.

QUARTER DAYS. The last days of each quarter of the year in which payments of interest or rent fall due. In England these are: Lady Day (25th March), Midsummer Day (24th June), Michaelmas (29th September), Christmas Day (25th December). Quarter days in Scotland differ from these.

QUORUM. The minimum number of members of a body necessary to form a meeting competent to transact business. In the British House of Commons the quorum is forty; in the House of Lords, thirty.

QUOTATION. An offer to sell goods at a price and under conditions that are stated. *See* ESTIMATE.

RACK RENT. A rent extended to the full annual value of the land or other property rented. It is the highest rent the property will bear.

RATE OF EXCHANGE. The price at which the currencies of foreign countries are bought and sold in terms of one another. *See* PAR OF EXCHANGE.

RATE OF TURNOVER. The number of times a trader's stock is sold in a given period. It is calculated by dividing the average stock held, valued at selling price, into the total value of sales.

Rate of turnover is important, because it determines total turnover, upon which gross profit depends. It varies considerably in different types of business; a fishmonger, for instance, may turn his stock over once a day, but a jeweller may do so only once a year.

RATES. The annual charge levied by a local authority on the ratable value of property in its area. Ratable value, last fixed in 1973 by the Valuation Department of the Inland Revenue, is calculated for land and houses by estimating the prospective rent if the property were let to a hypothetical tenant. This is termed the *gross value* of the property, from which certain percentage deductions for repairs and maintenance are made to arrive at the *net annual value*, i.e. the ratable value on which the rate is levied.

REAL PROPERTY (OR ESTATE). All interests in land, including buildings, other than leasehold interests (which are personal property).

REBATE. An allowance or abatement made from a bill or in the price of goods, etc.

RECEIPT. The stamp duty on receipts for amounts of £2 or over, required by the Stamp Act 1891, was abolished by the Finance Act 1970. Although the Cheques Act 1957 provides that a returned cheque duly paid by the bank may serve as a receipt, this does not in any way affect the debtor's right under the Act of 1891 to demand a receipt in addition if he wants one.

RECEIPTS AND PAYMENTS ACCOUNT. *See* INCOME AND EXPENDITURE ACCOUNT.

RECEIVING ORDER. The order made in BANKRUPTCY proceedings by the court, whereby all the property of an insolvent debtor is vested in the OFFICIAL RECEIVER. No person but the official receiver may then deal with the property.

RECONCILIATION STATEMENT. *See* BANK RECONCILIATION STATEMENT.

REFEREE IN CASE OF NEED. *See* CASE OF NEED.

REGISTERED CAPITAL. *See* CAPITAL.

RE-INSURANCE. An arrangement whereby an UNDERWRITER who has accepted a risk greater than he thinks it prudent to retain may relieve himself from it, or from some portion of it, by re-insuring with another underwriter.

REMITTANCE. The act of sending money from one person to another, usually by post; also the sum of money remitted.

RESERVE. An amount set aside out of profits or other surpluses and designed to meet contingencies. A reserve may be either a capital reserve or a revenue reserve.

(a) Capital reserve. One created out of capital profits (e.g. sale of shares at a premium), or out of profits made prior to INCORPORATION of a company. Such reserves are available for capital purposes only (e.g. extensions to premises).

(b) Revenue reserve. One set aside out of profits that might otherwise have been distributed as DIVIDEND. Such reserves, no matter under what name or heading, are available for any purpose, including if desired the subsequent payment of dividend.

(c) Provisions. A reserve aims to meet a contingency. It must be distinguished from a provision, which aims to provide for: *(i)* specific requirements (e.g. renewal of plant), or *(ii)* specific commitments and *known* contingencies where the amounts involved cannot be known in advance (e.g. depreciation of assets).

(d) Secret (or inner) reserve. A reserve not disclosed in the balance sheet, the usual purpose of which is to avoid fluctuations in the published profits. Such reserves are created by the undervaluation of fixed assets or stock, excessive provisions for bad debts and other contingencies, and by charging capital expenditure to revenue.

RESERVE FUND. A reserve represented by investments or other readily realizable and earmarked assets.

RESERVE (OR UPSET) PRICE. The lowest price an owner of goods is prepared to accept for them at an auction sale.

RESPONDENTIA BOND. Similar to a BOTTOMRY BOND, but pledges the cargo and not the ship as security for a loan. Like bottomry bonds, these bonds are now rare.

RETAIL TRADE. The sale of goods to the final consumer. Its particular function is to have available varied stocks from which the customer can meet his immediate requirements. Notwithstanding the growth of large-scale retailing, some 60 per cent of the separate shops in this country are owned by retailers operating on a small scale, and account for some 30 per cent of the total trade.

REVENUE. Income of a recurring nature from any source. The term is applied especially to the general income of a government from taxes, etc.

REVENUE EXPENDITURE. Expenditure chargeable against profits as being incurred in earning it, and not like capital expenditure adding to the value of the fixed assets of an undertaking. In practice, many minor items of capital expenditure are charged against profits as a matter of prudence.

RIGHTS ISSUE. A new issue of shares to existing shareholders in proportion to their present holdings. The issue is generally below the open market price, so SHAREHOLDERS profit by acceptance.

RING. A combination organized for the purpose of controlling the market and forcing up prices by restricting or withholding supplies. The operations are said to "corner" the commodity so restricted.

ROYALTY. The payment made to the owner for permission to use or take from his property, e.g. a payment by the lessee of a coal mine to the owner for each tonne of coal removed, or to a patentee for permission to use his patent. Royalties are also paid by publishers and producers to authors, playwrights, and composers.

RUMMAGING. The searching of a ship by customs officials to ensure that neither dutiable nor prohibited goods are concealed on board. See JERQUER.

SALARY. A fixed payment made periodically, usually monthly or quarterly, for regular services of a non-manual or non-mechanical kind, as opposed to wages paid to manual workers. See WAGES.

SALVAGE. A reward payable by the owners to persons, other than the ship's company, for saving ship or cargo from loss at sea due to pirates, enemies, fire, and perils of the sea. Claims based upon the danger involved and the value of the property saved are settled in the courts. The term is also used to denote the objects recovered from shipwreck, fire, etc.

SANS FRAIS. Words meaning *without expense*, sometimes added to continental BILLS OF EXCHANGE of small amount where the drawer has reason to believe that the bill may be dishonoured and does not wish to incur the expense of NOTING AND PROTESTING it. The words operate as an instruction to the bank not to incur these charges.

SANS RECOURS. Words meaning *without recourse*, added to the ENDORSEMENT of a BILL OF EXCHANGE by an endorser should the bill be dishonoured, e.g. by an agent endorsing for his principal.

SCRIP. Short for "subscription". A provisional or preliminary certificate of a person's holding in a JOINT STOCK COMPANY or government loan.

SECRET RESERVE. *See* RESERVE.

SECURED CREDITOR. One who holds a SECURITY sufficient to cover his loan should the debtor default.

SECURITY. Bonds, certificates, or other documents of value deposited with the creditor as cover for a loan. Sometimes the security takes the form of a GUARANTEE given by a third person. In the plural the word is used generically for stocks, shares, debentures, etc.

SEIGNIORAGE. The difference between the intrinsic and the face value of coins, consisting of the expenses of minting (termed *brassage*) and the profit made on the process, formerly claimed by the *seigneur* or ruler. Because of the low cost of cupro-nickel the profit of the British government on the minting of "silver" is quite considerable. The term is also applied to royalties on minerals.

SET-OFF. A claim set against another, as where each of two persons owes money to the other, so that only the balance is paid by the one who owes the greater sum.

SETTLEMENT DAYS. *See* ACCOUNT DAYS.

SHARE. A unit of the share capital contributed by the members of a company. Shares are classified according to their rights to participate in declared profits, as follows:

(a) *Preference shares*. Those with a prior claim on the profits. The fixed rate of DIVIDEND to which they are entitled must be met before any payment is made on the ordinary shares. Where dividends unpaid are carried forward the shares are termed *cumulative preference shares*, and where they carry the right to a further share of profits after the ordinary shareholders have received a specified return they are termed *participating preference shares*. A company may take power under its ARTICLES OF ASSOCIATION to issue preference shares repayable either on a specified date or on a date to be decided. Such shares are known as *redeemable preference shares*. They must be authorized by the articles and may be redeemed only if they are fully paid, and then only out of profits that would otherwise be available for dividend, or out of the proceeds of a new issue made for the purpose of redemption.

(b) *Ordinary shares*. Those entitled to profits after all preferential rights have been satisfied.

(c) *Deferred shares*. Those entitled to profits after the rights of preference and ordinary shareholders have been satisfied. Such shares are now fast disappearing. (Deferred shares necessitate a fixed rate of dividend on the ordinary shares.)

(d) *Founders' (or management) shares*. Sometimes issued to promoters and underwriters. They participate in profits only after all other shares have received fixed rates of dividend. Their value depends entirely on the success of the enterprise. Like deferred shares they are now rarely issued.

(e) *Bonus shares*. Shares representing accumulated profits, or undistributed reserves, issued to shareholders without payment, the issue being *pro rata* to their existing holdings. It does not make the shareholder better off financially, but regularizes the capital structure.

(f) *Forfeited shares*. Shares forfeited by decision of the directors by reason of calls being in arrear. Forfeiture does not extinguish the member's liability on such shares unless and until they are reissued.

SHARE CERTIFICATE. The certificate issued by a JOINT STOCK COMPANY stating that the person named thereon is the registered proprietor of the stated number of shares, of which the serial numbers are given. The certificate is usually signed by two directors and the secretary and bears the company's seal. It is *not negotiable*.

SHARE TRANSFER. An instrument transferring the ownership of shares in a registered company. It must be in writing, but is not by law required to be sealed, though the company's *articles* usually require that it must be so. Like a SHARE CERTIFICATE, it is *not negotiable*. The transfer is completed by registration at the company's registered office, which may be one of the banks.

SHARE WARRANT. A warrant issued by a registered company in exchange for fully paid shares, stating that the bearer is entitled to the shares specified therein. Such warrants are *negotiable* and transferable by mere delivery. Dividends are paid by means of coupons attached to the warrants.

SHAREHOLDER. One who holds a share or shares in a joint stock company. He has the right to attend and vote at meetings and to share in the profits of the company. On the other hand, he is liable for the amount unpaid on the shares he holds, and on shares he has transferred if the company is wound up within one year of the transfer.

SHERIFF. The sheriff, or *shire-reeve*, is a public official appointed annually by the Chancellor of the Exchequer to take charge of the Queen's business in each shire or county. His duties, now few, are to issue certain writs, to summon juries and to superintend parliamentary elections. In modern times these duties are performed mainly by an *under-sheriff*, usually a solicitor, who engages men, called sheriff's officers or *bailiffs*, to carry out the orders of the court. Certain old cities elect their own sheriffs, and the City of London elects two.

SHIPPING BILL. A form completed and officially passed by Customs when imported dutiable goods are re-exported or used as ship's stores. From it, the dockside Customs officer checks the goods on to the exporting ship.

SHIP'S HUSBAND. An agent appointed by shipowners to see to repairs, fittings, stores, and generally to look after the welfare of the ship while she is in port.

SHIP'S REPORT. A report that must be made to the Customs by the master of a ship within twenty-four hours of arrival from a foreign port. It is made on a prescribed form and provides a detailed description of the cargo. No goods may be landed until the report has been made.

SINKING FUND. Investments built up outside the business to meet the cost of replacing fixed assets or of redeeming liabilities, such as DEBENTURES. The method is to invest a periodical sum which, with accumulated interest, will produce the value of the asset to be replaced or the liability to be redeemed, the periodical sum for investment being obtained from sinking fund tables. Much of the NATIONAL DEBT of the British government is redeemed by sinking funds.

SLANDER. *See* LIBEL.

SLEEPING PARTNER. *See* PARTNERSHIP.

SLIP (INSURANCE). An informal memorandum prepared by an insurance broker as a preliminary to a marine insurance policy at LLOYD'S. It contains particulars of the proposed insurance and is presented to UNDERWRITERS in turn, who initial it for the amount of the risk they are prepared to accept. When the slip is fully underwritten the broker prepares the policy on a Lloyd's form.

SOFTWARE. Written or printed data, such as programs, essential to the operation of computers.

SOLD NOTE. *See* BOUGHT NOTE.

SOLVENT. Able to pay one's debts as they become due. *See* INSOLVENCY.

SPECIE. Coined money as distinct from paper currency. *See* BULLION.

SPECIFIC DUTIES. *See* DUTIES.

SPECIFICATION. This has three meanings: *(a)* the detailed description of an article which must be submitted with any application to the Patent Office; *(b)* a detailed statement of the work to be done and the materials to be used in the fulfilment of a contract, such a specification being commonly sent with a request for an ESTIMATE; *(c)* the declaration made on the official form deposited with the Customs authorities for statistical purposes when goods are exported.

SPOT. A slang word used in expressions like the following:

(a) Spot cash. Indicating that payment is due immediately possession of the goods is taken from the place where they lie.

(b) Spot price. Indicating that the price quoted is for the goods where they lie, and that their removal is at the buyer's expense. *See* EX WAREHOUSE.

(c) Spot sale. An indication that the goods are on hand and can be delivered immediately.

STAG. A speculator who applies for a new issue of stocks or shares, not with the intention of taking them up, but anticipating that they will rise to a premium before ALLOTMENT, and thus enable him to sell at a profit before he has to complete his purchase.

STAMPING OF AGREEMENTS. Most deeds (e.g. conveyances and leases) and also certain other contracts in writing (e.g. tenancy agreements and agreements for sale of a business) are charged with stamp duty under special headings according to the nature and value of the transaction. Agreements in writing executed under seal, not otherwise liable to duty, must be stamped with 50p duty. Agreements under hand only, not otherwise liable to duty, are exempt from stamp duty.

An agreement not stamped as required nevertheless creates a valid contract, but cannot be enforced at law. It may, however, be stamped subsequently, but only on payment of a penalty (usually £10) unless it is presented for stamping within thirty days from its date.

STANDARD COSTS. Costs predetermined on the basis of a detailed SPECIFICATION of all relevant factors. A standard cost differs from an estimated cost in that it specifies precisely what a given cost ought to be, thus providing a standard with which actual cost may be compared and efficiency measured.

STANDING ORDER. This has two meanings.

(a) Banking. An order authorizing a banker to pay from a CURRENT ACCOUNT a stated sum of money at specified intervals to the person named. It is useful where periodic payments such as subscriptions and insurance premiums are made and prevents their being overlooked.

(b) Meetings. Rules framed for permanent guidance as to procedure at meetings, etc., frequently adopted by local authorities and other bodies. In the Houses of Parliament standing orders regulate the procedure on bills and other matters.

STATEMENT. Short for *statement of account*, i.e. a statement sent at stated periods by a creditor to his debtor summarizing the receipts, payments, and allowances as they appear in the creditor's ledger for the period and showing the amount owing. It enables the debtor to check his own ledger against the particulars given, any errors discovered and agreed being adjusted by DEBIT and CREDIT NOTES. A statement must not be confused with an INVOICE, which gives detailed information about a particular transaction, whereas a statement gives a summary of every transaction during the period it covers. Again, unlike an invoice it *is* a demand for payment.

STATEMENT OF AFFAIRS. A statutory statement of his affairs submitted by a debtor to the OFFICAL RECEIVER within three days (seven days on a creditor's petition) from the RECEIVING ORDER made against him. The statement is in prescribed form and gives particulars of assets and liabilities, names and addresses of creditors and the SECURITIES held by them, and such other information as the official receiver may require.

STATISTICS. The classification, tabulation, and study of numerical data relating to persons and things, usually for the purpose of enabling conclusions to be drawn or forecasts to be made from them. They may be presented in tabular, graphical, diagrammatic, or pictorial form.

STATUTORY BOOKS. The records which, in addition to proper books of account, must be kept by a registered company; namely: *(a)* a register of mortgages and charges; *(b)* a register of members; *(c)* separate minute books for directors' and shareholders' meetings; *(d)* a register of directors' share-holdings; *(e)* a register of directors and secretaries.

STATUTORY COMPANY. A company incorporated by special Act of Parliament. Such companies are usually concerned with public utilities, such as railways, gas, electricity, and water. Their constitution and management are governed by their special Act of Parliament. (*But see* PUBLIC UTILITY COMPANY.)

STATUTORY DECLARATION. A declaration made before a COMMIS-SIONER FOR OATHS to take the place of other evidence that is lacking, e.g. a lost birth certificate. *See* AFFIDAVIT.

STEVEDORE. An experienced person engaged either as supervisor or labourer in the loading and unloading of ships' cargoes.

STOCK. Money contributed to the capital of an incorporated body, or advanced to the government and forming part of the national debt. The original capital of a registered company is always divided into shares, but when these are fully paid they may be converted into stock, each shareholder receiving an equivalent amount of stock. The essential difference between stock and shares is that the former may be transferred in fractional amounts, whereas shares cannot be sub-divided.

STOCK EXCHANGE. A voluntary association concerned with the buying and selling of stocks and shares. The affairs of the Stock Exchange in London are in the hands of two bodies: *(a)* the Managers, representing the shareholders of the property; *(b)* the Stock Exchange Committee, representing the members, by whom they are elected annually.

The members of the Exchange consist of:

(a) Jobbers. Members who buy and sell *on their own account*, their dealings with the public being through the medium of brokers only. A jobber as a rule specializes in a particular class of security, e.g. Government, oils, rubbers, foreign railways, etc.

(b) Brokers. Members who buy and sell, not on their own account, but *as agents for the public*. Whereas the jobber works for a profit, the broker works for a commission termed *brokerage*.

(c) Clerks. Authorized clerks are clerks with authority to

buy and sell for their principals. Unauthorized clerks are those privileged to enter the "House", but have no authority to buy and sell for their principals. Both authorized and unauthorized clerks may or may not be members of the Exchange.

Besides the Stock Exchange in London there were until 1973 a number of regional exchanges, but in that year they were integrated with the London exchange to function as a single organization known quite simply as *The Stock Exchange*. The trading floors in the larger cities continue to function as before, liaison being maintained through administrations based on the former regional exchanges.

The Stock Exchange is currently undergoing major changes in organization and procedures, but the details have not yet been finalized.

STOPPAGE IN TRANSITU. This is the right of a seller of goods who has not been paid as agreed in the contract to resume possession of goods still in course of transit. Repossession of the goods does not give the seller the right to resell them unless: *(a)* the goods are perishable, or *(b)* the intention to resell is notified to the buyer, and the buyer does not pay for the goods within a reasonable time, or *(c)* the right to resell was expressly reserved in the original contract.

SUBROGATION. The legal principle that entitles an insurer to any benefit received or that may accrue to the insured in respect of the loss insured against. It means that the person insured can recover only the actual amount of loss sustained. The principle applies only to contracts of pure INDEMNITY, under which payments to the insured are by way of compensation for actual loss sustained. It does not apply, for example, to contracts of life assurance, where the agreement is to pay a fixed sum.

SUBSCRIBED CAPITAL. *See* CAPITAL.

SUBSIDIARY COMPANY. Defined by the Companies Act 1985 as one of which another controls the composition of its board or holds more than 50 per cent of its equity capital, i.e. its ordinary shares. If the controlling company is itself a subsidiary of a third, then the first subsidiary is generally known as the sub-subsidiary of the third.

SUBSIDY. A payment made from national revenue to some enterprise or industry for the purpose of keeping down prices, e.g. the subsidy to farmers.

SUPERMARKET. A large self-service store. The Supermarket Association has about 300 members.

SURETY. One who undertakes to be answerable for the debt,

default, or miscarriage of another. If called upon to pay under the guarantee he has given he is entitled to refund by the person who has defaulted. *See* GUARANTEE.

SYNDICATE. A combination of capitalists or financiers entered into for the purpose of prosecuting a scheme requiring large sources of capital; especially one whose object is to control the market in a particular commodity.

TAKE-OVER. A take-over bid is an offer to buy shares from the public to enable the offeror to gain a controlling interest in the COMPANY concerned. If the SHARES are quoted on the STOCK EXCHANGE, the bidder is expected to comply with the terms of the City Code on Take-overs.

TALON. The last portion of a sheet of dividend coupons (similar to a sheet of postage stamps) attached to a bearer debenture or similar bearer security, by means of which the holder applies for a fresh sheet of coupons.

TARE. The weight of the case, crate, or other packing materials for goods. Deducted from the *gross weight* (i.e. the total weight of goods and packing) it gives the *net weight* (i.e. the actual weight of the goods themselves).

    Actual tare means that the packing has been weighed separately from the goods. Where the number of packages is numerous *average tare* is calculated by taking actual tare of a number of sample packages and calculating the average.

TARIFF. A list of charges or prices, e.g. a list of the Customs duties imposed on imported goods.

TEL QUEL RATE. The RATE OF EXCHANGE for foreign bills adjusted to fit the unmatured period of the bill. A bill with a longer period to run would be relatively cheaper than one for a shorter period, because it gives rise to a later claim.

TELEGRAPHIC TRANSFER. A telegraph message arranging for the transfer of money by a system of debits and credits to the accounts of the persons concerned. The system has been withdrawn and replaced by International Giro. (*See* CREDIT TRANSFER).

TENDER. There are two meanings: (*a*) a formal offer by a debtor of money due to his creditor or upon a BILL OF EXCHANGE; (*b*) an offer, usually in response to a public advertisement, to supply goods or to do work at prices quoted and under conditions stated in the tender; there is no implied undertaking to accept the lowest tender, but when the tender is accepted it naturally results in a binding agreement enforceable at law. *See* LEGAL TENDER.

testimonial. A certificate given by a responsible person bearing testimony to the character, qualifications, ability, conduct, or credit of another. Under the Statute of Frauds Amendment Act 1828, no person can be made liable on a *verbal* assurance as to the character of another given to enable that other to obtain credit, money, or goods.

TIME CHARTER. *See* CHARTER PARTY.

TIME POLICY. *See* POLICY.

TITLE. The right under which a person holds property of any kind. It may be acquired by gift, purchase, inheritance, or even by length of possession. It is a rule of COMMON LAW that no one can give a transferee a better title than he himself has in the thing transferred. Accordingly, a buyer who obtains goods from a seller whose title is defective (as where the goods have been stolen) will be obliged to pass them back to the owner without recompense. There are a number of exceptions to this rule, of which NEGOTIABLE INSTRUMENTS constitute the most important.

TITLE DEEDS. Deeds evidencing a person's right or title to land (including buildings). In law they are considered as REAL PROPERTY, and since the property to which they relate cannot be transferred without them, possession of them is important.

TOKEN MONEY. *See* MONEY.

TORT. *See* OFFENCES.

TRADE. *See* COMMERCE.

TRADE DISCOUNT. *See* DISCOUNT.

TRADE MARK. A distinctive mark or device placed upon or used in connection with goods to show that they are products of a particular manufacturer. A trade mark may be protected by registration at the Patent Office. The protection extends for seven years, subject to periodical renewal on payment of the prescribed fees.

TRAMPS. *See* LINERS.

TRANSIT. *See* STOPPAGE IN TRANSITU.

TRAVELLER'S CHEQUE. These are cheques for £10, £20, £50 and £100 obtainable at banks by persons who intend to travel either at home or abroad. They are universally accepted abroad at current RATES OF EXCHANGE not only by banks but also by hotels and other persons in payment of accounts. Each cheque contains a space for two signatures, one of which must be attached when the cheque is purchased and the other at the time it is tendered as payment. For the issue of such cheques the banks make an *ad valorem* charge.

TREASON. *See* OFFENCES.

TREASURE TROVE. Coins and other valuables of gold and silver found hidden in the earth or other private place and whose owner is not known. By law such property belongs to the Crown, but as an act of grace the finder is now usually given the market value.

TREASURY BILL. A short-term security issued by the British Treasury for amounts of £5,000, £10,000, £25,000, £50,000, £100,000, £250,000 and £1,000,000, and sold weekly by TENDER. They do not carry interest, but are issued at a discount and redeemed at their nominal value, the difference between the purchase price and the redemption price representing the investor's profit. No allotments are made at the weekly tender in amounts of less than £50,000.

TREASURY NOTE. A currency note issued by the British Treasury upon the outbreak of war in 1914 for amounts of 10s. and £1 and authorized as legal tender. Treasury notes were withdrawn in 1928 and superseded by notes issued by the Bank of England.

TRESPASS. Interference with another's property or person. There are three kinds: *(a) trespass on land*—unauthorized entry upon another person's land, the offence being actionable, even though no damage is caused; *(b) trespass to goods*—wrongful interference with another person's possessions; *(c) trespass to the person*—wrongful interference with a person's liberty, also injury or a threat of injury to a person.

TRINITY HOUSE. An ancient company performing many statutory duties relating to the marine, especially the appointment and licensing of pilots and the supervision of lighthouses, buoys, and beacons.

TRIPTYQUE. A document used for Customs identification purposes and issued by the motoring associations to those who take their cars abroad for touring purposes.

TRUST. *See* MERGER.

TRUSTEE. A person who holds property in trust for the use or benefit of another called the *cestui que trust*. It is unusual to appoint a sole trustee, though certain corporations, e.g. banks and insurance companies, offer themselves as trustees for remuneration.

Upon the issue of an ADJUDICATION ORDER in BANKRUPTCY the debtor's property, until then supervised by the OFFICIAL RECEIVER, vests in the trustee, who will normally be one of the creditors, or the official receiver himself.

TURNOVER. The total value of goods sold during a given period, usually one year. *See* RATE OF TURNOVER.

UBERRIMAE FIDEI. Certain classes of contract require *utmost good faith* by the parties making them. They are termed contracts *uberrimae fidei*. Each party must make a full disclosure to the other of all material facts bearing on the contract. Non-disclosure amounts to misrepresentation and makes the contract *voidable* at the option of the party prejudiced by the misrepresentation. Such contracts include insurance, contracts to take shares in companies or for the sale of land, contracts of family relationship, and contracts where a fiduciary relationship exists, as between solicitor and client, banker and customer, and agent and principal.

ULLAGE. Loss of liquid by leakage, evaporation, etc. The difference between the capacity of a cask and its contents.

UNDERWRITER. There are two classes.

(a) Insurance. A term used especially with reference to marine insurance to denote a person who subscribes his name to a policy of insurance, thereby accepting liability for the contingent loss. He is so called because he writes his name under the wording of the policy.

(b) Shares. One who guarantees a new capital issue by undertaking, in return for a commission, to purchase shares not subscribed for, up to an agreed number.

UNFUNDED DEBT. *See* FUNDED DEBT.

UNIT TRUST. Similar to an INVESTMENT TRUST, but confines its investments to the purchase of shares in a narrow range of carefully selected companies. Such trusts are known as *fixed trusts*, because they do not normally have power to invest in securities other than those agreed upon at time of formation. In recent years there has been a tendency to modify the fixed character of these trusts and to permit trust managers to sell securities and re-invest the proceeds, sometimes in named securities and sometimes in securities of their choice, thus giving rise to the type of trust termed a *managed unit trust*.

The trustees are usually banks known and respected in the world of finance. In the legal sense the funds are "vested" in them, and the banks as distinct from the management hold them on behalf of members of the public, who receive dividends from the bulk investment in proportion to the number of "units" or shares they hold in the trust.

UNVALUED POLICY. *See* POLICY.

UPSET PRICE. *See* RESERVE PRICE.

USANCE. The customary period of time for which BILLS OF EXCHANGE not payable on demand are drawn on particular places or countries. For most continental countries usance is three months, but the custom varies and the term means little nowadays.

USURY. The lending of money at exorbitant rates of interest. The laws against usury were repealed in 1854, and the lending of money at agreed rates of interest is now lawful, the only restraint being the provisions of the Moneylenders Acts, under which interest exceeding 48 per cent per annum on an unsecured loan is presumed excessive.

VALUE ADDED TAX. A type of sales tax levied at specified rates on the selling prices of products (including services) at each stage of production and distribution. It is payable in addition to the Customs and Excise DUTIES on wines and spirits, but not on imported services.

VALUED POLICY. *See* POLICY.

VISA. An endorsement on a PASSPORT by a CONSUL or other representative of the country to which an intended traveller is going. Visas are required only by certain countries.

VOUCHER. A document or other form of evidence attesting the performance of an alleged act, such as the payment of money.

VOYAGE CHARTER. *See* CHARTER PARTY.

VOYAGE POLICY. *See* POLICY.

WAGES. The remuneration paid, usually weekly, to manual workers of all kinds. The Truck Acts 1831–1940 made illegal the payment of wages *to workmen* otherwise than in LEGAL TENDER, but by the Payment of Wages Act 1960 it is now permissible, at the written request of the employee, to pay his wages by postal order, cheque, or direct into his banking account.

WALL STREET. The New York STOCK EXCHANGE—located in Wall Street.

WARD. An infant or minor, i.e. a person under eighteen, under protection or guardianship of the Court of Chancery, or under the protection or tutelage of some other guardian. *See* INFANT.

WAREHOUSE. A building in which *wares* or goods may be *housed* or stored in conditions that protect them from the weather and from thieves. Besides the warehouses privately owned by wholesalers and manufacturers there are numerous *public warehouses*, which may be used by anyone on payment of the charge for rent. Many public warehouses are specialized for the storage of meat, tea, sugar, wines, and tobacco. By holding back supplies in times of plenty and offering them in times of scarcity warehouses help to steady prices.

A *bonded warehouse* is a warehouse for the storage of dutiable goods. The warehouse proprietor enters into a bond with HM Customs as a guarantee that goods will not be removed till duty on them has been paid. The main commodities dealt with in this way are tea, tobacco, beer, wines, and spirits.

WAREHOUSE WARRANT. *See* DOCK WARRANT.

WAREHOUSEKEEPER'S ORDER. *See* CUSTOMS WARRANT.

WARRANTY. A contractual obligation which, unlike a CONDITION, does not go to the root of the contract, and which entitles the injured party to DAMAGES, but not to rescind the contract.

WASTING ASSETS. *See* ASSETS.

WATERED CAPITAL. *See* CAPITAL.

WHOLESALE TRADE. Trading in quantities larger than those dealt in by the retailer. The wholesaler is a middleman who buys goods in bulk from the producer and manufacturer and holds them ready to sell to the retailer.

WINDING UP. Putting an estate into liquidation for the purpose of distributing the assets among the creditors. The phrase is most commonly used in the liquidation of companies, which can be brought to an end: *(a)* compulsorily by the court; *(b)* voluntarily by the members; *(c)* under supervision of the court.

The bankruptcy laws do not apply to companies, and the person appointed to wind up a company is called a LIQUIDA-TOR, whose position is, however, equivalent to that of a TRUSTEE in bankruptcy.

WINDMILL. *See* ACCOMMODATION BILL.

WINDOW DRESSING. The attempts made to create favourable-looking financial statements; in particular, the practice at one time adopted by the joint stock banks of calling in loans towards the end of each accounting period in order to show large cash resources in their balance sheets.

WORKING CAPITAL. *See* CAPITAL.

WRIT. A document issued by the court directing a person to do or to refrain from doing some specified act. Almost all legal proceedings begin with the serving of a writ by the plaintiff upon the defendant, stating what the plaintiff demands.

WRITE OFF. To cancel a debt, thus treating it as if it were paid. In book-keeping it is the process of reducing the value of an asset or writing off a debt by debiting the profit and loss account.

YORK–ANTWERP RULES. A set of rules agreed at a conference of underwriters for use in the adjustment of shipping losses.

APPENDIX D

ABBREVIATIONS USED IN BUSINESS

Note: It is a matter of style whether certain abbreviations are followed by a full point. The reader is referred to p. 134 for a full discussion of the subject.

A

A1	first-class (ship in Lloyd's Register)
AA	Automobile Association
AB	Able-bodied Seaman
ABIM	Associate of the British Institute of Management
A/C	account current
a/c, acc., acct.	account
ACAS	Advisory Conciliation and Arbitration Service
ACCA	Associate of the Institute of Chartered Accountants in England and Wales
ACII	Associate of the Chartered Insurance Institute
ACIS	Associate of the Institute of Chartered Secretaries and Administrators
ACP	Associate of the College of Preceptors
ADP	automatic data processing
ad val.	*ad valorem* (L), according to value
AEA	Atomic Energy Authority
AIA	Associate of the Institute of Actuaries
AIB	Associate of the Institute of Bankers
AIC	Associate of the Institute of Chemical Engineers
AICS	Associate of the Institute of Chartered Shipbrokers
AIMTA	Associate of the Institute of Municipal Treasurers and Accountants
AInstP	Associate of the Institute of Physics
AKC	Associate of King's College, London

AMBIM	Associate Member of the British Institute of Management
AMICE	Associate Member of the Institution of Civil Engineers
AMIEE	Associate Member of the Institution of Electrical Engineers
AMIMechE	Associate Member of the Institution of Mechanical Engineers
AMInstT	Associate Member of the Institute of Transport
AR	all risks (insurance)
ARIBA	Associate of the Royal Institute of British Architects
A/S	account sales
a/s	after sight
ASCT	Associate of the Society of Commercial Teachers
ASLEF	Associated Society of Locomotive Engineers and Firemen
Asst.	Assistant
AUEW	Amalgamated Union of Engineering Workers

B

BA	Bachelor of Arts; Buenos Aires; British Association
BBC	British Broadcasting Corporation
BC	Before Christ; Borough Council; British Columbia
BCL	Bachelor of Civil Law
BCom, BComm	Bachelor of Commerce
BD	Bachelor of Divinity
b/d	brought down
BDS	Bachelor of Dental Surgery
B/E	bill of exchange
BEd	Bachelor of Education
Beds	Bedfordshire
BEng	Bachelor of Engineering
Berks	Berkshire
B ès L	*Bachelier ès Lettres* (Fr), Bachelor of Letters and Arts
B ès S	*Bachelier ès Sciences* (Fr), Bachelor of Science
b/f	brought forward
BHP, bhp	brake horse-power
B/L	bill of lading

BLitt	Bachelor of Literature
BMA	British Medical Association
BMus	Bachelor of Music
B/P	bill(s) payable
B/R	bill(s) receivable
Br.	British
B/S	balance sheet; bill of sale
BSc	Bachelor of Science
BSc Tech	Bachelor of Technical Science
BSI	British Standards Institution
BST	British summer time
BThU, Btu	British thermal unit
Bucks	Buckinghamshire
BUPA	British United Provident Association

C

C	*centum* (L), 100; centigrade
c	cent (USA); centime (France); centavo (Spanish Amer,); cubic; *circa* (L), about
CA	Chartered Accountant (Scotland); County Alderman
CAA	Civil Aviation Authority
Cambs	Cambridgeshire
Cantab	*Cantabrigiensis* (L), of Cambridge
CB	cash book; Companion of the Order of the Bath; County Borough
CBE	Commander of the Order of the British Empire
CBI	Confederation of British Industries
CC	continuation clause (insurance); County Council(lor)
cc, cu. cm, cm^3	cubic centimetre(s)
c/d	carried down
cent.	*centum* (L), hundred; Centigrade
cet. par.	*ceteris paribus* (L), other things being equal
cf., cp	compare
c.f.	cost and freight
c/f	carried forward
cfi	cost, freight and insurance
cg	centigram(s)
CH	Clearing House; Custom House; Companion of Honour
ChB	*Chirurgiae Baccalaureus* (L); Bachelor of Surgery

CID	Criminal Investigation Department
Cie	*Compagnie* (Fr), Company
cif	cost, insurance, and freight
cl	centilitre(s); class; clause
cm	centimetre(s)
CMG	Companion of the Order of St Michael and St George
C/N	credit note
Co	Company; County
COD	cash on delivery
Co. Derry	Co. Londonderry
C/P	charter party
cp., cf.	compare
CPR	Canadian Pacific Railway
CR	at company's risk
Cr.	credit; creditor; Crown
c/s	case(s)
CTL	constructive total loss (insurance)
cu., cub.	cubic
cum div.	with dividend
CVO	Commander of the Royal Victorian Order
CWO, c.w.o.	cash with order
CWS	Co-operative Wholesale Society
cwt	hundredweight

D

D	500
d.	*denarius, denarii* (L), old pence (pre-1971)
D/A	documents against acceptance
DBE	Dame Commander of the Order of the British Empire
DC	detention clause (insurance); direct current
DCL	Doctor of Civil Law
DCM	Distinguished Conduct Medal
DCVO	Dame Commander of the Royal Victorian Order
DD	Doctor of Divinity
d/d	days after date
deb.	debenture
def.	defendant; deferred
deld.	delivered
dely.	delivery
DEng	Doctor of Engineering
Dept.	Department

DFC	Distinguished Flying Cross
DFM	Distinguished Flying Medal
Dft	Draft
DHSS	Department of Health and Social Security
Dis., Disct.	discount
Div.	dividend
DL	Deputy Lieutenant
DLit ⎫ DLitt ⎭	*Doctor litteraturae* or *litterarum* (L), Doctor of Literature or Letters
dm	decimetre(s)
D/N	debit note; delivery note
D/O	delivery order
do	ditto (the same)
doz.	dozen
D/P	documents against payment
DPH	Diploma in Public Health
DPh	Doctor of Philosophy
Dr	debtor; doctor
d/s	days after sight
DSC	Distinguished Service Cross
DSc	Doctor of Science
DSIR	Department of Scientific and Industrial Research
DSM	Distinguished Service Medal
DV	*Deo volente* (L), God willing
D/W	dock warrant
dwt.	pennyweight (24 grains)

E

E	Eastern postal district
ea.	each
EC	East Central postal district
ECGD	Export Credits Guarantee Department
EDP	Electronic data processing
EEC	European Economic Community (known as the "Common Market")
EFTA	European Free Trade Association
e.g.	*exempli gratia* (L), for example
E & OE	errors and omissions excepted
EPNS	electro-plated nickel silver
ER	*Elizabeth Regina* (L), Queen Elizabeth
ERNIE	electronic random number indicating equipment
et al.	*et alibi* (L), and elsewhere; *et alii* (L), and others

et Cie	*& Compagnie* (Fr), Company
et seq.	*et sequens* (L), and that which follows
et sqq.	*et sequentes* or *sequentia* (plural of above)
etc	*et cetera* (L), and so forth
ETU	Electrical Trades Union
ex	from (e.g. *ex Montreal*)
ex div., e.d., x.div.	exclusive of dividend
ex int.	exclusive of interest
exor.	executor
exrx.	executrix

F

F, Fahr.	Fahrenheit
f.a.a.	free of all average
FACCA	Fellow of the Association of Certified Accountants
faq	fair average quality; free alongside quay
fas	free alongside ship
FBA	Fellow of the British Academy
FBI	Federal Bureau of Investigation
FBIM	Fellow of the British Institute of Management
FBOA	Fellow of the British Optical Association
FCA	Fellow of the Institute of Chartered Accountants in England and Wales
FCIS	Fellow of the Institute of Chartered Secretaries and Administrators
FCP	Fellow of the College of Preceptors
fcp, fcap	foolscap
FCS	Fellow of the Chemical Society
FCWA	Fellow of the Institute of Cost and Works Accountants
ff.	*folgende seiten* (Gr), folios, following; *fecerunt* (L), they made or did it; *fortissimo* (It), very loud
FFTCom	Fellow of the Faculty of Teachers in Commerce
FGA	foreign general average
FIA	Fellow of the Institute of Actuaries
FIB	Fellow of the Institute of Bankers
FIC	Fellow of the Institute of Chemistry
FICS	Fellow of the Institute of Chartered Shipbrokers
FIMTA	Fellow of the Institute of Municipal Treasurers and Accountants

FInstP	Fellow of the Institute of Physics
FIPA	Fellow of the Institute of Practitioners in Advertising
FO	firm offer; Foreign Office
fo., fol.	folio
fob	free on board
foc	free of charge
for	free on rail
fos	free on steamer
fot	free on truck
FPA, f.p.a.	free of particular average
fr.	franc (French coin)
FREconS	Fellow of the Royal Economic Society
FRIBA	Fellow of the Royal Institute of British Architects
FRS	Fellow of the Royal Society
FRSA	Fellow of the Royal Society of Arts
FRSE	Fellow of the Royal Society of Arts of Edinburgh
FSCT	Fellow of the Society of Commercial Teachers
FSS	Fellow of the Statistical Society
ft.	foot, feet
fwd.	forward

G

GA	general average (insurance)
GATT	General Agreement on Tariffs and Trade
GB	Great Britain
GBE	Knight or Dame Grand Cross of the Order of the British Empire
GC	George Cross
GCB	Knight Grand Cross of the Order of the Bath
GCIE	Knight Grand Commander of the Order of the Indian Empire
GCMG	Knight Grand Cross of the Order of St Michael and St George
GCSI	Knight Grand Commander of the Star of India
GCVO	Knight Grand Cross of the Royal Victorian Order
Gen.	General
Glam	Glamorgan
GLC	Greater London Council
Glos	Gloucestershire

GM	George Medal
gm, g	gram(me)
GMT	Greenwich mean time
Gov., Govt.	Government
GP	general practitioner
GPO	Genereal Post Office
gr.	grain; gramme; gross
grs.	grains; grammes
GV	*grande vitesse* (Fr), quick goods train

H

Hants	Hampshire
Herts	Hertfordshire
HL	House of Lords
HMC	Her Majesty's Consul, Customs
HMI	Her Majesty's Inspector
HMOW	Her Majesty's Office of Works
HMSO	Her Majesty's Stationery Office
Hon.	Honorary; Honourable
HP	Hire purchase
h.p.	horse-power
HQ	headquarters

I

IATA	International Air Transport Association
ib., ibid.	*ibidem* (L), in the same place
IBRD	International Bank for Reconstruction and Development (World Bank)
ICI	Imperial Chemical Industries
IDA	International Development Association
i.e.	*id est* (L.), that is
i.h.p.	indicated horse-power
IMF	International Monetary Fund
in.	inch(es)
inc., incorp.	incorporated
in re	in the matter of
INTELSAT	International Communications Satellite Consortium
INTERPOL	International Criminal Police Commission
inv.	invoice
IOM	Isle of Man
IOU	I owe you
IOW	Isle of Wight
IPFA	Institute of Public Finance and Accountancy
i.p.s.	inches per second

IQ	intelligence quotient
IRO	Inland Revenue Office
ISO	Imperial Service Order
ITA	Independent Television Authority
ital.	italic type

J

JP	Justice of the Peace
Jr., Jun., Junr.	Junior

K

KBE	Knight Commander of the Order of the British Empire
KC	King's Counsel
KCB	Knight Commander of the Order of the Bath
KCIE	Knight Commander of the Order of the Indian Empire
KCMG	Knight Commander of the Order of St Michael and St George
KCSI	Knight Commander of the Star of India
KCVO	Knight Commander of the Royal Victorian Order
KG	Knight of the Garter
kg, kilo	kilogram
km	kilometre(s)
KP	Knight of St Patrick
KT	Knight of the Thistle
kw	kilowatt (1,000 watts)

L

Lancs	Lancashire
lb(s)	*libra* (L.), pounds(s)
L/C	letter of credit
l.c.	lower case, i.e. small letters
LCCI	London Chamber of Commerce and Industry
LCP	Licentiate of the College of Preceptors
LDS	Licentiate in Dental Surgery
LEA	Local Education Authority
Leics	Leicestershire
Lincs	Lincolnshire
lit., l	litre
Litt D	*Litterarum Doctor* (L), Doctor of Letters
LLB	*Legum Baccalaureus* (L); Bachelor of Laws
LLD	*Legum Doctor* (L); Doctor of Laws

loc. cit.	*loco citato* (L), in the place cited
L'pool	Liverpool
LS	*locus sigilli* (L), place of the seal
Ltd, Ld	limited liability

M

M	1,000; *Monsieur* (Fr), Mr
m	metre(s); miles; minutes; million(s)
MA	Master of Arts
MB	Bachelor of Medicine
MBE	Member of the Order of the British Empire
MBIM	Member of the British Institute of Management
MC	Master of Ceremonies; metalling clause (insurance); Military Cross
M/C, M/chtr	Manchester
MCC	Marylebone Cricket Club
MCom	Master of Commerce (London and Birmingham)
MComm	Master of Commerce (Manchester)
MD	*Medecinae Doctor* (L), Doctor of Medicine; mentally deficient
Mdlle, Mlle	*Mademoiselle* (Fr), Miss
Mdlles, Mlles	*Mesdemoiselles* (Fr), The Misses
MEd	Master of Education
mega-	one million times; large
Messrs	*Messieurs* (Fr), Gentlemen
MICE, MInstCE	Member of the Institution of Civil Engineers
micro-	one millionth part of a unit; small
MIEE	Member of the Institution of Electrical Engineers
MIMechE	Member of the Institution of Mechanical Engineers
MInstT	Member of the Institute of Transport
MIWM	Member of the Institution of Works Managers
MM	*Messieurs* (Fr), Gentlemen; Military Medal
mm	millimetre(s)
MO	Medical Officer
MOH	Medical Officer of Health
MP	Member of Parliament; Metropolitan Police; Military Police
mpg	miles per gallon
mph	miles per hour
MPS	Member of the Pharmaceutical Society

Mr, Mrs	Mister; Mistress
MRI	Member of the Royal Institution
m/s	months after sight
Ms, M/s	Miss or Mrs
MS(S)	manuscript(s)
MSc	Master of Science
MusB(D)	*Musicae Baccalaureus (Doctor)* (L) Bachelor (Doctor) of Music
MVO	Member of the Royal Victorian Order

N

N	Northern postal district
n/a	no account (banking)
NAAFI	Navy, Army and Air Force Institute(s)
NALGO	National Association of Local Government Officers
NATO	North Atlantic Treaty Organization
NB	*nota bene* (L), mark well; New Brunswick; North Britain
NCB	National Coal Board
n.d.	no date; not dated
NE	North-Eastern postal district
NEDC	National Economic Development Council
nem. con.	*nemine contradicente* (L), no one contradicting
nem. dis.	*nemine dissentiente* (l), no one dissenting
no.	*numero* (L), number
Nom. Cap.	nominal capital
non seq.	*non sequitur* (L), it does not logically follow
Northants	Northamptonshire
Notts	Nottinghamshire
NP	Notary Public
NR	no risk (insurance)
n/s	not sufficient funds (banking)
NSW	New South Wales
NUR	National Union of Railwaymen
NW	North-Western postal district

O

o/a	on account (of)
OAP	old age pension(er)
OBE	Officer of the Order of the British Empire
OECD	Organization for Economic Co-operation and Development
OED	Oxford English Dictionary

OHMS	On Her Majesty's Service
OK	all correct (illiterate spelling of *orl k'rect*); *okeh*, so be it
OM	Order of Merit
O & M	Organization and Methods
OP	open policy (insurance)
op.	*opus.* (L), work
o/p	out of print
op. cit.	*opere citato* (L), in the work cited
OPEC	Organization of Petroleum Exporting Countries
OR	owner's risk
OS	old style; Ordinary Seaman; Old Saxon (language)
Oxon	*Oxonia* (L), Oxford; *Oxoniensis* (L), of Oxford (Bishop of Oxford's signature); Oxfordshire
oz(s)	ounce(s)

P

p	(new) pence
p., pp.	page; pages
PA	particular average (insurance); personal assistant; Press Association
P/A	power of attorney
p.a.	*per annum* (L), yearly
PAYE	Pay as you earn
PC	Police Constable; Privy Councillor
P/C	prices current
p.c.	*per centum* (L), per cent; postcard
pcl.	parcel
pcs.	pieces (cloth) ·
PCT	Pitman's Certificated Teacher
PEP	Political and Economic Planning (Club)
per	by
per cent.	*per centum* (L), by the hundred
per pro, p. pro, pp	*per procurationem* (L), on behalf of
pf	pfennig (German coin)
PhD	*Philosophiae Doctor* (L), Doctor of Philosophy
PL	partial loss (insurance)
PLC, plc	public limited company
P & L	profit and loss
PLA	Port of London Authority
p.m.	*post meridiem* (L), afternoon or evening
P/N	promissory note

PO	postal order; post office
P & O	Peninsular and Oriental (Steam Navigation Company)
POD	pay on delivery
POP	Post Office Preferred
PPI	policy proof of interest (insurance)
PPS	*post post scriptum* (L), a further postscript
pro.	for; professional
pro tem.	*pro tempore* (L), for the time being
prox.	*proximo* (L), next month
PS	*post scriptum* (L), postscript
PTO	please turn over; Public Trustee Office

Q

QC	Queen's Counsel
QED	*quod erat demonstrandum* (L), which was to be proved
QEF	*quod erat faciendum* (L), which was to be done
QMG	Quartermaster-General
qr	quarter; quire
q.v.	*quod vide* (L), which see

R

RA	Royal Academy
RAC	Royal Automobile Club
RADA	Royal Academy of Dramatic Art
radar	radio detection and ranging
RAF	Royal Air Force
RAMC	Royal Army Medical Corps
RAOC	Royal Army Ordnance Corps
RAPC	Royal Army Pay Corps
RASC	Royal Army Service Corps
RAVC	Royal Army Veterinary Corps
R/D	refer to drawer (banking)
RDC	running down clause (insurance); Rural District Council
re	with reference to
ref	reference
Rev., Revd	Reverend
RLO	Returned Letter Office
Rly	Railway
RM	Royal Mail; Royal Marines
rm	ream
RN	Royal Navy
RNVR	Royal Naval Volunteer Reserve

r.p.m.	revolutions per minute
RSA	Royal Scottish Academician; Royal Society of Arts
RSVP	*Répondez, s'il vous plaît* (Fr), Please reply
Rt Hon	Right Honourable

S

S	South
SAYE	Save as you earn
s. caps., s.c.	small capitals (printing)
sc.	*scilicet* (L), to wit, namely
ScD	*Scientiae Doctor* (L); Doctor of Science
Sch	schedule; school
SE	South-Eastern postal district
SERC	Science and Engineering Research Council
sic	(L) so written
SL	salvage loss (insurance)
SN	shipping note
s.o.	seller's option
SOS	Morse code signal for help
spec.	specification; speculation
sq.	square
SRN	State Registered Nurse
s.s. or s/s	steamship
St	Saint; strait; street
Staffs	Staffordshire
STD	subscriber trunk dialling
stet	let it stand
sup.	*supra* (L), above
SW	South-Western postal district

T

T/C	till countermanded
TD	Territorial Decoration
TGWU	Transport and General Workers' Union
TL	total loss (insurance)
TLO	total loss only (insurance)
TUC	Trades Union Congress

U

u.c.	upper case, i.e. capital letters
UDC	Urban District Council
UK	United Kingdom
ult., ulto.	*ultimo* (L), last month

UNCTAD	United Nations Conference on Trade and Development
UNESCO	United Nations Economic, Scientific and Cultural Organization
UNO	United Nations Organization
USA	United States of America
USSR	Union of Soviet Socialist Republics
u/w	underwriter

V

v.	versus, against
VC	Victoria Cross
verb. sap.	*verbum satis sapienti* (L), a word to the wise is enough
via	by way of, through
VIP	very important person
viz	*videlicet* (L), namely

W

W	Western postal district
WAAC	Women's Army Auxiliary Corps
W/B	way-bill
WC	West Central postal district
WEA	Workers' Educational Association
WHO	World Health Organization
Wilts	Wiltshire
WOB	washing overboard (insurance)
Worcs	Worcestershire
w.p.m.	words per minute
WRAC	Women's Royal Army Corps
WRAF	Women's Royal Air Force
WRNS	Women's Royal Naval Service
WVS	Women's Voluntary Service
W/W	warehouse warrant

X

x.c.	ex (without) coupon
x.d.	ex (without) dividend
x.i.	ex (without) interest

Y

YAR, Y/A	York–Antwerp Rules (insurance)
yd.	yard
YMCA	Young Men's Christian Association

yr.   year; your
YWCA   Young Women's Christian Association

@   at
&   and
©   copyright
®   registered trade mark
£   pound sterling
£E   pound Egyptian
$ dollar(s)
4to   quarto
8vo   octavo
%   per cent
‰   per mille, per thousand
number; space (in printing)
∵   because
∴   therefore
×   by
°   degrees
′   minutes
″   seconds
′.   feet
″   inches

Index